W9-AFA-695

PEOPLES OF OLD TESTAMENT TIMES

PEOPLES OF OLD TESTAMENT TIMES

Edited by

D. J. WISEMAN

for

THE SOCIETY FOR
OLD TESTAMENT STUDY

OXFORD
AT THE CLARENDON PRESS
1973

WINGATE COLLEGE LIBRARY
WINGATE, N. C.

Oxford University Press, Ely House, London W. 1

GLASGOW NEW YORK TORONTO MELBOURNE WELLINGTON
CAPE TOWN IBADAN NAIROBI DAR ES SALAAM LUSAKA ADDIS ABABA
DELHI BOMBAY CALCUTTA MADRAS KARACHI LAHORE DACCA
KUALA LUMPUR SINGAPORE HONG KONG TOKYO

© *Oxford University Press 1973*

LC 73-179589
4-10-74

Printed in Great Britain
at the University Press, Oxford
by Vivian Ridler
Printer to the University

PREFACE

IN 1925 The Society for Old Testament Study published its first volume, *The People and the Book* (Clarendon Press), edited by A. S. Peake. Now almost fifty years later it issues a volume designed to show our present state of knowledge about the peoples whose lives and lands touched upon that small but influential group of Hebrew peoples whose thought and actions are a primary concern of the Old Testament itself. So much information is available from documentary and archaeological sources that this book has had generally to exclude the people of Israel and Judah—themselves the subject of a mass of current literature—to concentrate upon the major ethnic groups of the ancient Near East whose contacts with them are an essential part of the fabric of Old Testament history.

The idea of this book is owed to the late Professor D. Winton Thomas who himself edited for the Society *Documents from Old Testament Times* (1958) and, to mark the Society's Jubilee, a companion volume *Archaeology and Old Testament Study* (1967). The latter discussed the places frequently mentioned in the Old Testament on which archaeology had relevant information to offer. He envisaged a third volume to complete the series with its emphasis on the peoples referred to in the Old Testament documents. His suggestion was readily accepted by the Society in 1968.

This volume of essays on Israel's neighbours and contemporaries aims to meet the needs of teachers and students of the Old Testament whether in college, school, or church. It is not primarily prepared for specialists but will provide them as well as the general reader with information which may not otherwise be readily accessible. For this reason bibliographies have been added at the end of each chapter.

All the contributors were asked to relate what is known about the people concerned from both biblical and extra-biblical sources. To show the place and character of any people in history it is often necessary to describe something of their history, language and literature, religion, law, sociology, economy, and other aspects of

59283

their civilization. No attempt has been made to impose a uniformity upon the various authors other than to ask that they show us what influence, if any, the people of whom they write had upon the Hebrews. All, however, follow a common chronology (see Table, pp. 358–9, based on the revised edition of *The Cambridge Ancient History* and on a revision of the chart prepared for *Archaeology and Old Testament Study*). While uniformity in the spelling of some personal and place names has not been possible, the variations should not prove a hindrance to the average reader and are noted in the Index.

I am grateful to Professor Winton Thomas, who was a constant source of encouragement until his death in 1970. Professor G. Posener of the Collège de France, Paris, has generously allowed the hitherto unpublished ostracon from Strasbourg to be used to illustrate the article on the Hebrews. The Revd. M. Couve de Murville, M.A., has kindly translated M. Cazelles's article from the French, and Professor G. Buccellati helped in a number of problems in the translation of the chapter by Professor Liverani from Italian. Thanks are due to the Revd. C. H. Southwood, M.A., Senior Lecturer in Religious Studies at Digby Stuart College of Education, who helped in the preparation of the Indexes, and to the publishers for their customary care and skill in the production of the volume.

My thanks are particularly owed to The Society for Old Testament Study for entrusting me with the editorship and to the individual contributors for their willing co-operation. Almost all are members of the Society and all are engaged in research upon the peoples of whom they write. They join me in the hope that this book will help in the understanding of the peoples of Old Testament times and thus of the Old Testament itself.

D. J. W.

London, June 1972

CONTENTS

CONTRIBUTORS

1. D. R. AP-THOMAS, M.A., B.D., Senior Lecturer in Hebrew and Biblical Studies, The University College of North Wales, Bangor.

2. J. R. BARTLETT, B.LITT., M.A., Lecturer in Divinity, Trinity College, Dublin.

3. H. CAZELLES, PH.D., D. TH., Professeur exégèse Ancien Testament à la Faculté de Théologie, Directeur de la Section Biblique, Institut Catholique de Paris.

4. H. A. HOFFNER, JR., M.A., PH.D., Associate Professor of Assyriology and Hittitology, Yale University, New Haven, Conn., U.S.A.

5. A. K. IRVINE, M.A., D.PHIL., Lecturer in Semitic Languages, School of Oriental and African Studies, University of London.

6. K. A. KITCHEN, B.A., Lecturer in Egyptian and Coptic, University of Liverpool.

7. W. G. LAMBERT, M.A., F.B.A., Professor of Assyriology, The University of Birmingham.

8. M. LIVERANI, D.LETT., Professor of the History of the Ancient Near East, University of Rome.

9. A. MALAMAT, M.A., PH.D., Professor of the History of the Biblical Period, The Hebrew University, Jerusalem.

10. A. R. MILLARD, M.A., M.PHIL., F.S.A., Rankin Lecturer in Hebrew and Ancient Semitic Languages, University of Liverpool.

11. H. W. F. SAGGS, M.TH., PH.D., F.S.A., Professor of Semitic Languages, University College of South Wales and Monmouthshire, Cardiff.

12. GEO WIDENGREN, F.L., T.D., D.TH., D.D., Professor of the History and Psychology of Religions, University of Uppsala.

13. R. J. WILLIAMS, M.A., B.D., PH.D., F.R.S.C., Professor of Egyptology and Hebrew, Department of Near Eastern Studies, University of Toronto.

14. D. J. WISEMAN, O.B.E., M.A., D.LIT., F.B.A., F.S.A., Professor of Assyriology, The University of London.

LIST OF PLATES

Between pp. 192–3

LIST OF FIGURES

ERRATUM

LIST OF FIGURES

6. Map of the Ancient Near East
for at end *read* 260

ACKNOWLEDGEMENTS

THE Editor wishes to thank the following for their kind permission to reproduce plates and illustrations:

Plates. The Trustees of the British Museum, Pls. I, III, VI *b*, VII *a*, *b*; The Brooklyn Museum, Pl. IV *a*; The Cairo Museum, Pls. V *a*, *b*; The Iraq Museum, Baghdad, Pl. IV *b*; Musée du Louvre, Paris, Pl. V *c*; The Oriental Institute, University of Chicago, Pls. II, VIII; Rykmuseum von Oudheden, Netherlands, Pl. VI *a*; Dr. C. F. A. Schaeffer, Pl. IV *c*.

Illustrations. Professor G. Posener, Fig. 1 (= Strasbourg ostracon Str. H 187 + H 183 + H 192; Mr. K. A. Kitchen kindly recopied the transcription given in the lower part of this Figure); I acknowledge with gratitude the help of the following: Mr. A. R. Millard for Fig. 2; Mr. K. A. Kitchen for Fig. 3; Professor A. Malamat for Fig. 4, and Professor H. A. Hoffner for Fig. 5 (after K. Bittel, *Hattuša* (O.U.P. 1970), fig. 3, pp. 26–7).

ABBREVIATIONS

A.A.S.O.R.	*Annual of the American Schools of Oriental Research.*
A.B.L.	R. F. Harper, *Assyrian and Babylonian Letters*, 1892–1914.
Ac.Or.	*Acta Orientalia.*
A.f.O.	*Archiv für Orientforschung.*
A.J.A.	*American Journal of Archaeology.*
A.J.S.L.	*American Journal of Semitic Languages and Literatures.*
Anat.Stud.	*Anatolian Studies.*
A.N.E.P.	J. B. Pritchard, *The Ancient Near East in Pictures relating to the Old Testament*, 1954; Supplement, 1969.
A.N.E.T.	J. B. Pritchard (ed.), *Ancient Near-Eastern Texts relating to the Old Testament*, 3rd edn., 1969.
A.O.A.T.	*Alter Orient und Altes Testament.*
A.O.F.	*Altorientalische Forschungen.*
A.O.T.S.	D. Winton Thomas (ed.), *Archaeology and Old Testament Study*, 1967.
A.P.E.F.	*Annual of the Palestine Exploration Fund.*
A.R.A.B.	D. D. Luckenbill, *Ancient Records of Assyria and Babylonia*, 1926.
A.R.I.	W. F. Albright, *Archaeology and the Religion of Israel*, 1953.
A.R.M.	*Archives royales de Mari.*
Ar.Or.	*Archiv Orientální.*
B.A.	*The Biblical Archaeologist.*
B.A.N.E.	G. Ernest Wright (ed.), *The Bible and the Ancient Near East* (Essays in honor of William Foxwell Albright), 1961.
B.A.S.O.R.	*Bulletin of the American Schools of Oriental Research.*
Bi.Or.	*Bibliotheca Orientalis.*
B.J.R.L.	*Bulletin of the John Rylands Library*, Manchester.
B.M.	British Museum.
B.M.B.	*Bulletin du Musée de Beyrouth.*
C.A.D.	*The Assyrian Dictionary of the Oriental Institute of the University of Chicago*, 1956–.
C.A.H.	I. E. S. Edwards, C. J. Gadd, and N. G. L. Hammond

	(eds.), *The Cambridge Ancient History*, 3rd edn., vol. I, parts i & ii (1970); vol. II is cited by author, title, chapter no., and fasc. no. and date of each part.
C.B.Q.	*The Catholic Biblical Quarterly.*
CP	A. Cowley, *Aramaic Papyri of the Fifth Century B.C.* (1923).
C.R.A.I.B.L.	*Comptes rendus de l'Académie des Inscriptions et Belles Lettres*, Paris.
D.Bh.	Darius, Behistun Inscription.
D.O.T.T.	D. Winton Thomas (ed.), *Documents from Old Testament Times*, 1958.
E.A.	J. Knudtzon, *Die El-Amarna-Tafeln*, 1908–15.
EB	Early Bronze.
E.T.	*Expository Times.*
H.U.C.A.	*Hebrew Union College Annual.*
HSS	Harvard Semitic Series.
I.Bo.T.	Istanbul Arkeoloji Müzelerinde Bulunan Bogazköy Tableteri.
I.D.B.	*The International Dictionary of the Bible*, 1962.
I.E.J.	*Israel Exploration Journal.*
I.L.N.	*The Illustrated London News.*
J.A.	*Journal Asiatique.*
J.A.O.S.	*Journal of the American Oriental Society.*
J.B.L.	*Journal of Biblical Literature.*
J.C.S.	*Journal of Cuneiform Studies.*
J.E.A.	*Journal of Egyptian Archaeology.*
J.E.O.L.	*Jahrbericht van het Vooraziatisch-Egyptisch Genootschap 'Ex Oriente Lux'.*
J.H.S.	*Journal of the Hellenic Society.*
J.K.F.	*Jahrbuch für kleinasiatische Forschung.*
J.N.E.S.	*Journal of Near Eastern Studies.*
J.P.O.S.	*Journal of the Palestine Oriental Society.*
J.R.A.S.	*Journal of the Royal Asiatic Society.*
J.S.S.	*Journal of Semitic Studies.*
J.T.S.	*Journal of Theological Studies.*
K	Tablets in the Kuyunjik Collection at B.M.
K.A.I.	H. Donner and W. Röllig, *Kanaanäische und Aramäische Inschriften*, vol. i, 1962; vols. ii–iii, 1964.
K.Bo.	Keilschrifttexte aus Boghazköi.
K.S.	A. Alt, *Kleine Schriften zur Geschichte des Volkes Israels*, 3 vols., 1953–9.

Mesopotamian history there is no general word for 'foreigner', for such terms as are sometimes so translated (lú.kur; *aḫum*, *nakrum*, *ubārum*) were not used to qualify specific persons in contrast with those considered natives. From the Ur III dynasty (*c.* 2000 B.C.) onwards the usual way of referring to foreigners was to state their provenance, either by the use of a gentilic adjective or by a description of the type 'man of/from the land/city of *X*'.[1] It is to be noted that in all periods where there are those peoples whom we would designate as 'foreigners' from other evidence, no ethnic description is used (e.g. Hurrians, see Chap. IX). In administrative records such persons are often listed without any indication that they were then considered 'foreigners', being already absorbed as 'citizens'. This may be because in Mesopotamian civilization the city as a political association or unity provided the status and protection for the individual and family and tribal relationships lost much of their importance.[2] Certainly, after the beginning of the Hebrew monarchy the clear distinction of peoples by their ethnic group or phratry (*mišpāḥāh*) disappears with the emphasis on a centralized administration working through town and village units to the individual family or 'clan' (*bêṯ 'aḇ*).[3] Despite this, there is evidence that groups of non-citizens, especially where associated in a trade, tended, like some social classes, to live in separate quarters or streets named after them, whether in Samaria in Israel or in Sippar in Babylonia ('the street of the people of Eshnunna').

The institution of resident aliens or 'sojourners' appears to be more prominent in the west, especially in the Old Testament (*gēr*)[4] and in Ugarit (Ras Shamra) where there is record of 'the men of Carchemish together with the people living within their gates'.[5] It has been surmised that the recognition of such resident aliens in the west is linked with the practice of hospitality based on nomadic tradition, evidence for which seems to be lacking in Mesopotamia.[6] Though the colour of skin was obviously recogniz-

[1] G. Buccellati, *The Amorites of the Ur III Period* (1966), pp. 324 f.

[2] A. L. Oppenheim, *Ancient Mesopotamia* (1964), p. 79.

[3] F. I. Andersen, 'Israelite Kinship Terminology and Social Structure', *The Bible Translator*, xx (1969), 29–39.

[4] Y. A. Seligmann, 'Gēr', *Encyclopaedia Miqra'it*, ii, cols. 546–9 (Heb.) *I.E.J.* xx (1970), pp. 201 f.

[5] J. Nougayrol, *Le Palais royal d'Ugarit*, iv (1956), p. 159 (RS. 18.115,22).

[6] A. L. Oppenheim, op. cit., p. 78.

able (Jer. 13:23), there appears to be little overt attempt in antiquity to differentiate between peoples as races by physical characteristics. Even modern attempts to do so remain merely hypothetical. Thus Grintz, contrary to the common but unproven view of Arabia as the place of origin of the Semites[1] and inducing the evidence of language, customs, and anthropology, argues for an original homeland in northern Mesopotamia. He considers the 'Armenoid' type with brachycephalic skulls as a distinguishing mark of the true Semite in all areas and periods. These he links with the indigenous Arab tradition which looks upon the 'pure Arab' (*al-ʿAriba*) as the descendants of Yoktan (Gen. 10:25–6; Kaḥṭān) in contrast to the 'sons of Ishma'ēl' who himself was son of a Hebrew father and an Egyptian mother (Gen. 16:3, 11).[2] But so categorical a physical distinction is not easily upheld.

Israel, as a nation, considered itself to be a 'congregation of peoples'. The term for 'people' (*ʿam*) was commonly used as an alternative to 'sons/children of Israel = Israelites'.[3] This word *ʿam* is primarily used of a group related genetically or with a common deity, and as such is used of other nations when qualified by name (as is the Akkadian *nišē*, 'men, people'). Foreign nations were usually referred to as 'nations' (*gôyîm*, sometimes translated, 'heathen' or 'gentile') or more rarely *lᵉ'umîm* (Isa. 34:1), the *gôy* being primarily a political unit of persons centred in a specific locality.

The Hebrews were conscious of their affinity with each other through the different 'families', 'clans', large kin groups, or phratries (*mišpāḥôṯ*) who all claimed descent from Abraham. These groups were the most stable unit of their society both in the bonds of recognized kinship and in organization which included inalienable land tenure (Josh. 13:23).[4] Emphasis on the larger

[1] S. Moscati, *The Semites in Ancient History* (1959).

[2] J. M. Grintz, 'On the Original Home of the Semites', *J.N.E.S.* xxi (1962), 200–4; cf. C. S. Coon, *The Origin of Races* (1963), pp. 1 ff.

[3] The argument that *ʿam ha'areṣ* is a technical term in pre-exilic times for a political entity of free landed citizens (so R. J. Coggins, *J.T.S.* xvi (1965), 124–7; S. Talmon, 'The Judean *ʿam ha'areṣ* in Historical Perspective', *Fourth World Congress of Jewish Studies, Papers*, i (1967), 71–6) has been strongly questioned by E. W. Nicholson, *J.S.S.* x (1965), 59–66; cf. P. R. Ackroyd, *Exile and Restoration* (1968), p. 150 n. 50.

[4] W. Johnstone, 'O.T. Technical Expressions in Property Holding', *Ugaritica*, vi (1970), 308–17.

date is possible since the text reflects the geographical horizon that could have been known to Moses at the Egyptian court in the fourteenth century B.C.[1] Whatever date and interpretation is followed, and the current divergence of views is reflected within this book, the chapter remains unique in ancient literatures whenever it was compiled between the Exodus and the Exile.

The 'Table of Nations' shows an awareness of the geographical distribution of people according to their countries. It is an ethno-geographical or ethnographical rather than ethnological presentation. Nevertheless, a merely geographical division of Japheth's descendants as the northern races, those of Ham as the southern peoples, and those of Shem as the central would require some additional explanations. The inclusion of Elam with the sons of Shem appears to be due to geographical proximity, unless there is some reflection of an early Semitic population in the region. The listing of Sheba, Havilah, and Lydians (Ludim) under both Shem and Ham might be explained by alliance by marriage. It has been suggested that under Shem are grouped all the 'sons of Eber', perhaps here the Hapiru in its broadest sense of semi-nomads (see Chap. I).

The Hebrews could recognize other peoples as 'foreigners' (Exod. 21:8), usually by their language: 'people of foreign speech and a hard language whose words you cannot understand' (Ezek. 3:5–6) or 'people of an obscure speech which you cannot comprehend, stammering in a tongue which you cannot understand' (Isa. 33:4–19; Ps. 114:1). Peoples could be distinguished by vocabulary (Deut. 3:9) and sub-groups by dialectal variations in pronunciation (Jud. 12:6), while others were bilingual (Isa. 36:11). They referred to them either individually or collectively as 'men' or 'people' (*'am*) of a particular territory (e.g. 'Egyptians', Gen. 41:40, Exod. 1:22, Neh. 9:10; 'Aramaeans', Amos 1:5) or of a particular god (thus the Moabites are the 'people of (the god) Chemosh, Num. 21:29; see Chap. X) or with particular customs (see Chap. V). In this, the practice of the Hebrews is identical with that of their neighbours throughout all periods of their history.

The Egyptians, always somewhat isolated from their neighbours, thought of themselves as 'men' and others as inferior 'humans' who could be accepted on learning their language. Throughout

[1] D. J. Wiseman, loc. cit., p. 25.

them or to the territory they inhabit, though with different connotations to that given in later texts.[1]

It is certain from the heading of the 'Table of Nations' ('These are the descendants [generations, genealogies, or family histories (*tolᵉdōṯ*)] of the sons of Noah', verse 1) and from the concluding catch-line or colophon ('These are the families (*mišpāḥôṯ*) of the sons of Noah, according to their generations, by their nations (*gôyîm*), and from these came the separate nations on earth after the flood', verse 32) that the differentiation of 'nations' was the main purpose. While the division of a nation into 'family' or 'clan group' (*mišpāḥāh*) is equally noted, less emphasis is placed on language (only mentioned in the 'colophons') and on territory ('land'). The 'Table' omits reference to race or physical type yet aims to show the unity of mankind, being primarily concerned with physical relationships. The expressions for the latter—'sons' or 'bore/begat'—have been used to distinguish two literary sources for this chapter (P and J respectively), but this is highly questionable in the light of the association of these terms in other documents. Indeed the terms normally employed for physical relationships are elsewhere used in Babylonian and Hebrew literature to denote political alliances.

The date of the compilation of Gen. 10 has been much discussed.[2] Most would consider this chapter to come from the seventh century B.C. on the grounds that some of the peoples mentioned (e.g. Cimmerians, Scythians, and Medes) are first named in Assyrian texts of that date. However, knowledge of groups bearing these names might have been conveyed through earlier peoples (e.g. Hurrians or Kassites) who are well known from contemporary sources of the mid second millennium and yet do not appear in this list. Others view this list as late Phoenician or classify it as very late and unreliable. However, a post-exilic date is unlikely because no reference is made to the Persians. On the basis of the first appearance of the Philistines in strength in the biblical world about 1200 B.C. (see Chap. III), many date Gen. 10 *c.* 1000 B.C. On the other hand it has been argued that an earlier

[1] J. J. Finkelstein, 'The Genealogy of the Hammurapi Dynasty', *J.C.S.* xx (1966), 95–118; A. Malamat, 'King Lists of the Old Babylonian Period and Biblical Genealogies', *J.A.O.S.* lxxxviii (1968), 163–73.

[2] J. Simon, 'The Table of Nations (Gen. X): its General Structure and Meaning', *Oudtestamentische Studien*, x (1954).

K.U.B.	Keilschrifturkunden aus Boghazköi.
LXX	Septuagint.
M.D.O.G.	*Mitteilungen der deutschen Orient-Gesellschaft zu Berlin.*
M.D.P.	*Mémoires de la Délégation en Perse.*
M.I.	Middle Iranian.
M.I.O.	*Mitteilungen des Instituts für Orientforschung.*
M.T.	Massoretic Text.
O.A.	*Oriens Antiquus.*
O.L.Z.	*Orientalistische Literaturzeitung.*
OP	Old Persian.
Or.	*Orientalia.*
Or.Suec.	*Orientalia Suecana.*
P.B.S.	Publications of the Babylonian Section, University Museum, University of Pennsylvania.
P.E.Q.	*Palestine Exploration Fund Quarterly.*
P.J.B.	*Palästinajahrbuch des deutschen evangelischen Institut für Altertumswissenschaft des Heiligen Landes zu Jerusalem.*
P.R.U.	*Le Palais royal d'Ugarit.*
Q.D.A.P.	*The Quarterly of the Department of Antiquities of Palestine.*
R	H. C. Rawlinson (ed.), *The Cuneiform Inscriptions of Western Asia* [vol. nos. shown I–V R].
R.A.	*Revue d'Assyriologie et d'Archéologie orientale.*
R.B.	*Revue Biblique.*
R.E.S.	*Revue des études sémitiques.*
R.H.A.	*Revue Hittite et Asianique.*
R.L.A.	*Reallexikon der Assyriologie.*
R.S.O.	*Rivista degli Studi Orientali.*
Stud.Or.	*Studia Orientalia.*
Ugar.	Ugaritic.
U.T.	Ugaritic Text.
V.T.	*Vetus Testamentum.*
W.O.	*Die Welt des Orients.*
W.Z.K.M.	*Wiener Zeitschrift für die Kunde des Morgenlandes.*
Y.G.C.	W. F. Albright, *Yahweh and the Gods of Canaan*, 1969.
Y.O.S.	*Yale Oriental Series.*
Z.A.	*Zeitschrift der Assyriologie.*
Z.A.W.	*Zeitschrift für die alttestamentliche Wissenschaft.*
Z.D.M.G.	*Zeitschrift der deutschen morgenländischen Gesellschaft.*
Z.D.P.V.	*Zeitschrift des deutschen Palästina Vereins.*

INTRODUCTION

PEOPLES AND NATIONS

THIS book is about peoples and nations in biblical times. One justification for its publication may well be the difficulty which exists in defining the term 'people' (Greek *ethnos*) and in tracing both development from 'people' to 'nation' (*demos*) and influence from one people to another. 'Nation' is largely a political term used of a distinct group of persons 'linked by a state or common will to a state'.[1] A 'people' may be characterized by common descent, a community of history, tradition, culture, custom, and language and occupy a definite territory. Religion may be an ethnic tie, but like 'civilization'—the structure of society distinguished by material and spiritual characteristics—it may override ethnic entities. Language may be a means of distinguishing a people, but while a change in language can mark assimilation into a new, normally more dominant, group, it is hazardous to base ethnological conclusions upon philological evidence alone. Language itself is no test of race since the same race may speak different languages and different races may speak the same language. 'Race'—the grouping of humans according to common physical characteristics—is properly the study of physical anthropologists. It is rarely mentioned in any document from the ancient Near East.

On the basis of language, modern research groups a number of the Old Testament peoples as 'Semito-Hamitic'. Thus the Hebrews are included with Akkadians, Amorites, Canaanites, Aramaeans, Phoenicians, Moabites, and Arabs (as 'Semites') and with Egyptians and Cushites ('Hamitic peoples'), all with languages which had a common origin.[2] The Hittites, as the later Persians, are classified as part of the Indo-European group of peoples, while the Sumerians, Hurrians, and Elamites are at present unassigned. Nothing outside the Old Testament references themselves is

[1] I. J. Gelb, 'The Function of Language in the Cultural Process of Expansion of Mesopotamian Society' in E. Kraeling (ed.), *City Invincible* (1960), p. 315.

[2] E. A. Speiser, *Interpreters' Dictionary of the Bible* (1962), sub. Man, ethnic divisions of.

known of a number of minor population groups (e.g. Hivites, Perizzites, Girgashites, Emim, Avim, etc.).

Historical evidence, supported by archaeological discovery, shows that, throughout the historical period at least, composite elements are to be found in most populations and languages of the biblical period. A mixed origin for the Hebrews themselves (as for their language) has been suggested by the intermingling with the Aramaeans (Deut. 26: 5), Amorites and Hittites (Ezek. 16: 3), Kenites (Exod. 18: 11), Canaanites (1 Sam. 7: 14), and Gibeonites (Josh. 9: 3).

A similar composite view can be seen in the so-called 'Table of Nations' (Gen. 10; cf. 1 Chron. 1: 5–23) which sets out a list of the descendants of Noah through his three sons, Shem, Ham, and Japheth, whose names have since been employed to designate both ethnic and language groups. In Genesis the list has been placed both as an introduction to the life of Abraham with whom the narrative focuses on the 'Hebrew' people and as the termination of the summary survey of the earlier history in a wider Near Eastern setting.

The 'Table' traces the sons of Noah in the reverse order to that of their birth. The sons of Japheth (verses 2–5) and Ham (verses 6–20) are followed by the lateral chosen line through the first-born Shem (verses 21–31) which is continued in the following chapter (Gen. 11). Each division of the list is followed by a statement that these were 'the sons of Japheth. . . in their own lands, each with their own language, by their families, by their nations' (verse 5); 'the sons of Ham by their families and languages, with their lands and nations' (verse 20); 'The sons of Shem, by their families, their languages, their lands and their nations' (verse 31). It has been suggested that these 'catch-phrases' may be traces of ancient colophons, a literary device found elsewhere in Babylonian and Hebrew texts to note the source from which the material had been abstracted or to link it with related information.[1] Lists, themselves a common early Mesopotamian literary form, giving personal and place names, including names of countries and mountains, are extant from the second millennium B.C. onwards. A genealogical ancestry of Hammurabi, king of Babylon (*c.* 1750 B.C.) contains names of individuals later applied to peoples descended from

[1] D. J. Wiseman, 'Genesis 10: some Archaeological Considerations', *Journal of the Transactions of the Victoria Institute* (1954), 14–25.

groupings of families or 'clans' rather than of 'tribes' (*šēḇeṭ*; *maṭṭeh*) comes with the Sinaitic covenant. The latter marked the first major step forward toward the birth of Israel as a 'nation'. The covenant treaty, with its roots in the Exodus-redemption concept which made Israel the people of the covenant (Exod. 12:6), was the historical basis which provided the necessary elements of nationality in common custom, government, a defined territory (Deut. 32:8–9), and above all common religious interests and practices. The Sinai covenant was the seal of Yahweh's choice of the people which went back to the time of Abraham (Gen. 12:1–3). Through this would be worked out their national role towards others in blessing. It held, however, the possibility of the loss of nationality through exile should the covenant ever be broken (Jer. 11:3–4). The Hebrews thought of themselves as the 'people of Yahweh' (2 Sam. 7:12), whose exclusiveness was to be marked among other ways by their care not to intermarry outside the kin groups (Ruth 1:22). This 'covenant-ideal' or attitude was to distinguish them throughout their history.

When the Hebrews settled in Palestine they found the military and political pressures such as to encourage a popular demand for that other contemporary expression of statehood—a governor or 'king like all the nations' around them (1 Sam. 8:5). This led to the territorial demarcation of their land and tribes and to the requirements made of any nation on the inter-state level. Such international agreements were often sealed by marriages between the respective ruling houses and by the exchange of trade and other missions. By the reign of Solomon the Hebrew kingdom was thus brought into contact with and dependence on the many peoples whose lands bordered it. The very phrases formerly used of close blood-relationship 'our brother, our flesh' (Gen. 37:27) are by now commonly used of non-kin and diplomatic activities. The relationship between Israel and Judah and other nations is a major theme in the Old Testament which is concerned with God and man in all his activities. There is thus a continuing interest for the Hebrews in the other peoples who surrounded them and whose presence was a constant temptation and, at times, a threat to their spiritual and physical existence. It is these peoples who are the subject of the following pages.

I

THE HEBREWS

H. CAZELLES

IT is important, in historical studies, to distinguish between Hebrews and Israelites. We are used to identifying them and, nowadays, one speaks of the Hebrew language,[1] not of the Israelite language. But this identification is late. A similar identification is that of the Jews with the Israelites, which only took place after the fall of Samaria; even at the time of the New Testament the Jews, or Judeans, are often distinguished from the Samaritans and the Galileans. In the same way the careful study of the Bible and archaeological discoveries has made it necessary to distinguish between Hebrews and Israelites.

The identification of the two terms seems to have come from the famous story of Joseph in Genesis, where the word Hebrew (*'iḇrî*) is very often applied to the Israelites (Gen. 39: 14–Exod. 10: 3). At first sight these texts seem to oppose Israelite and Egyptian nations. But further attention shows that the opposition does not lie precisely there. In the tradition represented by Exodus the Israelites did not depart alone, but with a large mixed group of non-Israelites (Exod. 12: 38; Num. 11: 4). It is the contrast between masters and servants that is here underlined, whether they are the servants of Potiphar or the servants of pharaoh; the texts concern the period when Egypt controlled Canaan, which contemporary scribes called Hurru, and where they made prisoners or recruited their personnel. In these texts 'Hebrew' is a very general term, which is used by the Egyptians or when someone is talking to Egyptians. The 'land of the Hebrews' (Gen. 40: 15)[2] is the land without political unity, 'the place of the Canaanites, the Hittites, the Amorites, the Perizzites, the Hivites and the Jebusites' (Exod. 3: 8). The God of the Hebrews (Exod. 3: 18; 5: 3; 7: 16; 9: 1, 13; 10: 3) is an expression used in the dialogue with pharaoh to distinguish him from the gods of pharaoh and from pharaoh himself. The same expression is found in cuneiform texts, and the Bible itself states that Israelites and Midianites together honoured him (Exod. 18). Finally the statement that 'the Egyptians might not eat bread with the Hebrews' (Gen. 43: 32) concerns a social rather than a national distinction, for Genesis 46: 34 says that 'every shepherd is an abomination to the Egyptians', the shepherds here being Jacob and his household. Koch does not accept 'Hebrew' as a sociological category. For him it designates a 'wider circle' of population than the Israelites.[3] A similar conclusion is reached later in this chapter. Koch believes that before the J redaction a 'Hebrew' story of the Exodus had already been written, and this was used by J for his 'Israelite' history.[4] As the term 'Hebrew' disappears before the Exodus (after Exod. 10: 3), reappears only in Numbers 24: 24 (as *'eḇer*), and is related to the Kittim, this postulated Exodus source for J is very doubtful. The term 'Hebrew' does not seem to have entered the biblical vocabulary from the Hebrew population itself, but from its use by Egyptians and their Philistine successors when alluding to Asiatic foreigners. The workers and prisoners called *'prw* in Egypt, as will be shown, do not seem to be identical with the *'br* peoples of Genesis 10: 25–30. The latter include the Arabian tribe of Yoktan and South Arabian tribes including Hadramaut and Ophir. The notion of an *'br* population wider than Israel does not seem to belong to the old Israelite traditions, but comes from an international concept by which Abraham, the father of nations (Gen. 17; P) or father of the Keturah tribes (Gen. 25; J), could include among his descendants more than Israel.

Indeed, those who speak of 'Hebrews' in the Bible, after the references by Egyptians, are the Philistines, who, traditionally, came from Câphtor (Crete) and are allied to other Sea Peoples. The Philistines were, for a time, the heirs of the pharaohs on the 'Palestinian' coast land. These city dwellers considered the Hebrews as a motley crew from the hinterland, to be treated with contempt (1 Sam. 4: 6, 9; 13: 3, 7; 14: 11; 29: 3). The Israelites are included, but other elements are meant as well. This is proved by three texts which have often been studied, most recently by Weingreen, Weippert, and Koch, and which can only be fully understood if a distinction is made between Israelites and Hebrews. 1 Samuel

14: 21[5] concerns the Hebrews 'who had been with the Philistines before that time' and the Israelites who were fighting with Saul and Jonathan; the Hebrews change sides and join the Israelites. In the previous chapter (13: 6 and 7) Hebrews and Israelites had taken different attitudes towards the Philistine army; the Israelites stayed where they were, even though they had to hide themselves in caves and among bushes and rocks, while the Hebrews crossed the Jordan to the land of Gad and Gilead. Finally there is 1 Samuel 13: 3, where the distinction is less clear. The text as we have it has perhaps been edited under the influence of the identification between Israelites and Hebrews, but the Greek text can be useful here. Saul wishes to let all the 'Hebrews' know of the victory of Jonathan over the Philistines; he also tries to attract to the side of the Israelites, who had become odious to the Philistines, a more numerous following.

After Saul the term 'Hebrew' practically disappears from the spoken language. Deuteronomy (15: 12) and Jeremiah (34: 9, 14) employ the term, but only in reference to an older text, the law concerning the 'Hebrew' slave in Exodus 21: 2. It is really only a quotation. As for Jonah 1:9, it is an isolated text from a period which tends to use archaic expressions; the hero, speaking with foreign sailors, is more or less in the same situation as Joseph speaking with the Egyptians, even if, with Koch, it is noted that Jonah's ship left Joppa on the Philistinian coast. But Joppa was never one of the five Philistine cities. According to the Eshmunazar inscription (l. 19), certainly by the fourth century B.C., it was a Phoenician city. One can say that after the reign of David, who built up the state by means of a policy of assimilation, and that of Solomon, who set up administrative districts[6] in areas where the Israelites constituted a minority of the population, the distinction between the various elements of the population fades, and the word 'Hebrew' is only used in texts which reproduce a more ancient tradition. Whatever their tribe, the Israelites consider themselves as 'sons of Israel'. The kingdom of Saul and David is the kingdom of Israel the ancestor (1 Sam. 24: 20), although they also considered themselves as connected with Abram the Hebrew (Gen. 14: 13), father of a multitude of nations, including the Midianites, the Dedanites, and many others (Gen. 25: 1–4).

(i) *The Discovery of the* ʿapiru/Ḫapiru

The distinction between Hebrews and Israelites is important because Egyptian texts discovered in the nineteenth century A.D. mention on the one hand Israel and on the other people whom the hieroglyphs indicate as *ʿprw*, the *w* being the sign of the plural. These texts do not all come from the same period. Merenptah, successor of Ramesses II, in the fifth year of his reign (*c.* 1230 B.C.), when he was campaigning between Canaan and Hurru, came across Israel near Yanoam, Ascalon, and Gezer. Israel was not sedentary at the time, since the text uses the determinative of the tribe and not that of the city. Neither Ramesses II nor Sety I, at the beginning of the same thirteenth century B.C., had come across Israel in their Asiatic campaigns. But they had met the *ʿprw*, or at least Sety I had, for he mentions their 'revolt' on one of the two stelas which he erected in Palestine itself, at Beth-Shan.

At least nine Egyptian texts clearly mentioning the *ʿprw* are now known. These texts range from the first quarter of the fifteenth century B.C. to the eleventh century B.C. They are therefore both earlier and later than the stela of Merenptah. The fifteenth-century texts mention either warriors in Canaan or captives employed as servants to 'strain wine'. In the twelfth century under Ramesses III they were prisoners given to the temples. Then, under Ramesses IV, *ʿprw* are found in the quarries of the Wadi Hammamat. In the eleventh century they disappear from Egyptian sources, just as they disappear from the living language of Israel in the tenth century.

The identification of the *ʿprw* of the Egyptian texts with the *ʿbrm* of the Bible seemed to imply no problems from the linguistic point of view since, after Müller and Burchardt, there was evidence for the correspondence of Egyptian *p* and Semitic *b*. The vowels were to prove more troublesome, however. The Egyptian texts do not record the vowels, but the fourteenth-century cuneiform texts found in Egypt do (Tell el Amarna letters). In the area where the pharaohs were fighting the *ʿprw*, and taking them prisoners, the diplomatic correspondence of the court of Amenophis III and Amenophis IV mentions rebels called *ḫabiru* or *ḫapiru* (the same syllable can be read *bi* or *pi*). Their name is written out in full in the letters sent to pharaoh by the King of Jerusalem (Amarna letters

286–90). It is clearly the same elements, or similar groups, who are called in other letters (Amarna 88, 34) SA.GAZ in ideographic (Sumerian) writing. These *Ḫapiru* were active in Canaan and also further north in Phoenicia. Later on evidence was discovered showing that these SA.GAZ/*Ḫapiru* were present in a much wider area, as far as Mesopotamia, beyond the Tigris and in Asia Minor. They are mentioned in texts which range from the third to the first millennium B.C. The later texts in fact reproduce ancient traditions and speak of these people and of their gods in the past.

Should one identify the Egyptian *ʿprw*, the cuneiform *Ḫab/piru* and the biblical *ʿbrm*? Scholars were divided on this question and they remain so. Many considered the vocalic elements in *ʿib̲rî* (pl. *ʿib̲rîm*, rarely *ʿib̲riyyîm* (Exod. 3: 18) and fem. *ʿib̲rīyah*) as incompatible with *Ḫabiru*. But, as Bruce has emphasized,[7] what mattered most in the discussion was the parallel which scholars tried to draw between the actions of the *Ḫabiru* and the conquest of Joshua. It was a false starting-point, and it soon became clear that it is impossible to reconcile the account of the conquest of Canaan in the book of Joshua with the movements of the *Ḫabiru* so far as they can be deduced from the Amarna letters.

However, the discovery of other texts from the fourteenth and thirteenth centuries B.C. has allowed some progress to take place, and has put an end to certain controversies. These texts, discovered at Ras-Shamra (Ugarit), are written in different languages and writings, one of these being close to the cuneiform of Amarna and the other close to Hebrew. One city called Halbi (like Aleppo) is given four names, which are perhaps the four quarters of the city. One of these names was written *Ḫal-bi* SA.GAZ in syllabic cuneiform and *ḫlb ʿprm* in West Semitic.[8] This provided the equation *Ḫapiru* = SA.GAZ = *ʿprm* (plural). There was no further objection to the identification of the *Ḫab/piru* of Amarna with the Egyptian *ʿprw*.

But to all appearances the gap had widened between these *Ḫapiru* and the biblical *ʿib̲r(iyy)îm*. However, the gap proved to be less than was at one time thought, at least as far as the consonants were concerned. The correspondence of the Hebrew ʿ to the *ḫ* was no problem, since the *ʿain* cannot be directly rendered in cuneiform. As for *b/p*, the passage from the unvoiced to the voiced consonant is frequent in Semitic dialects; moreover certain late Babylonian texts (end of the second millennium B.C.) have a rare rendering *Ḫa-bir-a* (which could not have been pronounced *Ḫapira*), and this makes it more probable that the pronunciation may have evolved towards the end of the second millennium B.C., the biblical texts having been composed, at the earliest, at the end of the same second millennium.

Biblical criticism has made progress too. It has not only established the distinction between Hebrews and Israelites; it has also discerned how the basic data have been edited differently during the centuries. It came to recognize as late Genesis 14, where Abram the Hebrew is mentioned at Hebron, and Genesis 23, where the same Abraham buys a cave at Hebron (*ḥbrn*) from Ephron (*ʿprn*) the Hittite. Nevertheless, the conclusions to be drawn from these observations are still under discussion. They prepare the solution to the problem, but one cannot yet say that they have given a solution. Before working out the relation of the Hebrews (and of the Israelites) to the *Ḫapiru* it is necessary to inquire who the *Ḫapiru* were.

(ii) *Expansion, Activity and Status of the* Ḫapiru/ʿprw

This inquiry is greatly helped by the publication of two collections bringing together and classifying the texts which concern the *Ḫapiru*: that of J. Bottéro (of which the numbering has been reproduced here as B.), and that of M. Greenberg (G.).[9] A few rare texts, already known, are missing from one or other of these collections. Others have since been published; they come from the Sumerian (Falkenstein),[10] from the ancient Hittite empire (Otten),[11] from Nuzi to the east of the Tigris (E. Cassin),[12] from Ugarit (Nougayrol[13] from Virolleaud),[14] Amarna (Edzard),[15] and Egypt (see p. 15).

The first question arising is this: It is certain that *ḫapiru* in certain places and at certain periods have been considered as being SA.GAZ. But it does not follow that we can read *ḫapiru* for every occurrence of the term SA.GAZ. Indeed the Mesopotamian and West Semitic lexicographers have never given in their list of equivalents the equation SA.GAZ (or its variants SAG.GAZ, SA.GAZ.ZA, SA.GA.AZ, GAZ) = *ḫapiru*. The Akkadian equivalent for the Sumerian SA.GAZ is always *ḫabbatu*, which means 'brigand, highway robber'. SA.GAZ does not mean anything in Sumerian; SAG.GAZ would mean something ('head-breaker'?) but it is an exceptional way of writing and is a late interpretation. B. Landsberger and A. Falkenstein therefore consider SA.GAZ to be a Sumerian adaptation of the Akkadian *šaggašu*, which means 'aggressor'; this interpretation is helped by the fact that GAZ can be read GAŠ. It seems to be confirmed by the description of the SA.GAZ in the text studied by Kramer and considered anew by Falkenstein: 'The SA.GAZ, these people without clothes who travel in dead silence, who destroy everything, whose menfolk go where they will, whose womenfolk have spindles . . . they established their tents and their camps . . . they spend their time in the countryside without observing the decrees of my king Shulgi.' At the end of the third millennium B.C. the SA.GAZ are therefore marauders on the edge of the ordered society dominated by the Third Dynasty of Ur. But the name can be applied to any non-sedentary population which is scarcely subordinate to authority.

The term SA.GAZ is thus a generic term which is wider in application than the *Ḫapiru*; we are not entitled to consider every SA.GAZ automatically as a *ḫapiru*. We must await the appearance of the word written out syllabically in full before we can treat of the *ḫapiru* and try to see why they were considered as SA.GAZ. Great caution is needed when dealing with the texts of Ur III and of the period of Agade. However, on a tablet from Tell Brak, which Gadd dated from the period of Agade, one finds the personal name *ḫa-b/pi-ra-am* (B. 6); this takes us to the Upper Habur, west of Nineveh. A little further north, in a text of Alishar from the Assyrian colony in Cappadocia, we meet with the *Ḫapiru*; this is from the latest period of Kultepe, probably under Warad-Sin, and these *Ḫapiru* are prisoners. They are described as *awīlu*, which is not necessarily an honorific title at that period, but they have sufficient wealth to buy themselves out of captivity (B. 5).

At about the same time (Larsa period, nineteenth century B.C.) the *Ḫapiru* appear in Southern Mesopotamia in administrative texts. They are generally referred to as SA.GAZ, but one text, identical in form to the others, spells out clearly *ḫa-pi-ri*. Whereas in the Laws of Lipit-Ishtar (*c.* 1934–1924 B.C.) one can still be doubtful as to the nature of the SA.GAZ, here it is clear that the SA.GAZ are *Ḫapiru*. They are soldiers (B. 16) with a chief

(B. 17), and they receive supplies of food. In a similar text found at Susa in Elam, sheep are recorded as supplied to them (B. 35) and to certain other groups as well; all these groups are called 'soldiers of the West', which is interesting.

At the same period one meets them in numerous texts from Mari on the Euphrates, to the west of Babylonia. These *Ḫapiru* (never written SA.GAZ) are also soldiers (B. 18, B. 20) with their chiefs, and one of their groups is recorded as having reached the number of 2,000 (B. 18). They pass from the service of one chief to another (B. 29) 'in the district of Shubat-Shamash'. As a result of this mobility they are identified by geographical element; they are 'from the (flat) country' (Bottéro), or 'from the country' (Kupper; *ša mâtim*) (B. 18), from Yamutbal (B. 19), from Suḫu (south of Mari) (B. 33), and one of them flees from Eshnunna (B. 30). They own donkeys (G. 15). They carry out raids in Idamaraz, and they capture towns like Iahmumum, Suruzum, Ashushik, and Luhaia, though they do not keep them. In order to stir up trouble they join other groups like the inhabitants of Talhaia and of Aslakka (B. 27). Disagreeable as they are to the king of Mari, they are sometimes even more so to the king of Assyria.

In a slightly later text (eighteenth century B.C.) found further west, at Alalakh in Syria, the *Ḫapiru* make peace with the King of the land, Irkabtum, under the leadership of a certain Šemuba. A treaty accompanied by oaths is also made between *Ḫapiri* and Hittite troops in two texts from the old Hittite empire, i.e. contemporary with or slightly later than the Mari period (Otten). Other texts from the old Hittite empire show the *Ḫapiri* as organized troops whom the Hittite king can employ. He is able to group as many as 3,000 of them, whom he employs on garrison duty. It is important to note that in the same chronicle, in archaic Hittite, a text which is unfortunately badly damaged mentions together a leader of the Hurrian army and 3,000 *Ḫapiru* soldiers. In no other text of this period are the *Ḫapiru* either the foes or the allies of the Hurrians: one is justified in asking whether the *Ḫapiru* do not constitute a Hurrian element (B. 72′).

We shall find the *Ḫapiru* again at the end of the sixteenth century B.C. and at the beginning of the fifteenth in the region of Alalakh, which was pervaded by Hurrian elements, so that Garelli can say that they constituted 'the overwhelming majority of the population'. The *Ḫapiru* have Hurrian names (B. 41, B. 44, B. 45, G. 50). When the word is written out in full it ends with the vowel *-i*, but the scribes usually employ the ideogram SA.GAZ. They are soldiers (B. 40, B. 41), or even quarrymen, under the orders of SA.GAZ leaders. One SA.GAZ from Tapduwa has fifteen soldiers under him; the SA.GAZ chief from Šarkuhe has twenty-nine; another has 1,436. They can form separate groupings, such as the one with which king Idrimi took refuge (B. 37); but they constitute an important social class, since in a list giving the names of offices (B. 39) the *Ḫapiri* come between a 'royal son' and an officer of the palace. We shall find the same situation in Canaan. They can own houses and, as in the Mari period, we can see them spread in different regions and places (B. 44). They are people who must be reckoned with.

During the course of the fifteenth century also the *Ḫapiru* appear in large numbers, but in different conditions, to the east of the Tigris in another Hurrian city, Nuzi. The documents, already numerous, have been increased by the work of Bottéro and Greenberg (E. Cassin). In certain respects the status of the *Ḫapiru* at Nuzi is similar to that at Mari or Alalakh, but in other ways it is different. At Nuzi *Ḫapiru* is always written out in full and never with the ideogram SA.GAZ, which was rather pejorative in Mesopotamian eyes. They can receive food rations, as do horses (HSS XV. 237), and clothing (HSS XIII. 123, 152) but they are capable of owning horses (HSS XIV. 53; XV. 239). They can be stone-carvers (*nurpiannuḫlu*, B. 64);[16] they can be 'decurions' (*emantuḫlu*, HSS XV. 62), an office which can refer to soldiers or to workers; they have a status which in the ration lists associates them with fishermen (HSS XIV. 102), carpenters (HSS XV. 237), and indeed with horses.

This status appertains to men and to women (B. 60, 61, 63, 65, 66). It is not always the same in all respects for men and women. Woman is more restricted than man, and it is in the case of women breaking a contract (*nabalkutu*, lit. 'transgress, turn away') that it is said: 'her eyes will be plucked out and she shall be sold.' It is not certain that the expression is to be taken literally. A man can go away as long as there is compensation, either in the form of a substitute (B. 60) or a tenfold substitute (B. 56), or else on payment of a rather large sum, one gold and one silver mina (B. 66 c). Neither men nor women were independent. They could be put at the disposal of the palace (B. 64) or of personages like Tehiptilla: Sukri-Teshup is able to take a *Ḫapiru* to the land of Arrapha, which was, however, not far away (B. 64). But their condition could become worse. In the case of theft or misbehaviour the *Ḫapiru* sank to the level of *wardu*, 'slave' (B. 54).

The *Ḫapiru* are not slaves, therefore, although their masters exercise 'lordship' (*ewurutu*) over them. There was, however, a difficulty of terminology at Nuzi on this point, for normally they enter '*ana warduti*', which should be translated 'into service' (B. 59). There is one case of a *Ḫapiru* entering into adoption (*ana martūti*), but this seems to be a case involving two contracts; the woman Watija enters the household of Paitae as adopted daughter and introduces her own son, who had been up till then *wardu* of Tehiptilla and who now becomes a *Ḫapiru* like his mother (able to depart as long as there is compensation). The important thing is that the *Ḫapiru* enters into this condition freely, 'of his own accord' (*ana ramānišu*) or 'from his mouth and from his lips'; he can keep it during his lifetime, but he can also leave it, under the conditions mentioned above. Sometimes the master has to pay a price to acquire the right of 'lordship' over them. The status of *Ḫapiru* is often acquired by people coming from another town (Lupti, HSS XVI. 396; Zarimena, HSS XIII. 152; Patwa, HSS XVI. 438), or from a foreign land like Assyria (B. 49, B. 50) or Akkad, i.e. Babylonia (B. 56, B. 63). In some cases they only enter into this status after a certain time (B. 56, in the year after arrival from Akkad).

Finally, it must be noted that the condition of the *Ḫapiru* at Nuzi can vary. We have seen that they could be stone-carvers or 'decurions'. They may also be *ubbutu* (HSS XV. 237, line 12). This term is associated with the *taḫlulu* (HSS XIV. 166) and with the *bīt kīli*, and has been studied by E. Cassin. It concerns 'men who are the object of bodily restraint and who perform thereby forced labour for the profit of a creditor'.[17] They were capable therefore, not only of buying themselves out, but also of contracting debts and of putting themselves into the legal situation known from Israelite institutions, the *'bṭ* (Deut. 15: 6; 24: 10; Joel 2: 7; Hab. 2: 6). This comparison is as important from the philological as from the historical point of view.

The *Ḫapiru* of Nuzi thus have obvious connections with the Hurrian population of the place, and one must ask whether it was not because of these connections that a better status than that of the slave was conferred on these refugees from Assyria, Babylonia, and elsewhere. Another connection must be noted. It can happen that a *Ḫapiru* provides as substitute a 'man of the Nullu', i.e. Lullu. Now other texts from the fifteenth century B.C., Hittite texts, provide at least thirteen examples where the parallel expressions are Lullu and *Ḫapiri*, the gods of the *Ḫapiri*[18] and the gods of the *Lulaḫḫi* (Hurrian ending *he/i*?). These gods are witnesses in treaties contracted between the Hittite kings and various other populations, not only those of the Middle Euphrates. The *Lulaḫḫu* were a people who lived to the east of the Hittites and not very far from Nuzi. It is tempting but perhaps erroneous to identify Lulaḫḫu with the land of Elaḫut; A. Goetze considers Elaḫut to be the same as the Luhaja which is mentioned in a Mari text as having been laid waste by the *Ḫapiru* and the people of Talhaiat.

However, another fifteenth-century Hittite text represents the *Lulaḫḫu* and the *Ḫapiru* as of an inferior social condition: this is a witchcraft text, which places the 'tongue' of the *Ḫapiri* and the *Lulaḫḫi* after that of the nobles, priests, and Awisili(?) men, but before that of the dead, the living, and the magicians. A Luwite text which lists related pairs has *Ḫapiri–Lulaḫḫi* after father–mother, brother–sister, slave–slave girl. Whereas the *Ḫapiru* had a status superior to that of the slave at Nuzi, we can see that in non-Hurrian Asia Minor they had an inferior status.

Historical texts are rare. One of them is probably a list of booty made up of prisoners: 600 SA.GAZ are given to the 'god of the temple' (*ili bîti*), just as we shall find them given to the Egyptian temples of the Delta by Ramesses III. An unfavourable Babylonian omen which did not mention *Ḫapiru* was translated into Hittite (B. 87), and the translation shows that the Hittites considered the *Ḫapiru* as dangerous foes who would 'enter the land' if the omen were to be fulfilled. Finally, a century later Mursilis II (*c.* 1334–1306 B.C.), in an arbitration treaty between Duppi-Teshub of Amurru and Tudhaliya of Carchemish,[19] recalls that the town of Jaruwatta in the land of Barga (probably south of Aleppo and west of the Orontes) had been captured by the king of the Hurrian country and given to the 'grandfather of Tette, the

SA.GAZ'. We thus find once more a Hurrian–SA.GAZ (or *Ḫapiru*) connection among the enemies of the Hittites. Mursilis I returns the town to Abiradda, whom the SA.GAZ had dispossessed.

These Hittite texts have taken us down to the fourteenth century B.C., and even later than the period of the Amarna letters. These letters reveal the activity of the SA.GAZ–*Ḫapiru* not only in Syria, but also in Phoenicia, near Sumur, Batrun and Byblos, in Upe near Damascus, and further south as far as Jerusalem. This is not surprising, since the Egyptians had met with *'prw* since Amenophis II in the fifteenth century B.C. In a campaign dating from the year 9 of his reign, which does not seem to have gone beyond North Palestine, he had taken prisoner '127 kings, 179 brothers of kings, 3,600 *'prw*, 15,200 Shasu alive, 36,300 Hurrians, 15,070 *ngś* alive, and 30,652 of their *'ḏt*(?)'.[20] This last element is a puzzle, and it is possible that the possessive pronoun refers to the people of Syria (*ngś* = *Nuḫasse*), previously mentioned. In any case, the sociological position of the *'prw* is clear. Both in numbers and in position they are between the kings and brothers of kings, on the one hand, and, on the other, the mass of the Shasu (nomads or semi-nomads) and of the Hurrians. They are thus the exact equivalent of the groups of military aristocracy that we have found at Mari, at Alalakh, and in the Hittite texts.

A similar sequence is found in an Amarna letter written about seventy years later by Biriawaza, governor of Upe, near Damascus, to Amenophis IV (B. 132). It gives Biriawaza, then his brothers, then the SA.GAZ, then the Sutu, who in the cuneiform texts are more or less the equivalent of the Egyptian Shasu. Once they are associated with the *ḫabbati*, highway robbers (Bottéro on B. 148), and are called 'wandering dogs' (*ḫalqu*) (B. 93). They can be bribed (B. 115). The name of any of their chiefs is never mentioned.

They are, however, a powerful military factor (ERIM, B. 93, B. 97, etc.). They are capable of winning over towns (Sumur, B. 99), mayors (*ḫazanu*, B. 96) and kings like the King of Hazor (B. 127). They were particularly hostile towards Rib-Addi, governor of Byblos, and made an alliance against him with Abd'Ashirta of Amurru, and later with Aziru his son. Sumur, Batrun, Shigata, and Ambi were taken and occupied (B. 99, 106).

Byblos and Ibirta suffered the same fate (B. 111), and so did the towns of Taḫši and Upe later on (B. 131). Labaya of Shechem grants them a territory (B. 145).

From the letters recently published by Edzard we know that some groups could come under the jurisdiction of the Egyptian king and be sent to 'the towns of Kašu to dwell there'. Is Kašu Nubia? This is not necessarily so here, since in the Posener Execration texts (E. 50–1) a country *Kwšw* is mentioned which is certainly in Asia and not in Nubia. Some biblical texts connect this Cush or Cushan with Midian and Judah (Hab. 3:7; Jud. 3:8);[21] the Kushite wife of Moses seems to have been the same as the Midianite Zipporah (Exod. 2: 21; Num. 12: 1). In the Amarna letters originating from Jerusalem *Kaša/u* does not appear to refer to a place so far off as Nubia. It is also said that the SA.GAZ *a-pu-ar-ra* will dwell in it (*ina libbišu*, (*ki*)?–*mu-ú ša aḫ-ta-bal-šu-nu-t*(*i*), 'an (St)elle derer, die ich weggeführt habe' (Edzard). It is noteworthy that the pharaoh uses the root *ḫabātu*, the equivalent of SA.GAZ in the Akkadian syllabaries. It is to be noted too that this transfer of population is similar to another transfer alluded to by Harmhab.[22]

They are in league with other 'lords' (*awīlū*). Thus one of them who has an Egyptian name, Amenhatpi, lord of Tushulti, takes them in after each more or less successful engagement against Mahzibi, Giluni, and Magdali (Migdol). He is compelled to hand over forty of them who have made their escape after their defeat before Hazi. He himself becomes suspect, however, and has to flee to some other SA.GAZ (B. 130). In the south the King of Jerusalem was hostile to them, although he is the only one to write their name out in full and not with the pejorative form SA.GAZ; perhaps this is because he himself has a Hurrian name, which Thureau-Dangin read as Abdi-Hebat.[23] Harabu, Suwardata of Kelle (the Keilah of the Bible), and Iapahi fight against them. But Iapahi's youngest brother goes to Muhhazi in order to come to terms with them (B. 147); it is likely that he is the Milki-ilu who, in league with Labaya of Shechem and his sons, will deliver his territory over to the SA.GAZ, preferring to come to terms with them rather than with pharaoh's commissioners. This gives the SA.GAZ more facility for taking action against Aialuna (Ayyalon) and Ṣarḫa (Samson's Zorah). However, it is not clear

WINGATE COLLEGE LIBRARY
WINGATE, N. C.

whether they kept the towns they captured any longer than did the *Ḫapiru* at Mari, or the sons of Jacob at Shechem (Gen. 34).

We know that about 1300 B.C. Sety I was obliged to cope with what he considered a revolt on the part of the SA.GAZ. They came from the mountain of Iarimuta and from Tjr, which are difficult to identify, and the pharaoh was compelled to afford protection against them to the Asiatics of *Rhm*(?). In the tale of the capture of Joppa, which was composed about this time by an Egyptian scribe, they constitute once again an element hostile to Egyptian power; there is the danger that they will insinuate themselves in liaison with the *maryannu*,[24] who are asking for fodder for their animals (the *maryannu* are an Indo-European element, and are often linked with the Hurrians; they are mentioned after the *ʿprw* in a list of Ramesses III, B. 189); however, the relation between the two is not clear and the text is damaged.

Posener has recently found a mention of the *ʿprw* in the first line of an ostracon in the Strasbourg Library (fig. 1).[25] These men are connected with the handling of stones. As the script seems to be that of Ramessid times (Nineteenth Dynasty), such an activity fits well with the *ʿprw* workers under Ramesses III and IV.

In the thirteenth century B.C. the *Ḫapiru* are known to us mainly by the texts from Ugarit in Syria. They are still foreign and untrustworthy elements, capable of destroying a castle (*dimtu*, B. 162), and in a text which reproduces an older tradition (B. 157) the SA.GAZ is placed between the thief and the evildoer. It was a privilege in a royal grant to receive the assurance that a SA.GAZ would not enter the house, and that the service of the royal messengers would not be required (i.e., probably, that they would not have to be given lodgings; B. 159).

The SA.GAZ, however, show a tendency towards settlement. We have already seen that in the territory of Ugarit there was a town or a district called Halbi of the *ʿprw*. A treaty between Hattusilis III the Hittite (1275–1250 B.C.) and the king of Ugarit mentions the territory of the SA.GAZ in the Hittite land, where fugitives from Ugarit could take refuge; the Hittite king undertakes to extradite them. A Hittite text mentions a town of the *Ḫapiru* (G. 137). A certain *Ḫapiru* is party to a lawsuit before the King of Carchemish and the king sends him elsewhere as he does not reside there (B. 158), but it would have been possible for him to do so. We learn from the personal names of Ugarit that nearly half of the population was Hurrian.[26] A note concerning a debt of oil has the name of a *Ḫapiru*, son of Kuiaba (B. 160), which reminds one of the Nuzi name, ARDU-Kubi; this should perhaps be read 'Abdu-Kubi', as Thureau-Dangin does for the name of the king

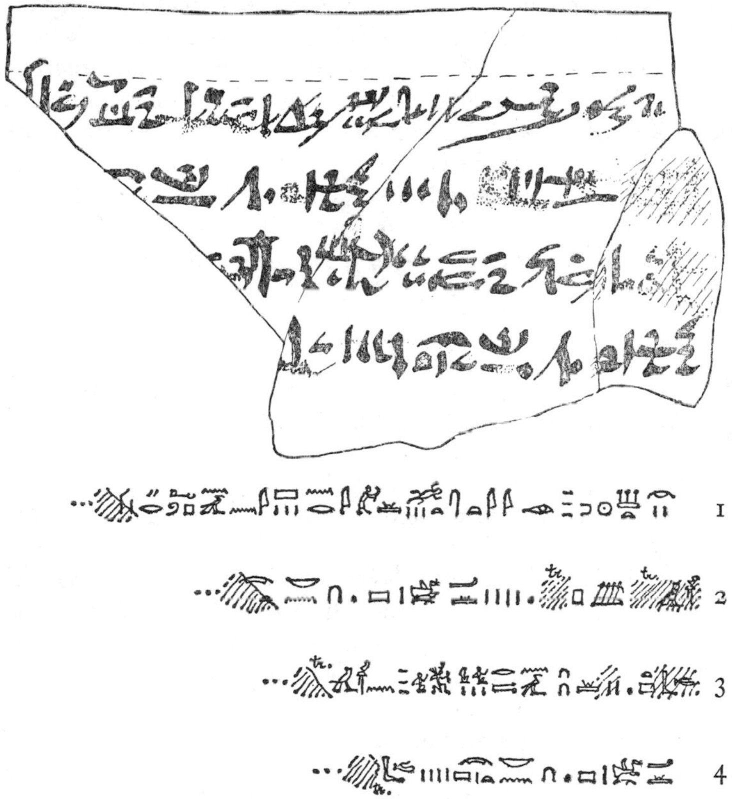

FIG. 1

of Jerusalem. Elsewhere, next to a certain Ari-Teshub who bears a characteristically Hurrian name, a *Ḫapiru* is mentioned (B. 163).

Other personal names of this type will occur; but they will disappear as a group. As J. Bottéro has noted, SA.GAZ in divination texts and lexicographical collections need not be rendered *Ḫap/biru*; it stands for *ḫabbatu*, 'dangerous brigands'. Certain isolated personal names occur with the epithet 'Habirean', and reading with *b* becomes more and more likely;[27] this is especially so in the case of *Ḫa-bir-a-a*, who is the beneficiary of a gift of real estate from Marduk-aḫḫē-eriba (*c*. 1060 B.C., B. 166); also in the case of *Ḫarbi-si*-ḪU, who is called the Habirean in a letter of Ninurta-nādin-šumati of Babylon (*c*. 1150 B.C.; B. 165), putting him at the disposal of the king of Assyria. It had been surmised that a neo-Assyrian text describing Nineveh mentions a god Ḫabiru, next to Kube, which would have paralleled the *Ḫapiri* gods of the Hittite texts. But there is now agreement that this refers to the gods *of the Ḫapiri*; W. von Soden prefers to see a reference to a deity *ḫa-wi-ru*, adored in the same temple. Just as there is no reference to contemporary Hebrews in texts of the first millennium from Israel, so, too, cuneiform and Egyptian texts of the same period do not know of any *ḫapiru*/*ʿprw* groups.

(iii) *Origin and Nature of the* ḫapiru/ʿprw

Having thus brought together the historical and geographical evidence, scholars have tried to discover the etymology of the name and the origins of the group.

Most of them have favoured a Semitic etymology. Since the form with *p* has proved to be older than the form with *b*, the root which is usually put forward at present is *eperu* (*epru*, *ḫaparu* at Amarna) in cuneiform texts, *ʿeper* in Massoretic Hebrew, which means 'dust'. E. Dhorme first put this forward, and the suggestion was taken up again forcefully by Borger. W. F. Albright supports it, and quotes in its favour the text of Falkenstein on the SA.GAZ who haunt the steppe and live in camps and tents.

However, this description is very like the accounts by the Babylonians of the Asiatics from the West, the Amorites and their god,[28] those whom the Egyptian wisdom text of Merikare[29] calls the 'miserable Asiatics'. This description hardly fits the *Ḫapiru* as such. It is strange, moreover, that the Egyptian scribes never used before *ʿprw* the determinative of the legs, of the land, or of the desert countries; not even that of the boomerang of the nomads. They used a determinative difficult to interpret (Gardiner Aa 20, 'doubtful'), used also for the verb *ʿpr*, meaning 'to equip, to provide' (an ideogram which is hard to explain).[30] This does not correspond to the Semitic 'dust' but to the Akkadian *epēru*. This was the etymology which W. F. Albright used to support; A. Goetze still seems to be in favour of it and adduces in support *ḫabatu*, meaning 'to receive subsidies from another', which is a homonym of *ḫabatu* = SA.GAZ. However, the existence of this *ḫabatu* has been called in question, and the homonyms given in B. 157 for AMA (Ugarit) require as equivalent to SA.GAZ not *ḫabatu* 'provide' but *ḫabbatu* 'brigand'. As for the verb *ḫapārum* (B. 5′), the relevance of which has been underlined by Landsberger, it is hardly mentioned in the current dictionaries. The Chicago Assyrian Dictionary (Ḫ, 217b, *sub ḫubullu*) proposes the translation 'went over'; this relates it to the Hebrew *'āḇar*, but does not fit in with the original *p* of the root, which is now well established.

It therefore seems established that there was an attempt on the part of the Akkadian scribes, or the scribes in their tradition, to link this term to a Semitic root. But they never knew exactly whether to see in it *ebēru*, *ḫabru* or *epēru*. They passed from one to another and they influenced the Egyptian scribes in the direction of *epēru*, 'provide'. It seems to me that B. Landsberger was right in seeing objections only where a Semitic etymology is concerned, and R. Dussaud was of the same opinion.

G. Dossin therefore considered the possibility of the Sumerian GABIRI meaning 'desert'. The *Ḫapiru* would have been warrior bands in the desert, the beduins of those times. For a long time I considered this opinion as valid, for want of a better.[31] But the Sumerian texts only know of SA.GAZ, and they describe them rather as MAR.TU, people of the West, than as *Ḫapiru*. The milieu where we find *Ḫapiru* is not a Sumerian one. The Susa tablet specifies that the *Ḫapiru* are soldiers from the West.

The milieu where we do find *Ḫapiru* is in fact a Hurrian one. They appear in Cappadocia as neighbours of the Hittites and of the Assyrian colonists; and it is now in the region north-east of the Tigris that scholars are looking for the first habitat of the Hurrians:

> The heaviest concentrations can be observed to the east of the Tigris, but there are also Hurrians in Upper Mesopotamia, where they control several small states, and they have gained a foothold on the western bank of the Euphrates. It looks as if, coming from a generally north-eastern direction, the Hurrians moved down in ever-increasing numbers from the mountainous border of the Fertile Crescent and advanced to meet the Amorites . . . (Kupper).[32]

The Hurrians appear in history as early as 2300 B.C., and it is in a region which is to become Hurrian-dominated, the region of the Upper Khabur, that the personal name *Ḫapiram* appears (Tell Brak). The language of the area from Urarṭu to the Caucasus will be related to theirs. Later we find Hurrians at Mari. Kupper estimates that nearly a third of the population of Chagar Bazar was Hurrian. Although for a time the Hurrian element was thought to have been minimal at Mari, round which *Ḫapiru* groups gravitated, Kupper has counted four or five princes with Hurrian names, like Arishenni of Nahur and Shukru-Teshub of Elahut.

We have to ask whether it is by chance that numerous *Ḫapiru* are found in the regions of Alalakh and Nuzi, which were extensively settled by Hurrians. Is it by chance that in Hittite texts the *Ḫapiri* are treated as strangers and intruders in the same way as the Hurrians? At the same period, the fifteenth century B.C., Egyptian texts reveal their presence in Canaan at a time when Egyptian scribes call the area 'Hurru'. In the Amarna period, it is the Hurrian king of Jerusalem who writes their name out in full and avoids using the pejorative ideogram SA.GAZ, even though he is their enemy. They then fade away and disappear, just as in the Bible the Hurrian wave of invasion is only a memory from the patriarchal age which has left hardly any trace, apart from 'the Horites, the sons of Seir in the land of Edom' (Gen. 36: 21).

The connection between the *Ḫapiru* and the Hurrians can therefore be considered as proven. But the texts do not permit the identification of the Hurrians with the *Ḫapiru*, well distinguished as they are from each other on the stela of Amenophis II. One can but follow the painstaking studies of Bottéro and Greenberg, for whom the *Ḫapiru* appear to be not an ethnic entity but a social category. It should therefore be asked whether the *Ḫapiru* are not the Indo-European aristocracy who, like Artatama, Suttarna, Biriawaza, and others,[33] lived alongside (or among) the Hurrian population both in Mitanni and in the Canaan of the Amarna letters. Unless this were the case, the Amenophis II list of prisoners would have ignored them. We know that Biriawaza of Upe speaks of his brothers and of his SA.GAZ in a list which resembles that of Amenophis II; Biriawaza himself has an Indo-European name. It is precisely 'to the man of Damascus' at Upe that pharaoh writes concerning the transfer of *Ḫapiru* in Kush 'in the place of people whom the pharaoh has removed from there' (EA 53, 63); these letters were studied by Edzard at the 1970 Congress at Munich. It remains to be seen whether the Kush mentioned there is to be identified with Kasi, hostile to the king of Jerusalem, as were the *Ḫapiru*. Finally, we may be able to find an Indo-European etymology, since the Hittite root *ḫapparija*[34] implies 'transfer', 'abandon', 'sale', 'market'. This root can explain *iḫpiur* in the Cappadocian text B. 5′, since it concerns a fugitive for debts.

Against this are the following considerations. The Egyptian scribes had a name for Indo-European warriors; they called them *maryannu*, even if one admits with Helck that in the minds of the scribes at the end of the second millennium B.C. *maryannu* meant mainly the cavalry and *ʿprw* was used for the infantry. Moreover, the Indo-European Šuwardata of the Amarna letters was an enemy of the *Ḫapiru*. Finally, what *Ḫapiru* names we know are not Indo-European but Hurrian names. J. Bottéro tells us that 'few' Alalakh names could be Semitic, 'most of the names are Hurrian' (p. 185), as are Akiptilla, Giddudu, and Hutanapu from Nuzi (E. Cassin). As E. Speiser had already pointed out: 'Hurrians and Hapiru were thus coextensive to a remarkable degree; apart from this their paths diverge sharply.'[35] The latest studies show us, however, that it is mainly from the sociological point of view that they differ from each other. Ipri-beli (B. 42; Alalakh p. 185) is particularly interesting in its Semitic form: 'Ipri is my lord'. The *ipri* or *ḫapiru* would be the Hurrian warrior aristocracy, capable of discussion with Hittite kings and of treating with them as with equals, capable of dominating Syria and penetrating Canaan as far as Jerusalem. Elements of this group, dispersed in the great Mitanni upheaval of the fifteenth century B.C., are scattered in Assyria and Babylon (Akkad), but receive a special status when they take refuge in the Hurrian area of Nuzi.

In view of this, one is compelled to look for a Hurrian etymology; since 'lord' is written in cuneiform Hurrian *ewri*, *epri* or *ibri*,[36] this hypothesis must be examined. But there is straightaway a tremendous difficulty. *ipri* is written with an *ʾaleph* and not with a *ʿain* in the cuneiform alphabet of Ugarit, whereas the equivalent of *Ḫapiru* is *ʿpr* with the *ʿain*. There is a second difficulty which is scarcely less serious, namely that certain ways of writing *ḫapiru* make it practically certain that the Akkadian and Hittite scribes intended to indicate a long *î* in the second syllable. Thus personal names are written *ḫa-pi-i-ri* on several occasions. For a long time these two objections seemed to me insuperable; I now think them less so, for three reasons.

Firstly, as Speiser[37] and Laroche[38] in particular have observed, Hurrian does not have a ʿain. It appears at Ugarit in Hurrian texts only for words of foreign composition. This is so for *ʿprm*=SA.GAZ. When the Ugarit scribes had to write down a Hurrian word used by the numerous Hurrian population, like *ewir* or *ipri*, they noted it with an aleph, e.g. *ewr-šr*. When they had to deal with *ʿprm*, who had been called *ḫapiri* for a long time in the scribal schools, they put in a ʿain.

Secondly, the resemblance between the *ubaru* or *ubru* and the *ḫapiru* has been noted. They are two distinct groups at Nuzi and at Ugarit. But there are strange analogies in their situation. They are strangers from outside the country but who can be guests; in his grants, the king can confer the exemption from having to lodge either group. The *ubaru* of the Hittite texts studied by von Schüler[39] is a protected person who has access to the king; he is a vassal of the Hittite empire and can take part in the cult. Any Semitic etymology is unlikely, since the Arabic word *wabara* means 'to halt' and, especially, 'to be hairy'. This hardly suggests the idea of a 'guest'. But the connection with the West Semitic *ʿpr* has become more likely since E. Cassin has found at Nuzi *ḫapiri ubbutu*, where the *ubbutu* corresponds to the Hebrew *ʿbṭ*; this increases the likelihood of an *ubru* or *upru* corresponding to *ʿiwri* or *ʿipri*.

Thirdly, concerning the long *î* in *ḫapiri*, this could come from the tendency of the scribes to create a *qâtîl* or *qattîl* form, just as they tended to attach the word to a Semitic root. It is striking that the Akkadian *i* of the second syllable disappears in Hebrew West Semitic. Abiram becomes Abram, Ahiab becomes Achab. Forms like ʿAmram, Elnathan, etc. would be transcribed by cuneiform scribes with an *i* in second position.

It is therefore not impossible that all these groups may have a common origin, as long as one admits that they evolved separately, so that they appear as distinct groups after five centuries of *Ḫapiru* wanderings. This common origin would be a military[40] Hurrian aristocracy, which was already without a stable habitat in the Mari period. They are fringe groups in relation to the major states, and even the minor states, of the second millennium B.C. Idrimi takes refuge with one of the groups for seven years as a fugitive. Kings make use of them, fight against them, and make treaties with them. They no longer belong to an organized ethnic group, and their status as foreigners or refugees becomes more marked before they tend to become assimilated.

(iv) ʿapiru *and Hebrews*

Weippert took up again the problem of the *ʿapiru* when he became aware of Mendenhall's theory on the establishment of the Israelites in Canaan. Mendenhall identified Israelites and *ʿapiru*, and he defined a member of the latter as a person who 'has renounced any obligation to the society in which he formerly had some standing and has in turn deprived himself of its protection'.[41] We have seen why this definition does not fit. Weippert was able to prove that the Israelites were not *ʿapiru*, and that one could not see in the Israelite conquest a sort of Peasants' Revolt against the Canaanite cities.

Weippert rightly underlined the importance of the law of the *ʿiḇrī* (pronounced *ʿivrī* or *ʿiwrī*) slave in Exodus 21: 1–11. As others had done before him, he showed the similarity of status between the *ḫapiru* at Nuzi and the *ʿeḇeḏ ʿiḇrî*; the latter also enters into an obligation for a limited period only, and is able to recover the status of *ḥop̄šî* (cf. the *ḫupšu* of Alalakh and Amarna) after a seven-year period. This period is the same as the time that Idrimi spent as a refugee with the *ʿapiru*; Weippert suggests that he may have become a *ʿapiru* himself.

Weippert has studied the phonetic problem more closely. He thinks that *ʿapiru* is a form of the *faʿîl* type which developed into a segolated form *faʿl* or *fiʿl*;[42] Brockelmann's *Grundriss* gives cases of the juxtaposition *malku/milku*. If one maintains that the original form is a Hurrian *ipri*, *iwri* or *ibri* (all of which are found in the texts) the problem is a little different. The Bible would then be nearer to the original form than the Akkadian scribes; these would appear to have wanted to take the term as the participle of a verb *ḫāpar* 'to pass', and have sometimes made it evolve into a verbal adjective of the *parîs* form. One can admit with Weippert that the length of the vowels depends on the cases of *scriptio plena* given by von Soden.[43] Moreover, Weippert gives about fifteen examples of words written with either *b* or *p* without alteration of the meaning. There is no insurmountable obstacle, therefore, in the way of maintaining that when the Israelites penetrated into Canaan they found there the remnants of the Hurrian military aristocracy, in a state of decay certainly, but having nevertheless afforded to the Egyptians and the Philistines the occasion of using their name as a generic term for the population of the hinterland. The Israelites even went so far as to adopt the old law of the *ʿib̲rî* servant for the cases when they might acquire servants and incorporate them into their families by the special rite carried out at the door of the house.

It is more difficult to determine how the Israelites defined their relations with these *ʿib̲rîm*.

Genesis 10: 21 ff. gives a table of peoples which considers *ʿeber* as a descendant of Shem through Arpachshad; the South Semitic tribes are linked to Eber through his son Joktan. Since Shem's eldest son is Elam, it is clear that this is a geographical rather than ethnic list. Arpachshad has long been compared with Arrapḫa, which is precisely where the Hurrians of Nuzi were to be found, as well as the *Ḫapiru* who took refuge at Nuzi. Joktan is linked to Eber through his brother Peleg, whose name is explained by the division of the earth, if that is really the meaning of the verb. It is anyway a sociological consideration, and we have seen how important these are in the question of the *Ḫapiru*/*ʿprm*.

There is a gap in the J tradition on the relation between Abram and Eber in chapters 10 and 11 of Genesis. But the P tradition in Genesis 10: 10–29 is clear; this leaves open the question whether it is the simplification of more complex relations.

In Genesis 14: 13 Abram is called *ʿib̲rî*. Weippert is right in drawing attention to the fact that the same text makes Mamre into an Amorite, whereas it was a geographical sacred place which was still in use as a market in the fourth century A.D. This episode presents a warrior Abram, with a rather different character from that in the other Genesis episodes, in which Abram is never a warrior. We have here what is really a typical *ḫapiru* of the Amarna type. The battle takes place at Hobah near Damascus, which is where we find the *Ḫapiru* of Amarna. The tradition reproduced in this episode is very ancient; but it appears to have been combined with another one, which refers to Jerusalem and Hebron where Abram buys from Ephron (*ʿprn*!) the cave of Machpelah (Gen. 23). All these elements are valuable, but it is impossible to disentangle all the historical and sociological elements which have been preserved in these chapters. I admit with Astour[44] that there has been a Deuteronomic edition of chapter 14, but it is not clear to me whether the epithet *ʿib̲rî*, given to Abram, is an editorial element to be connected with the P genealogy of Genesis 10. It does seem possible that the epithet *ʿib̲rî* given to Abram belongs to one or other of the two traditional elements which seem to me to underlie the story as we have it; that is, either the great coalition which ends in a battle north of Damascus, or the episode of Melchizedek further south. This is not the place for a discussion of the difficulties involved in an exegesis of Genesis 14; it is sufficient to remember that the editor gives as allies of Abram two geographical names, Mamre the sacred tree and Eshcol the valley. His intention is to evoke a pre-Israelite period, and he considers that Abram, the father of a multitude of nations and the descendant of Eber, according to P, was the sign of assembly for populations more numerous than the bʿnê-Yisrael; this is a confirmation of the genealogy in Genesis 25: 1–6, which gives the descendants of Abraham by Keturah. All the names of his descendants are of good Semitic formation, as is the name 'Abram' itself. But the population of Hebron was not necessarily Semitic, and the name of Ephron the Hittite evokes the *ʿprm* once more. It could be that the tradition or the documents employed by Genesis 14 underlined the geographical connections and not the ethnic ones, just as Genesis 10: 22 counts the non-Semitic Elam among the descendants of Shem.[45]

(v) *Conclusions*

In view of the present state of the information and of research, any conclusions must be extremely tentative.

The Hebrews of the Bible, *ʿib̲r(iyy)îm*, can be identified with the *Ḫapiru* of cuneiform texts, the *ʿprw* of Egypt and the *ʿprm* of Ugarit. They are not so much an ethnic group as a sociological phenomenon. This 'class' seems to be linked with the Hurrians, following their movements without being identified with them. They appear in Upper Mesopotamia at the end of the third millennium B.C. as a military aristocracy. These groups are a menace for their non-Hurrian neighbours, who call them SA.GAZ, 'brigands', even when they make contracts with them or make use of their services, either individually or collectively. They go down into Canaan at the time when Egyptian scribes call the country 'Hurru', but they are not thereby identified with the Hurrians. They disappear as distinct groups at the same time as the Hurrians disappear, at the end of the second millennium B.C. The Israelites are conscious of a certain common condition with them, especially in relation to the Philistines and the Egyptians, but this is a geographical rather than an ethnic link. However, the Israelites do not identify themselves with them, and, at the time of the monarchy, they cease to see in them a living population, even though they inherit certain of their customs dating from the patriarchal period.[46]

NOTES

1. On this point cf. M. Gray, op. cit. 188 ff.

2. D. B. Redford, 'The Land of the Hebrews in Genesis 40: 15', *V.T.* 15 (1965), 529–32.

3. K. Koch, 'Die Hebräer vom Auszug aus Aegypten bis zum Grossreich Davids'', *V.T.* 19 (1969), 37–81, esp. 46–9.

4. Ibid., 62.

5. The translations proposed by M. Kline (p. 50) are not convincing ('both' is not in the text and the 'selected troops' are presented as being the Israelite army), but the author's observations underline effectively the fact that for the biblical editor there was a common destiny between Israel and the Hebrews.

6. A. Caquot ('Préfets', *Supplément du Dictionnaire de la Bible*, 7, fasc. 43 (Paris, 1968), p. 284) prefers to attribute this 'integration' to David.

7. *A.O.T.S.* p. 13.

8. C. Virolleaud, *C.R.A.I.B.L.* (1939), 329; *R.E.S.* (1940), 74 ff.

9. The correspondence between the numbers in J. Bottéro (here B.) and M. Greenberg (here G.) will be found in *Bi.Or.* 13, nos. 3, 4 (1956), 149 f.

10. *Z.A.* 19 (1959), p. 286 n. 32. See also S. Kramer, *J.A.O.S.* lx (1940), 253, and F. R. Kraus, *Bi.Or.* 15 (1958), 77–8.

11. 'Zwei althetitische Belege zu den Ḫapiru (SA.GAZ)', *Z.A.* 18 (1957), 216–23. On B. 72 see *R.H.A.* 75 (1965), 35.

12. 'Quelques remarques à propos des archives administratives de Nuzi', *R.A.* 52 (1958), 16–28; 'Nouveaux Documents sur les Habiru', *J.A.* 246 (1958), 225–36.

13. *P.R.U.* iv (1956), 17.238 (pp. 107 ff.); 17.341 (pp. 161–3); 17.232 (p. 239).

14. *P.R.U.* v. (1965), 18.148 (no. 62, pp. 88–9).

15. At the Rencontre Assyriologique, Munich, July 1970, published in *Beiträge zur Altertumskunde* v (Bonn, 1970), pp. 52–62.

16. Cf. E. Cassin, *J.A.* 246 (1958), 236. On the equivalence: alphabetic ʿ = syllabic *ú* see A. Jirku, 'Die Umschrift ugaritischer Laryngale durch den akkadischen Buchstaben ú', *Ar.Or.* 38 (1970), 129 f.

17. Ibid., 231–2.

18. This is the correct translation, with A. Gustavs, 'Der Gott Hapiru', *Z.A.W.* xl (1922), 314; 'Was heisst *ilâni Hapiri*', *Z.A.W.* xliv (1926), 25–36, and the note by Weippert, p. 73 n. 3.

19. See H. Klengel, 'Der Schiedespruch des Mursilis II hinsichtlich Barga', *Or.* 32 (1963), 32–55.

20. On this text and the related bibliography see R. Giveon, *Les bédouins Shosu des documents égyptiens* (Leiden, 1971), pp. 12–15.

21. Cf. W. F. Albright, *B.A.S.O.R.* 83, p. 34 n. 8; not disproved in *B.A.S.O.R.* 95, p. 33 n. 19; B. Maisler (= Mazar), *Revue de l'histoire juive en Égypte* i (1957), 37 f.

22. Cf. W. Helck, *V.T.* xviii (1968), 476.

23. 'Le nom du prince de Jérusalem au temps d'El Amarna', *Mémorial Lagrange* (Paris, 1940), pp. 27–8. However the first sign is read, the goddess Heba or Hebat is a Hurrian deity.

24. For Helck (p. 530) the *ʿprw* are the infantry and the *mryn* are the cavalry.

25. Thanks are due to M. G. Posener for permission to publish this ostracon as fig. 1. In line 3 the *rmṯ mšʿ n jmnty* expression is quite close to the *ṣabē* (ERIM) of cuneiform texts. The men are Egyptian workers and are not the same *ʿprw* as in l. 1 even if they do similar work.

26. C. Schaeffer, *Ugaritica* iv (Paris, 1962), 87.

27. This is confirmed by *A Vienna Demotic Papyrus on Eclipse- and Lunar Omina*, edited by R. A. Parker (Brown University Press, 1959), which dates probably from the first Persian domination. It mentions four countries, Amurru, Egypt, Syria, and *ʿybr* (or *ybr* A II 18–24), no longer *ʿpr*. As in the case of the biblical texts, the root *ʿbr* may have exerted an influence. R. J. Williams (*J.N.E.S.* xxv (1966), 69) considers it to be the province of Eber-nâri, the *ʿabar-Nahara* of Ezra 4: 10.

28. See J. R. Kupper, p. 160.

29. See J. A. Wilson in *A.N.E.T.*, p. 416.

30. Posener (*apud* Bottéro, p. 166) compares this with *ʿprw*, meaning 'the crew' (of a ship, but also of workmen, *J.E.A.* 13, 75); Helck translates 'Abteilung'. Gunn and Gardiner translate 'gangs'. This administrative

letter (Sixth Dynasty) is interesting, since the *ʿprw* receive clothing (cf. B. 16, Larsa period) and the writer of the letter is a military leader.

31. There was an unfortunate trace of this in my *Syria* article, and M. Liverani deduced from the article an interpretation which differs from what the article was trying to say (p. 87).

32. 'Northern Mesopotamia and Syria', *C.A.H.*, rev. edn., ii, fasc. 14, p. 26.

33. See the study by P. E. Dumont in R. O'Callaghan's *Aram Naharaim*; M. Mayerhofer, *Die Indo-Arier im alten Vorderasien* (Wiesbaden, 1966), pp. 140–7.

34. See J. Friedrich, *Hethitisches Wörterbuch* (Heidelberg, 1952), p. 54. I. M. Diakonoff (*M.I.O.* (1967), 364) has noted in the different versions of the Hittite Code, § 48, *ḫipparas* = A.SI.RUM ('prisoner'); he compares with this the Hattusil III–Ugarit Treaty (B. 161). One wonders if *ḫipparas* is a Hittite adaptation of the word which is transcribed elsewhere *ḫapiru*.

35. 'Ethnic Movements in the Near East in the Second Millennium B.C.', *A.A.S.O.R.* xiii (New Haven, Conn., 1933), 34.

36. Cf. the *ḫipparas* in the Hittite Code, § 48.

37. 'Introduction to Hurrian', *A.A.S.O.R.* xx (1941), 44–9.

38. *Ugaritica* v, p. 527.

39. 'Hethitische Kultbräuche in dem Brief eines ugaritischen Gesandten', *R.H.A.* 72 (Paris, 1963), 45. On the analogies and differences between *ḫapiru* and *ubaru* cf. *Syria* (1958), 207–11.

40. ERIM, *ṣābe*, can be applied to non-military groups, but there is so much evidence of the military activity of the *ḫapiru* that it is best to leave these terms with their usual signification.

41. *B.A.* 25 (1962), 71.

42. Ibid., p. 84.

43. W. von Soden, *Grundriss der akkadischen Grammatik* (Rome, 1952), § 7e.

44. 'Political and Cosmic Symbolism in Genesis 14 and in its Babylonian Sources', *Biblical Motifs*, ed. A. Altmann (Harvard University Press, 1966), pp. 65–112.

45. The Kittim, *ʾšr* and *ʿbr* are mentioned together in the last Balaam oracle (J). In this I see a relation with the Sea Peoples and the Philistine settlement on the coast, together with the Aššurim of Gen. 25: 3 and of the Egyptian topographical list (*jsr*; Sety I and Ramesses II, in Simon's lists XVII. 4 and XXV. 8, with a spelling different from Assur), perhaps 2 Sam. 2: 9 and the word written *gšr* in Josh. 13: 2, on the border of Egypt. The Minean *ʾʾšr* in *Répertoire Epigraph. Sém.* 2771, 3–4, and 3022, 1, parallel to *mṣr* ('Egypt'), raises other problems. K. Koch rightly stresses the relation between *Shosu* and *ʿprw* in the two Sety stelae (Karnak and Beth-Shan, op. cit., 60). But for a necessary distinction between these two see R. Giveon, *Les bédouins Shosu des documents égyptiens* (Leiden, 1971), pp. 4, 14.

46. It has not been possible to consult the article on 'Habiru' by J. Bottéro since published in *R.L.A.* iv, i (1972), 14–27.

BIBLIOGRAPHY (*since* 1955)

Albright, W. F. 'The Amarna Letters from Palestine', in *C.A.H.*, rev. edn., ii (C.U.P., 1966), fasc. 51, pp. 14–20.

—— 'Abram the Hebrew', *B.A.S.O.R.* 163 (1961), 36–54.

—— *Yahweh and the Gods of Canaan* (London, 1968), pp. 64–79.

Alt, A. 'Bemerkungen zu den Verwaltungs- und Rechtsurkunden von Ugarit und Alalach', *W.O.* II. 3 (Göttingen, 1956), 237–43.

Astour, M. 'Les étrangers à Ugarit et le statut juridique des Habiru', *R.A.* 53 (1959), 70–6.

Baeck, L. 'Der Ibri', *Monatschrift für Geschichte und Wissenschaft des Judentums* 83, NF 47 (1939), (Tübingen, 1963), 66–80.

Borger, R., 'Das Problem der ʿapiru (Hebräer)', *Z.D.P.V.* 74 (1958), 121–32.

Bottéro, J. *Le problème des Habiru*, IVe Rencontre Assyriologique Internationale, Paris, 1954.

Campbell, E. F. 'The Amarna Letters and the Amarna Period', *B.A.* xxiii (1960), 10–12.

Cassin, E. 'Nouveaux Documents sur les Habiru', *J.A.* 246 (1958), 225–36.

Cazelles, H. 'Hébreux, Ubru et Hapiru', *Syria* 35 (1958), 198–207.

de Vaux, R. 'Les Patriarches hébreux et l'histoire', *R.B.* 72 (1965), 20; 75 (1968), 301–2.

Diakonoff, I. M. 'Die hethitische Gesellschaft', *M.I.O.* xiii (1967), 363–5.

Dossin, G. 'Les Bédouins dans les textes de Mari', ed. F. Gabrieli, *L'Antica Societa beduin* (Studi Semitici 2, Rome, 1959), pp. 35–51.

Edzard, D. O. 'Die Tontafeln von Kamid el-Loz', *Beiträge zur Altertums urkunde* (T. V. Bonn, Habelt, 1970), pp. 52–62, 12–14.

Eissfeldt, O. 'Ugarit und Alalah', *K.S.* III, pp. 273–6.

Finet, A. 'Iawi-ila, roi de Talhayum', *Syria* xli (1964), 140–2.

Garelli, P. *Les Assyriens en Cappadoce* (Paris, 1963), pp. 207 and 214.

—— *Le Proche Orient asiatique* (Paris, 1969), pp. 146 ff., 170 ff.

Gibson, J. C. L. 'Some important Ethnic Terms in the Pentateuch', *J.N.E.S.* xx (1961), 234–7.

Gray, Mary. 'The Habirû-Hebrew Problem in the Light of the Source Material Available at Present', *H.U.C.A.* xxix (1958), 135–202.

Greenberg, M. *The Hab/piru* (New Haven, Conn., 1955).

Helck, W. *Die Beziehungen Ägyptens zu Vorderasien im* 3. *und* 2. *Jahrtausend v. Chr.* (Wiesbaden, 1962), pp. 522–6.

—— 'Die Bedrohung Palastinas durch einwandernde Gruppen am Ende der 18 und Anfang der 19 Dynastie', *V.T.* xviii (1968), 472–80.

Kline, Meredith G. 'The Ha-BI-ru, kin or foe of Israel?', *The Westminster Theological Journal* 19 (1956), 1–24, 170–84; 20 (1957), 25–70.

Kupper, J. R. *Les Nomades en Mésopotamie au temps des rois de Mari*, (Paris, 1957), pp. 249–59.

LEWY, J. 'Origin and Signification of the Biblical Term "Hebrew"', *H.U.C.A.* xxviii (1957), 1–14.

LIVERANI, M. *Storia di Ugarit nell' eta' degli archivi politici*, Studi Semitici 6 (Rome, 1962), pp. 87–9.

MENDENHALL, G. E. 'The Hebrew Conquest of Palestine', *B.A.* xxv (1962), 71–84.

OBERHOLZER, J. P. 'The *'ibrim* in 1 Samuel', *Die Oud Testamentiese Werkgemeenskap in Suid-Afrika*, 3d metting (1960), p. 54.

O'CALLAGHAN, R. *Aram Naharaïm* (Rome, 1948), *passim.*

POHL, A. 'Einige Gedanke zur Habiru-Frage', *W.Z.K.M.* 54 (1957), 157–60.

ROWTON, M. B. 'The Topological Factor in the *Ḫapiru* Problem', *Studies in Honor of Benno Landsberger on his Seventy-fifth Birthday* (Chicago, 1965), pp. 375–87.

SCHAEFFER, C. *Ugaritica* 5, pp. 685–740.

WEINGREEN, J. 'Saul and the Habiru', *IVth World Congress of Jewish Studies* 1 (Jerusalem, 1967), pp. 63–6.

WEIPPERT, M. *Die Landnahme der israelitischen Stämme in der neueren wissenschaftlichen Diskussion* (Göttingen, 1967), pp. 66–102.

WINTON THOMAS, D. (ed.) *A.O.T.S.* (Oxford 1967), *passim* (especially the articles by F. F. Bruce and J. Gray).

YEIVIN, SH. 'The Origin and Disappearance of the Hab/piru', *Proceedings of the XXVth Congress of Orientalists* (Moscow, 1962), pp. 439–41.

—— The Age of the Patriarchs: I. The Patriarchs and the Hab/piru', *R.S.O.* 38 (Rome, 1963), 277–84.

II

THE CANAANITES

A. R. MILLARD

A TRUE picture of the Canaanites is hard for us to form because we lack sufficient records from an indubitably Canaanite source. There is nothing that can be recognized at once as Canaanite by modern man, nor is there any clear trace of any ancient distinguishing feature. The people are not known to have had a central or eponymous city or deity (as Ashur or Sheba), a separate culture or history, nor did they leave the stamp of an imperial rule on other lands. It follows that knowledge of the Canaanites and isolation of any traits as peculiar to them rests initially upon the witness of other peoples. As the promise, possession, loss, and partial recovery of Canaan form the central theme of the Hebrew Bible, the extent of the land occupies some place in it, but the inhabitants command little attention beyond the generality of their wickedness by which their extermination was justified. Documents in Egyptian and in the various languages employing the cuneiform script supplement the Hebrew records, albeit often in random fashion, the texts from Ugarit making the outstanding contribution.

While 'Canaanite' cannot be defined immediately, the territory 'Canaan' is more easily described, thus forming a basis for a survey of other aspects.

(i) *Canaan: the Land*

Canaan receives its first biblical definition in the Table of Nations, where the grandson of Noah is 'father' of Sidon and Heth (see pp. 197 f.), of the Jebusites, Amorites, Girgashites, Hivites, Arkites, Sinites, Arvadites, Zemarites, and Hamathites (Gen. 10: 15–19). The five names following Sidon are familiar as the inhabitants of the 'Promised Land' later in the Pentateuch (e.g. Exod. 13: 5). They occupied, presumably, the area enclosed by the border of verse 19, running south from Sidon towards Gaza, through Gerar, and across to the cities of the Dead Sea plain; no eastern limit is drawn.[1] To the north of Sidon lay the five remaining places, known from ancient sources as important coastal or inland (Hamath) centres. ʿArqa or ʿIrqata occurs in the Execration Texts (*c.* 1800 B.C.) and frequently thereafter. It lay a few miles south of the Eleutherus river, while the Zemarites' home, Ṣumur, was just to the north.[2] At a point where the coastal plain narrows, lies the offshore island of Arvad (Ruad), and beyond was Siyan of the Sinites, attested in tablets from Ugarit and in Assyrian inscriptions.[3]

Although the final settlement is an unlikely inclusion at first sight, Hamath is reached by two routes from the coast, one leading from ʿArqa, Ṣumur, and Arvad (now from Tartus and Tripoli), the other from modern Baniyas in the probable region of Siyan. The Hittite and Aramaic inscriptions of the first millennium B.C. found in Hamath, or relating thereto, do not rule out the possibility of an earlier or basically Canaanite population.[4]

Thus summarized, Canaanite territory covered western Palestine, with an extension northwards up the coast almost as far as Latakia and inland to Hamath. (It is not clear whether the hinterland between Galilee and Hamath was included.)[5] When the habitat of the various groups in the land is given in Numbers 13: 29, the coast and the Jordan valley are the Canaanites' domain, as distinct from those of the Amorites and the others. However, at the Conquest Canaan was evidently a name for the land as a whole (e.g. Num. 35: 10), a usage understandable in the light both of Canaan's place at the head of the peoples in Genesis 10: 17 and of the practice of extra-biblical writers in the latter part of the second millennium B.C. It is appropriate to survey the evidence from those sources next, then to consider the boundary records of the biblical Promised Land beside them.

Egyptian texts from the beginning of the second millennium B.C. refer to Palestine and southern Syria as Retenu (*Rṯnw*)[6] and its inhabitants chiefly as 'Asiatics' (*ʿ3mw*), only exhibiting more precise terms after *c.* 1500 B.C. The extensive records from the New Kingdom then confuse the picture by introducing several names. Retenu long continued in use, but there appeared beside

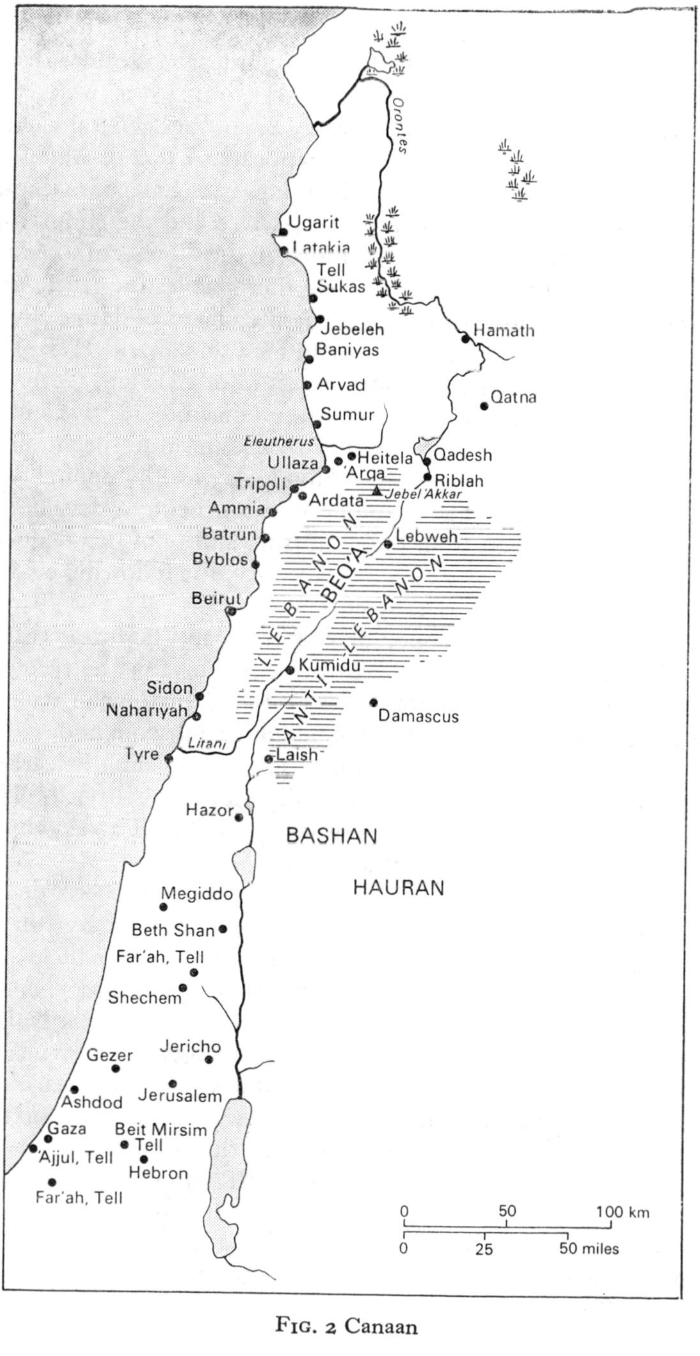
Orontes
Ugarit
Latakia
Tell Sukas
Jebeleh
Baniyas
Arvad
Sumur
Hamath
Qatna
Eleutherus
Ullaza
Heitela
'Arqa
Qadesh
Riblah
Tripoli
Ardata
Jebel 'Akkar
Ammia
Batrun
Byblos
Lebweh
LEBANON
BEQ'A
ANTI LEBANON
Beirut
Kumidu
Sidon
Nahariyah
Damascus
Litani
Tyre
Laish
Hazor
BASHAN
HAURAN
Megiddo
Beth Shan
Far'ah, Tell
Shechem
Gezer
Jericho
Ashdod
Jerusalem
Gaza
Beit Mirsim
Tell
'Ajjul, Tell
Hebron
Far'ah, Tell
0
50
100 km
0
25
50 miles

FIG. 2 Canaan

it the term Djahy (*Ḏȝhy*), the two being interchangeable. Inscriptions from the reign of Tuthmosis III utilize the word Huru (*Ḫwrw*), at first as a gentilic, presently as another general name for Syria and Palestine. Finally Canaan appears. A text of Amenophis II contains the earliest passage, listing 640 Canaanite captives between *maryannu* warriors and their wives and the children and women-folk of defeated princes.[7] Later, in the Nineteenth Dynasty, Canaan is a region embracing southern Palestine at least. A Ramesside papyrus speaks of 'Canaanite slaves of Huru',[8] while the 'Israel Stele' of Merenptah includes Canaan and Huru along with Israel, Hatti, Tjehenu, and the cities of Askalon, Gezer, and Yanoam.[9] From the position of the Canaanite captives in the Amenophis list it has been argued that Canaanite meant simply 'merchant' at that time, that is individuals wealthy enough to be classed with princes, the ethnic application being a development from it.[10] Quite apart from the doubtful validity of this deduction from the word order of a single occurrence, the following evidence from another source speaks against it.

Idrimi, prince of Aleppo, driven from his home, eventually found refuge in Canaan at the town of Ammiya, as he recounted afterwards in his autobiography.[11] The land of Canaan recurs as the home of persons listed in three tablets of subsequent decades—roughly contemporary with Amenophis II or slightly earlier—found at Alalakh, where Idrimi finally gained a throne.[12] There can be no doubt that a region was designated 'Canaan' by the middle of the second millennium B.C.

How large an area could be called Canaan has been debated since the recovery of the Amarna letters, many sent by rulers of Palestinian cities to the Pharaoh, a few directed to them, with allusions to the territory or denizens of Canaan ($^{m\bar{a}t}$*kinaḫḫi*, $^{m\bar{a}t}$*kinaḫna*, *kinaḫāyu*). Recently, careful study has clarified the data. As a result the limits of Canaan as an Egyptian province can be stated with some confidence. To the south the Sinai desert appears to have lain beyond Canaan, Gaza, the first major town on the road from Egypt, being known as 'the town of Canaan' and functioning as administrative centre.[13] To the east the Jordan and the Dead Sea formed a natural limit, like the Mediterranean to the west. How far these two lines continued northwards to enclose Canaanite terrain is more difficult to discern, for where the mountain ranges of Lebanon divide the land physically, the powers of Egypt and of Khatti—not to mention the ambitions of local princes—caused several changes in its territorial divisions. Idrimi's history shows that the coast as far north as Tripoli fell within Canaan in his day,[14] a situation continuing at the time of the Amarna correspondence. Beyond, the shore came under the control of Amurru, at least from the mid fourteenth century B.C. (the earlier situation was possibly that indicated by Genesis 10: 15–19, the coast being part of the same region as Sidon), the Egyptian governor having his seat at Ṣumur. Inland there were various principalities combined by Egypt to form the province of Upe, named after the Damascus area, but covering the Beqʿa as well, and governed from Kumidu.[15] Thus the northern limit of Canaan was formed by Upe and Amurru, at least in the Egyptian administration.

Biblical descriptions of Canaan take the same lines in the south, east, and west, as scrutiny of the key verses Numbers 34: 2–12 will show. For the northern edge more details are given than in the other sources. Despite some uncertainties of identification, there can be little doubt that the border ran over the northern end of the Lebanon range to Lebo-Hamath (now Lebweh) in the upper valley of the Orontes, and then, apparently, swept around Anti-Lebanon to the desert's edge and south through the Hauran to turn westwards to the Sea of Galilee. In its first section this line corresponds with the coastal extension of Canaan attested by the Idrimi and other texts.[16] By continuing east, on the contrary, it clearly embraces more than the Egyptian province of Canaan (cf. above); in fact, it includes the province of Upe (the Beqʿa and Damascus). That the whole area could be considered 'Canaan' in the eyes of the Egyptian administration is doubtful;[17] as late as the occasion of Ramesses II's marriage to a Hittite princess (*c.* 1271 B.C.) the governors of Canaan and Upe appear as equals, escorting the lady through their territory,[18] but there is no information from subsequent decades. The land of Canaan at the time of the Israelite conquest, therefore, stretched from the Negeb to the northern end of Lebanon,[19] embracing in addition the Damascene and Bashan to the east; in fact, all the territory held by Egypt following the peace treaty with the Hittites in 1284 B.C.

(ii) *The Name*

Until 1936 'Canaan' was usually derived from the root *knʿ* ('to be low', as 'lowland', *knʿ* is 'to bow, be low' in Aramaic; in Hebrew only the passive-reflexive and causative themes are attested: 'to be subdued, humble oneself; to make humble'). In that year E. A. Speiser linked the name with the term *kinaḫḫu*, used of a dye, in texts from the Hurrian-dominated town of Nuzi in eastern Iraq, dated *c.* 1500 B.C., and deduced that the name had been applied to the chief product of the land, purple dye.[20] Other scholars built on this association, notably W. F. Albright, who proposed first that the name itself was a Hurrian form from *iqnaʾu*, Ugaritic for 'blue purple', later positing a lost Semitic word **knʿ* for 'murex', whence *knʿn* denoted a 'purple-merchant', from which the land was named.[21]

Any relation of the name to the colour has been ruled out in a recent study of Sumerian and Akkadian words for dyes by B. Landsberger, the most rigorous linguist working in Assyriology during this century. He has shown how Sumerian *gìn* passed into Akkadian as *uqni-*, into Ugaritic as *ỉqnu* (also into Syriac as *qᵉnāʿ(a)*, *qunʿ(a)*, Greek as κύανος), yielding an adjective *qinaḫḫu* in the Hurrian-influenced dialect of Nuzi, and regularly exhibiting a *q*, not a *k*. Further, Landsberger remarked that the adjectival form 'Canaanite' would not be *kinaḫḫi*, but *kinaḫḫiu* or *kinaḫḫayu*, as in other cases.[22]

A satisfactory explanation of the name remains to be found. As far as is currently known, its advent coincided with the time of greatest Hurrian expansion in Syria and Palestine,[23] allowing one to surmise a Hurrian origin or use of the name. Some connection with the Semitic root *knʿ* could yet be argued; Noah's words 'cursed be Canaan, the lowest of servants shall he be to his brothers' (Gen. 9: 25) might involve a play on the name, supposing the nuance of subjection to lie within it.

(iii) *The Language*

On the premise of Hebrew and Phoenician descent from earlier Canaanite, some features of that language have been set out, together making it distinct within the Northwest Semitic family.[24]

A degree of guidance and control in reconstructing this 'Canaanite language' is provided by a limited store of original material in proper names, in the annotations made by local scribes to the Babylonian text of Amarna letters originating from Canaan, and in certain abnormalities in the same letters. There are drawbacks in using this material, for little is known of the mobility of scribes or of their particular schools and traditions. Continuing study of the linguistic remains from Syria and Palestine is clarifying the picture, but obscurities and differences of opinion remain common —caused in part by the accidents of preservation and discovery.

Egyptian sources (chiefly the Execration Texts) give strong evidence for use of a Northwest Semitic dialect by rulers of many Palestinian cities of the nineteenth century B.C., whose names are very similar to the 'Amorite' names of Mari and Syrian sites. So it is quite possible that 'Amorite' was the tongue of the whole area at that time. Some centuries later the situation had changed. Hurrian and Indo-European invaders gained control of various cities, imposing their own speech-forms on those they found there. However, one idiosyncrasy is evident at this period whereby bounds may be set to Canaanite. Where Semitic generally has *ā*, Canaanite has *ō*; e.g. the pronoun 'I' is *anāku* in Akkadian, '*ānōḵî* in one of the Amarna letters from Jerusalem (*E.A.* 287, 66, 69), as later in Hebrew.[25] Helpfully, this difference is contained in many place-names, prominently those ending -*ōn* (as Askelon, Sidon, contrasted with Siyan, Labnan), and a glance at any map or list of ancient towns will reveal an obvious division between north and south in this respect, in striking agreement with the topographical definition of Canaan reached already. It is impossible to tell whether this shift existed earlier, for the Egyptian sources mentioned above do not reveal the vocalization of the names. Slight traces are known from the Mari texts, too slight so far to justify a claim that 'Canaanite' was a separate entity so early.[26]

Ugaritic was the Semitic language of a leading Syrian port and its neighbourhood. It has been preserved in writing on clay tablets using an alphabetic cuneiform script found in the ruins of the city, destroyed about 1200 B.C. Since decipherment in 1930 the tongue has been classed widely as 'Canaanite', with a few dissenting voices.[27] Recent advances in knowledge allow a more balanced view.

By a multitude of features Ugaritic is placed squarely in the Northwest Semitic group, in numerous points evincing a pattern identical with Hebrew, therefore with Canaanite: e.g. third person pronouns with an initial *h*, *pôʿlēl* theme in 'hollow' verbs, and lexical community.[28] On the other hand, there are equally marked divergencies, as *š* to indicate the causative verbal theme where 'Canaanite' has *h*, different values for common aspects of the verb, and *ā*, not *ō* (*anāku* 'I').[29] Identity may be reckoned unlikely; cognate dialects are more probably in question (the location of Ugarit outside the territory of Canaan gives a little weight to the distinction, although land, language, and people are seldom coextensive). So long as the evidence available is as diffuse as the glosses and peculiarities of the Amarna letters, or as localized as the documents from Ugarit, it seems more satisfactory to treat Canaanite and Ugaritic as related and contemporary, but distinct. Indeed, a handful of texts written in a variant form of the alphabetic cuneiform testifies to some differentiation at Ugarit itself and in Palestine.[30]

(iv) *The People*

Our surveys of territorial and linguistic data have been limited by absence of evidence to the second millennium B.C., and largely to the later centuries thereof. No sure indication of Canaan or a Canaanite tongue older than that was found. Now we turn to the material remains to seek for any distinctively Canaanite relics, but before artefacts can be attributed to the people, limits are needed in terms of archaeological divisions. In the context of this volume the end of the Bronze Age is taken as the finishing point for 'Canaanite culture', although, in fact, the Phoenicians were but latter-day Canaanites (see pp. 263 f.).[31] A commencing date is more difficult to give, involving the identification of the 'Canaanites'.

Working backwards to find signs of major population movements or cultural change, we come upon none, except the Hurrian, until the obscure centuries prior to the beginning of the Middle Bronze Age. Archaeologists term the years *c.* 2200–1800 B.C. variously Middle Bronze I (W. F. Albright, G. E. Wright, R. B. K. Amiran), Intermediate Early Bronze (abbreviated EB—MB; K. M. Kenyon), or Intermediate Bronze Age (P. W. Lapp).

Throughout the Levant this is a period of sacked cities, yet of large cemeteries, and is normally understood as an age of nomadic incursions, the nomads being identified with the 'Amorites'. After a few centuries of disorganized and unsophisticated occupation there came a time of city-building characterized by superior pottery and bronze implements (Middle Bronze IIa in Albright's terms, Middle Bronze I in Miss Kenyon's). The distinctive forms suggest another invasion rather than a gradual transformation of nomads to citizens. Who brought the new culture, and whence they came, are questions receiving varied answers. Dr. Kenyon's recent theory argues that Amorites who overran the Syrian coast succumbed to the civilizing traditions of Byblos and diffused the resultant amalgamation throughout western Syria and Palestine. To this culture the name 'Canaanite' is attached; in fact the 'Canaanites were urbanised Amorites'.[32]

Objections have been raised to this simple picture, on the ground of the sharp break at the end of the Early Bronze Age, even at Byblos, and the new way of life has been seen instead as the result of Amorite drive.[33] Another hypothesis would maintain that the invaders of the 'Intermediate' period came from the Mediterranean, only the bearers of the Middle Bronze Age city-life still being viewed as Amorites.[34] None of these proposals is entirely satisfactory, yet each may contain some truth. That Amorites would contribute greatly to material progress is doubtful, in view of their performance in Babylonia, but that they could carry new ideas or techniques is very likely. Here Miss Kenyon's emphasis on Byblos may touch the root of the matter. As soon as Egypt began to recover from the disarray of the First Intermediate Period (*c.* 2181–2040 B.C.), timber began to be imported from Syria and soon expeditions were sent to fetch wood from the mountains of Lebanon. At the same time the kings of the Third Dynasty of Ur had agents in the west. Contact with these urban powers, one emergent, the other soon to fall, may be recognized as the catalyst, precipitating the urban development of Syria and Palestine. By 1850 B.C. the southern part of the region was supposedly subject to Egypt, its rulers responsible to the pharaonic court—their relationships are apparent in the Story of Sinuhe, and their insubordination in the Execration Texts. This north-western region did not stand alone. In Crete the great palaces of Middle

Minoan date were founded little later than 2000 B.C., presently giving testimony to contacts with Egypt and Syria, while there flourished important centres in Anatolia whose trade with Assyria is well-documented, but which are unlikely to have been restricted to that direction alone, and may have stimulated the bronze-working of the 'Amorites'.

In this way Palestine received a motley array of peoples and influences. Should the amalgam be designated 'Canaanite'?[35] If the name may be justified on cultural grounds, the usage of ancient sources, in particular the biblical texts, demands explanation. 'Canaan' was applied generally to Palestine and the south Syrian littoral in the Amarna period, as outlined above, but had a narrower primary reference to the coastland, if we may rely on the tradition in Genesis 10: 15 ff. Whether it was a territorial name or designated a people, in the first place, cannot now be determined. Its absence from earlier records is explicable in terms of the independent-city-state situation, which led to the use of a town-name more frequently than a comprehensive name as gentilic.[36] If the name was used by the natives of the area, then either they survived the various invasions, retaining some sense of identity (as suggested by P. W. Lapp),[37] or the name was assumed by their conquerors, or simply applied to any denizens or products of the region. A solution seems unattainable, but for the Old Testament interest an upper limit for Canaanite culture can be fixed at the beginning of the Middle Bronze Age city-life, *c.* 1850 B.C.

(v) *Culture and Society*

a. *The Middle Bronze Age*

Whatever the stimuli, the Middle Bronze Age saw a higher level of material achievement in Palestine than any other in the biblical period.[38] Whereas other eras yield some artefacts of high quality among large quantities of the mediocre, there is generally a better standard in this age. In the mundane context of the pottery this is most apparent. A technical innovation, the fast-spinning potter's wheel, contributed largely to this, bringing with it the need for well levigated clay. Crockery from the earlier part of the period (MB IIa, *c.* 1950–1750 B.C.—Albright etc.; *c.* 2000–1800 B.C.—Mazar; MB I, *c.* 1850–1800 B.C.—Kenyon) has a thin, hard fabric, imitating the shapes of metal vessels in a number of types. Yet, as so often with a new invention, the level of excellence gradually dropped, so that the wares of the later years and of the Late Bronze Age are inferior. In metal-working, too, there was an important advance, the alloying of copper with tin to make more durable bronze. Typical examples of the smith's craft are the wide-bladed daggers and the narrow-hafted axe-heads with straight sides found in many burials.

Developments in these two fields can be followed through the Middle Bronze Age without a break, but the evidence of city-defences indicates a major change in other aspects a little before 1700 B.C. Prior to that time fairly substantial walls of brick or stone surrounded the major cities, pierced by fortified gateways. These were then superseded by more massive systems, featuring a wall on top of a steeply sloped earth bank (glacis) stabilized with a plaster face, and held at the foot by a heavy stone wall. At some sites a ditch was dug beyond the wall, its spoil contributing to the bank, while at others the bank was made up of earth and rubbish cleared from the foot of the mound.[39] The chief cities were greatly enlarged, a bank and ditch enclosing enormous level areas beyond the *tell* (e.g. Tell el-Yahudiyeh in Egypt, Hazor and Dan in Palestine, Qatna and Carchemish in Syria). Carefully built gateways led through the ramparts, the vaulted passage sufficiently wide to allow a chariot to pass.

By and large restricted to fortifications, such changes are taken to show the rise to power of a folk new to the area and able to organize its labour-force for these huge construction works. The existence of one example of the large enclosures in Egypt (Tell el-Yahudiyeh), and the overthrow of the native rule by the Hyksos about 1720 B.C., link the erection of this type of defence unmistakably with the regimen of the 'foreign chiefs'. Although there is no certainty over the origin of the Hyksos, the introduction of horse-drawn chariotry suggests a relation with Amurru in Syria, where horse-raising commenced a little earlier. Also, pressure on North Syria by the rising Hittite power, and in the east by Hurrians and Kassites, may have precipitated a final southward surge from the Amorite homeland, the new arrivals combining with their compatriots already in Egypt to seize power.

A ruling class in firm control is thus predicated, each major city having a monarch. The second group of Execration Texts from

Egypt documents this situation, naming far fewer rulers than the earlier series, which hints at a patriarchal society. Texts of the rulers of Byblos, and mention of a Byblian king and Hazor's sovereign in the Mari tablets, agree with this. Within their fortress-cities the rulers occupied substantial palaces, and their dependants lived in well-built mansions, set amid the smaller, jumbled houses of the locals, much as in the familiar eastern pattern of today.

If we may judge by the furnishings of their tombs, the people of the land seem to have had adequate material goods, although the tombs cut in the rock obviously did not belong to the poorest persons. Peculiar circumstances have preserved wooden tables and dishes, basketry, and other perishables in the burials excavated at Jericho. With their aid a more complete picture of an early Canaanite home can be drawn than the indestructible pots and the metal objects alone recovered from other sites permit. Personal possessions were sparse: perhaps a locally made scarab set in a bronze ring, a long bronze clothes pin, a dagger or an axe for a man, a wooden toilet box inlaid with simply engraved bone plaques, a stone perfume jar, a wooden comb. Very little gold jewellery is known from Canaan at this time, nor are other objects of rare metal, ivory, or precious stones found outside the tombs of the princes of Byblos, with the exception of a silver cup laid in a tomb near Shechem.[40]

A noticeable lack of precious items characterizes Middle Bronze Age culture both in Canaan and in the whole of the Fertile Crescent.[41] Yet trade certainly flowered in all directions. Besides the continuous interchange with Egypt and Babylonia, merchandise was exchanged with Cyprus, and, on a smaller scale, with the Minoan and Middle Helladic world of the Aegean. A typical clue to Canaanite trade is the small jug of a dark fabric, decorated with incised lines and dots filled with a white paste ('Tell el-Yahudiyeh' ware), made in Canaan and carried to Egypt and Cyprus, containing perfume, a product, it has been conjectured, of the lower Jordan valley.[42] In exchange, we assume, Cyprus supplied the copper for the Canaanite smiths, as she did for those of Mari and Babylonia, while tin was taken westwards, in one instance to Hazor,[43] which itself transmitted unidentified cargoes to Crete.[44]

Babylonian influence is seen in the use of the cuneiform script at Hazor in this period, where, although the specimens are few, a school may have functioned. No archives of the time have been found nearer to Canaan than Alalakh (Tell Atshana on the lower Orontes), and the possibility of an equal or greater use of Egyptian on papyrus should not be disregarded—the Byblian princes concocted inscriptions in hieroglyphs on stone.[45] Use of Egyptian was a vital factor in the outstanding accomplishment of Middle Bronze Age Canaan, the production of the alphabet.

b. *The Alphabet*

Accidental discoveries are our only sources of information, but they have been sufficient to make an outline of the alphabet's early history possible.[46] None of the systems previously employed was well-suited for universal, rapid use, so the advantages of a simple and adaptable mode of communication, transcending time and space in the cosmopolitan trading centres of the Levant, are obvious.

Details of the place and time of the alphabet's birth are unlikely to be recovered, nor can we know the name of its inventor. Currently, evidence suggests the stimulus came from Egypt, where a sub-system of hieroglyphic had been developed to spell foreign names clearly by using only symbols for one consonant plus one vowel ('group writing' or 'syllabic orthography', e.g. B = ba, bi, bu). To isolate such signs from the hieroglyphic matrix was the essential step never taken in Egypt. We may imagine a scribe living about 1700 B.C. improvising a series of symbols in the familiar Egyptian pattern for the range of sounds in his local tongue.[47]

A few texts survive retaining the primary picture-form, though as yet unread (Shechem Plaque, Lachish Dagger, *c.* 1500 B.C.); many known from subsequent centuries show the evolution of the signs, and yield some sense, those discovered in Palestine sharing the same script as those clustered at the turquoise mines of Serabit el Khadem in Sinai and a stray from Egypt.[48] By the end of the millennium recollection of the original pictures had been lost, and the signs had gained conventional forms, their shapes dictated by writing materials and the need for speed. Brief notes of ownership, 'arrow of so-and-so', are found on copper arrow-heads,[49] longer records on stone are confined so far to Byblos (Ahiram sarcophagus, building texts).

The account of Wen-amun's mission to Byblos in the twelfth century B.C. tells of papyrus rolls taken there in quantity, surely for a chancellery or scriptorium. That documents of some length were written in the Canaanite script soon after its use began to spread can hardly be doubted, in view of the use made of the Ugaritic alphabetic cuneiform script, its imitator. Only the hazards of preservation have withheld examples from us.

c. *The Late Bronze Age*

As the alphabet was carried through from Middle to Late Bronze Age Canaan, so were most aspects of Canaanite culture. The division of Middle from Late is based, nevertheless, on new features, and on a major political change. Native forces expelled the Hyksos from Egypt, harrying them into Canaan and reasserting pharaonic rule there sometime in the third quarter of the sixteenth century B.C.[50] Many cities were sacked in the process, some abandoned for a while (Jericho, Tell Beit Mirsim), others quickly recovering under local princes. No doubt these rulers were kept in order as well as in power to some extent by the frequent marches of Tuthmosis III and Amenophis II, the slacker rein of their successors permitting petty quarrels to be settled by force, and giving scope to the ambitious. Again, the ruins of cities testify to several destructions. Vivid flashes of light are thrown on the events of a few decades by the El Amarna Letters and related tablets from Palestinian sites,[51] and by the archives from Ugarit. Canaan's population is revealed as a mixture, predominantly Semitic, with some Hurrians and Indo-Europeans, in so far as one may rely upon the evidence of personal names (see also Plates I, IV*c*, V*a*, VI*a*). In Syria dynasts of the Late Bronze Age claimed pedigrees reaching back into the previous era, showing no major disruption of the people over many centuries, and a resilient survival of various hostilities—unless we are to treat the claims with unwarranted scepticism.[52] And this situation can be projected, with due caution, into Canaan. Numerous city-states ruled the fertile districts or commanded the major highways, two cities rarely shared a king, and, although there were frequent alliances, none was ever strong enough to achieve a lasting hegemony (Hazor seems to have enjoyed some pretence to be 'head of all those kingdoms' (Josh. 11: 10), but they retained their identity as 'kingdoms'). Between the domains of the cities roamed the landless, the outlaws, the deserters, called comprehensively 'Habiru', sometimes banding together to attack the hapless townsfolk, and daily hindering merchants and couriers.

Within the city walls the aristocracy continued to occupy superior mansions, well furnished with foreign luxuries. Despite declining standards in most crafts, more objects of value survive from the Late Bronze Age, being found both in buildings and in tombs. Hoards of jewellery from Tell el-Ajjul, near Gaza, belong to the earliest phase of the period, perhaps being buried on the approach of Tuthmosis III's first invasion, *c.* 1468 B.C.[53] Megiddo has yielded numerous pieces, of varying dates, showing traits of almost every artistic style of the time, naturally with Egyptian dominant. The coalescence of Egyptian and Babylonian cultures in Canaan is seen most clearly in the cylinder seals, which combine features from the repertoires of each pictorially, or use the Babylonian cylindrical form and the cuneiform script to write a West Semitic name and title with a wholly Egyptian scene, as in the case of the fascinating seals of a king of Sidon and his son.[54]

As earlier, the best attested trade is that involving pottery. Cypriot and Aegean vessels preponderate, almost equalling the number of local productions in some tombs, and supplying helpful chronological links through their wider horizons. The El-Amarna Letters tell of goods passing in other directions, while the 'goodly Babylonish mantle' filched by Achan from Jericho (Josh. 7: 21) represents one item of trade leaving no material trace.

Information concerning the Canaanite cities of the thirteenth century B.C. is sparse, and has not been adequately synthesized recently. Many had evidently passed their heyday (e.g. Hazor), and resistance to invasions from the east (Israelites) and the west (Philistines) could not be consolidated, only the strongest holding out, notably Beth-Shan and Megiddo, where Egypt's power lingered. Yet the material culture of the Canaanites was not extinguished, for these invasions brought relatively minor changes at that level.

(vi) *The Religion*

Material remains and written documents contribute a fair quantity of information about religious practices and beliefs in Canaan, but are very far from supplying a complete picture. The facts are so diverse in nature and provenance that few generalizations can be made legitimately. For this reason alone it is dangerous to treat the rich data of Ugarit as typically Canaanite, and other objections have been raised already. Ubiquitous in the Hebrew reports of Canaanite cult are the 'high places'. Examples of artificial mounds which are reckoned to be 'high places' have been unearthed at Megiddo and other sites, yet no mention of a cultic 'high place' is known at Ugarit. Baal is titled 'Lord of Earth' there, while Phoenician sources name him 'Lord of Heaven'.[55] These are only examples of differences between Ugarit and other sources, cited to underline the need for caution in their use.

Devout Canaanites might worship in temples of various patterns. The 'high place' was at first apparently an open-air shrine on a hill-top, with trees nearby. In towns a mound of earth or stones could represent the natural hillock. One at Megiddo continued in use from the Early Bronze Age, one at Nahariyah, near Haifa, was built in the Middle Bronze II period, and an example at Hazor belonged to the Late Bronze Age. At Nahariyah traces of oil were observed, the remains of libations. Plans of other temples vary, few are complicated, most are small in size. One basic design has simply an ante-room and a holy place where the image or divine symbol rested; Beth-Shan, Tell Far'ah (north), and Hazor contain examples, the latter a more grandiose building with a porch. (When Solomon's Temple was planned it reproduced this arrangement, as did the Tabernacle in the wilderness.) Massive footings for walls enclosing a single pillared room, entered from a porch at one end, are believed to belong to shrines of more than one storey (hence termed *migdal* or 'tower' shrines by Mazar) of which models in terra-cotta exist, the latter serving as incense burners. A literary reference may be seen in the Keret story from Ugarit, where the king mounts a tower (*mgdl*) to offer sacrifice (Keret I. iii. 53 ff.). Shechem and Megiddo alone have yielded examples erected at the end of the Middle Bronze Age. The Shechem *migdal* was succeeded by a more conventional temple, with ante-room and holy place, the ante-room being smaller than the holy place, both entered from the long side. This is a well-known type, found beyond Canaan at Alalakh and Ugarit.[56] Finally, the discovery of a 15-metre-square temple, with rooms surrounding a sacred area, at Amman, dated to the Late Bronze Age, has brought recognition as a temple to a similar structure outside Shechem on the slopes of Mount Gerizim,[57] although the traces of foundation rites at Amman, involving multiple cremations, are absent from Shechem.

To identify the gods revered in these buildings is impossible at present. Inscriptions found *in situ* are so rare that only one temple can be assigned to a named deity with any plausibility, the temple of Mekal at Beth-Shan; otherwise the objects found allow merely conjectural attributions. In many places the ancients may have been vague themselves, as at Byblos, where the patron was simply *Baʿalat Gebal* 'The Mistress of Byblos', and could be identified according to the worshipper's background.

While numerous gods and goddesses are listed in texts, and the more popular ones are lauded or invoked in personal names, only a handful have well-defined characteristics. All are obvious personifications of natural powers and objects, except for those of foreign origin.

El, the head of the pantheon, plays little part in the poems of Ugarit, and is seldom found in names of the Late Bronze Age people, a development of the tendency in the Mari period, when, according to our sources, he was already giving way to Hadad. The greatest devotion was given to Hadad, the weather-god, under this, his West Semitic name; as Teshub, the Hurrian equivalent; or simply as *Baʿal* 'Master'.[58] Controlling the rains, mist, and dew, Hadad held the keys of good harvests, so the existence of a myth describing his battles with death, barrenness, and threatening flood waters among the texts of Ugarit is no surprise. How the myth should be interpreted is debatable. There is no hint of a special place in the cult of Hadad, and we may be doubtful about the theory that it was mimed at an annual festival. Like other ancient myths we understand it as recounting the archetypal event, which assures its hearers that the enemy has in fact been overcome long ago, so they should trust and adore the champion. Hadad is affiliated to El and to Dagan, the corn-god, in different Ugaritic writings—an indication of a fluidity of thought in the same place. His consort was Ashtart (Ishtar), goddess of battle, who is only occasionally distinguishable from Asherah, El's wife. Asherah can be identified hesitantly with the naked-mother figurines so frequently modelled in clay. There was another war-goddess, ʿAnat, also associated with Hadad. Among the remaining divinities were, for example, Reshef the god of war and the underworld,[59] Horon, lord of the underworld, Tirosh, god of new wine, Kathir and Hasis, hypostases of skill and art. All the chief members of the divine court had their own epithets, e.g. Asherah was called *Qudshu* 'Holy One'.

Small images in metal or clay are common finds at Canaanite towns. The majority average six inches in height and have rudimentary modelling of facial and bodily features. The cast-bronze figures, usually male, may hold weapons; sometimes they consist of male and female, in rare instances accompanied by a child. Gold or silver foil was added to indicate a kilt, a headdress, or an item of jewellery. Terra-cotta figurines are predominantly female, a simple silhouette being augmented to show the sex and face, the nose and ears especially being exaggerated. These figures, both metal and clay, are not found solely in sacred precincts, although many have such a provenance, and so can be considered personal or household equipment, amulets or good-luck charms.[60] Their use spans the whole of the Middle and Late Bronze Ages.

Temple paraphernalia included sacred pillars (*maṣṣēḇāh*) tree-trunks (*ʿᵃšērāh*) and incense altars (*ḥammān*). The pillars served as memorials in the first place, as in the Temple of Obelisks at Byblos, but inevitably attracted reverence as embodying the spirits of persons or gods connected with them. A few bear inscriptions naming persons commemorated; others, it can be suggested, were plastered, and then inscribed in ink or paint now lost through weathering (cf. Deut. 27: 2 f.). No *asherah* has survived from Canaan, nor is the significance of the symbol certain; the principle of life is supposed to have been represented by it, a view in harmony with the connection made between the goddess Asherah and the female figurines. Beside the statues, gods were symbolized by particular animals, notably the bull (related to El and Baal) and the lion (to Asherah), and they stand on or between their animals in some scenes.

Sacrifices offered on the altars consisted of animals and birds, slaughtered, presumably to secure divine favour, by any one at any time (*šlmm* at Ugarit, Hebrew *šᵉlāmîm* 'peace offerings'), and in special rites on holy days. Priestly experts examined the entrails to forecast the future and advise on conduct, using Babylonian techniques taught from models. How far the ordinary populace shared in these rites cannot be said; we may speculate on the existence of humble shrines, sacred wells and springs, and the services of witches, wizards, and necromancers as elements in the peasants' beliefs.

(vii) *Canaanite Influences on Israel*

The strict commands given to Israel for the extermination of the Canaanites and of Canaanite religious objects (e.g. Exod. 23: 24; 34: 13 ff.; Deut. 7) had the obvious motive of keeping Israel free from contagion. At the same time, notice should be taken of the absence of any injunction to destroy the material culture of the land (apart from the special case of Jericho). All that was captured in the way of domestic utensils, farm tools, wagons, buildings, weapons and armour, could be appropriated for Israel's use. And to a people newly settling down after a semi-nomadic life, wholesale adoption of these physical trappings would mean a major change in cultural identity, allowing, of course, for a period of time to become familiar with the more sophisticated techniques involved.[61]

If it is accepted that Israel inherited Canaanite civilization, what can be said of the two areas of Hebrew life where Canaanite influence is most strongly alleged, language and religion? The tremendous impetus given to Hebrew studies by the recovery of the Ugaritic texts, the nearest yet discovered to a corpus of Canaanite literature, has both clarified and complicated the picture. Hebrew, as we have seen, is most closely akin to the Canaanite dialects of the late second millennium B.C., and repeatedly may be better understood by comparison with them. Nevertheless, it remains distinctive, and cannot be assimilated to an earlier, hypothetical 'Canaanite' without far more data.[62] Striking similarities of phrase can be found between the Ugaritic poems and parts of the Old Testament, and it is quite conceivable that Israelite authors would take over expressions used in Canaanite poetry, but each case needs scrutiny within the wider range of ancient Semitic idiom, where equally close parallels may be traced.[63] Even the most compelling examples of Ugaritic–Hebrew community are strictly linguistic phenomena, generally isolated ones, and do not automatically involve transference of thought forms, as might easily be assumed.

Inheriting Canaanite culture, speaking a language close to Canaanite, the Israelites are frequently, and understandably, pictured as absorbing customs and beliefs from Canaan, too. Again, the discoveries at Ugarit have given an impulse in this direction. However, apart from common words (e.g. *khn*: *kōhēn* 'priest'; *dbḥ*: *zeḇaḥ* 'sacrifice'; *šlmm* cited above), no larger units of cultic expression or ritual can be traced from Canaanite sources into Hebrew. So firm is the conviction of Israel's separate and unique faith in the earliest of her traditions that it cannot be thought likely that the invaders would have adopted the alien practices of Canaan wholesale. There is no doubt that Canaanite attitudes gained a strong hold on Israel during the settlement, yet these things were recognized as intrusive by the upholders of Israel's own faith, and did not become a part of it.

NOTES

1. Understanding Lesha to be in the Dead Sea region; cf. J. Simons, *The Geographical and Topographical Texts of the Old Testament* (Brill, Leiden, 1959), § 271.

2. ʿArqa: E. Dhorme, *R.B.* xvii (1908), 509, now Tell ʿArqa. Ṣumur is probably Tell Kazel; see M. Dunand, N. Saliby, *Annales Archéologiques de Syrie* vii (1957), 3–16; xiv (1964), 3–14.

3. Siyan is written *syn* in Ugaritic (U.T. no. 1750); $^{\bar{a}l/m\bar{a}t}$*si-ya-na* in Akkadian texts from that neighbouring city, $^{\bar{a}l}$*si-a-nu* and $^{\bar{a}l}$*si-in-nu* in later Assyrian texts (*A.R.A.B.* §§ 611, 770, 772, 815, 821; ii, § 125 h). J. Nougayrol locates the place at Siano east of Jebeleh (*P.R.U.* iv. 16 f., following E. Forrer) although Jerome, in his *Questiones hebraicae in Genesim* (ed. J. P. Migne, *Patrologia Latina* xxiii (1844–64), col. 954), and others have put it further south, near ʿArqa. The name may be preserved in Nahr es-Sinn, between Jebeleh and Baniyas.

4. *'dnlrm*, the name of a governor in the eighth century B.C., could be Canaanite (text: *K.A.I.* no. 203).

5. Doubts about the precise value of this description may be licit, but the hints of antiquity within it, such as the complete unawareness of any Philistine presence in the south (contrast Exod. 13: 17; 15: 14), and the lack of clear limits to east and north (compare the details at the time of the Conquest, set out below), and its general agreement with other passages should be borne in mind.

6. Whatever the origin of the term, Egyptologists are agreed that A. Alt's equation with Lydda cannot be sustained; see Sir Alan H. Gardiner, *Ancient Egyptian Onomastica* vol. i (O.U.P., London, 1947), pp. 142 ff., and W. Helck, *Die Beziehungen Ägyptens zu Vorderasien* (Harrassowitz, Wiesbaden, 1962), pp. 272 ff.

7. See *A.N.E.T.*, p. 246.

8. Papyrus Anastasi III A. 5, 6—IV. 16, 4; R. A. Caminos, *Late Egyptian Miscellanies* (O.U.P., London, 1954), pp. 117, 200; A. Erman, *The Literature of the Ancient Egyptians* (Methuen, London, 1927), p. 210.

9. *A.N.E.T.*, pp. 376 ff.; *D.O.T.T.*, pp. 137 ff.; text now in K. A. Kitchen, *Ramesside Inscriptions* (Blackwell, Oxford, 1968), iv. 12–19.

10. B. Maisler, *B.A.S.O.R.* cii (1946), 9 ff.

11. S. Smith, *The Statue of Idrimi* (British Institute of Archaeology at Ankara, London, 1949), lines 19, 20 (*i-na ma-at ki-in-a-nim*^{ki} $^{\bar{a}l}$*am-mi-a*^{ki} *aš-bu*); *A.N.E.T.*, pp. 557 f.

12. D. J. Wiseman, *The Alalakh Tablets* (British Institute of Archaeology at Ankara, London, 1953), no. 48, 5, $^{\bar{a}l}$*ki-in-a-nim*^{ki} (Pl. XIII); no. 154, 24, $^{m\bar{a}t}$*ki-na-a-ni*^{ki}; no. 181, 9, $^{m\bar{a}t}$*ke-en-a-ni*^{ki} (*J.C.S.* viii (1954), 11).

13. See Sety I's texts in Kitchen, *Ramesside Inscriptions*, i, 8 § *c*; *A.N.E.T.*, p. 254c; cf. Y. Aharoni, *The Land of the Bible* (Burns and Oates, London, 1967), p. 62.

14. Ammiya is identified with Efneh, about 8 miles down the coast from Tripoli; see E. Dhorme, *R.B.* xvii (1908), 509, following Marmier.

15. Kamid el-Loz, in the Litani valley 12 miles north of Rasheya; see O. Weber in *E.A.* ii. 1214 f. The Beqaʿ proper was known as ʿAmq; see Y. Aharoni, *I.E.J.* iii (1953), 153–61; M. Weippert, in A. Kuschke, E. Kutsch, *Archaeologie und altes Testament, Festschrift für Kurt Galling* (J. C. B. Mohr, Tübingen, 1970), pp. 259 ff.

16. The Hor of Num. 34: 7, 8 is probably Jebel Akkar; cf. Ezekiel's Hethlon (47: 15) = Heitela, east of Tripoli.

17. Y. Aharoni, *The Land of the Bible*, pp. 146–53, 170–2, holds to this view; W. Helck, *Die Beziehungen . . .*, pp. 256 ff., argues for the position taken here, with more detail in *M.D.O.G.* xcii (1960), 1–13.

18. E. Edel, in *Geschichte und altes Testament, Festschrift für A. Alt, Beiträge zur historischen Theologie* xvi (1953), 55–63.

19. Cf. Josh. 13: 4, 'to the border of the Amorite', with the limits of Amurru; and Ezek. 6: 14, 'from the wilderness to Riblah', an even more northerly point (reading Riblah for M.T. Diblah).

20. *Language* xii (1936), 124 f.

21. *B.A.N.E.*, p. 356 n. 50, partly influenced by B. Maisler's view in this latter opinion; see n. 10 above.

22. *J.C.S.* xxi (1967), 166–7.

23. See R. de Vaux, *R.B.* lxxiv (1967), 489–92; H. Hoffner, below, p. 224; A. Goetze, *J.C.S.* xvi (1962), 52, takes the name as a Hurrian form *Kinaḫ* with plural article *na* suffixed.

24. See Z. S. Harris, *The Development of the Canaanite Dialects* (American Oriental Society, New Haven, Conn., 1939), pp. 29–30; A. Goetze, *Language* xvii (1941), 128–31.

25. S. Moscati, *An Introduction to the Comparative Grammar of the Semitic Languages* (Harrassowitz, Wiesbaden, 1964), §§ 8. 74, 83; 13. 7.

26. I. J. Gelb demonstrated the division in his valuable essay 'The Early History of the West Semitic Peoples', in *J.C.S.* xv (1961), 42 f., where some possible traces of early 'Canaanite' are discussed; *ḫamūṣam iḫmuṣ* (where *ḫamāṣam* would be expected), found in several exemplars of a royal inscription at Mari, is thought to be another; see S. Moscati, *Comparative Grammar*, § 8. 74; W. von Soden, *Akkadisches Handwörterbuch* (Harrassowitz, Wiesbaden, 1962), p. 315, s.v. *ḫamāṣu*, refers to G. Dossin, *Syria* xxxii (1955), 14, ii. 19. W. F. Albright, *B.A.S.O.R.* clxxvi (1964), 45, adduces Egyptian evidence from a slightly earlier date, but there are some questions concerning the vowels to be given to Egyptian signs; see K. A. Kitchen, *B.O.* xxvi (1969), 201.

27. Z. S. Harris, *Development*; H. L. Ginsberg, *The Legend of King Keret*, *B.A.S.O.R.*, Supplementary Studies 2–3 (New Haven, Conn., 1946); W. F. Albright, *B.A.N.E.*, pp. 328 ff.; J. Gray, *The Canaanites* (Thames and Hudson, London, 1964). The most notable objector is A. Goetze, *Language* xvii (1941), 127 ff.

28. The last emphasized by J. C. Greenfield, *J.C.S.* xxi (1967), 89–93, and *Proceedings of the International Conference of Semitic Studies 1965* (Israel Academy, Jerusalem, 1969), pp. 92–101.

29. *Ugaritica* v (1968), p. 234, no. 130, 12. F. Grondahl, *Die Personennamen der Texte aus Ugarit* (Pontifical Biblical Institute, Rome, 1967), p. 18, lists names from Ugarit showing the change *ā* to *ō*. At a sea-port linked in commerce and diplomacy with Canaan the presence of these names does not prove a *local* usage.

30. See D. R. Hillers, *B.A.S.O.R.* clxxiii (1964), 45 f. and n. 2.

31. They continued the name Canaan; cf. Matt. 15: 22 and Mark 7: 26, and perhaps a coin of Beirut cited by R. de Vaux, *J.A.O.S.* lxxxviii (1968), p. 23 n. 11. Punic inhabitants of North Africa called themselves *chanani*, according to Augustine (Z. S. Harris, *A Grammar of the Phoenician Language* (American Oriental Society, New Haven, Conn., 1936), p. 7).

32. K. M. Kenyon, *Amorites and Canaanites* (O.U.P., London, 1966); *C.A.H.* 2nd edn., 1, Part ii, pp. 567–94; II. Ch. iii (= fasc. 48 (1966)). The phrase comes from H. W. F. Saggs, *Bulletin of the School of Oriental and African Studies* xxx (1967), 404. Note also the detailed survey by W. G. Dever in *H.T.R.* lxiv (1971), 197–226.

33. R. de Vaux, *R.B.* lxxiii (1966), 605 f.; cf. 612 f.

34. P. W. Lapp, *The Dhahr Mirzbaneh Tombs* (American Schools of Oriental Research, New Haven, Conn., 1966), pp. 86–116; criticized by R. de Vaux, *R.B.* lxiv (1967), 471–4, and K. M. Kenyon, *Archaeology in the Holy Land*, 3rd edn. (E. Benn, London, 1970), pp. 340–1.

35. As K. M. Kenyon assumes in *Amorites and Canaanites*, *passim*; cf. T. C. Mitchell, in *A.O.T.S.*, p. 406 n. 38.

36. The few references to Canaanites at Ugarit illustrate this point, and make clear that the city was not reckoned in Canaan; see A. F. Rainey, *I.E.J.* xiii (1963), 43–5; xiv (1964), 101.

37. *Dhahr Mirzbaneh*, p. 96.

38. See the more comprehensive survey by B. Mazar in bibliography below, and K. M. Kenyon, *C.A.H.* 2nd edn., II. Ch. iii (see n. 32). For a discussion of recent studies see also G. E. Wright, *J.A.O.S.* xci (1971), 276–93.

39. On the glacis defences see P. J. Parr, *Z.D.P.V.* lxxxiv (1968), 18–45, even if his theory is to be rejected, as by Y. Yadin, *B.A.* xxxii (1962), 62 f.

40. I am indebted to Mrs. Miriam Tadmor for information of this discovery since published in *I.E.J.* xxi (1971), 178–81.

41. Cf. C. J. Gadd, *C.A.H.* 2nd edn., II. Ch. v, pp. 43 f. regarding Babylonia.

42. B. Mazar, *I.E.J.* xviii (1968), 77. A kiln containing Tell el-Yahudiyeh ware juglets has been unearthed at Afula; see R. Amiran, *The Ancient Pottery of the Holy Land* (Rutgers University Press, 1970), p. 120.

43. *A.R.M.* vii, no. 236; cf. A. Malamat, in J. A. Sanders (ed.), *Near Eastern Archaeology in the Twentieth Century; Essays in Honor of Nelson Glueck* (Doubleday, New York, 1970), pp. 164 ff.

44. A. Malamat, loc. cit., p. 168.

45. See K. A. Kitchen, *B.M.B.* xx (1967), 149–52; *La Siria nel Tardo Bronzo* (see bibliography), pp. 85 ff.

46. See F. M. Cross, *Eretz Israel* viii (1967), 8*–24*.

47. Cf. Kitchen, *La Siria*, pp. 85 f.; G. Posener, *Mélanges de l'Université Saint-Joseph* xlv (1969), 225–39 (reference by courtesy of K. A. Kitchen).

48. W. F. Albright, *The Proto-Sinaitic Inscriptions and their Decipherment* (Harvard Theological Studies xxii, Cambridge, Mass., 1966).

49. Discussed by F. M. Cross, *Eretz Israel* viii (1967), 12* ff., 19* ff.

50. On the date see Kitchen, *La Siria*, p. 79.

51. See, in general, W. F. Albright, 'The Amarna Letters from Palestine', *C.A.H.* 2nd edn., II. Ch. xx (= fasc. 51 (1966)).

52. D. B. Redford had drawn attention to Alalah, Qatna, Tunip, and Ugarit in *Or.* N.S. xxxix (1970), 16. Hazor might be added tentatively, by linking Ibni-Adad of the Mari texts with Jabin in Josh. 11; see A. Malamat in *Near Eastern Archaeology*, p. 168 and n. 22. The ancestry of Israel, too, is somewhat comparable.

53. O. Negbi, *The Hoards of Goldwork from Tell el-Ajjul* (Studies in Mediterranean Archaeology xxv, Goteborg, 1970). The chronology used here follows that of K. A. Kitchen; see note 50.

54. *Collection de Clercq, Catalogue*, I, nos. 386 *bis*, *ter*.

55. B. Mazar, 'The Philistines and the Rise of Tyre', *Proc. Israel Academy of Sciences and Humanities*, i. 7 (1964), p. 19; A. F. Rainey, *B.A.* xxviii (1965), 121.

56. G. E. Wright, *Shechem* (Duckworth, London, 1965), p. 99.

57. R. G. Boling, E. F. Campbell, G. E. Wright, *B.A.* xxxii (1969), 81–112.

58. The equation of Baʿal with Hadad has been demonstrated by A. F. Rainey, *I.E.J.* xviii (1968), 1–14.

59. P. Matthiae, *O.A.* ii (1963), 27–43.

60. Cf. Sir Leonard Woolley, *Alalakh* (Society of Antiquaries, London, 1955), pp. 244 ff.

61. The negative verdict of an archaeologist discussing the evidence for Israel's arrival in Canaan has to be read in this light (H. J. Franken, *C.A.H.* 2nd edn., II. ch. xxvi(b) = fasc. 67 (1968)).

62. Cf. (iii) above. While numerous advantages stem from comparison of ancient Semitic usage, and the West Semitic languages especially, the dangers need to be remembered and controls maintained to avoid introducing words or grammatical forms which would involve intolerable ambiguity within Hebrew; see J. Barr, *Comparative Philology and the Text of the Old Testament* (O.U.P., 1968); M. Greenberg, *J.A.O.S.* xc (1970), 536–40; P. Wernberg-Møller, *J.T.S.* N.S. xxi (1970), 447 f.

63. See P. C. Craigie, *Tyndale Bulletin* xxii (1971), 3–31, with references.

BIBLIOGRAPHY

The several chapters by K. M. Kenyon, M. Drower, and others on Syria and Palestine in *C.A.H.* 2nd edn., II give much information and full references. The following items are of particular value:

ALBRIGHT, W. F. 'The Role of the Canaanites in the History of Civilisation', in *B.A.N.E.*, pp. 328–62.

DE VAUX, R. 'Le Pays de Canaan', *J.A.O.S.* lxxxviii (1968), 23–30 (= American Oriental Series liii, *Essays in Memory of E. A. Speiser*).

LIVERANI, M. (ed.) *La Siria nel Tardo Bronzo, Orientis Antiqui Collectio*, ix (Rome, 1969).

MALAMAT, A. 'Syrien-Palästina in der 2. Hälfte des 2. Jahrtausends', *Fischer Weltgeschichte*, iii (Frankfurt, 1966).

MAZAR, B. 'The Middle Bronze Age in Palestine', *I.E.J.* xviii (1968), 65–97.

III

THE PHILISTINES

K. A. KITCHEN

AMONG the peoples of the Old Testament the Philistines are at once among the most familiar and the most elusive. They appear as mysterious aliens, entering to dispute Palestine with the Hebrews, in some of the finest and most graphic narratives in the Old Testament, involving such notable characters as Samson and Samuel, Saul and David—yet we learn little that is tangible about them, except the names of their chief cities under five 'lords', and their role as redoubtable adversaries of the Hebrews.

(i) *Origins and Background*

a. *The Framework of Old Testament Tradition*

Under Egypt, along with other names, Genesis 10: 13–14 notes the Casluhim, whence went forth the Philistines, and ends with the Caphtorim. It is interesting that the Philistines are here derived from the enigmatic Casluhim rather than the Caphtorim, although one may infer that the latter and the Philistines at least belong to the same general horizon.[1] Amos has the Philistines from Caphtor like Israel from Egypt (Amos 9: 7); Israel came out of Egypt, but did not originate there,[2] and so one may understand the Philistines arriving from Caphtor, but originating elsewhere (Casluhim with Gen. 10). Jeremiah 47: 4 confirms the link with Caphtor.

These associations of the Philistines with Caphtor and Casluhim underline the need to examine with them other related entities. The Caphtorim partly supplanted the even less known Avvim south from Gaza (Deut. 2: 23; cf. also Josh. 13: 3). Geographically, this coincides nearly with the Negeb of the Cherethites

(*Krētī*) mentioned in 1 Samuel 30: 14. 'Cherethites' later served as a poetic synonym for 'Philistines' (cf. Zeph. 2: 4–5 and Ezek. 25: 15–16). During most of Hebrew history the Philistines occupied South-West Palestine, under the lords of their five cities.

b. *The Background, from Extra-Biblical Sources*

1. *Origins.* While ancient Near-Eastern sources enrich several aspects of our knowledge of the Philistines, nothing very positive or convincing can yet be offered on the Casluhim.[3] However, Caphtor can now be definitively identified with Crete, and so the Caphtorim as Cretans.

The name 'Caphtor' recurs in cuneiform documents as Kaptara,[4] and is identifiable with Egyptian Keftiu.[5] People from Keftiu are represented in tomb-chapels at Thebes of the fifteenth century B.C.; those paintings that are demonstrably first-hand representations clearly depict the same people as feature in the frescoes at Knossos in Minoan Crete, and correspond to what is known of Minoans and Mycenaeans alike.[6] A Theban topographical list of Amenophis III (*c.* 1400 B.C.) demonstrates textually just what the Egyptians understood by Keftiu.[7] Two names on the right side—*Keftiu* and *Tanayu*—define the area(s) of the thirteen surviving names on the left side. *Tanayu* itself best corresponds to the Greek *Danaoi*,[8] used of Greeks in the Argolid and soon more widely.[9] The correspondence between Crete plus the Argolid and Aegean and the twelve names legible out of thirteen can be tabulated as follows.

Keftiu (*Crete*)	*Tanayu* (*Danaoi*)
1. Amnisos (i)	4. Mycenae
2. Phaistos (??)[10]	5. *Dqìs* = ?[11]
3. Cydonia	6. Messenia
– – – –	
10. Knossos	7. Nauplia
11. Amnisos (ii)	8. Cythera
12. Lyktos	9. *Wilia* (Ilios ??)[12]

This table speaks for itself.[13] Four names (one duplicated), perhaps five, clearly belong in Crete. Cythera leads one to the mainland, especially the Argolid, with three clearly identifiable names. Troy remains an alluring if doubtful possibility from further north.[14]

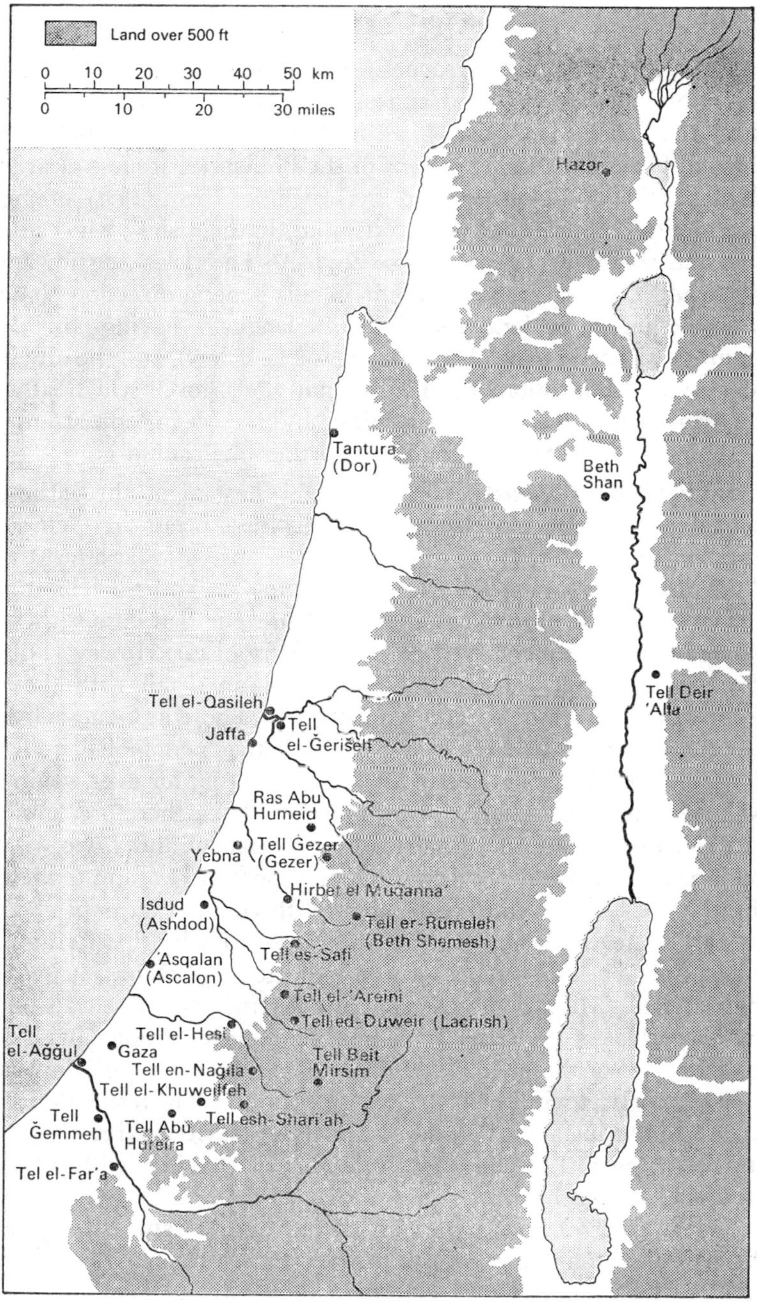

FIG. 3 PHILISTIA

Thus, if the Philistines reached Canaan from Caphtor, they did so from Crete—as did the Caphtorim of Deuteronomy 2: 23. In turn, the Cherethites (*Krētī*) can be 'Cretans' without qualms.[15] Beyond Crete, the further origins of the Philistines are less clear.[16] Ramesses III of Egypt (*c.* 1190 B.C.) includes them (*Prst*) among 'the foreign countries making a conspiracy in their isles', who came east and south through Syria to Egypt.[17] The 'isles', again, are Crete and the Aegean basin. Hints in this general direction come from the limited evidence for 'Philistine language' having possible affinities with west-Anatolian languages (see below), and the often-suggested identification of Philistines and 'Pelasgoi',[18] which latter are associated with western Asia Minor and Greece in some strands of the confused Greek traditions.[19] Further one cannot go.

2. '*Patriarchal Philistines.*' In the Old Testament the earliest narrative references to the term 'Philistines' occur in Genesis 21: 32, 34 and 26: 1, 8, 14–18. As external sources so far attest the Philistines *senso strictu* only from *c.* 1200 B.C., and the Hebrew patriarchs on any chronology must long precede that date,[20] these allusions have often been regarded as anachronisms. However, the 'Philistines' of Genesis do not correspond in detail with those securely attested from *c.* 1200 B.C. onwards. Those in Genesis live around Gerar, and under a king, not in the 'pentapolis' under 'lords' (*s*^{e}*rānîm*); they are relatively peaceable, not for ever waging wars, despite having an army commander. It is, therefore, more prudent to compare the 'Philistines' of Abraham and Isaac with such peoples as the Caphtorim of Deuteronomy 2: 23, and to view the term itself as a thirteenth- to twelfth-century term used of an earlier Aegean group such as the Caphtorim by the narrator. Thus, the Genesis references would indicate Aegean contacts with 'patriarchal' (Middle Bronze Age?) Palestine, and illustrate an overlap of use of the term 'Philistine' for Aegean peoples besides just the *Prst* of the later Egyptian sources. Such a proceeding is in harmony both with the Hebrew interrelation of the terms Philistines, Caphtorim, and Cherethites already seen (section (i) a above), and with the fact of close interrelations of the *Prst* with allied groups examined below.

Aegean interrelations with Canaan and the Levant as early as the Middle Bronze Age are, of course, well attested. The Mari archives have the King of Hazor sending gifts to Kaptara (i.e.

Crete);[21] conversely, Middle Minoan II pottery was found at Hazor and Ugarit.[22] In Middle-Kingdom Egypt, Middle Minoan Kamares pottery occurs at three sites, and related silverware in a temple-hoard.[23] Finally, on the linguistic plane, the mixture of names both Semitic (Abimelech, Ahuzzath) and non-Semitic (Phicol) in Genesis 26: 26 shows assimilation of aliens to a Semitic cultural milieu, such as later occurred with the Philistines themselves.[24]

3. *Philistine Entry into Canaan.* When the Philistines, in the narrowest terms (Egypt. *Prst*), reached Canaan under Ramesses III, they did not arrive alone and are never named alone. His Year 5 text associates them with the Tjekker, while that of Year 8 plus the Harris Papyrus I together add the names of five further groups, apart from the Lukka and Aḳaiwasha under Merenptah. Furthermore, in the great war scenes in the Medinet Habu temple of Ramesses III the Philistines, Tjekker, and Danuna are *all* dressed alike, with 'feathered' headgear and tasselled tunics[25]—but they are quite distinct from the Sherden in horned helmets and the Tursha in rounded caps. This point of identical dress is of some importance—it means that the clay coffins and other representations of people wearing 'feathered' headgear[26] cannot all be automatically and narrowly dubbed 'Philistine'; they can equally pertain to members of three related groups, and probably more.[27]

As some members of these groups (besides just *Prst*) did stay in Canaan subsequently,[28] but the Old Testament writers use only the one term 'Philistines', it is reasonable to suggest that they grouped these very similar peoples under the one term.

Furthermore, this closely related set of peoples to which the Philistines belong did not suddenly arrive in the Levant only in *c.* 1200 B.C. The Lukka (precursors of the Lycians) appear as raiders in the Amarna letters *c.* 1370 B.C.,[29] as Hittite allies against Ramesses II at Kadesh *c.* 1286 B.C.,[30] and then in Libya with Libyans and others in the first attack by 'Peoples of the Sea'[31] on Egypt, repulsed by Merenptah *c.* 1220 B.C.[32] Pa-luka, 'the Lycian', occurs as a personal name in Egypt under Ramesses III *c.* 1170 B.C.[33] Danuna is a land north of Ugarit in the Amarna letters,[34] before its peoples came south to meet Ramesses III; the name recurs much later in the Phoenician and Hittite Hieroglyphic (late Luvian) texts from Karatepe. Comprehensive study of all name-forms and contexts by Laroche shows clearly that Danuna is the region and people of Adana in Cilicia,[35] and not the far-western Danaoi as such.[36] Thirdly, the Sherden appear also in the Amarna letters,[37] and then as pirates raiding the Delta coasts until suppressed and taken over as slave troops by Ramesses II,[38] and employed at the battle of Kadesh.[39] Further, Sherden were among Merenptah's foes, who also included the Aḳaiwasha[40] (here only) and the Sheklesh and Tursha, who reappeared under Ramesses III. The Sherden appear on both sides in the wars of Ramesses III.

Thus, when the Philistines (*Prst*), Tjekker, and Weshesh appear with the Sherden, Danuna, Sheklesh, and Tursha under Ramesses III, they do so as part of a movement of peoples that had been affecting the Levant—Cilicia, Syria-Palestine, Egypt, and Libya—for over 150 years before *c.* 1200 B.C., merely reaching a migratory climax by the latter date. As the Sherden particularly were used as slave troops by the Egyptians, including in Palestine (e.g., up to Qadesh), a passage such as Joshua 13: 2 may already reflect the presence of Sea Peoples in South-West Canaan in the late thirteenth century B.C.,[41] with their troops used in Egyptian key garrisons in such well-attested administrative centres as Gaza. To this suggested picture can be added further lines of evidence.

The late second millennium B.C. saw Minoan and then emerging and dominant Mycenaean trade between the Aegean and the Levant.[42] But, more specifically, evidence has been suggested for members of the Sea Peoples being in Syria-Palestine and Egypt before the wars of Ramesses III, possibly going back into the late thirteenth century B.C. Thus a whole series of clay coffins, the lids decorated with faces and arms, have been attributed to 'Sea Peoples' or, specifically, Philistines of the twelfth–eleventh centuries B.C.[43] Two such were found in Tomb 570 at Lachish, but associated with pottery indubitably Late Bronze Age II in type, i.e. normally datable to the late thirteenth century B.C. Wright sees this as possible evidence, therefore, for members of the Sea Peoples or Philistines there at that time.[44] However, his further suggestion[45] that the Late Bronze 'bench tombs' at Tell el Farʿa are of Aegean origin, and so indicate related settlers at this period, is undermined by the fact that this class of tomb has native antecedents going back to the Middle Bronze Age.[46] The destruction of Ugarit by Sea Peoples has also been set as high as *c.* 1230 B.C.,[47] but this is not certain.

Rather better evidence may come from Deir 'Alla in the Jordan valley, where a twelfth-century level containing Philistine ware directly overlay one containing Late Bronze II pottery, a sanctuary yielding a faience vessel of Queen Tewosret (*c.* 1220/1200 B.C.), and small clay tablets inscribed with a script whose closest analogues are, for example, Cretan Linear A and B or 'Cypro-Minoan' script.[48] It has been suggested[49] that these late thirteenth-century tablets were written by members of the Sea Peoples if not actually Philistines, contemporaries of Queen Tewosret and perhaps also of her immediate predecessors.[50]

Finally, there is the sequence of Iron Age settlements at Beth-Shan.[51] Level VI shows pottery-forms linked more with Late Bronze II than with the fully fledged Iron Age I. To Level VI belong Egyptian monuments of Ramesses III and also the so-called 'Philistine' clay-coffin burials. 'Lower' Level V had entirely new buildings, further hieroglyphic texts, and saw re-erection and respect for the stelae of Sety I and Ramesses II and the statue of Ramesses III—*c.* 1100/1075 B.C. is the lowest feasible date for beginning 'lower' Level V. 'Upper' Level V is the Israelite period (tenth-century pottery) of David and Solomon, and IV reflects the Divided Monarchy.[52]

This sequence seems impeccable—except that there is no warrant at all to assume that Egyptian influence *c.* 1100/1075 B.C. would have led to such honour being paid to monuments of bygone kings—this is the age of Egyptian political bankruptcy exemplified by Wenamun! Therefore, an earlier date for founding 'lower' Level V must be predicated, and so also for Level VI. One might attribute VI to Ramesses III generally, and begin 'lower' V under, say, Ramesses VI (of whom a small bronze statue-base was found at Megiddo).[53] However, such minor objects as this small base and stray scarabs prove nothing much, as rightly stressed by Černý.[54] Nor is Ramesses VI known to have honoured his greater predecessors.

Therefore, one may rather suggest that 'lower' Level V was founded in or soon after Year 8 of Ramesses III (following on his defeat of the Sea Peoples); he would thus have reinstalled his own statue and—as a known admirer of Ramesses II—also have re-erected the stelae of that king and his father Sety I. Level VI would then represent the Egyptian regime at Beth-shan in Years 1 to 8 of Ramesses III, and probably in the last few years of the outgoing Nineteenth Dynasty. This would explain the affinities of Level VI pottery with that of Late Bronze Age II, and suggest that already at the end of the thirteenth century the 'Egyptian' garrison there was partly manned by close relatives of the Philistines. This would go well with the Lachish and Deir ʿAlla evidence, and earlier Egyptian and cuneiform data on Sea Peoples in the Levant, already considered above.

Thus, the over-all picture is of about 150 years (*c.* 1370–1200 B.C.) during which various peoples from the Aegean and western Asia Minor percolated in groups into the Levant, some via Crete (e.g. Philistines) and some as slave troops and as settlers in Egyptian-influenced parts of Palestine. Then in several waves,[55] at no great interval (end of thirteenth century B.C.), these 'Sea Peoples' took over Cyprus, and attacked North Syria (Ugarit, Alalakh). Thereafter,[56] migrating groups brought an end to the Hittite realm in Asia Minor (displacing part of the populace into North Syria),[57] while those already in Syria went south, regrouped in Amurru, and migrated southwards towards Egypt, a war-fleet skirting the coast while their families came overland in ox-carts (see Plate II). After defeat by Ramesses III, many stayed in Canaan (especially the Philistines and Tjekker), while others sailed back westwards, eventually to leave their names in Sicily, Sardinia, and as part of the Etruscan movement still later. Thus did South-West Canaan become in due course Philistia.

(ii) *Scope and Course of Philistine Settlement in Canaan*

a. *The Philistine Heartland*

Following on the eighth year of Ramesses III (*c.* 1200/1190 B.C.), the Philistines proper (*Prst*) would very quickly have taken control of not only the coastal region marked by the route and littoral towns of Gaza, Ashkelon, and Ashdod (being in part seafarers), but also the relatively rich grain-growing hinterland east of these.[58] As the west–east width of that hinterland to the edge of the low Shephelah hills averages little more than a dozen miles, there is no reason to date the Philistine settlement of inland Ekron and Gath (cf. below) much after their final establishment in the more coastal towns.[59]

Within a very few years of the Philistines' thus settling in South-West Canaan there appears in this region a distinctive new range of decorated pottery. This was inspired largely by Late Mycenaean pottery (of phase IIIc, Ib) in both form and decoration, incorporating also local Palestinian, Cypriote, and Egyptian elements.[60] From its concentration in Philistia and environs in the twelfth to eleventh centuries B.C. it has become known as 'Philistine pottery'. Correctly so, in view of its coincidence in space and time with the realm and heyday of the Philistines as known historically. It occurs throughout Philistia, following closely upon Late Bronze II levels in coastland sites,[61] but only after an interval on sites well inland.[62] In the south it occurs on the probable sites of Yurza, Sharuhen, and Gerar;[63] eastward it occurs in Philistine and Hebrew border-sites (Shephelah) from Debir (Tell Beit Mirsim) up to Gezer, and on the Mediterranean coast as far north as the vicinity of Joppa.[64] Outside this compact area very little of this pottery has been found, except in isolated cases.[65] By contrast, Beth-Shan, which was inhabited practically continuously from before the thirteenth century B.C. right through to the tenth century B.C., has so far yielded only one sherd.[66] Thus this pottery is first a convenient mark of the area inhabited by the Philistines, and secondly an indication of their influence in the borderlands of immediate neighbours, only rarely further afield.

It is equally instructive to note the limits of Philistine occupation as defined with reference to their neighbours (other than the Hebrews immediately eastward in the hills, and surviving Canaanite city-states). Thus, north of the anciently marshy and over-vegetated plain of Sharon,[67] the coastlands of Dor (Tantura) show nothing of Philistine pottery; but they were occupied *c.* 1090 B.C.[68] by the Tjekker, another of the Sea Peoples. This situation probably gives us the clue to conditions at Beth-Shan: its clay-coffin burials would be those of Tjekker, Sheklesh, or even some Sherden, not of Philistines (*Prst*)—hence the nearly total absence of Philistine ware at a town with a Sea Peoples' element in its populace.[69] When, after the battle of Gilboa, the victorious Philistines hung Saul's body on the wall of Beth Shan, they doubtless had the support of the local Canaanites and their own old Tjekker allies.

The precise topography of the Philistine 'pentapolis' still presents problems. Gaza (under modern town), Ashkelon ('Asqalan), and Ashdod (Isdud) are firmly located—but not so Gath and Ekron. Perhaps the best location so far offered for Ekron is Khirbet el-Muqanna'; it is well placed geographically, and seems to show a suitable occupation-history.[70]

Gath, however, remains an enigma. While, with Mazar, one may distinguish between Philistine Gath *par excellence* and a separate Gittaim north-west of Gezer (at Ras Abu Humeid),[71] yet it is prudent not to attribute too many biblical references too hastily to the lesser Gath-Gittaim.[72] Geographically ideal for Philistine Gath was the site known variously as Tell (Sheikh) el-'Areini, or 'Iraq el-Manshiyeh, or Tell Gath. However, excavations seem to indicate a very limited Philistine occupation upon a large mound of much earlier date, and so Gath is now often sought elsewhere. About a dozen miles southward, Tell en-Nağila might have suited—but excavation has again failed so far to produce a good Philistine occupation, despite initial surface finds of pottery.[73] After these meagre results scholars have sought further, both north and south. Northward, Tell es-Safi is favoured by Israeli scholars.[74] It is most unsuitable, because (i) it would put Gath much too far from Ziklag[75] (adjoining the Negeb-areas) for the immediate neighbourliness of David and Achish in 1 Samuel 27: 9–10; (ii) the six miles or so from an Ekron at Khirbet el-Muqanna' (or environs) to a Gath at Tell es-Safi is ludicrously short for the extensive if transient success of Israel on that border predicated by 1 Samuel 7: 14; (iii) a Gath on the very threshold of the vale of Elah does no justice to the pursuit as far as Gath *and* Ekron in 1 Samuel 17: 52. On the other hand, southward, G. E. Wright has suggested Tell esh-Shari'ah for Philistine Gath.[76] This location is also open to serious objection, although it amply fulfils point (ii) above. It fits (i) only if Ziklag be put at Tell el-Khuweilfeh rather than at Tell esh-Shari'ah itself. On (iii), so southern a Gath is unsuitable for 1 Samuel 17: 52, for the wounded would be falling all of some 20 miles along the roads before their Hebrew pursuers. Against Tell es-Safi, one may repeat its far superior identification with Libnah, so well put by Albright and Wright.[77] Against Tell esh-Shari'ah, one may additionally cite 2 Kings 12: 17, which implies that Gath guarded the entry to a good route for going up to attack Jerusalem; Wright's site offers an unrealistically long route right through Judea.[78]

Thus Gath remains unidentified at present. Topography demands a site at or near Tell el-ʿAreini or Tell en-Nağila, or between them; renewed fieldwork may some day provide one.[79]

b. *Philistine Expansion*

In the twelfth and eleventh centuries B.C. the Philistines and related groups expanded their activities northward and seaward, and eastward and inland. We need not assume any serious Egyptian control after Ramesses III, and none whatever after Ramesses VI.[80]

Having in part arrived by sea, the Philistines and their allies retained some seafaring propensities, as is indicated by Wenamun (*c.* 1090 B.C.), who was chased out of Phoenicia by the warships of the Tjekker prince of Dor. He names three other rulers with non-Semitic names—possibly the Philistine rulers of Gaza, Ashkelon, and Ashdod.[81] The Philistine coastal cities in the twelfth and eleventh centuries B.C. may have rivalled the re-emerging Canaanite centres of Tyre, Sidon, and Byblos in maritime trade.[82]

Inland the main clash between the two gradually expanding communities—Philistines and Hebrews—probably came not in the twelfth century B.C. but from *c.* 1100 B.C. onwards. Apart from the isolated incident of Shamgar ben ʿAnath (Jud. 3: 31), the Philistines play no part in the narratives of Judges until the last major story, that of Samson.[83] In this narrative, part of the Philistine–Hebrew boundary is between Timnah[84] and Ekron on the one side, and Zorah and Beth Shemesh on the other. It seemingly reflects a situation (*c.* 1070 B.C.?)[85] in which the Philistines perceptibly 'had rule over Israel' (Jud. 14: 4; cf. 13: 1, their dominance assigned 40 years), and exemplified by the Judeans' fear of offending the Philistines (Jud. 14: 11–12). Thus one may suggest that, from *c.* 1100 B.C. onwards, eastward expansion brought clashes in which the Philistines subdued western Judah contemporaneously with their maritime activities.

Further north, Philistine ascendancy over north-central Ephraim came similarly but more slowly. Israel's double defeat and temporary loss of the Ark of the Covenant (1 Sam. 4: 1–7: 1) may have brought a Philistine sack of Shiloh.[86] Some twenty years later

(1 Sam. 7: 2) Samuel and Israel achieved some success over the Philistines at Mizpah, recovering territory 'from Ekron even unto Gath' (1 Sam. 7: 14). By the time of his old age, however, the Philistines recovered their ascendancy (cf. 1 Sam. 9: 16), having garrisons at various points (cf. 1 Sam. 10: 5, 13: 3–4, 11–14). War between the Philistines and Saul was endemic (1 Sam. 14: 47, 52). In the course of repeated clashes (1 Sam. 14, 17, 18: 27, 30, 19: 8, 23: 1–5, 24: 1) neither side won a final victory, but the Philistines probably kept a tenuous supremacy most of the time. Not until the death of Saul at Gilboa did the Philistines seem at last to gain effective control over all north-central Israel west of the Jordan (1 Sam. 29: 1, 30–31; note 31: 7). Hebrew 'independence' was banished to the southern and eastern margins of their territory—David's first capital was at Hebron (South Judah), while Ishbosheth's was at Mahanaim over in Gilead (2 Sam. 2: 8–9) before his authority briefly and timorously reached back westward into Ephraim. Only with the reunion of all Israel under David was there any threat to the Philistine triumph.

(iii) *The Philistines and David and Solomon*

To that event and potential threat the Philistines reacted promptly (2 Sam. 5: 17 ff.), but their initial attempts to unseat David failed. Instead, he in turn eventually 'smote the Philistines and subdued them' (2 Sam. 8: 1), taking from them the enigmatic Metheg-ammah—perhaps Gath and district, as the parallel 1 Chronicles 18: 1 might suggest. As Malamat observed,[87] David thus broke Philistine power (reducing them to the defensive), restoring full Israelite independence—but not incorporating Philistia into his domains or actually ruling it. It remains, perhaps, a moot point whether David captured Philistine Gath (Achish becoming his vassal), or Gath-Gittaim, north-north-west of Gezer.[88] However, the Philistines were never again a major threat to Israel, despite at least one sustained attempt to recover their position.[89]

Nor did Philistine fortunes improve at David's death. In his early years Solomon made a marriage-alliance with the pharaoh of Egypt, receiving as dowry Gezer, which the pharaoh had sacked (1 Kings 9: 16; cf. 3: 1). Thus about 970/960 B.C. an Egyptian ruler must have subdued Philistia and rounded off his success by reducing Gezer, hitherto a Canaanite vassal of the Philistines. The pharaoh in question was certainly Siamun of the Twenty-first Dynasty[90]—and a fragmentary bas-relief of his from Tanis depicts the King slaying a foe, who grasps a double axe of a kind reminiscent of the Aegean and western Anatolian area,[91] i.e. of the general region whence came the Philistines and their allies. Weakened by their struggle with David, the Philistines thus fell to a new if ephemeral conqueror.[92] The alliance of Egypt and Israel caught the Philistines as in a vice, to the political and perhaps commercial benefit of both Egypt and Israel. By this time, also, Phoenician commerce was expanding; and so from the tenth century B.C. one may perhaps see the eclipse of the Palestinian Sea Peoples (in particular the Philistines) in both maritime trade and the control of land routes. That a treaty relationship existed between Israel and Gath under Achish may be indicated in 1 Kings 2: 39–40 (Shimei's recovery of two runaway slaves); but a vassal relationship is not necessarily implied.[93]

(iv) *The Philistines in the First Millennium* B.C.

a. *Mid Tenth to Mid Eighth Century* B.C.

During *c.* 950–750 B.C. Philistine history is traceable only in the fragmentary notices vouchsafed to us in the Old Testament. Conflicts continued between Philistia and her Hebrew neighbours, with the advantage passing first to one side then the other. Israel and the Philistines battled intermittently for possession of Gibbethon, twice with a change of ruler in Israel (1 Kings 15: 27, 16: 15 ff.).

With Judah, some Philistines had to pay effective respect to Jehoshaphat (2 Chr. 17: 11), but they and others plundered Judah under his son Jehoram (2 Chr. 21: 16–17). Similarly, Uzziah warred successfully, breaching the walls of Gath, Jabneh, and Ashdod, appropriating some Philistine territory (2 Chr. 26: 6–7), while in turn his grandson Ahaz lost both that and Hebrew territory to the Philistines (2 Chr. 28: 18). Isaiah threatened Philistine gains against Judah (9: 12), and Amos prophesied also the ruin of Philistia (Amos 1: 6–8), instancing that of Gath (6: 2). Hezekiah had a fleeting if far-ranging success against Philistia (2 Kings 18: 8).

b. *Mid Eighth to Sixth Century* B.C.

But from *c.* 745 B.C., with the accession of Tiglath-pileser III, these interminable and indecisive petty struggles were overshadowed by the advance of Assyria. For a century already, North Syria, central Syria, then Israel had successively been subdued to wavering vassalhood when not conquered outright; in *c.* 806/805 B.C. Adad-nirari III cast his eyes further south, alleging Philistia to be among his tributaries, but did not effectively reach beyond Damascus.[94] But sixty years later Tiglath-pileser III beat down the Syrian states within the five years *c.* 742–738 B.C.,[95] reaching to South Phoenicia.[96] In 734 Tiglath-pileser III intervened in southern Palestine, perhaps on the pretext of an appeal by Ahaz of Judah (2 Kings 16: 7–9; 2 Chr. 28: 16–21). He sacked Gaza, but re-instated its King Hanun as a vassal. Next year he subdued Ashkelon, enthroning there one Rukibti, in place of Mitinti I.[97] Assyrian rule was now a fact.

The accession of Sargon II was marked by an anti-Assyrian revolt in which Hanun of Gaza participated; it was quickly crushed (720 B.C.); Hanun was exiled. Thereafter Assyrian documents refer fleetingly to Philistine affairs,[98] until in 713/712 B.C. Assyrian replacement of Azuri by his brother Ahimetu as king in Ashdod precipitated a revolt. Sargon sent his commander to subdue Ashdod (cf. Isa. 20: 1); reliefs of the capture of Ekron and Gibbethon supplement the texts.[99] In conquered Ashdod, Sargon had a victory-stela erected,[100] and appointed an Assyrian governor alongside the local king.

Sargon's death encouraged renewed revolt, which in 701 Sennacherib duly suppressed. Mitinti of Ashdod quickly offered tribute. But the rebel upstart Sidqi was replaced in Ashkelon by a ruler with the Assyrian name of Sharru-lu-dari. Ekron was then conquered, and Hezekiah in turn obliged to release its king Padi, earlier put in his custody by the anti-Assyrian rebels in Ekron. Hezekiah remained unconquered, but Sennacherib transferred some of his lands to Philistine rule.[101]

Esarhaddon kept a firm hold on Philistia as a springboard against Egypt; the rulers of Gaza, Ashkelon, Ekron, and Ashdod are named in 677/676 B.C., but little else is said of them.[102] Ashurbanipal continued the Egyptian war, seeking to use Philistine aid in 667 B.C. Two Assyrian legal documents from Gezer, of *c.* 651,

649 B.C., are the last traces of Assyrian rule in this general area.[103] A renewed Egypt under Psammetichus I sought to expand into Philistia; Herodotus mentions a siege of Azotus (probably Ashdod) lasting twenty-nine years, the exact significance of which is uncertain.[104]

c. *The End of Philistine Independence*

Ashkelon sought to resist the Neo-Babylonian advance in 604 B.C.; Nebuchadrezzar II subdued it and exiled its king in Babylon, where his sons appear in the ration-tablets along with Jehoiachin of Judah and his relations. These, with mentions of kings of Gaza and Ashdod at the Babylonian court, are the last traces of Philistia as an entity, before her final disappearance as a political unit.[105]

(v) *Philistine Life and Culture*

a. *Language and Literature*

Very few indeed are the traces of the language(s) of the Sea Peoples in general, and of the Philistines in particular. Among personal names, that of Achish occurs in the forms '(*A*)*kashu*, '(*A*)*kasht*, in an Egyptian list of 'Keftiu' names of the sixteenth century B.C.; and it is seen in the name of Ikausu, King of Ekron, in 677, 667 B.C., being compared with Trojan Anchises in the *Iliad*.[106] Goliath (*Golyat*) is claimed as a dissimilated form of a Walwatta (cf. Lydian Alyattes), from a Luvian base *walwi*/*a*.[107] Also possibly of west Anatolian derivation are the Sea Peoples' names in the Wenamun papyrus.[108] However, in the first millennium B.C., Philistine rulers increasingly bear Semitic names—such are Hanun, Sil-Bel, Sidqi, Ahi-milki, Ahimetu, and others in the eighth and seventh centuries B.C.

Language traces outside of personal names are also slender, but consistent with them. The word *qōḇa'*/*kōḇa'*, 'helmet', may have entered Hebrew from Philistia and be of Anatolian origin (cf. Hittite *kupaḫḫi*).[109] The special word *seren*, used of the 'lords' of the Philistines, is often compared with *tyrannos* in Greek; a closer comparison is afforded by the title *tarwanas*,[110] commonly borne by Neo-Hittite kings in their late Luvian ('Hittite Hieroglyphic') inscriptions in the eleventh to the seventh centuries B.C.

Pending the discovery and decipherment of texts of some length,[111] our knowledge of Philistine literature is nil; even the Deir 'Alla tablets, if ever deciphered and proved relevant, are of very limited length and scope.

b. *Religion*

As has often enough been noted in the past, the only deities attributed to the Philistines bear Semitic names: the grain-god Dagon,[112] the Canaanite goddess 'Ashtoreth,[113] and Baal-zebub.[114] Dagon had temples at Gaza (Jud. 16: 21–23) and Ashdod (1 Sam. 5), while Baal-zebub was honoured at Ekron (2 Kings 1: 2). From the wording of 1 Samuel 31: 9–10, the temple of 'Ashteroth could be understood to be either in Philistia or at Beth-Shan; if verse 10 enlarges on verse 9, its order suggests that the temple was one in Beth-Shan.[115] Divination and soothsaying were held to be prominent practices of the Philistines (Isa. 2: 6), and this reputation doubtless influenced Ahaziah of Israel to make inquiry of Baal-zebub of Ekron (2 Kings 1: 2). Unlike their Semitic neighbours in Canaan, the Philistines were uncircumcised, an epithet then used in abuse of them by the Hebrews, marking them out as aliens (cf. Jud. 14: 3 and *passim*).

As noted above, the Philistines and their allies made some use of clay coffins with faces modelled on the headpieces; this type of object was derived by both Canaanites and Philistines from Egyptian usage.[116] Otherwise their funerary customs did not differ remarkably from that of their Semitic contemporaries (collective tombs, grave-goods, etc.). Of neither religious nor funerary ritual or beliefs have we any substantial traces.[117]

c. *Architecture*

Philistine architecture is still very little known. Recent work at Ashdod has uncovered traces of a massive mud-brick fort joining the city wall.[118] Little light can yet be thrown on the temple at Gaza having a colonnade of structural importance (Jud. 16: 23–27); a small temple is reported at Ashdod, but without any details.[119] Domestic architecture offers little remarkable; besides ordinary rectangular houses,[120] Ashdod has produced round houses.[121] The temples at Beth-Shan may rather belong to the main Canaanite population, and so not be properly relevant here.

d. *Material Culture*

Almost our sole evidence for dress comes from the reliefs of Ramesses III at Medinet Habu, already noted. The reliefs of Sargon II offer nothing special. The most distinctive Philistine artefact is undoubtedly their decorated pottery. Among weapons, Goliath boasted a helmet, body-armour, and greaves, plus javelin, spear, and shield. At Medinet Habu the Philistines and their allies have some kind of body-armour (in diagonal strips), often two spears, and round shields; the Sherden have horned helmets. These Sea Peoples also have long swords.[122] Comparable details are found in remains from Sardinia, and a sword from near Joppa in Palestine itself.[123]

e. *Philistine Society*

Philistine rule was seemingly vested in the oligarchy of five 'lords' (entitled *seren*) in their five principal cities.[124] In the course of time the term *seren* disappears in favour of the common designation 'king'.[125] Their subordinates in the ruling class were the *sārīm*, 'princes' or 'commanders' (1 Sam. 18: 30, 29: 3), below whom would come the main populace, including both native-born Canaanites and the descendants of the newcomers. Their military organization included chariotry, 'horsemen', and infantry (1 Sam. 13: 5), and the use of key garrisons in subdued territories, as with the Hebrews (see above, (ii) b, end).[126] The development of metallurgy, and particularly the use of iron, is reflected both in their monopoly of metalworking and weapon-production while dominating the Hebrews (1 Sam. 13: 19–22), and in excavated evidence for metalworking at various sites either Philistine or (in the twelfth to the eleventh centuries) under Philistine influence or control.[127]

f. *Cultural Assimilation*

During the twelfth century B.C. the Sea Peoples' settlers in Canaan must speedily have acquired the language of Canaan;[128] however, they also retained something of their old speech, or developed a patois of their own that persisted alongside the dominant Hebrew/Canaanite.[129] And, as often,[130] personal names show long retention of those from the old language (e.g. Achish, Ikausu) amid a flood of those taken from the adopted main language. The disappearance of *seren* in favour of 'king' may also reflect loss of older usage. The distinctive 'Philistine' pottery of the twelfth–eleventh centuries B.C. has virtually disappeared by soon after *c.* 1000 B.C. in favour of local wares. Thus, in many spheres, acculturation was so great as to replace the original culture of the Philistines and their relatives almost completely in about two centuries. However, less material aspects long outlasted these outward changes: the fivefold Philistine rule was never turned into a unified monarchy, for example, and Philistia retained a lively sense of independence, alongside other small states of the Levant, in opposition to Assyrian pretensions. Traces of that separate character survived the shock of empires even to the Hellenistic age.

NOTES

1. Classification of the Philistines under Egypt might be held to reflect their political subordination to Egypt (cf. G. E. Wright, *B.A.* xxix (1966), p. 71 n. 3). This would possibly be true in the late 13th/early 12th century B.C., and very briefly in the early 10th century B.C., but not at other periods.

2. As Hebrew tradition looks back to the patriarchs, Egypt being a land of sojourn, not of origins.

3. If *Kslḥ(m)* were a metathesized form for **Sklḥ(m)*, one might be tempted (with R. A. S. Macalister, *The Philistines* (1913), p. 28) to compare it with the Tjekker of the Egyptian sources. One could suggest that the *-ḥ* was a non-Semitic suffix; not Hurrian *-(ḫ)ḫi/e*, but rather something like Lycian-A *-ahi*, *-ehi*, etc. On former cf. J. Friedrich, *Handbuch der Orientalistik*, i. 2/2: *Altkleinasiatische Sprachen* (1969), p. 13, § 21 a; on latter cf. G. Neumann, ibid. 381, § 19, i. 10, and 383–4, § 24.

4. In late tablets referring back to Sargon of Akkad (*fl. c.* 2370 B.C.) cf. E. F. Weidner, *A.f.O.* xvi (1952/53), 1 ff.; C. J. Gadd, *C.A.H.*, rev. edn., i, Ch. xix, pp. 15–16; and M. Astour, *J.A.O.S.* lxxxiv (1964), p. 249 n. 109. More securely, Kaptara occurs in the Mari archives, 18th century B.C. (G. Dossin, *Syria* xxi (1939), 111–13), and later at Ugarit in Akkadian (J. Nougayrol, *P.R.U.* iii. 107) and in the epics (C. H. Gordon, *Ugaritic Textbook* (1965), p. 422, No. 1291).

5. See J. Vercoutter, *L'Égypte et le monde égéen préhellénique* (1956), pp. 106–14, esp. pp. 109–12; by a well-attested rule of 'phonetic decay' in Egyptian, one may posit the original Egyptian form as *Kaftaru becoming *Kaftaiu, Kaftiu.

6. For a definitive study of the Egyptian evidence see the comprehensive work of Vercoutter in preceding note; for an outline cf. his *Essai sur les relations entre Égyptiens et Préhellènes* (1954).

7. Preliminary publication, K. A. Kitchen, *Or.* xxxiv (1965), 5–6 and Pls. II, IX; full publication, see E. Edel, *Die Ortsnamenlisten aus dem Totentempel Amenophis III* (1966), pp. 33 ff. and Pl. III. Subsequent studies include: Astour, *A.J.A.* lxx (1966), 313–17; Kitchen (with Albright), *B.A.S.O.R.* clxxxi (1966), 23–4; Edel, *Archeion koinōniologias kai ēthikēs* x (1967/8), 37–48; P. Faure, *Kadmos* vii (1968), 138–49; W. Helck, *Göttingische Gelehrte Anzeigen* ccxxi (1969), 72–86; Kitchen, *Bi.Or.* xxvi (1969), 198–202, and cf. id., *J.E.A.* lv (1969), 223–5.

8. So already Helck, op. cit. 73, and Faure, op. cit. 146.

9. For the narrower and wider uses of Danaoi cf. Sir A. H. Gardiner, *Ancient Egyptian Onomastica* i (1947), p. 125* and refs., and Helck, op. cit. 73.

10. So Edel, *Ortsnamenliste* p. 42 (reading a vertical *t* for 'seated man'); cf. id., *Archeion*, pp. 41–2; Faure, op. cit. 139–40, doubts Edel's reading, but his own suggestions seem at least as hypothetical.

11. Not yet identified; see Faure, op. cit. 141–2.

12. So Edel, *Ortsnamenliste*, pp. 46–8, and *Archeion*, pp. 44–5. Others (e.g. Faure, op. cit. 143) are chary of looking so far afield as Troy.

13. Wainwright's long-defended thesis locating Keftiu/Caphtor in Cilicia must now, therefore, be finally and completely dismissed.

14. In favour of this identification, Edel, *Ortsnamenliste*, pp. 48–53, cites *Drd[ny]* from a Karnak topographical list of Amenophis III; same as *Drdny* under Ramesses II (Qadesh), and phonetically equivalent to the *Dardanoi* of the *Iliad*; for such Egyptian knowledge reaching to the Troad cf. C. W. Blegen, *Troy and the Trojans* (1963), pp. 140–6.

15. Although the origin of the name remains obscure. Among possible early references, the only plausible ones so far are the pl. geographical term and the personal name *ke-re-te* and *ke-re-te-u* (*Kretheus*) in the Linear B tablets from Pylos (refs.: cf. (e.g.) M. Ventris and J. Chadwick, *Documents in Mycenaean Greek* (1956), indexes, 148, 420).

16. On the 'Cretan hieroglyphic' Phaistos Disc, of about the 16th century B.C., one of the commonest signs is that of a man's head with a 'feathered' crest much like that of the Philistines in the Egyptian reliefs. At least their kind of headgear was known there then, whether or not Philistines were actually present.

17. Great Inscription of the Year 8, Medinet Habu (Epigraphic Survey, *Medinet Habu I* (1930), Pl. 46, ll. 15 ff.; K. A. Kitchen, *Ramesside Inscriptions* v, 1 (1970), pp. 39 ff.; trans. W. F. Edgerton & J. A. Wilson, *Historical Records of Ramses III* (1936), pp. 53 ff.); cf. also Year 5 Inscription, ll. 50 ff. (*Med. Habu I*, Pl. 28; Kitchen, op. cit. 25 f.; Edgerton & Wilson, op. cit. 30 ff.).

18. First proposed in the 18th century (cf. Macalister, *Philistines*, p. 2); cf., latterly, V. Georgiev, *Jahrbuch für kleinasiatische Forschung* i (1950), 137, and W. F. Albright, *C.A.H.* ii, Ch. xxxiii, pp. 29–30.

19. Cf. Albright, loc. cit. The Illyrian thesis, represented by G. Bonfante, *A.J.A.* l (1946), 251 ff., fails (in his case) because based on secondary *n*-forms instead of on the *P-l-s-t* of the early data.

20. A total evaluation of all the available lines of evidence would best place the patriarchs Abraham to Jacob somewhere in the first half of the second millennium B.C. (*c.* 1900–1700 ?); cf. K. A. Kitchen, *Ancient Orient and Old Testament* (1966), pp. 41–56, with refs.

21. Dossin, quoted by A. Pohl, *Or.* xix (1950), 509.

22. Hazor; see Y. Yadin *et al.*, *Hazor II* (1960), p. 86 and Pl. 115: 12–13, and A. Malamat, *J.B.L.* lxxix (1960), 18–19. Ugarit; cf. C. F. A. Schaeffer, *Ugaritica* i (1939), 54 ff.

23. At Kahun, Harageh, Abydos, hoard from Tod; cf. H. Kantor, in R. W. Ehrich (ed.), *Chronologies in Old World Archaeology* (1965), pp. 19–22 and refs.; for reverse traffic cf. S. S. Weinberg, in Ehrich, op. cit. 308.

24. See section (v) f below. The name Phicol remains an enigma; perhaps cf. Anatolian names in *Pig/k-* (cf. E. Laroche, *Les Noms des Hittites* (1966), pp. 142–3, Nos. 990–5), but with the greatest reserve. For Anatolian contact with Syria-Palestine in the early second millennium B.C. cf. Luqqa ('Lycian'), son of Kukun, at Byblos, references in Kitchen, *Ancient Orient and Old Testament* (1966), p. 52 n. 90—for Kukun as an indubitable Anatolian name cf. Laroche, op. cit. 95–6, Nos. 601–7, and L. Zgusta, *Kleinasiatische Personennamen* (1964), p. 253, § 724.

25. See Epigr. Survey, *Medinet Habu I*, Pls. 43 (Tjekker) and 44 (Danuna, Philistines). For Sherden and Tursha see (e.g.) *Medinet Habu VIII* (1970), Pl. 600 B, and W. Wreszinski, *Atlas zur altägyptischen Kulturgeschichte*, ii, Pl. 160 A/B.

26. For other examples of this headgear cf. refs. given by T. C. Mitchell, *A.O.T.S.*, pp. 412–13, and R. D. Barnett, *C.A.H.*, rev. edn., ii, Ch. xxviii, 19.

27. *Med. Habu I*, Pl. 44, shows a third, unlabelled row of captives, but the vertical text names the Sheklesh besides the Philistines and Danunim, and this suggests they are here depicted; so also, Edgerton & Wilson, *Historical Records*, p. 47 n. 15 a.

28. The Tjekker inhabited the district of Dor *c.* 1090 B.C. (Wenamun); at about this date the Onomasticon of Amenemope knows of Sherden, Tjekker, and Philistines, but without clearly locating them (Gardiner, *Ancient Egyptian Onomastica*, i. 194*–205*, Nos. 268–70).

29. *E.A.* 38, in which the King of Alashiya (Cyprus) refers to their raids.

30. *Poem*, §§ 4, 45, 86 *ter*, 150; *Bulletin*, § 45; *Reliefs*, § 65. Text, K. A. Kitchen, *Ramesside Inscriptions*, ii, 1–3 (1969–70), pp. 4, 17, 32, 50, 111, 143: 64. Trans. Sir A. H. Gardiner, *The Ḳadesh Inscriptions of Ramesses II* (1960), pp. 7, 8, 10, 29, 44; cf. p. 58. For *Pa-luka* as a personal name under Ramesses III cf. Gardiner, *Onomastica* i. 128*.

31. A term coined by the Egyptians under Merenptah and Ramesses III; cf. Gardiner, *Onomastica* i. 196*.

32. Great Libyan War inscription, ll. 1, 14 (K. A. Kitchen, *Ramesside Inscriptions*, iv, 1 (1968), pp. 2, 4; trans. Breasted, *Ancient Records of Egypt* iii, §§ 574, 579). Luk(k)a also in Hittite records and at Ugarit.

33. Cf. note 30 above.

34. *E.A.* 151, l. 52, giving Danuna, Ugarit, Qadesh, and Amurru from north to south.

35. See his paper in *Syria* xxxv (1958), 263–75, overlooked by some recent writers.

36. However, Mycenaeans did reach Cilicia in the later part of the Late Bronze Age, especially at Tarsus, which has produced Mycenaean IIIB and IIIC pottery (cf. V. R. d'A. Desborough, *The Last Mycenaeans and their Successors* (1964), pp. 205–6); other surveys may confirm this (cf. M. V. Seton-Williams, *Anat. Stud.* iv (1954), 134). Such settlers or visitors could have moved south to become the Danuna of Ramesses III.

37. *E.A.* 81: 16, 122: 35, 123: 15. It should be noted that Albright, *A.J.A.* liv (1950), p. 167 n. 18, would take the word as for *šerdu*, 'servant'; this is conceivable in *E.A.* 122, 123, but hardly fits the case in 81.

38. Stela 'Tanis II', ll. 13 ff.: '. . . the Isles of the Aegean fear him, . . . the Sherden, rebellious of heart, . . . they came bold-[hearted, they sailed] in ships of war from the midst of the Sea, . . .' (but Ramesses II vanquished them); K. A. Kitchen, *Ramesside Inscriptions*, ii, 6 (1971), pp. 289–90, and cf. J. Yoyotte, *Kêmi* x (1949), 66–9. Aswan Stela, Year 2, l. 8: 'He has seized the warriors of the Great Sea, and the Delta rests and it sleeps' (Kitchen, ibid. 345). Papyrus Anastasi I, 17: 4 presupposes use of Sherden (and other) troops in W. Asia (*A.N.E.T.*, p. 476 b).

39. *Poem*, § 26; text, Kitchen, *Ram. Inscriptions*, ii, 1 (1969), p. 11, trans. Gardiner, *Ḳadesh Inscriptions of Ramesses II* (1960), p. 7. For illustration cf. (e.g.) C. Kuentz, *La bataille de Qadech* (1929–34), Pl. 34 (below king). Cf., further, Papyrus Anastasi II, verso of 7, 8 (R. A. Caminos, *Late-Egyptian Miscellanies* (1954), p. 64; cf. pp. 45–6 on 5: 2). Under Ramesses III, see note 25 above.

40. Controversy still rages over the possible identity of Egyptian Aḳaiwasha, Hittite Ahhiyawa, and Greek Achaeans. In favour, cf. G. L. Huxley, *Achaeans and Hittites* (1960). Critical, with good over-all survey, see G. Steiner, *Saeculum* xv (1964), 365–92. Texts of Merenptah's wars, Kitchen, *Ram. Inscriptions* iv, 1 (1968), pp. 1–24, iv, 2, pp. 33 f.; translations, cf. Breasted, *Anc. Records* iii, §§ 569–617.

41. Josh. 13: 3 may simply be a defining expansion of verse 2 by the narrator (cf. the placement of brackets in RSV), in terms of Philistine centres from *c.* 1200 B.C. onwards. Jud. 3: 3 would likewise reflect Philistine fivefold chiefship from about that date. The 'way of the land of the Philistines' (Exod. 13: 17) and 'sea of the Philistines' (Exod. 23: 31) is probably the terminology of *c.* 1200 and on, perhaps replacing an earlier '. . . of the Caphtorim' or suchlike.

42. See the works of Vercoutter cited in nn. 5, 6 above, and cf. F. H. Stubbings, *Mycenaean Pottery in the Levant* (1951).

43. See G. E. Wright, *B.A.* xxii (1959), 53–66; T. Dothan, *Antiquity and Survival* ii, 2–3 (1957), pp. 151–64 *passim*, and her *The Philistines and their Material Culture* (1967), pp. 211–46 (Hebrew).

44. G. E. Wright, *B.A.* xxii (1959), 59–60, 66; *B.A.* xxix (1966), 74.

45. *B.A.* xxix (1966), 74; developed by Mrs. J. Waldbaum, *A.J.A.* lxx (1966), 331–40.

46. See W. H. Stiebing, *A.J.A.* lxxiv (1970), 139–43.

47. By Albright, *C.A.H.* ii, Ch. xxxiii, p. 31, depending on link with Assyria.

48. Note the summary accounts by Wright, *B.A.* xxix (1966), 73, and by Albright, op. cit. 27 (but with both levels in one stratum). For reports on Deir ʿAlla see H. J. Franken, *V.T.* xi (1961), ff., and *Excavations at Deir ʿAlla I* (1970). For the tablets cf. Franken, *V.T.* xiv (1964), 377–9, 417–22, and *P.E.Q.* xcvi (1964), 73 ff.

49. Wright, Albright, opp. citt., and others whom they mention.

50. Her cartouche on the Deir ʿAlla vase is as pharaoh, true only of her last two regnal years (having taken over the regnal years of King Siptah at his death); she was previously queen-consort of Sety II.

51. Frances James, *The Iron Age at Beth Shan* (1966).

52. In brief, James, op. cit. 133–9, 149–54, summarizing her detailed findings in the body of that work.

53. Bibliography, see Porter & Moss, *Topographical Bibliography of Ancient Egyptian Hieroglyphic Texts, Reliefs and Paintings*, vii (1952), p. 381.

54. See J. Černý, *C.A.H.* ii, Ch. xxxv, pp. 11–12.

55. R. D. Barnett, *C.A.H.* ii, Ch. xxviii, p. 19.

56. In Ugarit, Alalakh, etc., the last Mycenaean pottery is IIIB; continued occupation of sites in Cyprus, Cilicia, and at Beth-Shan (see n. 60 below) is marked by occurrence of IIIC.

57. On which see K. A. Kitchen, *Hittite Hieroglyphs, Aramaeans and Hebrew Traditions* (forthcoming), Ch. iii.

58. Cf. D. Baly, *The Geography of the Bible* (1957), pp. 138–42.

59. Given the very limited size of the area concerned and the quite large-scale impact of the Sea Peoples' invasion, the view of a gradual expansion towards the zone of Ekron S. to Gath—barely 12 miles away! —seemingly implied by B. Mazar, *The Philistines and the Rise of Israel and Tyre* (1964), p. 10, seems unrealistic, and should probably be discarded. However, expansion beyond these limits is quite another matter, as it would be opposed by the Hebrews and Canaanite city-states.

60. For discussions of the Mycenaean derivation of Philistine pottery see A. Furumark, *The Chronology of Mycenaean Pottery* (1941), pp. 118–22; V. R. d'A. Desborough, *The Last Mycenaeans and their Successors* (1964), pp. 209–14, 237–41; T. Dothan, works cited n. 43 above, pp. 151 ff. and Ch. iii respectively. For fragments of Mycenaean IIIC pottery from Beth-shan cf. V. Hankey, *A.J.A.* lxx (1966), 169–71 and pl. 45.

61. As at Ashkelon, Tell Ğemmeh (Albright, *A.A.S.O.R.* xii (1932), 54, 55), and probably Ashdod (*B.A.* xxvi (1963), 136).

62. As at Beth Shemesh and Tell Beit Mirsim (Albright, loc. cit.), both Israelite rather than Philistine sites.

63. i.e. Tell Ğemmeh, el-Farʿa S., and Hureira.

64. Cf. (briefly) Albright, loc. cit., and summary of evidence, Dothan, *The Philistines* (1967), Ch. ii, esp. pp. 45 f. (Hebrew).

65. Megiddo is one such; cf. Dothan, op. cit. 47 f.

66. See F. James, *Iron Age at Beth Shan* (1966), p. 150 and Fig. 24.

67. Cf. D. Baly, *Geography of the Bible* (1957), pp. 133–7.

68. The Wenamun papyrus (e.g. *A.N.E.T.*, p. 25b) dates to a 'Year 5' which is *not* that of either Ramesses XI or the Twenty-First Dynasty's founder, Smendes, but belongs to the so-called 'Renaissance Era' (Year 1 = Year 19 of Ram. XI), and is equivalent to Year 23 of Ramesses XI. Given that Ramesses II acceded in 1304 or 1290 B.C., and that there was *no* kingless interregnum between the 19th and 20th Dynasties (careers of officials in both forbid it), and the need for minimal-length reigns in both dynasties (to allow for attested lifespans of officials), this dateline for Wenamun can hardly be moved a decade either side of *c.* 1090 B.C. Dates for him at *c.* 1070 B.C. and later are excluded.

69. Cf. F. James, *Iron Age at Beth Shan*, p. 136–8. For references to Canaanites at Beth-shan see Josh. 17: 11–13, 16; Jud. 1: 27–28.

70. See J. Naveh, *I.E.J.* viii (1958), 166 ff.; B. Mazar, *I.E.J.* x (1960), 106 ff.; and cf. 'context' of other sites, in Y. Aharoni, *P.E.Q.* xc (1958), 27–31.

71. *I.E.J.* iv (1954), 227–35; leaving aside other Gaths with distinctive epithets (Hepher, Padalla, Rimmon . . .).

72. Cf. on this point H. E. Kassis, *J.B.L.* lxxxiv (1965), 259–71.

73. Cf. (e.g.) Wright, *B.A.* xxix (1966), 79.

74. E.g. Y. Aharoni, *The Land of the Bible* (1966), p. 250.

75. Sometimes located at Tell el-Khuweilfeh (cf. F.-M. Abel, *Géographie de la Palestine* ii (1938), p. 465), but probably better at Tell esh-Shariʿa (cf. Aharoni, *Land of the Bible*, p. 259 and n. 7).

76. *B.A.* xxix (1966), 78–86.

77. In *A.A.S.O.R.* ii–iii (1923), 12–17, and *B.A.* xxix (1966), p. 80 n. 23, respectively.

78. On routes up to Jerusalem cf. Albright, op. cit. 13 f., and Kassis, *J.B.L.* lxxxiv (1965), 260–1, 271.

79. In *C.A.H.* ii, Ch. xxxiii, p. 26 and n. 3, Albright retains Tell ʿAreini for Gath, and goes back to ʿAqir for Ekron; the latter is surely a counsel of despair, given the unsuitability of the site (Albright, *A.A.S.O.R.* ii–iii (1923), 1–3).

80. Ramesses VI is the last ruler to leave monuments in Sinai; thereafter Suez to El-Arish was doubtless Egypt's eastern limit; cf. also Černý (n. 54 above), p. 12.

81. See Mazar, *The Philistines* (1964), pp. 2–4.

82. Ibid. 4–6; Mazar suggests that Ashkelon was the leading Philistine port down to this period, and clashed with Tyre.

83. Jud. 13–16 (Jud. 17–21 are simply two 'appendices' on isolated incidents in the whole Judges' period).

84. Cf. Aharoni, *P.E.Q.* xc (1958), 27–8.

85. The chronology will be dealt with elsewhere.

86. *Inter alia* one finds the priests and cult at Nob in Saul's time (1 Sam. 21, 22).

87. *J.N.E.S.* xxii (1963), 14.

88. As Malamat suggested (op. cit. 15).

89. Four successive conflicts in Gob or Gath (which ?); cf. 2 Sam. 21: 15–22.

90. The 22nd Dynasty began *c.* 945 B.C. (935 is too low), and Psusennes II before it reigned some 14 years (959–945) and Siamun some 19 years, i.e. *c.* 978–959 B.C. See K. A. Kitchen, *Third Intermediate Period in Egypt* (1972).

91. Cf. at random Lydian double-axe forms (R. Dussaud, *Prélydiens, Hittites et Achéens* (1953), p. 136, Fig. 32). Siamun relief: see P. Montet, *Le Tombeau d'Osorkon II* (1947), Pl. 9A (photo), and his *L'Égypte et la Bible* (1959), p. 40, Fig. 5 (sketch).

92. Often cited is a scarab of Siamun from Tell el-Far'a S. (e.g., Malamat, op. cit. (n. 87), 12); destruction-levels at Tel Mor near Ashdod and at Gezer itself have been attributed to Siamun's raid (ibid. 12 f.).

93. A point made by Malamat, op. cit. 15.

94. Cf. his Nimrud inscription (*A.N.E.T.*, p. 281b; probably not the Saba'a stela—see H. Tadmor, *I.E.J.* xix (1969), 46–8); the new text from Tell al-Rimah (S. Page, *Iraq* xxx (1968), 139–53) omits *Palashtu.* Cf., further, H. Donner, in *Archäologie und altes Testament* (*Festschrift Galling*) (1970), pp. 49–59.

95. Precise dates still in dispute; cf. E. R. Thiele, *Mysterious Numbers of the Hebrew Kings*, 2nd edn. (1965), pp. 90–117, and H. Tadmor, *Scripta Hierosolymitana*, viii (1961), pp. 232–71, and forthcoming edition of the annals of Tiglath-pileser III. For an excellent treatment of relations between Philistia and Assyria see his paper in *B.A.* xxix (1966), 86–102.

96. Where an Assyrian official reported on his master's trade embargo against Egypt and Philistia (Saggs, *Iraq* xvii (1955), 127 f.; Tadmor, *B.A.* xxix (1966), 88).

97. Texts, cf. *A.N.E.T.*, pp. 282–4, plus D. J. Wiseman, *Iraq* xiii (1951), 21–4, and *Iraq* xviii (1956), 117–29. Cf. also H. Tadmor, *I.E.J.* xii (1962), 114–22, and Y. Aharoni, *Land of the Bible* (1967), 328–33.

98. See references given by H. Tadmor, *B.A.* xxix (1966), 92–3.

99. Ibid. 94, with Figs. 9 and 10.

100. Its fragments are illustrated, ibid., p. 95 Fig. 11.

101. *A.N.E.T.*, pp. 287–8.

102. Ibid. 290–4, plus refs.; *B.A.* xxix (1966), 99–100.

103. Ibid. 101.

104. Ibid. 102 and refs. For an Egyptian envoy, Pediese son of ʿApy, to Canaan and Philistia, of 22nd–26th Dyn. date, cf. G. Steindorff, *J.E.A.* xxv (1939), 30–3 and Pl. 7.

105. For principal refs. cf. Tadmor, op. cit. 102.

106. Writing-board; cf. T. E. Peet in S. Casson (ed.), *Essays in Aegean Archaeology* (1927), pp. 90–9.

107. Albright, *C.A.H.* ii, Ch. xxxiii, p. 30, citing forms from Goetze, *J.C.S.* xvi (1962), 49b, to which add E. Laroche, *Les Noms hittites* (1966), p. 204, No. 1486 (Walwaziti).

108. Details in *Studies Presented to D. M. Robinson*, i (1951), pp. 228–9 and cf. Albright, loc. cit.

109. Cf. already T. C. Mitchell, *A.O.T.S.*, p. 415.

110. Probably meaning 'judge' or similar (cf. E. Laroche, *Les Hiéroglyphes hittites*, i (1960), pp. 197–8, No. 371; P. Meriggi, *Hieroglyphisch-Hethitisches Glossar* (1962), p. 125: 2). On a broader plane, cf. the Hebrew 'judges' and Phoenician 'suffetes'.

111. Very recently (Autumn 1970) some eight scrolls from near Hebron(?) have been reported to carry texts in a script seemingly in a language related to the west-Anatolian group, and probably going back to the seventh century B.C. (cf. *P.E.Q.* ciii (1971), pp. 62–3). The reference is by courtesy of Mr. A. R. Millard. One may compare the probable use of Carians in the Judean royal guard in the 9th century B.C. (2 Kings 11: 4, 19). Earliest occurrence of the term is as Karkiya/Karkisa (cf. Old Persian Kark-) in the Hittite records; cf. Albright, *A.J.A.* liv (1950), p. 168 n. 122. On Carian cf. V. Ševeroškin, *R.H.A.* xxii, 74 (1964), 1–55; many new data are forthcoming from Egypt (Saqqara excavations).

112. On Dagon cf. M. H. Pope & W. Röllig, in H. W. Haussig (ed.), *Wörterbuch der Mythologie*, i (1965), pp. 276–8; cf. also pp. 49–50.

113. On Ashtoreth and related entities cf. Albright, *Archaeology and the Religion of Israel* (1953), pp. 74 ff., and Pope & Röllig, op. cit. 250–2.

114. On whom see Macalister, *The Philistines*, pp. 91–3.

115. So identified by A. Rowe, *Four Canaanite Temples of Beth Shan* (1940).

116. See Albright, *A.J.A.* xxxvi (1932), 304–6.

117. Gleanings of very uneven value indeed were gathered from 'late classical' and Church writers, on temples, legends, etc., by Macalister, *Philistines*, pp. 93 ff., but this material is virtually unusable for the early periods of Philistine history. For libation-spouts see *B.A.* xxvi (1963), p. 32 Fig. 14.

118. Cf. D. N. Freedman, *B.A.* xxvi (1963), 136–7.

119. Cf. ibid. 137.

120. The three-roomed variety is claimed to be distinctively Philistine by Mazar, *Philistines* (1964), p. 6.

121. Cf. *B.A.* xxix (1966), p. 86, Fig. 8.

122. See *Medinet Habu I* (1930), Pls. 34, 39 (also in Y. Yadin, *The Art of Warfare in Biblical Lands* (1963), pp. 336/7, 340/1).

123. Sardinia; cf. Albright, *B.A.S.O.R.* xcv (1944), 38, and Barnett, *C.A.H.* ii, Ch. xxviii, pp. 12, 16. For Joppa sword see R. D. Barnett, *Illustrations of Old Testament History* (1966), pp. 29, 31, Fig. 16.

124. On the Philistine 'league' cf. B. D. Rahtjen, *J.N.E.S.* xxiv (1965), 100–4.

125. Achish is 'King' of Gath from David's time (1 Sam. 21: 10, 12, etc.), and so in the Assyrian records later.

126. Cf. also the suggestions of Mazar, *Philistines*, p. 10.

127. Note references collected by Mazar, op. cit., p. 13 n. 18, and the possibility of craft-guilds among the Philistines.

128. As often noted in the past, Delilah spoke equally easily to Samson and the lords of the Philistines; and David and Achish seem to converse easily enough.

129. We hear of the speech of Ashdod as late as Nehemiah (13: 24).

130. A phenomenon already noted above (section (i) b 2, end, and n. 24). Cf. also the situation at Sam'al in North Syria, where an Aramaeanized realm and dynasty has among its royal names not only the expected Aramaean names but also residual late Luvian names, such as Panammu (Pana-muwa).

BIBLIOGRAPHY

Further detailed references are to be found in the foregoing Notes and in the works here listed.

ALBRIGHT, W. F., 'Some Oriental Glosses on the Homeric Problem', *A.J.A.* liv (1950), 162–76.

—— 'The Eastern Mediterranean about 1060 B.C.', *Studies Presented to David Moore Robinson*, i (1951), pp. 224–31.

—— 'Syria, the Philistines, and Phoenicia', *C.A.H.*, 2nd (rev.) edn., ii, Ch. xxxiii (= fasc. 51 (1966)), pp. 24–33.

BARNETT, R. D., 'The Sea Peoples', *C.A.H.*, 2nd edn., ii, Ch. xxviii (1969).

DE VAUX, R., 'La Phénicie et les peuples de la mer', *Mélanges de l'Université Saint-Joseph* xlv (1969), 481–98.

DOTHAN, T., 'Archaeological Reflections on the Philistine Problem', *Antiquity and Survival*, ii (1957), pp. 151–64.

—— *The Philistines and their Material Culture* (1967) (Hebrew).

EDGERTON, W. F., & WILSON, J. A., *Historical Records of Ramses III* (1936).

HESTRIN, RUTH, *The Philistines and Other Sea Peoples* (1970).

MACALISTER, R. A. S., *The Philistines, their History and Civilization* (1913, repr. 1965).

MAZAR, B., 'The Philistines and the Rise of Israel and Tyre', *Proceedings, Israel Academy of Sciences and Humanities*, i, 7 (1964).

MITCHELL, T. C., 'Philistia', in D. Winton Thomas (ed.), *Archaeology and Old Testament Study* (1967), pp. 404–27.

TADMOR, H., 'Philistia under Assyrian Rule', *B.A.* xxix (1966), 86–102.

WEIPPERT, M., *Göttingische Gelehrte Anzeigen* ccxxiii (1971), 1–20.

WRIGHT, G. E., 'Philistine Coffins and Mercenaries', *B.A.* xxii (1959), 53–66.

—— 'Fresh Evidence for the Philistine Story', *B.A.* xxix (1966), 69–86.

YADIN, Y., *The Art of Warfare in Biblical Lands* (1963), pp. 248–53, 336–45.

IV

THE EGYPTIANS

RONALD J. WILLIAMS

By the time that the Israelites first emerged as a nation, the Egyptian civilization had reached its zenith and was already on its decline. The central position of Syria-Palestine between the great powers of Egypt and Mesopotamia rendered it vulnerable to the changing political fortunes and prey to the ambitions of its neighbouring states. It was inevitable that the Hebrews should inherit much from these older centres of culture.[1] The biblical references to 'all the wisdom of Egypt' (1 Kings 4: 30; Acts 7: 22) bear witness to the deep impression left by the attainments of the Egyptians.

The dominant feature of the Egyptian landscape is the Nile. From the confluence of the Blue and White Niles at Khartoum the great stream winds its way north across the desert, cutting its path deep through the soft limestone and sandstone until it finally pours into the sea almost two thousand miles distant. At intervals, ridges of hard granite form natural barriers which result in a series of six rocky cataracts. The first of these, at Aswan, was regarded as the southern border of Egypt in ancient times, and the region lying between the first and third cataracts is designated as Nubia. Still further south, beyond the fourth cataract, is the area known as Cush, also called Ethiopia by the Greeks.

To the north the river divided originally into at least five branches which fanned out towards the Mediterranean. The marshy delta thus formed contrasted sharply with the long narrow valley, rarely more than twelve miles wide and bordered by high cliffs. This natural division between delta and valley fostered the differences between the inhabitants, so that Upper and Lower Egypt were always conscious of a deep-seated distinction. Consequently it required a strong and highly centralized government to hold these two disparate areas together as a unified nation.

The inevitable result of the vast stretches of desert to the east and west of the valley, the cataracts impeding the passage of ships to the extreme south, and the Mediterranean Sea to the north, was to isolate Egypt from the outside world to a remarkable degree. To this factor must be attributed the amazing conservatism and resistance to foreign influences which characterized Egyptian civilization.

The ancient Egyptians were of Mediterranean stock, short and small-boned. Their language belongs to the Hamito-Semitic family and seems to occupy a position between the two main groups of languages. It is of unusual interest linguistically, in that it provides us with written records spanning a period of some four and a half millennia. The original hieroglyphic system of writing was very early supplemented by a cursive variant known as hieratic, which by the Persian period had been further simplified to the still more cursive demotic script. Finally, the Greek alphabet was adopted to write the latest stage of the language, referred to as Coptic.

During its long history the spoken language had undergone a steady and inevitable development. The written language, however, was standardized to conform with the dialect of the ruling group: Old Egyptian in the Old Kingdom, Middle Egyptian during the First Intermediate Period and subsequent Middle Kingdom, and Late Egyptian in the New Kingdom and later period of decline. That different dialects were a feature of the spoken vernacular is clear from the Middle Kingdom tale of Sinuhe, which notes that the speech of the Delta was unintelligible, or at least difficult, to a man from Upper Egypt. By the time the demotic script is in full use, some dialectal differences may already be discerned, and the latest phase of the language, written in Greek letters, is clearly divisible into several well-marked dialects.

There are evidences of human habitation in the Nile Valley from Palaeolithic times. Gradually, as the process of desiccation set in and the forests thinned out, hunting gave way to farming. The basis of the agricultural economy was the annual inundation of the Nile. Fed by the yearly rains in the Abyssinian highlands, the river rose steadily and overflowed its banks. The regular deposits of silt left by the receding waters, combined with the fructifying warmth of the sun, resulted in an exceptional fertility of the soil. The necessity for irrigation and the large-scale draining of marshes required extensive co-operation, and created the earliest social organization. An agricultural calendar was introduced that has been described as 'the only intelligent calendar which ever existed in human history'.[2] With minor modifications it is the calendar still in use today.

An efflorescence of civilization at the end of the fourth millennium was the result of cross-fertilization from Western Asia. This is revealed in the adoption by the Egyptians of certain features developed by the burgeoning civilization in Mesopotamia: monumental brick architecture with characteristic recessed panelling, artistic motifs and designs, cylinder seals, and the basic principles of a pictographic writing system.

The successful unification of the two parts of the land was finally achieved about 3100 B.C., when the Delta was conquered by the rulers of Upper Egypt. In his valuable history of Egypt, written in Greek during the third century B.C., but unfortunately preserved only in citations by later authors, Manetho divided the ruling houses from this period down to the conquest by Alexander the Great in 332 B.C. into thirty dynasties, later increased to thirty-one. Although this division did not always correspond with a change of royal family, it is a convenient and useful device which has been adopted by modern historians.

The first major period of Egyptian power, known as the Old Kingdom, was ushered in by the great pyramid-builders of the Third Dynasty (*c.* 2686–2613 B.C.). King Djoser's step-pyramid at Saqqara, designed by his famous vizier Imhotep, marks the beginning of monumental stone architecture. This truly magnificent engineering accomplishment was possible only in a highly centralized state, headed by a powerful and autocratic ruler. The tradition was continued in the Fourth Dynasty by the pyramids at Gizeh.

Trade was carried on from very early times with the Phoenician coast, especially Byblos, since it was the source of the valuable coniferous timber eagerly sought by the inhabitants of a land sorely denuded of large trees. During the Fourth Dynasty an Egyptian temple was constructed at Byblos and remained there as late as the period of the empire, although it had to be rebuilt at least once.

At the same time the cult of the sun-god Rēʿ at Heliopolis was growing in power and importance. Whether a change of royal line was forced by the Heliopolitan priesthood or not, it is certain that in the course of the Fifth Dynasty (*c.* 2494–2345 B.C.) the divine ruler became subservient to Rēʿ, with a consequent loss of prestige. This is reflected in the decrease in size of the royal pyramids, and their inferior workmanship, as contrasted with that of the magnificent sun-temples which were erected. From now on the worship of Rēʿ was to be the official cult of the royal house.

During the reign of the last king of the Fifth Dynasty the Pyramid Texts were first inscribed on the walls of the royal pyramids. This extensive body of funerary literature was of great antiquity, having been about a thousand years in the making. Divided into 714 spells, it included ancient rituals, hymns, prayers, and magical charms, all intended to ensure the continuing welfare of the king in the after-life, and thus it preserved some of the earliest religious concepts of the Egyptians.

The complex administrative structure necessitated by the highly organized state created in the Old Kingdom demanded an efficient bureaucracy to cope with the practical problems of census-taking, taxation, labour corvées, and tribunals. The engineering knowledge and sophisticated logistics entailed in the vast building projects bear witness to the degree of skill required. In order to train the large number of scribes needed for government service, officials personally instructed promising boys in their own homes, and schools were later set up in the palace. Such pupils, who received instruction in reading, writing, and elementary mathematics, were regularly referred to as 'sons' of their teachers.

Many officials composed didactic treatises in order to provide teaching aids. Such a collection of aphorisms and wise counsels was attributed to the vizier Imhotep, who flourished at the beginning of the Third Dynasty, but it has not been preserved. Similar works have survived in whole or in part from the Old Kingdom, chief of which is that of the Fifth Dynasty vizier Ptahhotpe.[3] In addition to being textbooks of style, they sought to impart rules of court procedure and moral values. Thus the pattern was set for a long series of such literary works, which were to be produced until as late as the first century A.D. and which left their mark on the biblical writings.[4]

Great advances were made in medicine, which reached heights in the Old Kingdom never surpassed in ancient Egypt. Although most treatises of the period still combined magical spells and incantations indiscriminately with medical prescriptions, one work dealing with surgical cases is unique in its unusually scientific approach to the matters of diagnosis and treatment with a minimum of magical procedures. It was this high standard of achievement in the Old Kingdom that resulted in the much later deification of Imhotep as the patron of medicine, and the Greek traditions of indebtedness to Egypt in this sphere.

In mathematics the Egyptians were less advanced, largely because of their primitive mode of calculation and the use of unit fractions. Nevertheless, their practical techniques were surprisingly adequate for the engineering problems they encountered, and their methods were sufficient for them to to be able to compute the volume of a cylinder or a truncated pyramid.

The eclipse of the Old Kingdom was the result of many factors. The building exploits of the rulers had been an intolerable burden to the nation, and the establishment of perpetual endowments for the upkeep of the tombs of royalty and the nobility contributed in large measure to the depletion of the treasury. Even more serious was the steady growth in power of the provincial governors or nomarchs, whose offices had become hereditary, and who had arrogated to themselves many of the powers and perquisites of the king himself. The latter was forced to placate them with royal gifts to win their loyalty, until the state was so impoverished that he was reduced to offering them mere titles. The ninety-four-year reign of Pepy II towards the end of the Sixth Dynasty left the country for many years with an ineffective ruler. Consequently civil war broke out in the area surrounding the capital city of Memphis, and this insurrection was accompanied by an overthrow of the social order. The new spirit of social justice and responsibility for the less fortunate is well expressed in the 'Tale of the Eloquent Peasant' composed during this period.[5]

About 2160 B.C. Khety I, the nomarch at Heracleopolis, set up a rival house, known as the Ninth and Tenth Dynasties, which overthrew the tottering Memphite power. Since the south was now under the control of the nomarchs of Thebes, and the Delta had been gradually infiltrated by bedouin tribesmen from the Sinai peninsula, Egypt was effectively divided into three. At length the rulers of the Tenth Dynasty were successful in asserting their control over the Delta. However, the rivalry between the Heracleopolitan and Theban houses flared up in intermittent fighting, which resulted eventually in the triumph of the Theban ruler Mentuhotpe II about 2040 B.C.

The literature produced during this troubled age, referred to as the First Intermediate Period, is marked by a spirit of disillusionment and pessimism. One text, which takes the form of a debate between a man and his *bai* (a term usually rendered inadequately as 'soul'), makes an attack on the established ideas and practices with respect to death.[6] In another, the deceased king Khety III is represented as writing a treatise of instruction for his son Merikarēʿ.[7] It is evident that the optimistic faith of the Old Kingdom in the certainty of material rewards for virtue has given way to a projection of these into the after-life. The latter had by now been extended to a wider group than royalty alone, and the ancient Pyramid Texts were adapted and inscribed in the tombs of nobles. The concept of a judgement after death, in which a man's deeds on earth will be the determining factor of his immortality, is another feature of the text. An upright character is extolled as of paramount importance. This interesting work is also one of the early attempts at political propaganda, being designed to improve relations with the south.[8]

The reunification of the land under the Theban ruler Mentuhotpe II of the Eleventh Dynasty marks the beginning of the Middle Kingdom. His vigorous rule of more than half a century, in which the powers of the nomarchs were drastically curtailed, made possible a resurgence of Egyptian prosperity and culture. After a brief period of anarchy at the end of this dynasty the throne was seized about 1991 B.C. by the usurper Amenemhet I, who was probably a former vizier. It is likely that he depended on the support of the disgruntled nomarchs for his rise to power, with the result that, despite his efforts to curb the territorial ambitions of the latter, they were again to pose a threat to the central authority. It was left to his successors to terminate for good the powers which the nomarchs had appropriated.

Establishing a new royal residence near Lisht, Amenemhet I proceeded to organize an efficient administrative system. During his reign the pressure of Asiatic nomads on his eastern border forced him to build a fortification known as the 'Wall of the Ruler' at the isthmus of Suez. It is significant that some years earlier the Sumerian ruler Shu-Sin of the Third Dynasty of Ur had found it necessary to construct what he called the 'Wall of the Amorites' in the region north-west of Baghdad to counter a threat of invasion by western Semites. The subsequent attempts of Semitic tribesmen to cross the Egyptian border were probably the result of the Amorite movements in Syria.

Early in his reign Amenemhet commissioned the writing of a clever propagandist tract known as the 'Prophecy of Neferti'.[9] Purporting to be composed in the reign of Snofru, the first king of the Fourth Dynasty, more than six hundred years before the time of Amenemhet, the work predicts a period of anarchy which will be brought to an end by the accession to the throne of a man of non-royal blood, named Ameny, who would restore order and build the 'Wall of the Ruler'. By this means the assumption of royal authority by Amenemhet is justified as divinely ordained from antiquity.

On his western border also troubles developed, this time with the Libyans. While his son and co-regent Senwosret was engaged in leading the army in Libya, a court conspiracy succeeded in murdering Amenemhet. Prompt action on the part of Senwosret was required to ensure his succession. In order to bolster his claim to the throne, he had a scribe named Khety compose the 'Teaching of Amenemhet'.[10] This very moving document is presented in the form of a message from the deceased king revealed in a vision to his son. The perfidy of the courtiers responsible for the assassination is vividly described, and Senwosret's right to the throne is clearly affirmed.

Another work which refers to this episode is the celebrated 'Tale of Sinuhe', which recounts the fortunes of a high court official who fled for his life to Syria on learning of the court conspiracy, lest he should be wrongfully accused of involvement.[11] Of special interest to Old Testament scholars is the description given of the semi-nomadic life in Syria, which provides a welcome corroboration of the biblical descriptions of conditions in the age of the contemporary patriarchs.

The renowned scribe Khety to whom we have alluded above also composed a work for his son which set the style for a new type of literature. In this 'Satire on the Trades' he passed in review various occupations and declared them all to be inferior to that of the scribe alone.[12] His lead was followed by many others in later ages, and early in the second century B.C. the Hebrew writer Ben Sira adapted the theme to his own purposes (Ecclus. 38: 24–39: 11).

The Twelfth Dynasty achieved a position of domination over Syria-Palestine which was at least economic, if not also political to some degree. Egyptian officials were stationed in such cities as Byblos, Ugarit, and Megiddo. Senwosret III led a campaign into Palestine and probably attacked Shechem. There was a continual movement of nomadic Semites between Egypt and Palestine, as graphically depicted in a contemporary tomb-painting at Beni Hasan showing thirty-seven tribesmen, headed by a sheikh with the Hebrew name Abishai (Plate III). The migrations of the Hebrew patriarchs to and from Egypt recorded in Genesis 12: 10 ff. were part of this constant traffic. A papyrus of the Thirteenth Dynasty lists a number of Semites attached as servants to an Egyptian official's household, who had become sufficiently assimilated to their new environment to give Egyptian names to their children.

A large and important group of documents to be dated to the late Twelfth or early Thirteenth Dynasty reveals the extensive influence of the Middle Kingdom in Syria-Palestine. Known as Execration Texts, they are inscribed on pottery bowls and clay figurines, and contain curses against the foes of Egypt. Jerusalem, Shechem, and Ashkelon are some of the cities mentioned in them. From them we learn that the early patriarchal organization had not yet given way to that of the city-state. The texts also indicate dissension within the royal harem, and testify to the unsettled conditions of the time which foreshadowed the end of the prosperous Middle Kingdom.

The Second Intermediate Period began about 1786 B.C., when the Twelfth Dynasty was followed by two houses ruling concurrently: the Thirteenth Dynasty which continued in the Memphite area, and the Fourteenth which established itself at Xoïs, in the marshlands of the western Delta. Both dynasties consisted of numerous kings with brief reigns. Nevertheless, Egyptian power and prestige seem to have been substantially maintained for another century or more.

During a period of more than half a century there was a continuous infiltration of Asiatics into the eastern Delta. This was very likely part of the mass migrations of peoples into the Fertile Crescent during the eighteenth century. Manetho described the invaders as Hyksos, a term which he translated as 'shepherd-kings'. In fact, the name is derived from the Egyptian *ḥḳȝw-ḫȝśwt*, 'rulers of foreign lands', a term applied to Asiatic sheikhs during the Twelfth Dynasty and even earlier. About 1720 B.C. the Hyksos had become sufficiently strong to establish themselves as a ruling house at Avaris, which is referred to as the Fifteenth Dynasty. A contemporary group of Hyksos chieftains is known as the Sixteenth Dynasty. Eventually, in about 1674 B.C., they succeeded in dislodging the Thirteenth Dynasty rulers from the Memphite region and forced them to seek refuge in Upper Egypt. However, the Hyksos power was confined mainly to the territory north of Memphis.

The military superiority of the Hyksos lay in the fact that they possessed bronze body-armour and weapons of a new type, as well as the powerful composite bow, which put their archers beyond the range of enemy arrows. The use of the horse and chariot gave a greater mobility to their forces and also contributed to their success. Apart from the arts of war and metallurgy, however, the Hyksos had little to contribute. As has frequently been the case, the victor was himself vanquished by the culture of the conquered. The Hyksos retained the Egyptian system of administration, they adopted the local customs, they used the hieroglyphic script, and sometimes they even assumed Egyptian names.

By the end of the seventeenth century the Fourteenth Dynasty in the western Delta had been brought to an end. There is ample evidence for the expansion in this period of Hyksos influence into western Asia. This was made possible by the fact that Babylonian power was at a low ebb and the Assyrian state was feeble. During the era of Hyksos domination Semitic tribes continued to move into Egypt, and the episodes described in the biblical account of Joseph are to be placed at the end of the Hyksos period, although many of the features contained in it may reflect a later date.[13]

Upper Egypt was but little affected by the Hyksos presence in the north. A native family had established itself securely at Thebes as the Seventeenth Dynasty and held undisputed possession of the south. It was only at the end of the dynasty that organized resistance to Hyksos authority was instituted by Seqnenrēʿ II. His son Kamose managed to clear the Hyksos from Middle Egypt, recapturing Memphis and driving the enemy back to their capital at Avaris. On his death, his brother and successor Ahmose completed the expulsion of the Hyksos from Egypt about 1567 B.C., and at the same time achieved the reconquest of Nubia, so vital for Egyptian trade. With his reign Manetho begins the Eighteenth Dynasty, which was to inaugurate the New Kingdom, a period of unprecedented magnificence.

The outstanding achievement of this dynasty was the creation of an empire which, at its greatest point, stretched from the fourth cataract in the south to beyond the Euphrates in the north. This was a legacy of the Hyksos occupation that alerted Egypt for the first time to the danger of foreign invasion. Her cherished illusions of security had been for ever shattered, and the control of Palestine as a buffer state was seen as the best means of avoiding any further threat from Asia. Although Thutmose I, early in the dynasty, had launched a campaign which took him to the upper Euphrates, it remained for a later ruler to establish effective Egyptian supremacy.

When he was able finally to free himself from the domination of his strong-willed stepmother, the dowager queen Hatshepsut, Thutmose III set out to accomplish this task. He began by defeating a confederacy of native chieftains, headed by the ruler of Kadesh and supported by Sausshatar, the King of Mitanni. This great victory at Megiddo, about 1482 B.C., was followed by a series of sixteen military expeditions over the next thirty years, in which he pushed into Phoenicia, gained control of the Phoenician littoral, and finally advanced into Mitanni. On his eighth campaign he had boats constructed at Byblos which were transported overland to Carchemish. By this means his troops were enabled to cross the Euphrates river, the first time in recorded history that such a feat had been accomplished. On the walls of the temple at Karnak Thutmose had long lists inscribed of the names of conquered city-states in Palestine, such as Aijalon, Gezer, Megiddo, and Taanach.

So decisive were the victories of Thutmose III that his immediate successors required but a few minor campaigns to maintain the empire. His son Amenhotpe II concluded with Mitanni the first recorded international treaty of friendship.

The administrative centre of the newly acquired Asiatic empire was located at Gaza. A substantial degree of autonomy was accorded to the city-states, although resident commissioners and garrisons of Egyptian troops were installed in certain of them, and a heavy tribute was exacted from them annually. The sons and brothers of local rulers were frequently taken to the capital city of Thebes, where they were educated and indoctrinated in Egyptian ways. Not only were they thus held as hostages to ensure the loyalty of the Palestinian vassal states, but they were also thoroughly imbued with an appreciation of things Egyptian.

The worship of the god Amūn had already come into some prominence during the early Middle Kingdom. When, as a result of the syncretistic tendency in Egyptian religion, the creator and sun-god Rēʿ was fused with Amūn in the form Amon-Rēʿ, the new deity assumed the position of dynastic god at Thebes, the capital throughout the New Kingdom. It was doubtless the recently achieved status of Egypt as an imperial power that elevated the national god Amon-Rēʿ to the position of a universal god. The great 'Hymn to Amūn', which was composed about the middle of the fifteenth century B.C., stresses this aspect of the deity.[14]

By the time of the New Kingdom the process of democratization with respect to the after-life begun in the First Intermediate Period had advanced to a stage where all who could provide themselves with the necessary funerary accoutrements might be assured of immortality. The ancient Pyramid Texts had, by the Middle Kingdom, been expanded and revised to become the Coffin Texts, and were now inscribed on the interiors of the coffins. The process of revision, interpretation, and expansion of these texts continued, until they became the extensive corpus of magical charms, intended to ward off the dangers of the journey to the underworld, known to the Egyptians as the 'Book of Coming Forth by Day', and familiar in modern times as the 'Book of the Dead'. Chapter 125, the celebrated 'Affirmation of Innocence', offers us a valuable insight into the ethical code of the day.[15] It was the tragedy of Egyptian religion that the lofty moral concepts expressed in this text were at the same time nullified by the conviction that magical means were available to enable one to escape the consequences of one's misdeeds. The fear of the unknown led to a proliferation of other mortuary texts, such as the 'Book of Him who is in the Underworld', the 'Book of Gates', the 'Book of Caverns', and the 'Book of the Two Ways'.

The reign of Amenhotpe (Amenophis) III, which began about 1417 B.C., was one in which Egypt enjoyed many years of peace and prosperity, and in which the pharaoh's grandiose architectural schemes were given full scope. The great temple to Amon-Rēʿ at Luxor was one of the many products of his bounty. It is significant, however, that he also built a shrine at Thebes to the new god Aten. A pleasure-boat and a palace were called 'Splendour of Aten' after the same deity, and two of his children bore names which included the name of this god (Plate IV*a*). There is some evidence that the worship of Aten goes back to the reign of Amenhotpe's father Thutmose IV, but it was only in the time of the former that it attained such prominence.

His son Amenhotpe IV was probably associated for some years with him as co-regent. On his accession to power, about 1379 B.C., the growing rivalry between Amon-Rēʿ and Aten came to a head. The youthful pharaoh, with a frail physique but an indomitable will, espoused the cause of the new god with the zeal of a fanatic. For him Aten was the physical sun-disc, shorn of the accretions of centuries which had clustered about the figure of the sun-god Amon-Rēʿ, and hence was portrayed only as a disc from which the rays extended as arms offering mankind the hieroglyphic symbol for life.

Thebes, the centre of the worship of Amon-Rēʿ, having become most distasteful to him, Amenhotpe IV founded a new residence city at Tell el-Amarna, which he called the 'Horizon of Aten'. He endeavoured to remove the hated name of Amūn wherever it appeared on temple walls, and even changed his own name to Akhenaten. It may be questioned whether the term 'monotheist' can properly be applied to him, but it is undeniable that he gave homage to Aten alone, even though acknowledging the existence of other gods in his great 'Hymn to Aten'.[16] This magnificent poem owes much to the earlier 'Hymn to Amūn', but is a finer literary creation. The striking similarity of Psalm 104 to it can hardly be the result of direct acquaintance by the Hebrew poet, but rather of familiarity with later Egyptian works which were permeated with phrases and concepts drawn from it.

At the new site of Tell el-Amarna the royal archives were found, consisting of almost 400 clay tablets inscribed in cuneiform Akkadian, the language of international diplomacy at the time.[17] These were originals or copies of letters which passed between Egypt and her vassal states in Syria-Palestine during the reigns of Amenhotpe III and Akhenaten. They are of interest to students of the Hebrew language for the frequent Canaanite glosses they contain. But more important is the fact that they reveal the disintegration of the Asiatic empire won at such pains by Thutmose III. This was fomented by the Hittite king Šuppiluliuma, who encouraged the separatist tendencies of the North Syrian states, and abetted by the invasions of the Habiru in Palestine. These Semitic people appear as *ʿprw* in Egyptian inscriptions from as early as the time of Thutmose III, when they were employed in work-gangs.

Attempts were made, perhaps even before the death of Akhenaten, to effect a reconciliation with the Amon-Rēʿ priesthood. At all events, by the time of Tutankhamūn the site of Tell el-Amarna was for ever abandoned and the Atenist heresy at an end. The religious exclusiveness of the faith ran counter to the Egyptian temperament, and its doctrine was far too intellectual for general acceptance. This remarkable Amarna period had lasted for a brief span of only two decades. Its influence, however, was destined to linger on in art and literature.

Harmhab, the vigorous commander of Akhenaten's army, who had never been a convert to Atenism, brought the Eighteenth Dynasty to an end. His efforts were directed mainly towards the stabilization of the government. On his death his aged vizier laid claim to the throne, and, as Ramesses I, initiated the Nineteenth Dynasty about 1320 B.C. In little more than a year he had died and was succeeded by Sety (Sethos) I, who turned his attention once more to western Asia, where the Hittites were now the dominant power. Peace terms were probably concluded with the Hittite ruler, and control in Palestine was restored by means of several campaigns. From Beth-Shan, where an Egyptian garrison was stationed, come two stelae of Sety I, one describing his 'liberation' of the town from the control of Hamath, and the other referring to the "*prw* of Mount Jarmuth'.[18]

The growing Hittite threat was passed on to his son and successor Ramesses II, a young man of vigour and courage, but impetuous and bombastic. In his fifth year, about 1299 B.C., he set forth against a powerful Syrian coalition formed by Muwatallis, the Hittite king. At Kadesh on the Orontes he fell into a clever trap, and only with the greatest bravery was able to extricate himself and his troops from probable annihilation. In characteristic fashion, this was later proclaimed in his royal inscriptions as a glorious victory. After two decades of continuous fighting Ramesses concluded a non-aggression pact with the new Hittite ruler Hattušili III. According to the terms of the treaty, the Egyptian sphere of influence was restricted to Palestine and southern Syria, and both parties agreed to engage in mutual defence against another attacking power and to extradite any political refugees.

Whatever might be his shortcomings, Ramesses succeeded during the course of a very long reign in bringing a large measure of peace and prosperity to Egypt. His building exploits were prodigious. In the north-eastern Delta, from which the royal family had sprung, a summer residence was established, known as Per-Ramesse, and appearing as 'Raamses' in the Old Testament. His construction of the neighbouring town of Pithom at the same time makes it certain that it was at this period in the first decade of the thirteenth century B.C. that the Hebrews served their harsh taskmasters before the exodus from Egypt (Exod. 1: 8–11).

Merenptah, one of the numerous sons of Ramesses II, ascended the throne about 1236 B.C. His accession was marked by an uprising in Palestine which he quickly subdued. But far more serious was the situation that soon developed on his western border, where some Libyan tribes, joined by numbers of Sea Peoples who had sought a foothold on the Delta coast, threatened the security of Egypt. These Sea Peoples were folk of Indo-European stock who had left Europe in search of new homelands. Among their numbers were such varied groups as the Lycians, Achaeans, Tyrsenians, Sardinians, and Sicilians. Merenptah drove the invaders back and thus postponed the danger for nearly forty years. In celebration of his triumph he prepared a stela on which he had hymns of victory inscribed.[19] This furnishes us with the sole occurrence of the name Israel in Egyptian texts, written with a hieroglyphic determinative which suggests that the Israelites were not yet a settled people. This monument would be contemporary with the campaigns of Joshua.

Merenptah was followed by several weak rulers, and a state of anarchy ensued until Sethnakhte restored order once more. His reign marks the beginning of the Twentieth Dynasty, but after a brief period of only two years he was succeeded by his son Ramesses III about 1198 B.C. The last of the great pharaohs, he sought to pattern himself in every way possible on his famous predecessor Ramesses II, as his adopted name, his numerous buildings, and his lengthy inscriptions amply testify.

A further attempt at occupation of the western Delta by the Libyans, once more in league with the Sea Peoples, was foiled. But about 1190 B.C. the Sea Peoples, having earlier accomplished the downfall of the Hittite empire, moved south through Palestine to the borders of Egypt. Augmented by yet other kindred groups, such as the Teucrians and the Philistines, they attacked by land and sea, only to be thrown back by superior Egyptian forces and compelled to settle elsewhere in the eastern Mediterranean. Despite one or more campaigns into Asia, Ramesses was unsuccessful in dislodging the Philistines from the Palestinian coastal plain, where they remained to plague the Hebrews.

The enormous cost of his wars, his building projects, and the lavish gifts made to the priesthoods drained the royal treasury of much of its resources. This resulted in a state of unrest among the populace which found expression in strikes on the part of the necropolis workmen, and a series of impudent caricatures of the king sketched on potsherds. Finally, intrigue in the court resulted in an abortive attempt on the pharaoh's life. On Ramesses' death a little later, his son succeeded to the throne and the conspirators were tried and punished. The loss of the empire during a dreary succession of seven ineffectual pharaohs, all named Ramesses, further impoverished the state and led to the collapse of the New Kingdom. An important cause of her downfall was the fact that Egypt lagged behind western Asia in clinging to the use of bronze until the seventh century, whereas iron was in general use by 1150 B.C. in the rest of the Mediterranean area.

Literature and the arts flourished during the New Kingdom. The tradition of the short story, first developed by the Egyptians as a literary form, was continued by many examples. One of these, the 'Tale of the Two Brothers',[20] relates an episode which appears as a theme in several later Greek and Latin works, but above all in Hebrew literature (Gen. 39: 6–20).[21]

Didactic treatises likewise were still being produced, the most outstanding one being that of Amenemope, which was perhaps written at the end of the Nineteenth Dynasty or slightly later.[22] It is noteworthy for its unusually high moral tone and insistence on personal piety, and is of particular interest for Old Testament studies, inasmuch as the collection preserved in Proverbs 22: 17–23: 14 gives evidence of literary dependence on it.[23]

The increase in personal piety was a characteristic of the Nineteenth Dynasty, with its submergence of the individual in the impersonal, authoritarian state. Peculiar to this period are some compositions which are reminiscent of the Hebrew and Mesopotamian penitential psalms.[24] Another feature of the later New Kingdom was the appearance of love songs, of which several collections have been preserved.[25] It is quite possible that the biblical Song of Songs may owe something to this literary genre. One last work, which was a product of the closing days of the Twentieth Dynasty, recounts the misfortunes of a temple official named Wenamūn who was sent on a mission to Byblos.[26] With sardonic humour it portrays Egypt's loss of prestige in the Mediterranean world, and contains an episode which demonstrates that the phenomenon of ecstatic prophecy was to be found in Syria as well as in Israel.

With the establishment of the Twenty-first Dynasty about 1085 B.C. the fortunes of Egypt were at a low ebb. The vizier of Lower Egypt, Nesbanebded, proclaimed himself pharaoh at Tanis in the northern Delta, while effective power in the south was exercised by Piankh, who succeeded Hrihor, the vizier of Upper Egypt, who had previously assumed the office of High Priest of Amūn at Thebes. The division of the land was averted by an alliance. During this period the contacts between the Egyptians and the Hebrews grew steadily in importance. The political asylum afforded to the Edomite Hadad in the time of David (1 Kings 11: 14–22) was probably granted by Siamūn towards the close of the dynasty. It was probably the same king who gave his daughter in marriage to Solomon (1 Kings 3: 1), and bestowed on him as a dowry the city of Gezer, which he had recently captured in an expedition (1 Kings 9: 16).

About 945 B.C. Sheshonk I, whose name appears in Hebrew sources in the form Shishak, seized the throne and founded the Twenty-second Dynasty, which was of Libyan ancestry, with its centre at Bubastis. It was to his court that Jeroboam fled for refuge from Solomon (1 Kings 11: 40). In Rehoboam's fifth year Sheshonk invaded Palestine and sacked the temple at Jerusalem (1 Kings 14: 25 f.), recording on the walls of the Karnak temple 156 of the towns he claimed to have captured. The ensuing reigns of his dynasty were rent with strife, and two minor dynasties, perhaps contemporaneous, intervened before order was restored. During these unsettled times many Hebrews abandoned the Northern Kingdom to settle in Egypt (Hos. 7: 11, 9: 6), and King Hoshea frantically dispatched envoys to an official (perhaps the vizier)[27] of the pharaoh before the fall of Samaria in 721 B.C. (2 Kings 17: 4).

Meanwhile the ruling family in Cush, far to the south, had been gradually acquiring a foothold in Upper Egypt. At last Piankhy grasped the opportunity to challenge the tottering power of the rulers in the Delta and captured Memphis. On his return to Cush, the Delta revolted, and it fell to the lot of Piankhy's son Shabaka to overthrow the Delta regime. By this time Assyria was menacing Egypt and was held at bay with great difficulty. Matters came to a head during the reign of Taharqa; Esarhaddon invaded Egypt in 671 B.C. and captured Memphis, whereupon Taharqa fled into Cush. Returning on hearing of Esarhaddon's death, he was routed once more by Ashurbanipal. Two further insurrections were crushed by the latter, who proceeded to sack Thebes, an event referred to with some relish in the Bible (Nahum 3: 8–10). This marked the end of the Twenty-fifth Dynasty and of Cushite power in Egypt, while Thebes was never to regain her position of eminence.

Taking advantage of the preoccupation of Ashurbanipal with affairs at home, a family from Sais in the Delta once more established stable conditions in Egypt in 663 B.C., with the aid of Greek mercenaries. This period witnessed the founding of a colony of

Jewish mercenary soldiers on the island of Elephantine. Many important documents written in Aramaic during the later Persian domination have been recovered from this site and elsewhere, which reveal religious practices at variance with biblical prescriptions, above all the presence of a local temple to Yahweh.[28]

Necho, the second ruler of this Twenty-sixth Dynasty, in 609 B.C. marched into Palestine in a futile attempt to bring aid to the Assyrian forces in their last-ditch stand before the combined onslaught of the Babylonians and the Medes. In the course of events Necho put to death Josiah, King of Judah, who had vainly sought to halt the Egyptian forces at Megiddo.[29] Necho himself selected the brother of the lawful heir to rule as a vassal of Egypt (2 Kings 23: 29–35). Three years later, at the battle of Carchemish, Necho was roundly defeated by Nebuchadrezzar. When Jerusalem was captured by the latter, many Hebrews emigrated to Egypt (Jer. 41: 16–18, 43: 5–7).

After the fall of Assyria to the Babylonians, the Persians emerged as a new threat. With the capture of Babylon by Cyrus in 539 B.C. the handwriting was on the wall for Egypt. The invasion and occupation of the land by Cambyses in 525 B.C. spelled the end of effective Egyptian independence. Despite several unsuccessful attempts at rebellion, this Twenty-seventh Dynasty retained control until the reign of Darius II, when Amyrtaeus raised the standard of revolt, and on the death of Darius in 404 B.C. proclaimed himself king. His six-year reign comprised the Twenty-eighth Dynasty; but two more native dynasties, with the aid of Sparta and Athens, were to maintain a temporary independence, until the Persians under Artaxerxes III once more subjugated the land in 341 B.C.

Their triumph was short-lived, for Alexander the Great invaded Egypt in 332 B.C., and after his death it passed to the long line of Ptolemies. Under the first ruler of this name Palestine again came under the control of Egypt in 301 B.C., to remain thus for a century. As a result of his campaigns in Palestine numbers of prisoners were carried off to Egypt, and many Jewish mercenaries were later settled there. Of special interest is the tomb of Petosiris, an Egyptian official of the late fourth century. On its walls are carved hieroglyphic inscriptions which betray the influence of the Old Testament writings, particularly Psalm 128.[30]

About 160 B.C., when the High Priest Onias IV had been deposed and murdered in Jerusalem, an emigration of Jews took place to the Delta, where a temple was constructed at Leontopolis. Meanwhile the city of Alexandria attracted an ever increasing Jewish population, for whom the Greek Septuagint version of the Hebrew Scriptures was made. It was fortunate for textual critics of the Old Testament that the Septuagint was much later rendered into Coptic, the native vernacular, for this translation is an important witness to the pre-Hexaplaric text of Origen.

Ptolemaic control came to an end with the incorporation of Egypt as a province of the Roman Empire in 30 B.C., a status which it was to retain until the accession of Constantine in A.D. 324. Native Egyptian culture, however, was still creative. As late as the Roman period several literary works were current in demotic, forming a cycle of tales the hero of which was Petubastis, a ruler of the Twenty-third Dynasty. Two other demotic tales, from the Ptolemaic and Roman periods, relate stories concerning Khamwēse, one of the sons of Ramesses II. The later of the two contains an episode which is a prototype of the biblical parable of Dives and Lazarus (Luke 16: 19–31).[31] There are even two almost intact examples of didactic treatises, likewise in demotic.

Perhaps this is an appropriate point at which to take leave of our subject. Egypt had ceased to exist as an independent nation and the grandeur of her past was but a memory. Yet the vitality of the Egyptian literary muse was unabated, and would continue down into Coptic times.

NOTES

1. For a fuller discussion of the Hebrew people's debt to Egypt see the present writer's 'Egypt and Israel' in *The Legacy of Egypt*, J. R. Harris (ed.) (O.U.P., Oxford, 1971), pp. 257–90; and 'Some Egyptianisms in the Old Testament', in *Studies in Honor of John A. Wilson* (Univ. of Chicago Press, Chicago, 1969), pp. 93–8.

2. O. Neugebauer, *The Exact Sciences in Antiquity*, 2nd edn. (Brown Univ. Press, Providence, R.I., 1957), p. 81.

3. *A.N.E.T.*, pp. 412–14.

4. This is especially marked in the Book of Proverbs. For examples see the first work cited in n. 1.

5. *A.N.E.T.*, pp. 407–10.

6. Ibid., pp. 405–7; *D.O.T.T.*, pp. 162–7; R. O. Faulkner, in *J.E.A.* 42 (1956), 21–40; R. J. Williams, in ibid. 48 (1962), 49–56.

7. *A.N.E.T.*, pp. 414–18; *D.O.T.T.*, pp. 155–61.

8. Cf. the present writer's 'Literature as a Medium of Political Propaganda in Ancient Egypt', in *The Seed of Wisdom*, W. S. McCullough (ed.) (Univ. of Toronto Press, Toronto, 1964), pp. 14–30.

9. *A.N.E.T.*, pp. 444–6.

10. Ibid., pp. 418 f.

11. Ibid., pp. 18–22.

12. Ibid., pp. 432–4.

13. For the most recent views on the Egyptian background of the Joseph story see J. Vergote, *Joseph en Égypte* (Louvain, 1959) and especially D. B. Redford, *A Study of the Biblical Story of Joseph* (Leiden, 1970).

14. *A.N.E.T.*, pp. 365–7.

15. Ibid., pp. 34–6.

16. Ibid., pp. 369–71; *D.O.T.T.*, pp. 142–50.

17. *A.N.E.T.*, pp. 483–90; *D.O.T.T.*, pp. 38–45.

18. A town situated to the north of Beth-Shan, mentioned in Josh. 21: 29.

19. *A.N.E.T.*, pp. 376–8; *D.O.T.T.*, pp. 137–41.

20. *A.N.E.T.*, pp. 23–5; *D.O.T.T.*, pp. 168–71.

21. Cf. the present writer's 'Ancient Egyptian Folk Tales', in *Univ. of Toronto Quarterly* xxvii (1958), 256–72.

22. *A.N.E.T.*, pp. 421–4; *D.O.T.T.*, pp. 172–86.

23. Cf. the remarks of the present writer in *J.E.A.* 47 (1961), 100–6, and those of B. Couroyer in *R.B.* 70 (1963), 208–24.

24. *A.N.E.T.*, pp. 380 f.; *D.O.T.T.*, pp. 151–4.

25. *A.N.E.T.*, pp. 467–9; *D.O.T.T.*, pp. 187–91.

26. *A.N.E.T.*, pp. 25–9.

27. So S. Yeivin in *V.T.* 2 (1952), 164–8.

28. *A.N.E.T.*, pp. 491 f.; *D.O.T.T.*, pp. 256–69.

29. The preposition *'al* in the Hebrew text cannot mean 'against' but must be intended for *'el*, 'to' (so R.S.V.), as shown by the Babylonian Chronicle.

30. Edited by G. Lefebvre, *Le Tombeau de Petosiris* (Inst. français d'archéol. orient., Cairo, 1924).

31. Cf. n. 21.

BIBLIOGRAPHY

BREASTED, J. H. *A History of Egypt* (Scribners, New York, 1905).

ČERNÝ, J. *Ancient Egyptian Religion* (Hutchinsons, London, 1952).

DRIOTON, E., & VANDIER, J. *L'Égypte* [Les peuples de l'orient méditerranéen, ii], 4th edn. (Presses universitaires de France, Paris, 1962).

GARDINER, Sir A. H. *Egypt of the Pharaohs* (Clarendon Press, Oxford, 1961).

HARRIS, J. R. (ed.) *The Legacy of Egypt* (Clarendon Press, Oxford, 1971).

SMITH, W. S., *The Art and Architecture of Ancient Egypt* [Pelican History of Art] (Penguin Books, Harmondsworth, 1958).

WILSON, J. A. *The Burden of Egypt* (Univ. of Chicago Press, Chicago, 1951).

V

THE AMORITES

M. LIVERANI

THE 'Amorite whose stature equalled that of the cedars, whose strength equalled that of the oaks . . .': this definition given by Amos (2: 9) in a poetic and imaginative style shows how, in the middle eighth century B.C., the memory of this people had become so vague as to be thrown back into a mythical past in which men assume gigantic proportions and can be defeated only by direct divine intervention. In the days of Amos the term had no specific value when applied to contemporary reality, and remained only as a generic denomination for the people of the entire Syro-Palestinian region; but the memory, or rather the opinion, was still lingering that, much earlier, before the conquest of the 'promised land' by the tribes of Israel, this term had designated a specific people, present in that land along with so many others. Nearly all memory of the specific characteristics of the individual populations had been lost, and consequently it would not be possible now to reconstruct them within the context of the Old Testament. Modern criticism would have remained unable to distinguish, within the populations of pre-Israelite Palestine, which were the purely mythical elements, which elements could be connected with historical reality (and in what measure), and what changes could have occurred in the process of traditional and historiographical transmission. However, the discovery of earlier and contemporary texts in other regions of the Near East has permitted a reconstruction, within certain limits, of the history of some of these named peoples, in particular that of the Amorites, and to set them in a more precise historical framework. In this new light it is possible today to evaluate the specific meaning of the Old Testament references.

This task is not a simple one, as records of the Amorites are spread over a long period of time; indeed, they cover more than two millennia, and often refer to different entities. An undifferentiated and uncritical use of the documentation can lead, and has only too often led, to a simplistic levelling of the historical perspective which results in the attribution to the Amorites of the Old Testament of characteristics proper to Amorites of other groups of texts (or vice versa). The picture thus given is as false as one which would today attribute to the Romans of antiquity characteristics of the contemporary Rumanians, or to the Franks characteristics of the French.

The heart of the problem is whether or not it is possible to establish a rigid equivalence between the name and the ethnic entity. It is clear that this rigid equivalence is found in ancient historiography, which is rather nominalistic in its character. The historians of antiquity (and they are historians, not contemporary 'witnesses') who in the eighth and seventh centuries attempted to give a picture of the ethno-political situation in Palestine at the time of the Israelite conquest, received from tradition the name of the Amorites, and were in no doubt that one specific entity corresponded to that denomination. Undisturbed by the fact that many names were given by tradition, names which seem to overlap, they solved the problem by concluding that each name corresponded to a separate ethnic group, and that consequently the ethnic situation in pre-Israelite Palestine was extremely composite (Kenites, Kenizites, Kadmonites, Hittites, Perizzites, Rephites, Amorites, Canaanites, Girgashites, and Jebusites).[1] All these peoples would then have been swept away, so they claimed, by the Israelite conquest.

Modern scholars for a long time accepted without question the substance of this ancient view that Amorites, Canaanites, and others were so many different peoples who inhabited pre-Israelite Palestine. The diversity was due, they thought, either to the peoples' speech deriving from different linguistic sources, as in the case of the Hittites, or, as in the case of the Canaanites and Amorites (both Semitic peoples of the north-west), to their coming from two different waves of Semites who poured into Palestine from the Syro-Arabian desert about the years 3000 and 2000 B.C. respectively.

But today one is reluctant to think that the displacements of populations necessarily go with the displacements of their names.

Nor is it accepted that the constitution of an ethnic group necessarily corresponds with the first use of a determinate name, or that this ethnic group should be considered as having ceased to exist once the name is no longer in use. There is today a greater awareness of the fact that the history of an ethno-geographical name can evolve in a particular way, detaching itself from the history of an ethnic unit which can be identified, and that it rests mainly on the basis of cultural factors which develop according to both external influences and internal changes. As regards the Amorites in particular, it has only recently become clear that the 'Canaanite' dialect is but a local derivation of the 'Amorite', and that the cultural elements known from archaeology and associated with the Canaanites (the Syro-Palestinian Late Bronze period) are a local development of elements to be traced back to the Amorites (the Syro-Palestinian Middle Bronze period). It seems therefore that the Amorites and Canaanites should not be separated into two peoples, whether by origin, culture, or date of arrival. We should admit instead that 'Canaanite' came into use at least from the middle of the second millennium B.C., to indicate, at least in part, those populations which had before been referred to by the term 'Amorite'. The situation is, however, still not simple, for both terms also designate specific coexisting regions, and the use of both terms persists for a long time, with the inevitable deformations deriving from changes in the political field as well as from the conditioning of the terms one by the other.

(i) *Documentary evidence*

The oldest and most numerous evidences of the Amorites come from Mesopotamian documentation, which is almost the only source of information about them during the period in which they formed a distinct ethnic group. The name of the Amorites is Martu in Sumerian and *Amurru(m)* in Akkadian;[2] the relationship between these names is firmly attested by lexical lists as well as by analogous use, and presents no problem apart from that of their linguistic correspondence and their etymology, which remain obscure.[3] In Sumerian and Akkadian texts two different uses of the term Martu/Amurru appear to have been current from very early antiquity. First, a geographic use, to indicate one of the four cardinal points of the compass (West). Second, an ethnic use, to refer to single persons or groups of people originating from regions outside the Sumero-Akkadian world (in its strictest sense, namely lower Mesopotamia), and coming apparently from the west.

The first of these uses, which continued for a very long time in Mesopotamian documents, was already established in the Old Akkadian period. Thus the obelisk of Maništusu (*c.* 2300 B.C.), in the description of some fields, referred to the western side as tu_{15} mar-tu.[4] This is found in other sources of the Old Akkadian and Ur III periods, proving that it was well established during the second half of the third millennium B.C.[5] It is reasonable to deduce, on the basis of the use of the same term to designate a region and the people inhabiting it, that the use of the term for a cardinal point is secondary, even though very ancient. Thus the west was referred to as Martu/Amurru because west of Mesopotamia there was a region called Martu/Amurru. This is not a unique case, and later it became general, the north being known as Subartu, the east as Elam, and the south as Sumer, so completing a cosmic-geographical picture which had Akkad/Babylon as its centre.[6] The very ancient testimony for the use of Martu/Amurru to designate the west is important for locating the general direction of the provenance of the Amorites in Mesopotamia. In the past this factor has often been neglected by those scholars who maintained that the Amorites came from the north-east.[7] The problem is today considered solved.

References in texts for the ethnic use of the term 'Martu' are older still. In an archaic text from Fara (*c.* 2600 B.C.) a list of farmers names one É-ág-gid mar-tu, who is the first Amorite to be specifically mentioned.[8] During the Akkadian period references to single people or to groups of people defined as Martu become more frequent, at Lagash, Umma, Adab, and Susa.[9] From the contents of the texts and comparison with the later texts of the Ur III period it becomes clear that the people in question were immigrants—presumably from the west—who, in their search for work with city administrations in lower Mesopotamia, moved to these towns. They were known by a term (Martu) which emphasized their position as foreigners and immigrants, as opposed to the majority of people working there, who were of local origin. The mention, from Old Akkadian times, of officials called ugula mar-tu and nu-bànda mar-tu-ne, 'inspector of Martu',[10] shows that the presence of these immigrants, with their own particular character, constituted an organizational problem for the city administrations.

The documentation seen so far gives evidence at the level of single individuals or family units. But a date formula of Šar-kali-šarri (*c.* 2250 B.C.) shows that during the Old Akkadian period the Amorites already had relations as a group with the Mesopotamian city-states, and were a political or tribal unit. This date formula reads, 'the year in which [the King] defeated the Martu at Mount Basar'.[11] This alludes to a battle that took place outside Mesopotamia, and, more precisely, at Jebel Bišrī, in Syria, west of the Middle Euphrates, just in the area known in Mesopotamia as Amurru. There is other evidence for the connection between Jebel Bišrī and Amurru in, for example, the explicit definition of Gudea: 'Basalla mountain of Amurru' (ba_{11}-sal-la ḫur-sag Mar-tu),[12] or the explanation of ^{KUR}*Ba-šár* as ^{KUR}*A-mur-ri-i* in the *lipšur*-litanies.[13] The location of the battle in a mountainous region, outside urban and agricultural areas, and the identification of the Martu with nomads, which come out clearly in texts from the following period, make the episode appear to be a punitive expedition of the armies of Akkad against groups of nomads responsible for incursions and raids.

After these sporadic first references, which already contain precise information, the evidence becomes more continuous, more plentiful, and more differentiated under the Third Dynasty of Ur.[14] It consists mostly of references in administrative texts to individuals qualified as Martu, in the same manner and with the same implications as shown for the Old Akkadian period. The greater number and internal differentiation of the data enable us to reconstruct some of the characteristics of Amorite presence in various centres of the empire of Ur. A major part of the information comes from Drehem (Puzriš-Dagan), the large centre for collecting livestock, near Nippur, and one of the centres of economic administration of the empire of Ur. The Martu people appear in the Drehem texts principally as suppliers of sheep and goats. This fits in with their nomadic life as shepherds; the times for bringing in the supplies seem to point to a seasonal pattern, which could mean that their presence in the area was due to a practice of periodical transhumance.[15]

The evidence from other centres is less. In Isin the Martu people appear as buyers of leather goods; in Lagash they receive food rations, probably in exchange for what appears to be work done, and the same seems to be the case at Umma. In general terms it seems that in the more northerly locations (Drehem, Isin), which are those nearest to the place of origin of the Martu people, the latter appear in the sources as foreigners, whose contact with the Ur administration was a commercial one (sale of livestock, buying of manufactured products). On the other hand, in Sumer proper the Martu people appear as residents and dependants of the administration of Ur through the specific work they undertook. These are immigrants in process of assimilation into the local society, although they are still regarded as distinct from the rest of the population. The same difference can also be seen from the point of view of language, at least in so far as it is possible to judge on the basis of names. The Martu people from Drehem and Isin generally bear western-Semitic ('Amorite') names, while the Martu people from Lagash and Umma more often bear Sumerian and Akkadian names, that is, names customary in the area in which they have settled and where they work. It is obvious that small groups of immigrants, and, even more, individuals, tended inevitably to assimilate themselves to the local population through mixed marriage, by learning and using the local language,[16] and through the loss of old customs. Because of this the 'second generation' Martu people were soon well assimilated into the Sumero-Akkadian world which received them.

What opinion did the other inhabitants of Mesopotamia have of the Amorites? We are given a good idea of this by extracts from texts dating from the Ur III period, or the years immediately following, which give descriptions—even though stereotyped, and with a simple structure—of the Amorites. The most detailed and best known is that of the 'Myth of Martu', which gives a description of the god Martu,[17] who evidently represents the characteristics of the people of the same name: he is 'one who lives in a tent, exposed to wind and rain, who digs truffles at the foot of the mountain, who does not bend a knee, who eats raw foods, who has no home during his lifetime, and no tomb at his death'.[18]

Other texts confirm this picture, recording 'the Martu who does not know grain', 'the Martu who does not know houses, who does not know cities, the uncouth man who lives in the mountains, may he bring sheep and fat-tailed sheep', 'the Martu who has the impetus of the southerly wind and does not know cities', 'the Martu, people of raiders, with animal instincts, like wolves'.[19] The general picture is clear: a people living in the mountains, that is on the barren ground, far from the valleys with their irrigated agriculture; a people of nomadic shepherds, ignorant of the cultivation of land and of city life; a people culturally unsophisticated, who do not participate in any part of the characteristic life of the urban society of Mesopotamia.

The value of this evidence has often been partly misunderstood. It must be remembered that it is neither direct nor impartial testimony concerning the way of life and the technological and cultural baggage of the Amorites, but simply a vivid picture of how they were seen by the Mesopotamians. It is a picture subject to all the misunderstandings and generalizations that always go with general descriptions of 'the foreigner' in strongly ethnocentric civilizations. If some of the elements which form this picture come from direct experience ('the Martu who lives in a tent'), however drastically generalized ('who does not know grain'), other data derive only from prejudice or from ignorance ('who has no tomb', 'who eats raw foods').[20] The experience which the people of Mesopotamia had of the Amorites was somewhat distorted, because it was of Amorites who came to the towns in search of work, or of groups of raiders which interfered with the traffic of merchants and messengers when these had to leave the towns and valleys and cross the 'mountains'. But it is doubtful whether all the Amorites, taking into consideration also those still in their land of origin, Syria, would correspond to the 'type' described by the Mesopotamians, who had little knowledge of Syrian culture.

The problem of whether the Amorites were all nomads (and thus corresponded to the 'type' described by the Mesopotamians), or whether beyond the 'mountains' there were other Amorites living in cities, belonging to a political and social organization, and having the technology and economy which went with a city life not very different from or inferior to the Mesopotamian, can be investigated in two ways. An analysis of the archaeological data from Syria, that is from the land of origin of the Amorites, can give us a more balanced view of the cultural situation of Amurru than the repetitive and tendentious view given by the Sumerian literary texts. Further, a linguistic analysis of the Amorite onomastica can show whether this language was one of many coexisting languages and dialects used by people differing both in orgin and in their way of life, or whether it represented the entire western-Semitic language group during the period around the end of the third and the beginning of the second millennium. There is a tendency to think that the Amorites, being nomads and forming an ethnically compact population, could be opposed to another people, the Canaanites, who were sedentary and already present in Syria for some time when the Amorites arrived there about the year 2000 B.C. This theory of the arrival of nomadic Amorites in Syria and Mesopotamia from the Syrian desert *c.* 2000 B.C. is closely bound to the view that Semitic nomadism involved the displacement of large groups of people, as with Central Asian nomadism, and also to the opinion that the Semitic people spread from the desert in periodic large-scale waves.[21] Both opinions are hard to defend today, as it is now known that nomadism during the Bronze Age was more a pastoral transhumance over short distances by groups belonging to a 'dimorphic' society which was both agrarian and pastoral; the differentiation between the two components was purely technical and economic. The nomads and farmers formed together one ethnic unit.[22]

In coming to any linguistic investigation one must note that, until the middle of the second millennium, there is no trace of opposition between 'Amorite' and 'Canaanite' dialects, such as could point to a difference in origin or in time of arrival in the Syro-Palestinian region. Amorite is the only northwest-Semitic dialect attested between the years 2300 and 1600 B.C. It is in fact the name by which the northwest-Semitic language of that period is referred to today. There is no trace of 'Canaanite' before the middle of the second millennium; and, in addition, the characteristics which would oppose 'Canaanite' to 'Amorite' are innovations found in Canaanite, and are a development which occurred *in loco* near the middle of the second millennium. About this time the general unity of Amorite begins to break up into dialects in a more obvious manner, beginning a process which goes on into the first millennium, and leads to a distinction between the 'Aramaic' and 'Canaanite' dialects. There is certainly no justification for projecting such a situation back in time, thus making Amorite into a sort of 'proto-Aramaic', characteristic of the nomads and opposed to the 'Canaanite' characteristic of sedentary people.[23]

The general linguistic unity of the Semites in Syria during Amorite times is contrasted with the evidence of written as well as archaeological sources for the intermingling of an agricultural and urban civilization with the mode of life characterizing groups of nomads. The inscriptions of Sargon and Naram-Sin, as well as the administrative texts of the Third Dynasty of Ur, attest the presence in Syria of cities such as Ibla, Armanum, and Gubla, which were in commercial and political contact with the Mesopotamian empires, the latter sometimes exercising a certain control over them.[24] Archaeological excavations in the ʿAmuq, Hama, and now especially in Tell Mardikh, have confirmed the existence there of fully developed cities in the last centuries of the third millennium, similar to those more amply evidenced in Palestine. These cities of the final phase of the Early Bronze Age possess a rich culture, with marked Mesopotamian influence in the figurative arts, and a very well developed architecture in their palaces, temples, and fortifications. These same characteristics of urban development, agricultural economy, palace type of political organization, and commercial and diplomatic relations with Mesopotamian centres, are also found in the Syro-Palestinian culture of the Middle Bronze Age (first half of the second millennium). Reading texts from Mari and Alalakh VII we know this culture to have an ethnic basis which is mostly Amorite. A culture known as 'Intermediate Early Bronze–Middle Bronze' is chronologically situated in between these two urban cultures, and scholars (Kenyon in particular) tend to attribute it to nomadic populations.[25] This transition period with its nomadic character is placed about 2000 B.C. Comparison with Sumerian texts which describe the Amorites at that very time has led to the conclusion that this 'Intermediate' culture is the archaeological trace of the 'Amorites'. In fact, this theory should be received with scepticism. As has been shown, the pressure of the Amorites into Mesopotamia is attested from 2600 B.C. (Fara texts), and was already very strong during the dynasties of Akkad and Ur III; further, as will be shown, this pressure continues for a long time. Consequently, we note that the Amorite drive towards Mesopotamia is a phenomenon much older than the 'Intermediate' Syro-Palestinian culture. Moreover, the thoroughly nomadic character of the latter is to be rejected, particularly as regards Syria. If the abrupt change between the Early and Middle Bronze Ages implies some large socio-political upheaval, it is still impossible to establish a connection between the place and direction of origin of the innovatory elements in material culture and the place of origin of the presumed Amorites.[26] Although Kenyon's theory fitted well with the old idea of waves of invasions by Semitic peoples, and in particular with the arrival in Syria-Palestine of the Amorite nomads about 2000 B.C., it does not correspond any longer with the idea of the nomads as a social (rather than migratory) phenomenon in a 'dimorphic' society, and with the ethno-linguistic identity between the nomadic and sedentary peoples of Syria during the Bronze Age. Consequently we must give up the precise identification of the Amorites as carriers of this 'Intermediate' civilization. Instead, both this Intermediate period and the urban civilization at the end of the Early Bronze Age (and later the Middle Bronze Age) must be thought of as the environment in which the Amorites lived, partly as nomads and partly as citizens.

It is obvious that a marked difference exists between the abundant and direct evidence for the pressure exerted by the nomadic Amorites on the Mesopotamian city-states, and the circumstantial and scarce evidence for the sedentary Amorites of Syria. This divergence is caused by the type of evidence, which is Mesopotamian in origin, and cannot be transferred on the historical plane. Although the phenomenon most apparent in our sources for the period around 2000 B.C. is the movement of nomadic peoples towards the valley of the Tigris and the Euphrates, the centre of the Amorite world remained in Syria. Explicit evidence for sedentary Amorites in Syrian localities is not lacking: we have, for example, the 'two Amorites of Nihriya' in a text from Cappadocia, or the merchants of Ibla paying with 'Amorite silver'.[27]

The drive towards Mesopotamia came to a violent climax *c.* 2000 B.C., during the last years of the Third Dynasty of Ur. There had been warnings, as such incursions had taken place since the time of Šar-kali-šarri. There are many lists of loot taken by kings of Ur from the Amorites[28] which point to battles and military expeditions. One of these is recorded in an inscription of Šu-Sin (2037–2029 B.C.)[29] which is detailed and explicit. The military activities of the kings of Ur against the Amorites seem to have been their response to continuous attacks by the latter. The situation, however, must have been very serious, since the kings of Ur took the trouble to build a great line of fortifications joining the Tigris to the Euphrates, and so protecting the cities of Akkad and Sumer from any Amorite attacks from the north.[30] The building had already been begun in the reign of Šulgi (2094–2047). As is known from letters (or rather copies of them) exchanged between the king and his officials, the defence wall was completed in the fourth year of Šu-Sin, a year known by the name: 'Year in which Šu-Sin, King of Ur, built the Amorite wall [known as] "the one which keeps away Did(a)num"'. Another letter from an official to the king gives more information, in particular the length of the wall, which was 280 km. long.

The wall was effective in checking and controlling the entry of Amorites into Mesopotamia so long as the organization of the Ur empire was able to devote sufficient attention to it and to provide military personnel to man the fortifications. But during the reign of the last King of Ur, Ibbi-Sin (2028–2004 B.C.), the empire was shaken by a major crisis. It is difficult to ascertain the origin of this crisis, which was to have considerable effects. The empire's provincial centres had already ceased to depend entirely on the central administration, and to send in their dues, in the first years of Ibbi-Sin. A serious agricultural crisis and the inability to obtain provisions from the north caused an alarming increase in the prices of staple commodities in the capital—grain prices increased sixty-fold, fish fifty-, and oil six-fold.[31] The overrunning of the fortifications by the Amorites is part of this general picture, as is their subsequent spreading into the country, which was now defenceless and lacking resources.[32] The economic crisis and the Amorite invasion caused political division, since each city was working for its own defence and its own supplies, none of which was any longer forthcoming from the capital. An official of Ibbi-Sin, Išbi-Erra, declared himself independent at Isin, and Naplānum, an Amorite, seized power at Larsa. Towns on the periphery of the empire, such as Susa, Mari, and Eshnunna, became autonomous. Ur was thus left with very limited territory to control, until it fell under fierce attack by the Elamites and was destroyed in a manner which made a strong impression on the world of the time.[33] The Amorites played an important part in this break-up and in the introduction of a new political order.[34] In some instances we find them acting in groups, even if the definition 'the Amorites' may simply allude to a small group (or a tribe) or an informal group (such as a mercenary army), and not necessarily to a political entity acting in coherent unity. Ibbi-Sin himself calls on the help of the Amorites against his new enemy, Išbi-Erra.[35] The same Išbi-Erra proclaims the destruction of an Amorite city in a date formula.[36] The first kings of Eshnunna record in their year-date formulae various episodes in their relations with the Amorites: 'year in which Martu struck the land of Ibbi-Sin', 'year in which Martu pillaged Išur', 'year in which Martu struck Bab-Iba'um', 'year in which Martu entrusted the power over Išur to Bilalama', 'year in which Bilalama, the *iššakku* of Eshnunna, struck Martu on the head', 'year in which Martu submitted himself'.[37] These are all only echoes of the military and predatory activities of the Amorites in the vacuum of political power which followed their breaking through the fortified line. However, the force, lacking central direction, was used by the different kings for their own varied ends, and so finally spent itself.

At the same time, individual Amorites attain high positions, and even royal power. These are identified individually as Amorites by their personal names. The phenomenon does not happen all at once on a large scale, but the repetition of single occurrences becomes gradually more and more marked. The first known instance is that of Naplānum at Larsa, followed by others in Babylon (Sumu-abum, Sumu-la-El), Marad (Yamsi-El, Sumu-Numhim), Sippar (Bunu-tahtun-Iia, Mana-balti-El), and Kish (Abdi-Erah, Sumu-ditana, Yawium), at Mari (Yaggid-Lim, Yahdun-Lim), and elsewhere.[38] It is doubtful if this phenomenon was linked with the invasion of the Amorites in the reign of Ibbi-Sin and with their subsequent war activities; doubtful too if these Amorites reached power as a result of military and political action by their tribe. They seem rather to be isolated personal cases, these people having achieved power from within. It is obvious, however, that their position as immigrants, and their belonging to a warlike and turbulent people united in family and tribal life, assisted their seizure of power. The Sumerian and Akkadian population seems meanwhile to have remained passive because of the breakdown of authority which followed the fall of Ur. The Amorites, then, had greater political initiative, diligence, and readiness to take in hand a situation when there was breakdown and crisis. The increased political influence of the Amorites can be seen even at royal level, since kings now bore such titles as ad-da kur mar-tu, 'father of Amurru', and ad-da e-mu-ut-ba-la, 'father of Yamut-bal' (an Amorite tribe), both borne by Kudur-Mabuk of Larsa; it is also seen in the title lugal mar-tu, 'King of Amurru', used by Hammurabi of Babylonia.[39] Sometimes the Amorite element is joined with the Sumero-Akkadian urban element to denote all the king's subjects, as when Sin-kašid calls himself by the title of 'King of Uruk, King of Amnanūm' (an Amorite tribe),[40] or when an official from Mari writes to his king, 'If you are King of the Haneans (another Amorite tribe) you are also King of the Akkadians'.[41] This seems to be carried out more systematically in Syria, judging by the following list of adversaries of Yahdun-Lim: 'La'um King of Samanum and of the land of the Ubrabūm, Bahlukulim King of Tuttul and of the land of the Amnanūm, Ayalum King of Abattum and of the land of the Rabbūm'.[42]

From now on, after centuries of slow infiltration, and after the violent invasion during the fifth year of Ibbi-Sin and the further gradual infiltration which followed, the Amorites became a numerically conspicuous element in the Mesopotamian population. This was particularly so in the more exposed areas, such as the Middle Euphrates valley, Assyria, and the Diyala basin, but even the heart of Mesopotamia—the land of Sumer and Akkad—was very noticeably affected by the immigration. On the whole it is more difficult to follow this now than during the Ur III period, because, after the reigns of Išbi-Erra and his successor, the administrative texts cease to define the Amorite immigrants as 'Martu'. This is certainly a sign that less attention was now paid by the palace administration to a characteristic which was no longer unusual. It shows too that in Mesopotamia the Amorites were customarily looked upon with greater indifference. It is only possible to trace the diffusion of proper names which are linguistically Amorite. This source of information naturally tends to make less of the position, because of the tendency towards assimilation of the Amorites in the Sumero-Akkadian society, as seen already at the time of Ur III. Then, as during the Old Babylonian period, many Amorites and sons of Amorites are disguised under Akkadian names assumed in their new place of residence.[43]

It has even been doubted whether the persons qualified as Martu in the Ur III texts belonged to the same ethnic group as those who bore Amorite (western Semitic) names in the Old Babylonian texts.[44] There is no longer any doubt as to that identity, because an analysis of proper names of the Martu has revealed a strong affinity with western names of the Old Babylonian period,[45] and also because a long Old-Babylonian-period list of Martu contains exclusively west-Semitic names.[46] It is certain that the qualification 'Amorite' must have become too general and consequently of little use. More particular qualifications are more frequently found, which enable something more to be seen of the inner organization of the great Amorite group. These are tribal qualifications, such as Haneans (*Ḫa-na*), Benjaminites (DUMU *Ya-mi-na*), and Suteans (*Su-ti-um*, *Su-tu-u*), and lesser groups—the Amnanū, Rabbū, Ya'ilanū, DUMU Sim'al, Yahrurū, and others.[47] In a world which is by now generally Amorite these are the most significant designations. It is understandable that such specifications should be more frequent in the Mari texts, as this city was in closer contact with these tribes, because of its geographical location where the Euphrates and its tributaries adjoin the area in which the nomad tribes led their lives as shepherds and raiders.

The Mari texts enable us for the first time to observe the western nomads, that is the various tribes of Amorite origin, in their actual environment, and not only at the time of their disintegration after contact with the cities. What was only barely glimpsed before is now clearly attested. Their livelihood was based on the breeding of small livestock (sheep and goats), while the camel was not yet bred (at least not on a large scale), and the donkey was used as beast of burden.[48] The nomadism itself was very dependent on places where there was water and pasture, and undertaken in regions near cultivated land. The nomads, too, had limited agricultural experience; they sometimes sowed and reaped, stopping for this in one place for the necessary time, or leaving part of the group behind to complete the work. It is not surprising that their settlements took the form of villages, which, although small in size and modestly built, testify to a certain stability.[49] The various groups had an internal organization built on kinship, which grouped families into clans, tribes, and tribal confederations.[50] The elders maintained the traditions and were called on to pass judgement or give directives on behaviour for the whole group.[51] There are also references to chiefs in a privileged position which was probably held only occasionally. They are referred to as 'kings', which is certainly an improper extension of a terminology otherwise typical of sedentary groups.

Relations with city kingdoms show us different aspects which partially repeat, and so clarify, observations already made of the Third Dynasty of Ur. On one hand there is the constant threat by the nomads to communications between towns, and their persistent aim to appropriate agricultural lands better provided with water and pasture than their own arid steppe land. On the other there is the continuous flow of nomads into the cities in search of work. This mostly consisted of service in the army as mercenaries, though there was also some work under the palace administration or in agriculture. Finally, there is an attempt by the palace administration to make use of the tribe and to oppress it through military call-up, forced labour, and taxation.

The Mari texts are a good source for observing the nomads throughout northern Mesopotamia. They also provide direct and abundant information about city kingdoms of Amorite ethnic origin in Syria. In this way the Amorites' two different ways of life become apparent: as nomads and shepherds, where this is dictated by natural conditions, and as citizens and peasants, where agricultural activity is possible. So we learn of the great centres of Carchemish, Aleppo (Yamhad), Qatna, Alalakh, and Hazor, all fully integrated into the political and commercial world of the time, and participants, together with the Mesopotamian centres, in a common homogeneous culture, though with local variants.[52] This is not the place for a study of the history of the particular Amorite kingdoms in Syria, but it is important to remember their 'dimorphic' type of existence to avoid adopting the simplistic view that all Amorites were nomads. A city official in Aleppo could have been as much an Amorite as a shepherd from the Habur valley or from the Tadmor steppe.

We have now reached a watershed in our account of the history of the Amorites. We can still call them Amorites, inasmuch as they carry names substantially the same as those of the Martu of earlier times. They are the heirs of earlier ways of life and continue the historical process set in motion by the Martu. Yet they are no longer very conscious of belonging to a unique *ethnos*. Instead, it is the sense of belonging to a specific tribe or city which is what really counts. In Mesopotamia itself, as has been seen already, the word 'Amorite' is used less and less, though increasingly it has secondary uses. Thus, for example, the Babylonian titles of *wākil Amurrî*, 'overseer of the Amorites', *rab Amurrî*, 'chief of the Amorites', *tupšar Amurrî*, 'scribe of the Amorites',[53] found in the administrative, and especially the military, hierarchy of the kings of Babylon and Mari, presuppose a use of the word 'Amorite' to indicate mercenaries, or at least a situation in which the Amorites (but not only the Amorites) were at the service of the city-state. This is also found at Susa, which is on the extreme eastern periphery of Amorite presence. Two documents concerning the allotment of land to 'shepherds, soldiers, Amorites'[54] show how far the use of the word has deviated from its original ethnic sense to a new functional significance. These documents are dated towards the end of the Old Babylonian period. However, at the same time, a well-known text of Ammi-ṣaduqa, King of Babylon (1646–1626 B.C.), an edict for the restoration of justice, shows that the word is still in use in its ethnic meaning. In this edict 'Amorite' is used in opposition to 'Akkadian', to indicate the western-Semitic element which coexisted with the Mesopotamian part of the population, thus showing the numerical importance of the Amorites after the centuries of infiltration and invasions, and their complete assimilation into Babylonian society, in which they were by now considered the equal of the local inhabitants.[55]

The opposition of Akkadians to Amorites which is so explicit in the text of Ammi-ṣaduqa is also the last reference to the Amorites as an individual ethnic group. The significance of the term changes during the middle of the second millennium, partly because of the historical circumstances, and partly because our evidence now comes from the west, the land of Amurru itself. The Amorite infiltration into Mesopotamia ceased gradually, and the earlier immigrants were absorbed into the more numerous and more technically experienced Akkadian population. The thrust of western nomads does not, however, cease entirely—it was in fact a constant aspect of Mesopotamian history, connected with factors of geography and economy—but is known under other names, some used before and probably representing a part of the Amorite group, but which now became more individualized. The nomads are now known as Ahlamu in upper Mesopotamia, as Suteans in Syria, and the whole question of contact between nomads and sedentary groups is raised again; the same characteristics are involved, though the name changes.

In Syria itself, as local evidence becomes more abundant, the term 'Amurru' is seen to be used in further different ways. It is certain that, as now used there, it cannot stand for the west in general or all the west-Semitic peoples; for this was the Mesopotamian point of view. What emerges progressively is the use of the designation 'Amurru' for a specific region within Syria. This sense of the word is already found in the Mari texts, where it was evidently derived from Syria. In one text the 'messengers of the four Amorite kings' are associated with the messengers of Hazor; in another we find the geographical sequence 'land of Yamhad, land of Qatna, and land of Amurru'.[56] Amurru is consequently an area (not unified politically) of southern Syria. The seventeenth-century texts of Alalakh allude to Amurru as a particular region, situated most probably in central or southern Syria.[57] The term is still somewhat vague, and though it seems to refer to a specific region it does not designate a political entity.

Later on, at the end of the fifteenth century, this same region took on a definite political shape, with the beginning of the kingdom of Amurru under Abdi-Aširta and his descendants.[58] This kingdom was at first mostly in the mountains—northern Lebanon and southern Jebel Ansariyya, between the valleys of the rivers Orontes and Litani on one side and the coastal strip on the other—that is to say, a mountain region, surrounded by intensely urbanized and cultivated areas. The original population of Abdi-Aširta's kingdom must have been sparse, given to tending sheep on the mountain pastures, and isolated from the more lively agricultural and urban economy, as well as from the social and political contacts which characterized the neighbouring kingdoms. The pastoral character of the people and the isolation of the region that now became the kingdom of Amurru are elements which favour the connection between this use of the term 'Amurru' and the former one. The link can be seen in that the population of the Lebanon range was the direct heir of the Amorite tribes, not having taken part in the historical evolution of the town areas. Or, more simply, the term 'Amurru', previously used of Syria in its entirety, was now free to be used to designate the mountainous part of the interior after the other parts had assumed specific names, just as they assumed a specific political order, namely as kingdoms (Mukiš, Niya, etc.), as confederations of small kingdoms (Nuhašše), or as Egyptian 'provinces' (Kinahni, Ube). Consequently the term was adopted by the most recently formed state, which held less attachment than the others to any specific urban centre. During the Amarna period the state of Amurru is carrying on political activity of distinctive character. Abdi-Aširta was more a local leader than an actual king; he did not reside in a 'palace' or in a fixed capital; at his death the power passed collectively to his sons, and not, as was usual, to a designated heir. Only later did Aziru attain such power as to be virtually the only king of Amurru and to have his title recognized. Some of his brothers, however, continued to play a considerable role. The geographical and demographical conformation of the land of Amurru, with its forests and pastures and a sparse and mobile population, lent itself ideally to the reception of exiles in great numbers. These (called *ḫabiru* in the terminology of the time) had abandoned their lands for economic or political reasons (being mostly debtors threatened with imprisonment) and were in search of a place of refuge away from the control of the city-states.[59] Abdi-Aširta and Aziru enlisted large numbers of these exiles during their wars of expansion against the coastal states (especially Byblos), and also against the inland cities of Tunip and Niya. That this struggle was one of social vindication is clear from some passages of the political propaganda aimed by Abdi-Aširta at the peasants of the region he was claiming ('Kill your masters and become like us: then you will have peace'), as well as at his army of exiles ('Unite yourselves and let us fall on Byblos. No one will save her from our hands. We will drive out the governors from the land, and all the lands will go over to the exiles').[60]

This 'heroic' phase in the formation of the kingdom of Amurru was followed, after the death of Abdi-Aširta and the seizure of power by Aziru, by a more normal integration into international politics. This took place during the troubled Amarna period, when Amurru was in the difficult position of buffer state between regions dominated by Egyptian and Hittite influence.[61] Initially Amurru was under Egyptian control, and Aziru's ambition was to see his position recognized officially by the Egyptian court. However, with the appearance of Šuppiluliuma on the political scene, the King of Amurru saw his chance of leading a life politically independent of the Egyptians, with the support of the Hittites. His reckoning proved faulty, for the Hittite power became so strong that Aziru had to recognize the sovereignty of Šuppiluliuma, who imposed a vassal treaty upon him, and whose yoke resulted in a stricter and more stringent rule than that of the Egyptians.

A few remarks will suffice regarding the history of the kingdom of Amurru. Under Aziru it grew to include such cities as Tunip and Sumura. It remained under firm Hittite domination, and was governed by the descendants of Abdi-Aširta until the end of the thirteenth century. The names of the successive kings are known (Ir-Tešub, Duppi-Tešub, Bentešina, Šapili, Bentešina once again, then Šaušgamuwa). The mode of their dependence on the Hittites is known from the treaties imposed on them (apart from that of Šuppiluliuma) by Muršili II, Hattušili III, and Tudhaliya IV.[62] We know something too of the relations of Amurru with its richer, though weaker, northern neighbour Ugarit, on the political, commercial, and family (matrimonial) level.[63]

But all this refers to a state which was only one among many then in Syria. Although it bore the name of 'Amurru', it was not particularly different from its neighbours. In addition to this limited sense in which 'Amurru' was used it also seems to have retained its larger sense as a designation of Syria in its entirety. It is sometimes difficult to distinguish between these two uses in the instances where materials and other products are defined as 'Amorite' in Egyptian, Hittite, and Ugaritic texts.[64] There is similar uncertainty in the case of the 'Amorite donkeys' of some Middle Babylonian documents,[65] or in the matter of the loot said to have been taken in Amurru by Tukulti-Ninurta I.[66]

(ii) *Geographical Factors*

The great invasions and the social and political crisis which occurred in Syria about 1200 B.C. put an end to the existence of Amurru as a separate state,[67] and interrupted all documentation of Syrian origin. However, when Tiglath-pileser I made an expedition *c.* 1100 B.C. to the Mediterranean to get cedar logs, the name 'Amurru' was still applied to the region of Arwad and Sumura, that is, to the area which had seen the development of the kingdom of Amurru:

> Having reached mount Lebanon, I cut and took away cedar logs for the temples of Anu and Adad, the great gods, my lords. I went back to Amurru and conquered it in its entirety. I received tribute from Byblos, Sidon, and Arwad. I left on ships of Arwad of the land of Amurru and crossed from Arwad, which is in the middle of the ocean, to Sumura which is in the land of Amurru—a journey of three double hours by land.[68]

It is remarkable that the area specifically referred to as Amurru lies opposite the northern part of inner Syria known as Hatti: 'During the return journey I took into my possession the land of Hatti in its entirety; I imposed tribute and [the payment of] cedar on Ini-Tešub King of greater Hatti [i.e. Carchemish].'[69] The situation seems to be a direct continuation of what it had been during the fourteenth and thirteenth centuries. Amurru is the coastal zone north of Byblos, with the mountains behind the coast; Hatti was the area which had been directly controlled by the Hittites during the time of their empire (Carchemish and Mukish), and was still in the hands of dynasties of Hittite origin (Carchemish and Hattina).

There is a long break in Mesopotamian documentation concerning Syria, and when reports start again with Ashur-naṣir-apli II (883–859 B.C.), the memory of the situation before 1200 B.C. has not yet entirely been lost. A passage in his annals seems to give a restricted sense to Amurru, which it locates between Byblos and Arwad, even though the more general use of the term to designate Syria is found in the very same passage: 'I went up to the land of Amurru. I washed my weapons in the Great Sea, and I made offerings to the gods. I received tribute from the kings of the coast-lands, from Tyre, Sidon, Byblos, Mahallata, Maiṣa, Kaiṣa, Amurru, and Arwad which is in the middle of the sea. I received silver, gold, tin, bronze . . . in tribute from them.'[70] However, in the inscriptions of Ashur-naṣir-apli II and Shalmaneser III (ninth century), and later in those of Adad-nirari III, Sargon II, and Sennacherib (eighth century), the name 'Amurru' is generally used to designate the entire area of Syria-Palestine. It describes a geographically and politically composite entity, as is shown by the expressions 'the kings of the land of Amurru, all of them', 'Amurru in its entirety', 'the large land of Amurru'. When the term is clarified by more detailed lists of localities, these all fall within the region from the Euphrates to the borders of Egypt. Thus in a text of Shalmaneser III the kings of Hattina, Carchemish, Sam'al, Bīt-Agusi, and Kummuh (that is, the neo-Hittite and Aramaean kings of northern Syria) are referred to as being 'kings of Amurru'.[71] In a text of Sennacherib, however, it is the Phoenician kings of Sidon, Arwad, and Byblos, the Philistine kings of Ashdod and Ashkelon, and the Transjordanian kings of Beth-Ammon, Moab, and Edom, who are known as 'kings of Amurru'.[72] Finally, Sargon II mentions 'Damascus of the land of Amurru' and 'Hatti of the land of Amurru',[73] showing that then the term 'Hatti' was thought of as more restricted. Sennacherib tells us something about the language of Amurru: 'I built a portico, made like a Hittite palace, which in the language of Amurru they call *bīt-ḫilāni*.'[74] In modern terminology one would say 'a north-Syrian palace' and 'in the northwest-Semitic language'.[75]

The last Assyrian kings make little use of the term 'Amurru', and then almost only in stereotyped expressions which have little meaning from the geopolitical point of view. Esarhaddon calls himself 'King of Subartu, Amurru, Gutium, the great land of Hatti . . . King of the kings of Dilmun, Magan, Meluhha, King of the four parts of the world',[76] and Ashurbanipal says that Šamaš-šum-ukin of Babylon allied himself with 'the kings of Gutium, Amurru, Meluhha'.[77] Not only Amurru, but also Gutium, Magan, and Meluhha are terms which had had a precise meaning in the past, but which were now used to indicate in a completely abstract manner 'a part of the world', or to designate in an archaic manner new political entities. In this way 'Gutium' will refer to the Medes, and 'Meluha' to Egypt.

It was the astrologers and the interpreters of omens who kept these archaic terms alive and suggested their reinterpretation and identification with existing political entities. As they naturally used a very archaic and abstract cosmo-geographical terminology, which they found in their canonical 'series' of texts (which came from an old tradition), they had to translate these into 'modern' terms in order to apply the omens to their own time and permit the king to make current use of them. In some cases the 'translation' of the archaic term into a modern one is easy and explicit (with annotations such as 'the Umman-Manda are the Cimmerians'); in other cases it was more difficult. This applies to Amurru, which was often mentioned in astrological reports, because, being one of the four parts of the world,[78] it always appeared whenever some phenomenon indicated the west. It is for this reason that reports made to Esarhaddon and to Ashurbanipal are full of indications concerning the fate and behaviour of a 'king of Amurru', whose identity is not clear:

'When Mars in his journey from the head of the Lion passes over Cancer and Gemini, this is what it means: end of the reign of the King of Amurru.'[79]

'When the planet Mars approaches Perseus, there will be a rebellion in Amurru, brother will kill brother.'[80]

'When the moon appears, and its left side is dark in the sky, there will be a good market in the country, there will be a rebellion in Amurru . . . when the moon appears her right side is Amurru.'[81]

'When the moon appears on the 30th day of Sivan, Ahlamu will devour the abundance of Amurru. The month of Sivan is Amurru, [consequently] it is bad for Amurru.'[82]

'The moon eclipse which has taken place concerned the [foreign] lands. All its evil is accumulated against Amurru. Amurru is Hatti, or Chaldea.'[83]

'This eclipse of the moon which took place in the month of Kanunu concerns Amurru. The King of Amurru will die, his land will decrease or fall to ruins. In regard to Amurru, the experts will tell the King my lord that Amurru is Hatti or Sutu or else Chaldea; one of the kings of Hatti or Chaldea or of the Arabs will bear [the consequence of] this omen. . . . The King of Ethiopia, or the King of Tyre or Mugallu will die a natural death, or will be taken a prisoner by the King my lord.'[84]

If sometimes the omen was left undetermined, at other times the interpreters tried to give a 'translation' which was politically up to date. The obvious identification with Syria (Hatti) is satisfactory only in certain instances, because Syria as part of the Assyrian kingdom does not have a 'king' or a political fate different from that of Assyria. Therefore the preferred identification of Amurru was with nomads originating in the west, that is the Aramaeans (Sutu), the Chaldeans (even though these are in the south), and the Arabs. Historically these are shrewd identifications, as they show a typological connection between the Amorites of antiquity and the people now going through a similar historical process.

This progressive reduction of 'Amurru' to an archaic term, used in a cryptic terminology to designate a cosmic rather than a geographical entity (a quarter of the world), is necessarily accompanied by the appearance of another term to indicate Syria as a whole. This term is 'Hatti', which in the inscriptions of the last Assyrian kings and in the later neo-Babylonian inscriptions (eighth–sixth centuries) lost its specific connection with neo-Hittite northern Syria, and was used for the whole territory from the Euphrates to the Egyptian frontier. An inscription of Nebuchadrezzar says 'The governors of the land of Hatti, beyond the Euphrates, towards the setting sun . . . brought large cedar logs from mount Lebanon to my city Babylon.'[85] In the inscriptions of Nabonidus 'Hatti' refers to practically the whole western half of the empire, as opposed to 'Akkad', which is the eastern half, that is Mesopotamia. He wrote 'Shamash made the people of Akkad and Hatti faithful to me in word and heart. . . . I gathered the peoples of Akkad and Hatti whom Sin king of gods had entrusted to me from the frontiers of Egypt on the Upper Sea (Mediterranean) and to the Lower Sea.'[86] Still more clearly, the term 'Hatti' is used repeatedly in a chronicle of the Persian period to indicate the Syro-Palestinian region. It is a vast and mixed region ('Hatti in its entirety', 'the kings of the land of Hatti'), which extended from Carchemish to the Egyptian border, including Hama, Ashkelon, and Jerusalem, and was bordered by the desert inhabited by the Arabs.[87] In the middle of the first millennium 'Amurru' was completely supplanted by the term 'Hatti' to designate Syria-Palestine. The reference in an inscription of Cyrus (539–530 B.C.) to 'the kings of Amurru who live in tents'[88] is perhaps only a learned reminiscence. The intention was probably to allude to the new nomadic peoples from the west, the Arabs, according to the exegesis used in the interpretation of omens. It is significant that Mesopotamian documents ended with an indication similar to the ones with which they had begun:[89] the nomads came from the west, their ways and their technical assets differing from those of the sedentary peoples.

(iii) *Old Testament References*

After this historical examination of extra-biblical sources we can examine the references to Amorites in the Old Testament on a firmer basis. Two of the four significances of the term 'Amurru' cannot be applied to biblical passages: the original one of the Amorites as a Semitic people of the north-west in the years between the third and second millennium B.C., with a sedentary part in Syria and a semi-nomadic part pushing towards Mesopotamia, is obviously too distant chronologically from the biblical texts, which are about a millennium later. The connection is similar to that between the Romans and the Rumanians mentioned earlier, etymological but historically altered. The significance of 'Amurru' as 'west' is also out of the question, because it is only relevant from one point of view, the Mesopotamian point of view, certainly not the Palestinian one, Palestine having the sea to its west. The other two significances (Amurru as a state and later as a specific region of Syria, north of Byblos; Amurru as a general designation of Syria and Palestine) are, on the contrary, reasonably comparable with the biblical use, and can contribute to clarify the exact significance.

Amurru as a specific zone north of Byblos could still be the Amurru used in early biblical texts, since this significance, in full vogue in the fourteenth and thirteenth centuries (when there was a political entity corresponding to the name), was still used by Tiglath-pileser I (*c.* 1100), and even occasionally during the time of Ashur-naṣir-apli II (*c.* 850), after which it fell out of use completely, and for ever. In terms of Israelite history, this is the prevailing significance at the time of the conquest of the 'promised land'. The definition of the border of Canaan given in Joshua 13: 4–5 ('All the land of Canaan, from Ara of the Sidonians to Afqa [Aphek], [that is] to the Amorite border, and the land of Byblos with Lebanon to the east, from Baal-Gad at the foot of the Hermon to Lebo'-Hamath')[90] keeps the exact memory of the situation during the fourteenth and thirteenth centuries, that is, of the period to which the passage refers. Amurru is the region north of Afqa (namely north of the Nahr el-Kelb), south of which are the kingdom of Byblos and the land of Canaan; the eastern extremity of the border is also correct: Lebo'-Hamath is a locality in a wooded area which acts as a border between the Beqa and the zone of Kadesh on the Orontes.[91] This line from Afqa to Lebo'-Hamath is the frontier between the Egyptian province of Canaan (*Pꜣ Knʿn*) and the kingdom of Amurru, a vassal of the Hittites. It had been an essential frontier between two worlds opposed to each other politically from the campaigns of Šuppiluliuma (*c.* 1370) till the invasion of the Sea Peoples (*c.* 1190).

The passage of Joshua now being examined is the only one in which the term 'Amorite' alludes to the region of Amurru (in its strict sense), which was so active during the Late Bronze Age. In all the other passages the term is used either very generally or with reference to specific zones which were not connected with the name 'Amurru' in the extra-biblical sources. The numerous references contained in stereotyped lists of the pre-Israelite populations of Palestine are obviously vague: 'the Amorite' always appears in them (even if in different positions) because of its notoriety in comparison with other, less well-known terms. No specific information is to be found in these lists, which, on the contrary, show substantial ignorance of the ethnic and political situation in pre-Israelite Palestine. Also, the systematized genealogy attempted in the 'Table of the Nations', in which the Amorite is one of the sons of Canaan (Gen. 10: 16), is clearly artificial, creating a symbolic explanation of historical relations. Other references to the Amorite as the only representative of pre-Israelite populations in Palestine are equally very general, as in Deuteronomy 1: 44 ('The Amorite who inhabits these mountains . . . has come out . . . and defeated you in Seir'), Genesis 48: 22 ('Shechem . . . which I took from the Amorites'), and Joshua 10: 5 ('five Amorite kings, the kings of Jerusalem, Hebron, Jarmuth, Lachish, and Eglon, united and left on an expedition'). These may be considered to be the most correct references, those which best reflect the real sense of the word. It might appear at first that there are other references more specific, alluding, as they do, to Amorite areas with particular ecological or topographical characteristics. Of this type is the connection of the Amorites with mountains which one finds in Judges 1: 34 and in Joshua 11: 3, and which is very clearly expressed in Numbers 13: 29: 'the Amalekite occupies the Negev, the Hittite, the Amorite, and the Jebusite occupy the mountain, the Canaanite occupies the edge of the sea and the banks of the river Jordan.' Of the same kind also is the localization of the Amorites in Transjordania, and in particular the definition of two Transjordanian kings Og and Sihon as Amorites, repeated over and over in biblical texts, and thus acquiring a prominence which is not in proportion to the tradition from which it was derived. All of these cases are deceptively specific, because they seem to preserve memories of actual Amorite settlements. In fact, we think that the occurrences of the word 'Amorite' should be analysed in conjunction with the use of the other terms, and in particular the term 'Canaanite'. The problem can be worded as follows: Why did the author of a certain passage use the term 'Amorite' instead of the word 'Canaanite' (this being the principal alternative)? Considered this way, the problem allows of reasonably satisfactory answers. A first solution is that the use of one term rather than the other is due to the preference of the author or of the tradition on which he depends. It is generally assumed that the use of 'Amorite' was preferred by the Elohist tradition and the word 'Canaanite' by the Yahwist tradition.[92] Even though it is reasonable to doubt that the correlation applies exactly in all cases, it is also reasonable to accept the more general value of this now time-honoured observation: the implication of this is that in a text as composite as the Old Testament the choice between functionally equivalent terms can correspond to elements of tradition and of style. A second explanation is that the term 'Amorite' was applied preferably to geographical entities which the term 'Canaanite' did not fit. This is evidently the case with Transjordania, because the border of Canaan continues that of the homonymous Egyptian 'province' of the fourteenth–thirteenth centuries, which did not extend further than the river Jordan (except perhaps the Bashan zone), and corresponds to the area occupied by sedentary inhabitants during the Late Bronze Age.[93] So the term 'Canaanite' is reserved for the Jordanian and coastal zone, and the term 'Amorite' is the only one available to indicate in a general way the pre-Israelite population of Transjordan; in other words, it is specific only in appearance.[94] In a similar way we can explain the connection of the 'Amorites' with mountains; since the pattern of settlement characteristic of the Late Bronze Age consisted in the concentration of population in the valleys and on the coast,[95] the 'Canaanite' cities were generally situated in those regions and not in the mountains. These, on the other hand, had a more scattered pastoral population, more directly heir to the ancient 'Amorite' people. It is interesting to note that even the kingdom of Amurru of the fourteenth and thirteenth centuries was distinct from the Canaanite kingdoms of the valleys and the coast, as it was mountainous, pastoral, and not urban. It is difficult to be more precise, but it is tempting to establish a historical constant stemming from the Sumerian texts, in which the Martu lived 'on the mountain' (outside agricultural Mesopotamia), through the Late Bronze situation, with the kingdom of Amurru mountainous in character, down to the situation outlined in Numbers 13: 29.

Further precision seems impossible without resorting to hypothesis or conjecture. If the use in the Old Testament of the term 'Amorite' remains in most cases vague, this is the result not only of our lack of knowledge but mostly of the fact that during the time when it was used by biblical authors the term itself was vague and shifting. One characteristic point should be stressed, as it places the Amorites in their correct position, and is valid for all the Old Testament references to the term. Whenever the Old Testament refers to the Amorites, the reference is always to the past; the present knows Philistines and Aramaeans, Moabites and Edomites, Sidonians, Assyrians, and Egyptians, but does not know Amorites, who did not correspond to any historical reality at the time when the text was composed. The Amorites are situated in the age of the conquest or before, the age that can be defined as the mythical era of the origins of Israel (mythical in a phenomenological sense, just as origins are always mythical). Israel did not know the Amorites in actual history—it did not know any ethno-political entity identifiable with the 'Amorites'—but projected them into the past, making of them an integral element of Palestine at the time of the conquest, namely at the time when the history of Israel can be said to begin, and making them an element which was brushed away by the conquest, at the start of 'history'.

NOTES

1. Gen. 15: 19–20. There are also other lists, briefer and with a different order; cf. F. Böhl, *Kanaanäer und Hebräer* (Leipzig, 1911), pp. 63 f.

2. Sumerian kur mar-tu as a region and lú mar-tu as an ethnic appellative; Akkadian *amurru(m)* as region and *Amurrû* (fem. *Amurrîtu*) as ethnic appellative.

3. Cited in the relevant lexical lists in *C.A.D.* i, 92–4. For a recently proposed etymology see G. Buccellati, *The Amorites of the Ur III Period* (Naples, 1966), pp. 133–4.

4. V. Scheil, *Textes élamites–sémitiques* (*M.D.P.* ii, Paris, 1900), 12 (A ix 16), 20 (B vi 16), 29 (C xiii 23), 36 (D ix 5). For a full bibliography see H. Hirsch, 'Die Inschriften der Könige von Agade', *A.f.O.* xx (1963), 14–15, n. 147.

5. Cf. F. R. Kraus, 'Provinzen des neusumerischen Reiches von Ur', *Z.A.* li (1955), 46 (l. 12), 52.

6. The conception of the world as made up of four regions orientated to the cardinal points was considered in various ways according to the period; cf. in general K. Tallquist, 'Himmelsgegenden und Winde', *Stud. Or.* ii (1928), 105–85; P. Neugebauer & E. F. Weidner, 'Die Himmelsrichtungen bei den Babyloniern', *A.f.O.* vii (1931–2), 269–71. Already in the epic of Enmerkar (S. N. Kramer, *Enmerkar and the Lord of Aratta* (Philadelphia, 1952), ll. 141–6; cf. D. O. Edzard, *Die 'zweite Zwischenzeit' Babyloniens* (Wiesbaden, 1956), p. 31) the sequence Subartu—Sumer—Akkad—Martu is found, and in the 'Curse of Akkad' (A. Falkenstein, 'Fluch über Akkade', *Z.A.* lviii (1965), 52–3, 66 (ll. 45–50); English trans. by S. N. Kramer in *A.N.E.T.*, p. 648) the order Sumer—Martu—Meluhha—Elam—Subartu was intended to supply a comprehensive picture of the world in which Sumer is the centre.

7. B. Landsberger, 'Über die Völker Vorderasiens im dritten Jahrtausend, 4: Amurru', *Z.A.* xxxv (1923), 236–8; T. Bauer, *Die Ostkanaanäer* (Leipzig, 1926).

8. A. Deimel, *Wirtschaftstexte aus Fara* (Wissenschaftliche Veröffentlichung der deutschen Orient-Gesellschaft xlv, Leipzig, 1924), no. 78, l. 10.

9. Cf. J. R. Kupper, *Les nomades en Mésopotamie au temps des rois de Mari* (Paris, 1957), 150–1; for texts published later see I. J. Gelb, *Sargonic Texts in the Ashmolean Museum, Oxford* (*Materials for the Assyrian Dictionary* V, Chicago, 1970), nos. 5, 16; 13, 6; 18, 15; 71, 2–3.

10. J. R. Kupper, op. cit. 150; I. J. Gelb, op. cit. no. 13, 6.

11. H. Hirsch, loc. cit. 28–9 (no. 2); cf. J. R. Kupper, op. cit. 149 (n. 3)–150; D. O. Edzard, op. cit. 33 (2a).

12. Gudea statue B vi 5–6; cf., most recently, A. Falkenstein, *Die Inschriften Gudeas von Lagaš*, i (Rome, 1966), pp. 51 f.

13. E. Reiner, 'Lipšur Litanies', *J.N.E.S.* xv (1956), 134 (l. 39).

14. The evidence has been collected and fully discussed by G. Buccellati, op. cit.; later evidence has been published successively by e.g. H. Limet, 'Tablettes inédites du Musée du Louvre', *R.A.* lxii (1968), 1–15; M. Lambert, *Tablettes économiques de Lagash* (Paris, 1968), nos. 50, 6; 139, 3; 276, 11. See also notes 28–9.

15. M. Liverani, *R.S.O.* xliii (1968), p. 121 n. 2.

16. On the problem posed by the linguistic differences between Amorite immigrants and the Sumerian population see the reference to an 'Amorite interpreter' (eme-bal mar-tu) in G. Buccellati, op. cit. 328–9, and also the lexical text cited by S. J. Lieberman, 'An Ur III Text from Drehem Recording Booty from the Land of Mardu', *J.C.S.* xxii (1968–9), p. 55 n. 22, which distinguishes 'the language of Akkad' (eme Uri), 'the language of Elam' (eme Elam-ma), 'the language of Amurru' (eme Mar-tu), and 'the language of Subartu' (eme Su-bir$_4$).

17. On the god Martu/Amurru and its connection with the Amorites cf. J. R. Kupper, *L'iconographie du dieu Amurru dans la glyptique de la 1ère dynastie babylonienne* (Brussels, 1961); J. Lewy, 'Amurritica', *H.U.C.A.* xxxii (1961), 31–74.

18. E. Chiera, *Sumerian Epics and Myths* (Chicago, 1934), no. 58 iv, 24–9; cf. G. Buccellati, op. cit. 92 f.

19. For references to these texts see G. Buccellati, op. cit. 92–5.

20. Cf. M. Liverani, 'Per una considerazione storica del problema amorreo', *O.A.* ix (1970), 22–6, where it is shown that other aspects of this literary description are contradicted by texts keeping closer to reality: e.g. the lack of sedentary stability or the practice of agriculture.

21. For the history of this question, and for a more recent presentation, see S. Moscati, *The Semites in Ancient History* (Cardiff, 1959).

22. On the types of Near Eastern nomadism, and on the concept of 'dimorphic society', see M. B. Rowton, 'The Physical Environment and the Problem of the Nomads', in J. R. Kupper (ed.), *La Civilisation de Mari* (Paris, 1967), pp. 109–21. Also helpful, though relating to a slightly later period, is G. E. Mendenhall, 'The Hebrew Conquest of Palestine', *B.A.* xxv (1962), 66–87.

23. These views on the classification of northwest-Semitic dialects in the second millennium go back to proposals by S. Moscati, 'Il semitico di nord-ovest', *Studi orientalistici in onore di G. Levi Della Vida*, ii (Rome, 1956), pp. 201–21; id., 'Sulla posizione linguistica del semitico nord-occidentale', *R.S.O.* xxxi (1956), 229–34; id., 'Sulla più antica storia delle lingue semitiche', *Rendiconti dell'Accademia Nazionale dei Lincei*, (serie viii), xv (1960), 79–101. See, more particularly, M. Liverani, 'Elementi innovativi nell'ugaritico non letterario', ibid. xix (1964), 173–91.

24. For royal inscriptions of the Akkad dynasty see H. Hirsch, *A.f.O.* xx (1963), 38 (Sargon), 74–5 (Naram-Sin). For administrative texts of Ur III cf. D. D. Luckenbill, 'A Messenger from Ibla', *A.J.S.L.* xxxix (1922–3), 65–6; I. J. Gelb, 'Studies in the Topography of Western Asia', *A.J.S.L.* lv (1938), 77; A. Goetze, 'Four Ur Dynasty Tablets Mention-

ing Foreigners', *J.C.S.* vii (1953), 103–7; E. Sollberger, 'Byblos sous les rois d'Ur', *A.f.O.* xix (1959–60), 120–2.

25. Cf. the synthesis by K. M. Kenyon, *Amorites and Canaanites* (London, 1966); id., 'Syria and Palestine, c. 2160–1780', in *C.A.H.* 1/2, (Cambridge, 1971), fasc. 29, (1965), pp. 38–61. See also the reconstruction by W. F. Albright, 'Abram the Hebrew: a New Archaeological Interpretation', *B.A.S.O.R.* clxiii (1961), 36–54; and by R. de Vaux, 'Les Patriarches hébreux et l'histoire', *R.B.* lxxii (1965), 5–28.

26. P. Lapp, *The Dhahr Mirzbaneh Tombs* (New Haven, Conn., 1966), has noted that the innovations in the material culture are of Mediterranean derivation, while the presumed Amorite invasion must have started from the Syro-Arabian desert.

27. The texts are respectively given in S. Smith, *Cuneiform Texts from Cappadocian Tablets*, ii (London, 1924), no. 49a, 13–14, and B. Kienast, *Altassyrische Texte* (Berlin, 1960), no. 32, 17–22. On the Amorites in Old Assyrian texts cf. J. Lewy, 'Zur Amoriter-Frage', *Z.A.* xxxviii (1928), 243–72 (especially 256–7); id., *H.U.C.A.* xxxii (1961), 31–74 (on the text cited here see pp. 66, 70 and n. 221).

28. Cf. (most recently) S. J. Lieberman, *J.C.S.* xxii (1968–9), 53–62.

29. M. Civil, 'Šu-Sîn's Historical Inscriptions, Collection B', *J.C.S.* xxi (1967), 31–2.

30. R. D. Barnett, 'Xenophon and the Wall of Media', *J.H.S.* lxxxiii (1963), 1–26; C. J. Gadd, 'Babylonia c. 2120–1800 B.C.', in *C.A.H.* 1, Part ii (1971), pp. 612–13 (= fasc. 28 (1965), pp. 17–18); and especially C. Wilcke, 'Zur Geschichte der Amurriter in der Ur-III-Zeit', *W.O.* v (1969), 1–31, where all the pertinent texts are given in transcription and translation.

31. This is reconstructed by T. Jacobsen, 'The Reign of Ibbī-Suen', *J.C.S.* vii (1953), 36–47 (for the prices cf. p. 42 n. 49).

32. *P.B.S.* xiii, no. 9; transcription and translation by T. Jacobsen, *J.C.S.* vii (1953), 39–40, and by C. Wilcke, *W.O.* v (1969), 12–13.

33. Cf. the two lamentations on the destruction of Ur translated by S. N. Kramer, *A.N.E.T.*, pp. 455–63, 611–19.

34. The treatment of this question by D. O. Edzard, op. cit., is basic.

35. *P.B.S.* xiii, nos. 3, 6 (line 35); cf. A. Falkenstein, 'Ibbīsîn-Išbi'erra', *Z.A.* xlix (1950), 59–79 (esp. pp. 62–3, ll. 35–6).

36. G. Buccellati, op. cit. 93.

37. T. Jacobsen, *The Gimilsin Temple and the Palace of the Rulers at Tell Asmar* (Chicago, 1940), 175–82 (nos. 55, 64–8, 70, 81).

38. Cf., in general, D. O. Edzard, op. cit. 99–184.

39. J. R. Kupper, op. cit. 174–7; see also J. Lewy, *H.U.C.A.* xxxii (1961), 58–61.

40. See, most recently, A. Falkenstein, 'Zu den Inschriftenfunden der Grabung in Uruk-Warka, 1960–1961', *Baghdader Mitteilungen*, ii (1963), pp. 1–82 (especially p. 23); G. Pettinato, 'Unveröffentlichte Texte des Königs Sînkāšid von Uruk', *O.A.* ix (1970), 97–112.

41. *A.R.M.* vi, no. 76, 20–1.

42. G. Dossin, 'L'inscription de fondation de Iaḫdun-Lim, roi de Mari', *Syria* xxxii (1955), 14 (iii, 4–9).

43. Cf. statistics in G. Buccellati, op. cit. 100.

44. Cf. n. 7.

45. G. Buccellati, op. cit. 213–31.

46. I. J. Gelb, 'An Old Babylonian List of Amorites', *J.A.O.S.* lxxxviii (1968), 39–46.

47. Cf. J. R. Kupper, op. cit.

48. For the place of these nomadic Amorites in the problem of Semitic origins see J. Henninger, *Über Lebensraum und Lebensformen der Frühsemiten* (Köln–Opladen, 1968)—this has a full bibliography on individual problems (e.g. the camel). But see also the review in *O.A.* ix (1970), 362–4.

49. On the agricultural experience of the nomads see J. R. Kupper, op. cit. 58, and H. Klengel, 'Halbnomadischer Bodenbau in Königsreich von Mari', *Das Verhältnis von Bodenbauern und Viehzüchtern in historischer Sicht* (Berlin, 1968), pp. 75–81. On the 'city of nomads' cf. e.g. 'the city of Haman, race of Haneans, which all the fathers of the Haneans had built', in G. Dossin, *Syria* xxxii (1955), 15 (iii, 28–9).

50. To give a single example, Ubrabu, Yahruru, and Amnanu are three tribes in the great Benjaminite confederation, according to *A.R.M.* iii, no. 50, 10–13. For a comparison of the social organization of the Amorite tribes with that of the Patriarchs see, among others, M. Noth, *Die Ursprünge des alten Israels im Lichte neuer Quellen* (Köln–Opladen, 1961); A. Malamat, 'Mari and the Bible: Some Patterns of Tribal Organisation and Institutions', *J.A.O.S.* lxxxii (1962), 143–50.

51. H. Klengel, 'Zu den *šībūtum* in altbabylonischer Zeit', *Or.* xxix (1960), 357–75.

52. On the Amorite city-states in Syria-Palestine see F. Michelini Tocci, *La Siria nell'età di Mari* (Rome, 1960); J. R. Kupper, 'Northern Mesopotamia and Syria', *C.A.H.* II, rev. edn. (Cambridge, 1963), fasc. 14; H. Klengel, *Geschichte Syriens im 2. Jahrtausend v.u.Z.* i–ii (Berlin, 1965, 1969).

53. On these titles cf. J. R. Kupper, *Nomades* 185–95; B. Landsberger, 'Remarks on the Archive of the Soldier Ubarum', *J.C.S.* ix (1955), 122–8; E. Salonen, 'Zum altbabylonischen Kriegswesen', *Bi.Or.* xxv (1968), 160–2; J. M. Sasson, *The Military Establishments at Mari* (Rome, 1969), pp. 12–13.

54. V. Scheil, *Actes juridiques susiens* (*Mémoires de la mission archéologique de Perse*, xxiii, Paris, 1932), pp. 147–51 (nos. 282–3).

55. F. R. Kraus, *Ein Edikt des Königs Ammi-ṣaduqa von Babylon* (Leiden, 1958); English trans. by J. Finkelstein, *A.N.E.T.*, pp. 526–8.

56. G. Dossin, 'Kengen, pays de Canaan', *R.S.O.* xxxii (1957), 37–8; J. R. Kupper, op. cit. 178–9; H. Klengel, *Geschichte Syriens*, ii. 182.

57. J. R. Kupper, op. cit. 179–80; H. Klengel, op. cit. ii. 182–3.

58. In general, E. Dhorme, 'Les Amorrhéens', *R.B.* xxxix (1930), 168–78; xl (1931), 161–72 (= *Recueil E. Dhorme* (Paris, 1951), pp. 128–52); H. Klengel, op. cit. ii. 178–325.

59. M. B. Rowton, 'The Topological Factor in the Hapiru Problem', *Studies in Honor of B. Landsberger* (Chicago, 1965), pp. 375–87; M. Liverani, 'Il fuoruscitismo in Siria nella tarda età del bronzo', *Rivista Storica Italiana* lxxvii (1965), 315–36.

60. M. Liverani, 'Implicazioni sociali nella politica di Abdi-Aširta di Amurru', *R.S.O.* xl (1965), 267–77.

61. H. Klengel, 'Aziru von Amurru und seine Rolle in der Geschichte der Amārnazeit', *M.I.O.* x (1964), 57–83.

62. E. F. Weidner, *Politische Dokumente aus Kleinasien* (Leipzig, 1923), no. 4 (Šuppiluliuma–Aziru), no. 5 (Muršili II–Duppi-Tešub), no. 9 (Hattušili III–Bentešina); H. Freydank, 'Eine hethitische Fassung des Vertrages zwischen dem Hethiterkönig Šuppiluliuma und Aziru von Amurru', *M.I.O.* vii (1960), 356–81; O. Szemerényi, 'Vertrag des Hethiterkönig Tudhaliya IV mit Ištarmuwa von Amurru', *Oriens Antiquus* (Budapest, 1945), 113–29.

63. Cf., as the latest, M. S. Drower, 'Ugarit', *C.A.H.* ii, rev. edn. ch. xxi (b) (Cambridge, 1968), fasc. 63, pp. 14–16.

64. e.g., A. Gardiner, *Ancient Egyptian Onomastica*, i (Oxford, 1947), 187*; R. Caminos, *Late Egyptian Miscellanies* (Oxford, 1955), pp. 117, 200–1; A. Goetze, 'The Inventory IBoT I 31', *J.C.S.* x (1956), 32 (ll. 2–3); J. Nougayrol, *P.R.U.* iii (Paris, 1955), p. 183 (l. 11).

65. L. W. King, *Babylonian Boundary Stones* (London, 1912), no. 7, 17 (Marduk-nadin-aḫḫe, 1098–1081); A. Ungnad, 'Zur Geschichte und Chronologie des zweiten Reiches von Isin', *Or.* xiii (1944), 86–8 (*Y.O.S.* i. 37, 7; Marduk-šapik-zeri, 1080–1068), and commentary pp. 90–5. In Babylonian texts of the fourteenth–thirteenth centuries a use of 'Amurru' as a specific designation may be met, e.g. the statement of the Kassite Kadašman-Enlil, 'They kill my merchants in the land of Amurru, and in the land of Ugarit', quoted in Hattušili III's letter in K. Bo. I. 10, 14′–15′ (cf. trans. by A. L. Oppenheim, *Letters from Mesopotamia* (Chicago & London, 1967), p. 144).

66. E. Ebeling, *Keilschrifttexte aus Assur juristischen Inhalts* (Leipzig, 1927), 180, 14; cf. H. Klengel, *Geschichte Syriens* ii. Nr. 227. For the dating cf. E. F. Weidner, 'Der Kanzler Salmanassars I', *A.f.O.* xix (1959–60), 34.

67. The famous inscription of Ramesses III clearly attests the passage and stay of the Sea Peoples in Amurru, and the consequential damage; cf. W. Edgerton & J. Wilson, *Historical Records of Rameses III* (Chicago, 1936), p. 53.

68. E. F. Weidner, 'Die Feldzuge und Bauten Tiglatpilesers I', *A.f.O.* xviii (1957–8), 343 f. (ll. 16–24); see also 350 (ll. 24–28).

69. Ibid. 344 (ll. 26–8); see also 350 (ll. 28–30).

70. Cf. L. W. King, *Annals of the Kings of Assyria*, i (London, 1902), pp. 372 f. (iii. 85–8); in inscriptions on the colossi (pp. 199–200, ll. 23–39), Amurru is put before Byblos.

71. The Monolith inscription, with the first edition of the Annals; trans. in *A.R.A.B.* i. § 601.

72. D. D. Luckenbill, *The Annals of Sennacherib* (Chicago, 1924), p. 30 (ll. 50–64).

73. *A.R.A.B.* ii, §§ 6, 9.

74. D. D. Luckenbill, op. cit. 97 (l. 82).

75. *Ḫilāni* is Ugar. *ḫln*, Heb. *ḥallôn*, 'window': the suggestion in *C.A.D.* vi. 184 that the word is 'possibly Hitt[ite]' is certainly wrong.

76. R. Borger, *Die Inschriften Asarhaddons Königs von Assyrien* (Graz, 1956), p. 80 (ll. 27–9).

77. *A.R.A.B.* ii, § 789.

78. Cf. n. 6, and schemes like 'the right of the moon is Akkad, the left Elam, the upper Amurru, the lower Subartu' (R. Campbell Thompson, *The Reports of the Magicians and Astrologers of Niniveh and Babylon* (London, 1900), no. 268, obv. 11–12; *A.B.L.*, no. 1006, 11–13), which is a citation from the canonical series (C. Virolleaud, *Astrologie chaldéenne, Second Supplément* (Paris, 1912), pp. 126 f., ll. 24–5); and still more clearly 'The south is Elam, the north is Akkad, the east is Subartu and Gutium, the west is Amurru' (C. Virolleaud, op. cit. 126 f., l. 22).

79. *A.B.L.*, no. 519, 3′–7′; see, now, S. Parpola, *Letters from Assyrian Scholars to the Kings Esarhaddon and Assurbanipal* (Neukirchen, 1970), no. 13.

80. *A.B.L.*, no. 679, 9–10; S. Parpola, op. cit., no. 300.

81. R. Campbell Thompson, op. cit., no. 43, 5–5′.

82. Ibid., no. 67, 1–3.

83. *A.B.L.*, no. 337, 11′–16′; translated in *C.A.D.* i, Part ii, 507; S. Parpola, op. cit., no. 278.

84. *A.B.L.*, no. 629, 15–3′, 6′–8′; translation in *A.N.E.T.*, p. 626; S. Parpola, op. cit., no. 279.

85. S. Langdon, *Die neubabylonischen Königsinschriften* (Leipzig, 1912), pp. 148 f. (iii. 8–18).

86. C. J. Gadd, 'The Harran Inscriptions of Nabonidus', *Anat. Stud.* viii (1958), 60 f. (ii. 6–8); 64 f. (iii. 18–21), cf. 58 f. (i. 32–3).

87. D. J. Wiseman, *Chronicles of Chaldean Kings* (London, 1961), pp. 66–75.

88. F. H. Weissbach, *Die Keilinschriften der Achämeniden* (Leipzig, 1911), pp. 6 f. (ll. 29–30).

89. *āšib kuštari*, 'who live in tents', is the exact translation of the Sumerian expression za-lam-gar ti applied to the Amorites in E. Chiera, *Sumerian Epics and Myths* (Chicago, 1934), no. 58, iv. 24. (For the lexical equivalents see W. von Soden, *Akkadisches Handwörterbuch* (Wiesbaden, 1965), p. 517, sub *kuštāru*; *C.A.D.* i, Part ii, 386–7 (sub *ašābu*). Cf. also the earliest Assyrian kings 'who lived in tents' (*āšibūtu kúl-ta-re*) according to the king lists (I. J. Gelb, 'Two Assyrian King Lists', *J.N.E.S.* xiii (1954), 210 (line 10).

90. Cf., in general, Y. Aharoni, *The Land of the Bible* (London, 1966), pp. 66 f., 216 f., and, most recently, R. de Vaux, 'Le pays de Canaan', *J.A.O.S.* lxxxviii (1968), 29.

91. i.e. 'the forest of Labwa' of the texts of Amenophis II (*A.N.E.T.*, p. 246) and of Ramesses II (J. Breasted, *Ancient Records of Egypt*, iii (Chicago, 1906), § 340). On *L^{e}bo'-Ḥamāṯ* see O. Eissfeldt, 'Der Zugang nach Hamath', *O.A.* x (1971), 269–76.

92. Cf. e.g. M. Noth, 'Der Gebrauch von *'mry* im AT', *Z.A.W.* xxvii (1940–1), 182–9. [See now also J. van Seters, 'The Terms "Amorite" and "Hittite" in the Old Testament', *V.T.* xxii (1972), 64–81, with whose general conclusion I am in partial agreement, but in which many particular points seems to me questionable.]

93. Y. Aharoni, op. cit. 61–70.

94. The definition of Og and Sihon as 'Amorites' is substantially no more definite than the same appellation for the kings of Ammon, Moab, and Edom in the inscriptions of Sennacherib cited in n. 72 above. [See now the important study by J. R. Bartlett, 'Sihon and Og, Kings of the Amorites', *V.T.* xx (1970), 257–77.]

95. See the basic study by A. Alt, 'Die Landnahme der Israeliten in Palästina', *K.S.* i. 89–125, and later detailed studies like that of S. Yeivin, 'The Third District in Tuthmosis III's List of Palestine-Syrian Towns', *J.E.A.* xxxvi (1950), 51–62; now also, Y. Aharoni, op. cit., *passim*.

BIBLIOGRAPHY

BAUER, TH., *Die Ostkanaanäer* (Leipzig, 1926).

BÖHL, F., *Kanaanäer und Hebräer* (Leipzig, 1911).

BUCCELLATI, G., *The Amorites of the Ur III Period* (Naples, 1966).

DHORME, E., 'Les Amorrhéens (à propos d'un livre récent)', *R.B.* xxxvii (1928), 63–79, 161–80; xxxix (1930), 161–78; xl (1931), 161–84.

GELB, I. J., 'La lingua degli Amoriti' *Rendiconti dell'Accademia Nationale dei Lincei, Serie* VIII, xiii (1958), 143–64.

—— *The Early History of the West–Semitic Peoples, J. C. S.* xv (1961), 27–47.

HALDAR, A., *Who were the Amorites?* (Leiden, 1971).

HUFFMON, H. B., *Amorite Personal Names in the Mari Texts* (Baltimore, 1965).

KENYON, K. M., *Amorites and Canaanites* (London, 1966).

KUPPER, J. R., *Les nomades en Mésopotamie au temps des rois de Mari* (Paris, 1957).

LIVERANI, M., 'Per una considerazione storica del problema amorreo', *O.A.* ix (1970), 5–27.

MAISLER, B., *Untersuchungen zur alten Geschichte und Ethnographie Syriens und Palästinas*, i (Giessen, 1930).

MOSCATI, S., *I predecessori d'Israele* (Roma, 1958).

VI

THE ARAMAEANS

A. MALAMAT

In the last quarter of the second millennium B.C. a west-Semitic people, speaking various Aramaic dialects, spread out from the fringes of the Syro-Arabian desert (though it is sometimes held that they came from the north), fanning out over the Fertile Crescent, from the Persian Gulf to the Amanus mountains, the Lebanon, and Transjordan. This burgeoning forth—unparalleled in the ancient Near East—was held in check by the great powers of the day, till their decline let it loose over the civilized regions of Hither Asia. Originally nomadic or semi-nomadic, the Aramaeans rapidly became an important political and economic factor. Though their earliest historical appearance remains controversial, the Bible notes the kinship of these Aramaeans with the Hebrew Patriarchs, and records a vital, 300-year relationship, both friendly and hostile, between the two peoples in later times. In the course of time the Aramaic language became thoroughly entrenched in Hebrew culture; it was the language of parts of the Bible (in the books of Ezra and Daniel) and remained in everyday use among the Jews for over a millennium.

(i) *History*

Aram is mentioned as a place-name as early as the twenty-third century B.C., in an inscription of Naram-Sin of Akkad, which refers to a region on the Upper Euphrates, and in *c.* 2000 B.C. in documents from Drehem, as a city on the Lower Tigris. It occurs as a personal name in the latter documents, in the Mari texts (eighteenth century B.C.), at Alalah (seventeenth century), and at Ugarit (fourteenth century). One of the Ugaritic texts mentions the 'fields of Aram(aeans)', though its ethnic character here is doubtful.[1] Aram is also mentioned in Egyptian sources, as a place-name (*pꜣ-ỉrm*) in Syria, in a recently discovered topographical list of Amenophis III (first half of the fourteenth century B.C.);[2] and again in an Egyptian frontier journal from the time of Merenptah, about 1220 B.C. (thus the name should not be emended, as is often done, to Amurru). Yet these isolated references are inconclusive in establishing such an early appearance of the Aramaeans, especially since the name Aram is later frequent as an onomastic and toponymic element even in entirely un-Aramaean contexts.

The earliest definite extra-biblical reference to the Aramaeans is from the time of Tiglath-pileser I of Assyria (1116–1076 B.C.). This king's consistent reference to the compound name Aḫlamē-Ar(a)māya in his inscriptions has led to the consideration that the Aḫlamu were actually Aramaeans, and that the latter's first appearance thus stemmed back to the early attestation of the Aḫlamu near the Persian Gulf at the beginning of the fourteenth century B.C.[3] This identification, however, is untenable, for the Aramaeans are mentioned quite separately from, and alongside, the Aḫlamu (and the Sutu) in an inscription most likely attributable to Ashur-bēl-kala (Tiglath-pileser I's successor),[4] while the Assyrian kings Adad-nirari II and Ashur-naṣir-apli II (tenth–ninth centuries B.C.) refer to the Aḫlame-Armaya alongside the Aramaeans *per se*. The compound Aḫlame-Armaya rather denotes an association of nomadic groups, in analogy with similar couplings of tribal names, such as the Old Babylonian references to Amnanu–Yaḫrurum, Ḫana–DUMU.MEŠ-Yamina, Amurru–Sutium.[5] One such component name may well have come semantically to denote the generic concept 'nomad'—as probably happened with the names Aḫlamu and Sutu. Moreover, the term Aram displays a particular tendency for coupling, as in the biblical Aram-Naharaim, Aram-Zobah, Aram-Damascus, Aram-Beth-Rehob, and Aram-Maacah. At any rate, the close historical relationship of the Aḫlamu and the Aramaeans led occasionally in late cuneiform sources to the Aramaic language and script being referred to as 'Aḫlamu'.[6]

Tiglath-pileser I's inscriptions deal with the Aramaeans in two separate contexts: in the Annals for his fourth year (1112 B.C.) he boasts that he 'went forth into the desert [here the west-Semitic term *mudbara* is employed], into the midst of the Aḫlame–Armaya.

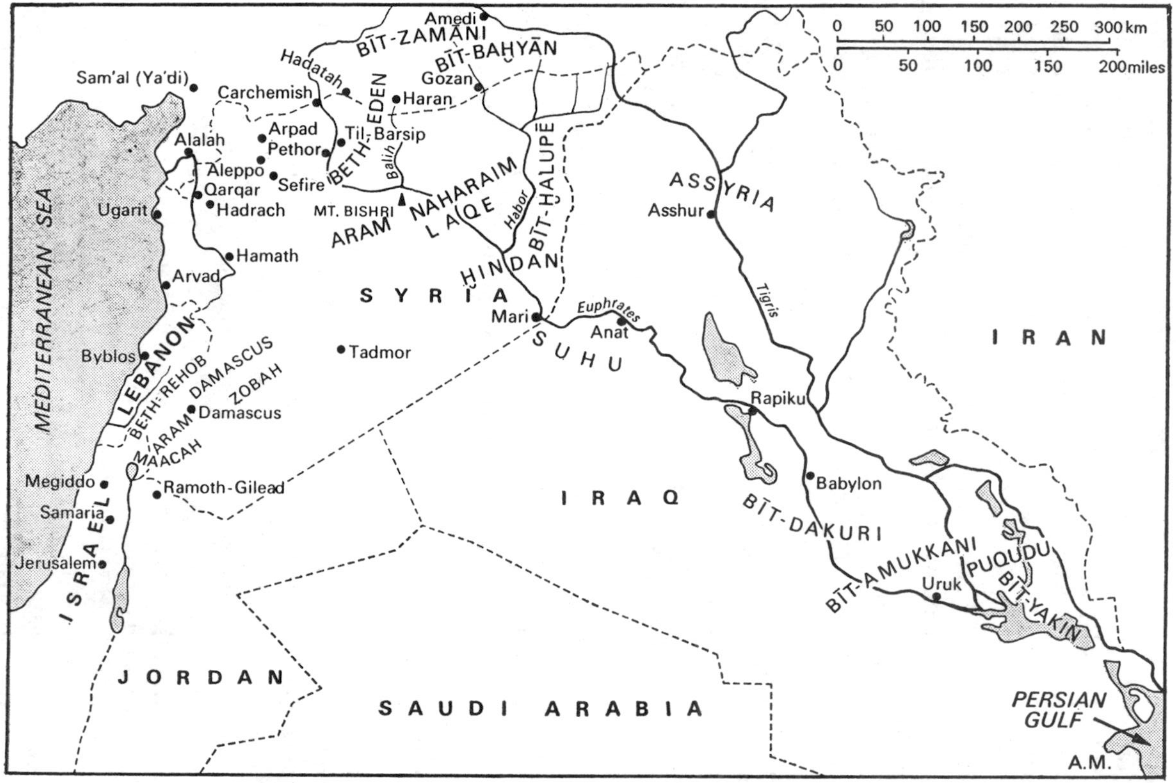

FIG. 4 The Aramaean cities and states.

. . . The country from Suḫu [on the Middle Euphrates—biblical Shuaḥ, Gen. 25: 2] to the city of Carchemish I raided in one day' (*A.R.A.B.* i, § 239). Crossing the Euphrates, he sacked six Aramaean villages in the Mount Bishri district—mentioned in documents as much as a millennium earlier as a perennial breeding ground for nomadic tribes. This is taken as a clear indication that the Aramaeans had already become settled in the area south-east of the great bend of the river, whence they subsequently spread.

The other reference to the Aramaeans underlines their steadfast resistance to the Assyrians: Tiglath-pileser I relates that, in the course of repeated campaigns to subdue the Aramaeans in the west, he had to cross the Euphrates no less than twenty-eight times. 'From the foot of the Lebanon mountains,[7] from the town of Tadmar [biblical Tadmor, later Palmyra] of the country of Amurru, [towards] Anat of the country of Suḫu, as far as the town of Rapiqu of the country of Karduniash [Babylonia], I defeated them' (cf. *A.R.A.B.* i, § 287). Here the Aramaean tribes are already associated with Mount Lebanon—three or four generations prior to their entanglement there with Saul and David. An Assyrian chronicle clearly testifies to the extreme danger posed by the Aramaeans towards the end of Tiglath-pileser's reign, when they penetrated even into Assyria proper, seizing cities and disrupting communications.[8]

Tiglath-pileser's son, Ashur-bēl-kala (1073–1056 B.C.), mentions the Aramaeans (unassociated with the Aḫlamu) in his Annals and related documents, referring specifically (in *c.* 1070 B.C.) to the 'land of Aram' (*māt Arime*, a genitival form of the nominative *Arumu*, *Aramu*, affected by vowel harmony), the exact location of which it is difficult to fix. If the so-called 'Broken Obelisk' from Nineveh is actually to be attributed to Ashur-bēl-kala, as seems reasonable,[9] then the Aramaeans (who figure most prominently in it) were spread over the vicinity of the Kashiari mountains (modern Tur-'Abdin) towards the Tigris, in the north, and along the Habur valley, to the south. In this period, an Aramaean usurper (a 'son of a nobody') bearing the Babylonian name Adad-apla-iddin even managed to seize the throne of Babylon.[10]

The Aramaeans thus came to achieve historical significance at the end of the second millennium and the beginning of the first millennium B.C., at which time a cluster of independent Aramaean states arose.[11] Those in Syria (to which we shall return below) are known from the combined evidence of Assyrian, Aramaean, and biblical sources; those in Mesopotamia almost entirely from Assyrian documents, beginning in the late tenth century B.C. The most important among the latter were Bît-Adini (biblical Beth-Eden; Amos 1: 5) above the great bend of the Euphrates, on both banks (capital: Til-Barsip); Bît-Baḫyan (capital: Gozan; cf. 2 Kings 17: 6) on the Upper Habur, and Bît-Ḫalupe on the Lower Habur; Laqe, Ḫindan, and Suḫu on the Middle Euphrates; Bît-Zamani in the Kashiari mountains to the north (capital: Amedi, modern Diarbekir); and Bît-Amukkani, Bît-Dakuri, and Bît-Yakin, near the Persian Gulf.

Only a cursory outline of the later fortunes of the Aramaeans is possible here, though two of their major states, which rose in the west and became fatefully entangled with the Israelites, will occupy us later. The climax of the Aramaean threat to Assyria came during the century spanning the turn of the millennium, when Assyria reached a nadir under Ashur-rabi II (1012–972 B.C.) and Tiglath-pileser II (966–935 B.C.). Aramaean power in the west now became severely curtailed, however, on account of the rising kingdom of Israel (see below), which relieved Assyria somewhat on its western flank. Indeed, towards the end of the tenth century B.C. Ashur-dan II (934–912 B.C.) was able to repel the Aramaean states on the Upper Habur, and Adad-nirari II (911–891 B.C.) had success there and also on the Middle Euphrates.

Ashur-naṣir-apli II (883–859 B.C.) and, in particular, Shalmaneser III (858–824 B.C.) dealt the Aramaeans further blows. Apart from their renewed campaigns in northern Mesopotamia, the Assyrians overran the Aramaean states between the Habur and the Euphrates, and after successive attempts even the stubborn kingdom of Bît-Adini fell (in 855 B.C.), thus removing the last major stumbling-block towards the west into Syria. This brought Shalmaneser III, and later Adad-nirari III (810–783 B.C.), into a direct confrontation with the powerful kingdom of Aram-Damascus, resulting in its subjugation (see below). Yet the final blow came from Tiglath-pileser III (744–727 B.C.), who reduced the Aramaean states in Syria to mere Assyrian provinces, such as Sam'al, Arpad, and Hadrach (cf. Zech. 9: 1) in the north, and Aram-Damascus in the south.

In spite of occasional revolts (see below), the Assyrians held tightly on to Syria, thus terminating independent Aramaean history in the west: around the second half of the eighth century B.C. the focus of Aramaean history shifts to Babylonia. Since the eleventh century B.C. various Aramaean and closely related tribes (such as the Suteans and the ethnically mixed Chaldeans) had infiltrated in increasing numbers into Babylonia, rising to play a prominent role in the days of Tiglath-pileser III.[12] His inscriptions attest to heavy Aramaean settlement around the Persian Gulf, and specify some thirty-five different tribes—among whom are the Puqudu (the Pekod of Jer. 50: 21 and Ezek. 23: 23). These tribes, whose chieftains were frequently designated by the term *nasīku* (cf. the Hebrew cognate *nāsīḵ*, applied to the Midianite tribal leaders), were a bane to Tiglath-pileser III and the succeeding Sargonid dynasty. They were subjugated only after repeated attempts, and then exiled in large numbers (e.g. 208,000 by Sennacherib in 703 B.C.). Even so, the Aramaeans ultimately came to the fore as a dominant factor within the neo-Babylonian empire.

(ii) *Origins and Affinities in Biblical Tradition*

An obscure tradition preserved in Amos 9: 7 traces the origin of the Aramaeans to a place called Kir, possibly near Elam (cf. Isa. 22: 6), though Amos 1: 5 and 2 Kings 16: 9 give this as the place to which the Aramaeans of Damascus were destined to be exiled. The passages in Amos imply that, after almost half a millennium of Aramaean settlement in Syria, there still circulated a national account of the Aramaean migration, much like the chronicle of the Israelite exodus from Egypt or that of the Philistines from Caphtor.[13] They further point to the historical consequences of Aramaean 'misbehaviour', leading to their return to their ancestral homeland—reminiscent of the threat to a disobedient Israel of being sent back to Egypt (cf. Deut. 28: 68; Hos. 8: 13).

In the Table of Nations (Gen. 10: 22–23), the eponymous ancestor Aram, on a par with Elam and Ashur, is descended directly from Shem, reflecting the Aramaeans' rise to importance in the Near East in the first third of the first millennium B.C. Four 'sons' ('brothers' in the parallel version in 1 Chr. 1: 17) are assigned to Aram: Uz, Hul, Gether, and Mash (LXX and Chronicles:

Meshech; Samaritan Pent.: Massa), whose identity and location are uncertain. The Qumran *War Scroll* (II. 10, rendering Massa, and Togar instead of Gether) places these 'beyond the Euphrates'. The previously modest standing of the Aramaeans is reflected in the genealogical table of the Nahorites (Gen. 22: 20–24), where Aram is made a grandson of Nahor and son of Kemuel (whose significance eludes us) through the lineage of Nahor's wife and not his concubine, thus placing them in Mesopotamia, not southern Syria.[14] Here, too, Aram is merely a 'nephew', rather than the 'father', of Uz.

The Bible closely links the Hebrew Patriarchs with the Aramaeans: not only is Abraham a brother of Nahor, but Isaac and Jacob marry daughters of their cousins Bethuel 'the Aramaean' and Laban 'the Aramaean', respectively (Gen. 25: 20; 31: 20). It is thus that the narrator attributes to Laban the Aramaic equivalent for the Hebrew word *gal'ēd*: *y^{e}gar śāh^{a}dūtā*, 'the stone-heap of witness' (Gen. 31: 47), an etiology for the place-name Gilead.[15] In one instance a Patriarch himself (apparently Jacob) is designated as *^{a}rammī 'ōḇēḏ*, 'a roving Aramaean' (Deut. 26: 5; for a similar expression in Assyrian inscriptions see p. 149 and n. 40).[16] This tradition conforms with the later Hebrew names for the ancestral habitat of the Patriarchs, the district of Harran: 'Paddan-Aram' (Gen. 25: 20, etc.; Akkadian *paddan*, denoting a 'road'), the 'field of Aram' (*ś^{e}dē Aram*; Hos. 12: 12) or 'Aram-Naharaim', i.e. mainly the 'Jezireh', the Habur, and both banks of the Euphrates, further west.

As noted above, the appearance of the Aramaeans in the Patriarchal period is not confirmed in extra-biblical sources, at least not as an element important enough to warrant naming the entire Jezireh after them. Indeed, epigraphic sources of the fifteenth–twelfth centuries B.C. refer simply to Naharaim (Egyptian *Naharin(a)*; Akkadian *Naḫrima/Nārima*), but never to *Aram*-Naharaim.[17] Thus the latter appellation, as well as the alleged Aramaean affinity of the Patriarchs, appear to be anachronistic concepts, introduced under the influence of the later entrenchment of the Aramaean tribes in the Jezireh region (end of the second millennium B.C.).[18] The various arguments, particularly the linguistic ones, put forward to prove that the Patriarchs were 'proto-Aramaeans' have justly been rejected.[19]

That Aram or Aram-Naharaim was the country of origin of Cushan-Rishathaim, the first oppressor of Israel in the period of the Judges (Jud. 3: 8, 11; to be dated *c.* 1200 B.C.), or of the still earlier Balaam (Num. 23: 7; Deut. 23: 4), seems also to be anachronistic. As for Balaam, whose ancestral home was Pethor (some 20 km. south of Carchemish, on the western bank of the Euphrates), the anachronism here may well have come about in the tenth or first half of the ninth century B.C., when this city was an actual Aramaean possession. This is evident from Shalmaneser III's Annals for his third year (857 B.C.):

The city of Ana-Aššur-utēr-aṣbat, which the people of Hatti [i.e. the Syrians] called Pitru [Pethor], which is on the Sagur river, on the other side of the Euphrates, and the city of Mutkinu, on this side of the Euphrates, which Tiglath-pileser my ancestor . . . had settled—which in the reign of Ashur-rabi, king of Assyria, the king of the land of Arumu had seized by force—those cities I restored to their (former) estate.

(*A.R.A.B.* i, § 603; for the date of this conquest see p. 142.)

(iii) *Aram-Zobah and the Struggle with David*[20]

By about 1100 B.C. the Aramaean tribes had not only expanded in Syria, but certainly also had penetrated, like the Israelites, into underpopulated northern Transjordan. Only with the rise of kingship in Israel, however—late in the eleventh century, when the Aramaeans were already consolidated into various states—did unavoidable conflict break out between the two growing neighbouring nations. The kingdom of Zobah now rose to lead the Aramaeans in southern Syria, and indeed Saul lists it among his enemies (1 Sam. 14: 47; the M.T. refers merely to 'kings of Zobah', while the LXX has 'king', in the singular, mentioning in addition Beth-Rehob).

Early in David's reign Aram-Zobah had reached the peak of its power under the vigorous Hadadezer 'the son of Rehob' (2 Sam. 8: 3), i.e. a native of Aram-Beth-Rehob, who apparently amalgamated this kingdom with Zobah into a *Personalunion*. While Aram-Beth-Rehob was apparently located in the southern Lebanon valley, Aram-Zobah lay in the north, extending north-east of the Anti-Lebanon into the Syrian desert, towards Tadmor. In his heyday Hadadezer ruled over vast territories, founding an empire of complex political structure, comprising even Aram-Damascus and other vassals and satellites, such as the kingdom of (Aram-) Maacah, in upper Gaulan, and the land of Tob, somewhere in northern Transjordan (2 Sam. 10: 6, and cf. v. 19; 1 Chr. 19: 6–7). In the south his sphere of influence reached as far as Ammon, while in the north-west he was checked by the kingdom of Hamath (2 Sam. 8: 9–10).

Hadadezer's expansion in the north-east, up to the Euphrates and even 'beyond the river' (2 Sam. 8: 3; 10: 16; 1 Chr. 19: 16), might well be reflected in the above-cited inscription of Shalmaneser III (p. 141), according to which a 'King of Aram' conquered areas on both sides of the Euphrates below Carchemish in the days of Ashur-rabi, the Assyrian contemporary of Hadadezer. In a similar retrospective statement, in the Annals of Ashur-dan II, the places conquered by the Aramaeans are in a different area, though most likely also north of the Upper Euphrates bend.[21] If the Aramaean king in both these Annals was indeed Hadadezer, his conquests along the Euphrates must be dated between the accession of Ashur-rabi (1012 B.C.) and Hadadezer's wars against David, in the first two decades of the tenth century B.C.

David's threefold victory over Hadadezer and his allies sealed the fate of this first Aramaean empire in Syria and brought its territories under Israelite control. The chronological chain of events may be reconstructed as follows: (*a*) Israel's initial war against the allied Ammonite and Aramaean forces, who had reached even the plain of Moab (2 Sam. 10: 6 ff.; 1 Chr. 19: 6 ff.); (*b*) the battle of Helam (somewhere in northern Transjordan), where the Aramaeans employed auxiliaries from beyond the Euphrates (2 Sam. 10: 15 ff.; 1 Chr. 19: 16 ff.); (*c*) the final, deep penetration which took David into central Syria, utilizing Hadadezer's absence in the Euphrates region, when the auxiliary forces from Aram-Damascus were defeated. David took as booty especially quantities of copper (paralleled later by the Assyrians in their successes against Aram-Damascus) from three of Hadadezer's cities in Coele-Syria: Tebaḥ (Tibḫath-Tubiḫi), Cun, and Berothai (2 Sam. 8: 3 ff.; 1 Chr. 18: 3 ff.; and cf. Ps. 60: 2).

The kingdom of Aram-Zobah thus disappears from the historical scene, being replaced by Aram-Damascus. The name Zobah, however, occurs later, on bricks found at Hamath, inscribed in

Aramaic and apparently referring to a district within the kingdom of Hamath (cf. Hamath-Zobah in 2 Chr. 8: 3); it especially occurs as the name of an Assyrian province (Ṣubatu/Ṣubutu/Ṣubiti) in the late eighth and seventh centuries B.C., after the final fall of Aram-Damascus and Hamath.

(iv) *The Rise of Aram-Damascus*

The kingdom of Aram-Damascus, which became the foremost Aramaean state in Syria during the ninth–eighth centuries B.C., was founded in the latter days of Solomon by Rezon the son of Eliadah, who removed Damascus from under Israelite control, making it his capital (1 Kings 11: 23 ff.). This state was also referred to simply as 'Damascus' or as 'Aram' *par excellence*—in the Bible, in Assyrian sources, and in Aramaic inscriptions (the votive stele of Bar-Hadad and the Zakir inscription both mention the 'King of Aram'). Neo-Assyrian documents refer to this kingdom by the enigmatic appellation (*ša-*)*imēri-šu* (sometimes even spelt syllabically), literally '(the land) of (his) donkey(s)';[22] though used interchangeably with the name Damascus, it most probably refers only to the country as such.

The rise of Aram-Damascus was greatly facilitated by the division of the united kingdom of Israel, and fully exploited the continual disputes between Judah and Israel. The biblical source well illustrates this in 1 Kings 15: 18–19, referring to the war between Baasha of Israel and Asa of Judah (in the period 890–880 B.C.), when the latter induced 'Ben-Hadad the son of Tab-Rimmon, the son of Hezion' to change sides. The biblical passage first informs us of the dynastic line at Damascus (the Hezion there may possibly be the above-mentioned Rezon, founder of the kingdom),[23] and then of the changes in allies—the first alliance is between Tab-Rimmon and Asa's father, Abijah of Judah; the next between Ben-Hadad and Baasha of Israel; and finally there is the proposed military pact between Ben-Hadad and Judah, which was followed by an Aramaean campaign wresting eastern Galilee from Israel (v. 20).[24]

Aramaean pressure on northern Israel increased even to the point of threatening its very existence. The Upper Transjordan region, to Ramoth-Gilead in the south, a buffer-zone with a mixed

Israelite-Aramaean population (cf. 1 Chr. 2: 23; 7: 14), changed hands every so often, as is evident during the Omride dynasty in Israel. Ben-Hadad (II, apparently), in attempting to attack the Israelite capital at Samaria with the auxiliary forces of thirty-two vassal kings, was repulsed by King Ahab; shortly afterwards he was again defeated at Aphek in southern Gaulan (1 Kings 20). The subsequent treaty returned those towns in Transjordan conquered by Ben-Hadad I, and granted Israelite merchants preferential rights in Damascus, like those enjoyed previously by the Aramaeans at Samaria (1 Kings 20: 34). Ben-Hadad II, forced to reconstitute his army and his kingdom, also in reaction to a new Assyrian threat, reduced his vassal states to mere provinces (cf. 1 Kings 20: 24–25), and thereby consolidated his empire.[25]

To meet the menace posed by Shalmaneser III of Assyria, a league of twelve western kings, including Irḫuleni, King of Hamath, and Ahab of Israel, was initiated and led apparently by Ben-Hadad II (probably the Adad-idri of the Assyrian sources). The first clash occurred in 853 B.C. at Qarqar in the land of Hamath. The allies had under Adad-idri 1,200 chariots, 1,200 riding horses, and 20,000 infantry; under Irḫuleni 700 chariots, 700 riding horses, and 10,000 infantry; and under Ahab 2,000(!) chariots and 10,000 infantry. The enormous force under Ahab may have included auxiliaries from Jehoshaphat of Judah (cf. 1 Kings 22: 4, and also 2 Kings 3: 7), and from vassals such as Ammon and Moab. The only other independent Aramaean king participating in this battle was Baasha, 'son of Rehob', from the land or mountain of Amana (^{KUR}*A-ma-na-a-a*—which cannot be Ammon, written in Assyrian sources always as *Bît-*, but once *Ba-an- Am-ma-na-a-a*, with geminated *m*, as in the Bible), probably referring to the Anti-Lebanon, biblical Mount Amana (Song. 1: 4). As this Baasha may have combined under his rule two separate entities, Aram-Beth-Rehob (see p. 141, on Hadadezer son of Rehob) and the mountainous region to the east, only a single contingent of infantry is ascribed to him (analogous to the combined forces of Beth-Rehob and Zobah in the war against David, mentioned in 2 Sam. 10: 6).[26]

A war between Ahab and Ben-Hadad at Ramoth-Gilead (as in 1 Kings 22) is unlikely so short a time after the battle of Qarqar, for this western alliance of kings seems to have remained intact, meeting Shalmaneser III again in 849, 848, and 845 B.C.[27] Only

Hazael, who overthrew the Ben-Hadad dynasty, reversed Aramaean policy towards Israel, clashing with Ahab's son Joram in 842 B.C. at Ramoth-Gilead (2 Kings 8: 28 f.; the alleged encounter here in the days of Ahab probably reflects this later event). This disintegration of the western alliance finally enabled Shalmaneser to defeat Aram-Damascus in 841 and 838 B.C., in the first instance destroying the plantations and orchards surrounding Damascus, and then proceeding through the Hauran and Galilee to Mount Ba'al-rasi ('Ba'al of the Summit', possibly Mount Carmel).

Hazael, however, was able to consolidate his realm after the Assyrian pressure ebbed, bringing Aram-Damascus to the peak of its power, and later giving his name to the synonymous appellation Beth-Hazael, after the dynastic founder (Amos 1: 4; and in Tiglath-pileser III's inscriptions, for which see below). In the south Hazael first seized Transjordan down to the Arnon brook (2 Kings 10: 32 f.), then raided into western Israel, bringing it to its knees (2 Kings 13: 7, 22), and finally reached the borders of Judah, which was forced to pay a heavy tribute (2 Kings 12: 17 f.). These developments are well reflected in the Elisha cycle (which assigns the prophet a part in the overthrow of the Ben-Hadad dynasty; 2 Kings 5–7; 8: 7–15; and cf. also the condemnation of Aramaean atrocities against Israelite Gilead, in Amos 1: 3–5). The Aramaeans were able to retain their position into the reign of Hazael's son, Ben-Hadad III (2 Kings 13: 3; and cf. 2 Chr. 24: 23 f.), who formed an extensive coalition, encompassing even southern Anatolia, against Zakir, King of Hamath and La'ash.

The tide turned, however, when Adad-nirari III renewed campaigns against the Aramaeans in Syria in 805–802 B.C., primarily against Damascus and its king, 'Mari' (the Aramaic word for 'Lord', probably referring to Ben-Hadad III). On a stele recently found at Tell el-Rimah, Adad-nirari III records the heavy tribute extracted from Aram-Damascus (silver, copper, iron, and fine garments), in connection with an expedition to the Mediterranean in 802 B.C., or one against the district of Manṣuate (in the Lebanon valley) in 796 B.C. (both campaigns are listed in the Assyrian Eponym Chronicle). Among the tributaries here is, for the first time in an Assyrian source, 'Iu'asu the Samaritan', i.e. King Joash of Israel;[28] his appellation as 'the Samaritan' may imply (as with the later Menahem 'the Samaritan') that his kingdom was initially limited through earlier Aramaean conquests to the district of Samaria alone. Because of Damascus' weak position Joash was able to deal Ben-Hadad a threefold blow and recover many cities lost to the Aramaeans by his father Jehoahaz (2 Kings 13: 19, 25).

Jeroboam II pursued his father Joash's aggressive policy towards the Aramaeans, who were further weakened by Shalmaneser IV during his campaign to Damascus in 773 B.C. Jeroboam succeeded not only in freeing all Transjordan but even in imposing Israelite domination over Damascus (2 Kings 14: 25, 28). Aram-Damascus had one final flicker of glory under its last king, Rezin, who is mentioned as a vassal of Tiglath-pileser III in about 738 B.C. He rebelled and invaded Transjordan, annexing it as far south as Ramoth-Gilead, and even raided Elath (2 Kings 16: 6). Forcing Pekah of Israel to join him, he pressed upon Jotham, King of Judah, and his son Ahaz, who appealed to Assyria for deliverance (2 Kings 15: 37; 16: 5, 7 ff.; Isa. 7: 1 ff.). Tiglath-pileser III crushed Aram-Damascus once and for all in his campaigns of 733 and 732 B.C., boasting that he destroyed 591 cities in sixteen districts and exiled numerous inhabitants (cf. 2 Kings 16: 9, where Rezin's execution is noted). 'The widespread [land of Beth-]Hazael in its entirety from m[ount Leba]non as far as the town of [Ramoth-] Gilead, which is on the borderland of the land of Beth-Omri, I restored to the territory of Assyria. I appointed over them officials of mine as governors.'[29]

Aram-Damascus was then broken up into Assyrian provinces: Damascus in the centre; Hauran, Qarnini (biblical Karnaim), and Gilead in the south; Manṣuate in the west; and Ṣubatu in the north (see p. 143). An unsuccessful rebellion broke out in Damascus in 720 B.C., in conjunction with similar events in Samaria, Arpad, and perhaps also Sam'al, which were all quelled by Sargon. The destruction of the erstwhile flourishing kingdom of Damascus left a deep mark in the oracles of doom uttered by Amos (1: 3–5), Isaiah (17: 1–3), and Jeremiah (49: 23–27).[30]

(v) *The Legacy*

a. *Political organization*

The combined evidence of the Aramaic, Assyrian, and biblical sources provides an insight into the structure and political groupings of the various Aramaean states, at least in Syria. We can thus follow the continual rivalries and constantly changing alliances among them, as well as the Aramaization evolving in the tenth–eighth centuries B.C. in the neo-Hittite states, such as Ya'dy-Sam'al (capital: modern Zinjirli), Til Barsip (later capital of Bît-Adini) in the north, and Hamath in middle Syria.[31] Though the vast Aramaean expansion in Hither Asia failed to lead to pan-Aramaean political or cultural unity, confederations of considerable extent, but of changing leadership, did periodically rise in Syria: Aram-Zobah—*c.* 1000 B.C.; Aram-Damascus—ninth century B.C.; Arpad (mentioned in 2 Kings 18: 34; 19: 13, *et al.*; capital: modern Tell Refād, some 30 km. north of Aleppo)—mid-eighth century B.C. The stature of Arpad about this time is attested in the Aramaic treaty inscriptions from Sefire (south of Aleppo),[32] which contain such indicative terms as 'all Aram' and 'Upper and Lower Aram'. Such pliant and internally loose confederations, however, readily distintegrated under outside pressure.

b. *Language*

Of the few traces of Aramaean culture left among the peoples with whom the Aramaeans intermingled, Aramaic and its script are the outstanding ones. There appear Aramaic inscriptions, chiefly in Syria (and interestingly also in the Jordan valley), as early as the ninth–eighth centuries B.C.[33] Though adopting the Phoenician alphabet, Aramaic developed its own specific form, and occasionally was even written in other scripts (in cuneiform on a tablet from Uruk, and in demotic on Egyptian papyri). 'Imperial' Aramaic became the *lingua franca* of the Persian period, and eventually spread over an area from Asia Minor and the Caucasus to India, Afghanistan, northern Arabia, and Egypt.

Aramaic clearly played an important role in the realm of administration and diplomacy already in the Babylonian, and even the Assyrian, empire. There are several indications of this (apart from the Aramaic inscriptions and many loan-words from Mesopotamia), such as the mention of an 'Aramaic letter' (*egirtu armītu*, employing an Aramaic loan-word) by an Assyrian official in the second half of the ninth century B.C.; of 'Aramaic documents' (*nibzi armaya*, using the Aramaic term *nbz*) in the late eighth century B.C.; frequent references to 'Aramaean scribes' alongside Assyrian; and depictions of them in pairs on reliefs and in wall-paintings from the time of Tiglath-pileser III onwards (the one writing on a tablet in cuneiform, and the other on papyrus or leather—certainly in Aramaic).[34] The Bible notes the diplomatic use of Aramaic in Palestine as well (cf. 2 Kings 18: 26 ff.—*c.* 700 B.C.), as is confirmed by a letter found at Saqqara in Egypt (600 B.C.; most likely sent from Philistia).

The spread of Aramaic, facilitated by its simple script, was furthered by large-scale population movements: mass deportations of Aramaeans, and their resettlement within the Assyrian empire;[35] their service within the Assyrian army and administration; and their widespread mercantile activities. The latter, along the international trade routes, and Aramaean settlements at the major caravan stations, coupled with their inherent wanderlust, placed them to the fore of Middle Eastern commerce from the ninth century B.C. onwards.

c. *Religion*

Aramaean religious influence on other peoples is obscure, for the Aramaeans themselves were readily influenced by their adopted surroundings. Thus many foreign deities (e.g. the Canaanite Baʿal-Shemayin, Reshef, and Melqart; and the Mesopotamian Shamash, Marduk, Nergal, and Sin) appear in Aramaean inscriptions. The principal Aramaean deity in Syria was the ancient west-Semitic storm-god Hadad, worshipped, e.g., at Damascus (cf. the dynastic name Bar/Ben-Hadad). At Sam'al, the Aramaeans worshipped Hadad alongside the dynastic gods Rakib-El, Baʿal Hamman, and Baʿal Ṣemed, as well as Baʿal Harran, whose cultic centre was at Harran. Other deities venerated among the Aramaeans are revealed by the theophoric elements in personal names, especially at Elephantine and other colonies in Egypt; these include such gods as Nabu, Bethel, and the female deities Malkat-Shemayin and Banit, who also had shrines in the Aramaean colony at Syene.[36] Traces of Aramaean religion in the Hellenistic period appear at such places as Baalbek and Hierapolis, the main cult centre of Atargatis, the female deity whose name combines *ʿatar* (as in Aramaic names, e.g. at Sefire (Atarsamak) and Elephantine) and *ʿatta* (Anat).

Among the Israelites the influence of Aramaean worship is evident in Ahaz's introduction of the Damascus cult at Jerusalem, as reflected in the Damascus-style altar (2 Kings 16: 10–13; and cf. 2 Chr. 28: 23). The 'sacrifice' of Ahaz's son (2 Kings 16: 3; and cf. 2 Chr. 28: 3) may be further evidence for such influence, since this was a cult practice among the Aramaeans exiled to Samaria from Sepharvaim; the Adrammelech of this cult (2 Kings 17: 31) was almost certainly the god Adad-melek, who, at the Aramaean centre of Gozan, was also the subject of such rites.[37] Note also the worship of Hadad-Rimmon, the local deity of Damascus, in the Megiddo plain (Zech. 12: 11; cf. 2 Kings 5: 18). On the other hand, Aramaean susceptibility to Israelite religious influence is evident in the episode of Naaman, army commander of the King of Aram-Damascus (2 Kings 5: 15–17). In a later period Aramaean religion made itself felt among the Jewish colonists at Elephantine, and, in turn, Jewish influence is seen in such names as Shabbetai in the Aramaean community at nearby Syene.

d. *Material culture*

Excavations at such centres as Tell Halaf (Gozan, in the ninth century B.C., during the reign of King Kapara),[38] Arslan Tash (Ḫadatha) and Tell Aḥmar (Til Barsip), Zinjirli (Sam'al), Tell Refād (Arpad), Hamath, have revealed the Aramaean cultural achievement, especially in architecture, sculpture, and other arts.[39] The Aramaeans were always strongly influenced by the specific local environment, in Mesopotamia by the remnants of the Mitanni culture and by the Assyrians, and in Syria by the neo-Hittites and Phoenicians. Though such evidence is difficult to interpret, the zenith of Aramaean material culture seems to have been reached in the tenth–eighth centuries B.C.

The Aramaeans—though seen by their enemies as 'fugitives, treacherous, a roving people',[40] and in spite of their lack of an original, creative culture—certainly hold their special place in history as a major catalyst of civilization in the ancient Near East.

NOTES

1. For refs. see A. Dupont-Sommer, *V.T.* Supplement i (1953), 40 ff.; J. R. Kupper, *Les Nomades en Mésopotamie au temps des rois de Mari* (Brussels, 1957), pp. 112 ff. The mention of Aram in one of Naram-Sin's inscriptions has recently been disproved; cf. E. Sollberger, *R.A.*

lxiv (1970), 173. For a further reference to Aram (in the land of Suburtu) in the reign of Ammi-ṣaduqa see A, Pohl, *J.K.F.* ii (1965), 364.

2. Published by E. Edel, *Die Ortsnamenlisten aus dem Totentempel Amenophis III* (Bonner Bibl. Beiträge 25, Bonn, 1966), pp. 28 f. (list DN, no. 7); cf. W. Helck, *Göttingische Gelehrte Anzeigen* ccxxi (1969), 81.

3. See P. B. Cornwall, *J.C.S.* vi (1952), 137 ff., for two Kassite letters noting the marauding Aḫlamu. Cf. also Kupper, *Les Nomades*, pp. 108 ff.

4. Published by E. F. Weidner, *A.f.O.* vi (1930–1), 88 ff. (Assur no. 6796a = VAT 9539); and cf. A. Malamat, *The Aramaeans in Aram Naharaim and the Rise of their States* (Jerusalem, 1952), pp. 11 ff. (Hebrew), where another document is also treated, mentioning the Aramaeans alongside the Aḫlamu (K 4525; Winckler, *A.O.F.* ii (1900), 574 f. = *A.B.L.* no. 1013). For a new, parallel inscription (B.M. 134497) see now A. R. Millard, *Iraq* xxxii (1970), 169, which preserves the name of the mountain—^{šad}*Labnani*—in the line after the mention of the Sutu; at the end of line 5 we may perhaps restore [*Ta-ad*]-*mi-ra-ia*^{meš}, i.e. reading 'the Tadmorites who are at the foot of Mt. Lebanon'.

5. Cf. S. Moscati, *J.S.S.* iv (1959), 303 ff.; I. J. Gelb. *J.C.S.* xv (1961), 37 and n. 32; A. Malamat, *XVe rencontre assyriologique internationale* (Liège, 1967), p. 138 and nn. 1 and 2.

6. Cf. *C.A.D.* i/1, 192 f., s.v. *aḫlamatti*, *aḫlamu*; and cf. also, in a late text from Uruk, the interesting note on 'Aba-enlil-dari whom the Aḫlamû call Aḥiqar' (i.e. in Aramaic), by J. van Dijk, *A.f.O.* xx (1963), 217b.

7. The words *ištu šēp* ^{šadê}*Labnani* are mentioned only in a single version of the many parallel inscriptions of Tiglath-pileser I, for which see Weidner, *A.f.O.* xviii (1958), 342 ff. (Text I, ll. 31 ff.); and Malamat, *Studies . . . B. Landsberger* (*A.S.* xvi, Chicago, 1965), p. 372 n. 35.

8. Cf. Weidner, *A.f.O.* xvii (1956), 384; H. Tadmor, *J.N.E.S.* xvii (1958), 133 f.; and D. J. Wiseman, 'Assyria and Babylonia (*c.* 1200–1000 B.C.)', *C.A.H.* II, rev. edn., Ch. xxxi (= fasc. 41 (1965)), pp. 22, 25.

9. See, for the latest discussions of the 'Broken Obelisk', K. Jaritz, *J.S.S.* iv (1959), 204 ff.; R. Borger, *Einleitung in die assyrischen Königsinschriften*, i (H.d.O., Leiden, 1961), 135 ff.; J. A. Brinkman, *A Political History of Post-Kassite Babylonia* (Rome, 1968), pp. 383 ff.

10. For this ruler and the Aramaean thrust into Babylonia see A. Malamat, *The Aramaeans*, pp. 14 ff.; Wiseman, *C.A.H.* rev. edn., Ch. xxxi, pp. 26 ff.; and bibliographical refs. in both works.

11. For this period up to Ashur-naṣir-apli II, and on the various Aramaean states, see in detail Malamat, *The Aramaeans*, and the documentation and bibliographical refs. there.

12. See J. Brinkman, *A Political History of Post-Kassite Babylonia*, pp. 267 ff., and for the Aramaean expansion there, in a still later period, see M. Dietrich, *Die Aramäer Südbabyloniens in der Sargonidenzeit* (Neukirchen, 1970).

13. Cf. C. H. Gordon., *J.B.L.* lxxiv (1955), 289.

14. See the commentaries on Genesis, and in particular B. Mazar, *B.A.* xxv (1962), 99; cf. Malamat, *XVe rencontre assyriologique*, 129 ff.

15. The element *ʿd* here in Hebrew *glʿd* may well have had originally the meaning of 'pact, agreement' (perhaps to be read *ʿad*, as in Gilead; and stemming from a root different from *ʿēd*, 'witness'?), in accord with the Aramaic cognate (which latter appears as a loan-word in the neo Assyrian form *adû*). Cf. already J. Hempel, *Z.A.W.* l (1932), 78; and recently F.O. Garcia-Treto, *Z.A.W.* lxxix (1967), 13 ff. If so, the Aramaic phrase would be a late interpretation, as perhaps is to be inferred also from the use of the Aramaic definite article in *śāhᵃdūtā*.

16. Cf. M. A. Beek, *Oudttestamentische Studiën* viii (1950), 193 ff.; H. Seebass, *Der Erzvater Israel* (Berlin, 1966), p. 4; L. Koehler & W. Baumgartner, *Hebräisches und aramäisches Lexikon zum alten Testament*, 3rd edn. (Leiden. 1967), p. 2b, who, however, accept the usual translation of *'ōḇēḏ* here—'wandering, errant, perishing'.

17. For the term in biblical and extra-biblical sources see R. T. O'Callaghan, *Aram Naharaim* (Rome, 1948), pp. 131 ff.; J. J. Finkelstein, *J.N.E.S.* xxi (1962), 73 ff.

18. Cf. J. C. L. Gibson, *J.S.S.* vii (1962), 53 f., and recently B. Mazar, *J.N.E.S.* xxviii (1969), 78, dating these anachronisms to the end of the 11th century B.C. (whereas numerous scholars would insist on the real Aramaean extraction of Israel's forebears; see also next note).

19. The 'proto-Aramaean' hypothesis has been put forth by M. Noth; see his final statement in *Die Ursprünge des alten Israel im Lichte neuer Quellen* (Köln–Opladen, 1961). The meagre linguistic evidence drawn from the Mari texts is not convincing, however; cf. the critical remarks by D. O. Edzard, *Z.A.* N.F. xxii (1964), 142 ff.; M. Wagner, *V.T.* Supplement xvi (1967), 355 ff.

20. For further details and bibliographical refs. on this section see M. F. Unger, *Israel and the Aramaeans of Damascus* (London, 1957), pp. 42 ff.; and see the present writer's studies in *B.A.* xxi (1958), 100 ff., and *J.N.E.S.* xxii (1963), 1 ff.

21. The Annals were published by Weidner, *A.f.O.* iii (1926), 151 ff., who locates the region conquered by the Aramaeans in northern Syria, at later Arpad (p. 156), while E. Forrer (*R.L.A.* i. 291) places them east of the Tigris. We should prefer to consider, however, the area of later Bît-Adini; cf. A. Malamat, *The Aramaeans*, pp. 20 and 46 f.

22. For more recent but still tentative attempts to explain this obscure appellation cf. Malamat, *Tarbiz* xxii (1950–1), 64 (Hebrew); E. A. Speiser, *J.A.O.S.* lxxi (1951), 257 f.; C. H. Gordon, *I.E.J.* ii (1952), 174 f.; F. M. Tocci, *R.S.O.* xxxv (1960), 129 ff.; *C.A.D.* vii. 115.

23. Cf. B. Mazar, *B.A.* xxv, p. 104 n. 12, who opines that Hezion was the proper name of the king, and Rezon his royal title, since the Hebrew *rzn* denotes 'ruler, prince' (note further the Phoenician cognate in the Azitawanda Inscription iii, l. 12). We may have here, however, little more than two variants of the same name or title, if the existence of a *ḥ/r* phonetic change is admitted, as suggested by B. Landsberger

(who further pointed to Hebrew *rāzōn*, *rōzᵉnīm* = Akkadian *ḫazan(n)u*, 'mayor, potentate'); cf. *W.O.* iii (1964), 60. A late spelling of the latter word has the form *ḫaziyānu/ḫaziyannu* (e.g. in el-Amarna), which occurs in neo-Assyrian also as a personal name—as if derived from a root *ḫzy*; for this 'secondary and backward development' cf. I. J. Gelb, *Glossa* ii (1968), 101. Thus, Hezion—like Rezon—could simply mean 'potentate' or the like.

24. In *B.A.S.O.R.* lxxxvii (1942), 23 ff., W. F. Albright ascribes to this Ben/Bar-Hadad a votive stele dedicated to the god Melqart, found north of Aleppo, on the basis of his highly doubtful restoration of the King's ancestors as Tab-Rimmon and Hezion. The stele, however, seems to refer to one of the later Ben-Hadads, both of whom were of considerable influence far to the north (see below), as witnessed *inter alia* by the find-spot of this same inscription. E. Lipiński, *Annali dell'Instituto Universitario Orientale di Napoli* xxxi (1970), 101 ff., who attributes this stele to Ben-Hadad son of Hazael, now reads *'Attar-hapēš* as the name of his (grand)father. Also problematic is the new reading and historical interpretation of this inscription by F. M. Cross, *B.A.S.O.R.* ccv (1972), 36 ff.; 'Bir-Hadad, son of 'Ezer, the Damscene, son of the King of Aram'.

25. Cf. Mazar, *B.A.* xxv, 109 ff. and *J.B.L.* lxxx (1961), 25 f., who attributed far-reaching implications to this reform, assuming *inter alia* that the Aramaic idiom of this newly formed state later developed into 'Imperial' Aramaic (see below).

26. For the battle of Karkar, and Ahab's participation at the head of a minor coalition, see Malamat, 'The Wars of Israel and Assyria', in *The Military History of the Land of Israel in Biblical Times*, ed. J. Liver (Jerusalem, 1964), pp. 246 ff. (Hebrew). On p. 258 n. 22 there we considered a reading showing this last ally, Baasha, to have been King 'of (Beth-)Rehob, of Amana'; if our conjecture that this ruler headed a union of two neighbouring lands is correct, then a long-standing problem in this inscription has found its solution (and without assuming that anything dropped out): the anti-Assyrian league would then add up to 12 political units, as summed up in the inscription, though only 11 kings are mentioned.

27. Cf. A. Jepsen, *A.f.O.* xiv (1942), 154 ff.; J. M. Miller, *J.B.L.* lxxxv (1966), 441 ff.; *V.T.* xvii (1967), 307 ff.; and now also E. Lipiński, in *5th World Congress of Jewish Studies*, i (Jerusalem (1969), 157 ff.), who, on different grounds, dissociate Ahab from *all* his Aramaean wars, dating them instead as late as Jehoahaz or Joash of the Jehu dynasty. Lipiński in particular regards the Ben-Hadad of Ahab's time as a mere prolepsis of the later king of this name, the son of Hazael (see below).

28. The new stele was published by S. Page, *Iraq* xxx (1968), 139 ff.; and see the studies by H. Cazelles, *C.R.A.I.B.L.* (Jan.–Mars, 1969), 106 ff.; H. Donner, in *Archäologie und altes Testament: K. Galling Festschrift* (Tübingen, 1970), pp. 49 ff.; J. A. Soggin, *V.T.* xx (1970), 366 ff.; A. Cody, *C.B.Q.* xxxii (1970), 325 ff.; E. Lipiński, op. cit. (above, n. 27); and B. Oded, in *Studies in the History of the Jewish People and the*

Land of Israel, ii (Haifa, 1972; Hebrew, in press). And cf. A. Malamat, *B.A.S.O.R.* cciv (1971), 37 ff., for the probable Assyrian transcription of King Joash's name as *Iu-'a-su* (instead of the usual transliteration *Ia-'a-su*), which represents a closer rendering of the Hebrew.

29. This quotation is based on new fragments of Tiglath-pileser III's inscriptions from Nimrud, published by D. J. Wiseman, *Iraq* xvii (1956), 120 ff., and on a reconstruction by H. Tadmor, *I.E.J.* xii (1962), 114 ff. For Tiglath-pileser III's liquidation of Aram-Damascus, and its subsequent split into Assyrian provinces, cf. most recently B. Oded, *J.N.E.S.* xxix (1970), 177 ff.

30. On the prophecies against Aram see the biblical commentators. For Amos, in particular, see now J. A. Soggin, *Near Eastern Studies in Honor of W. F. Albright* (Baltimore, 1971), pp. 433 ff., who surveys the strife between Aram and Israel in the ninth–eighth centuries B.C.

31. For the possibility of a reverse sequence, i.e. a neo-Hittite imprint upon Aramaean states, in particular Bît-Adini, cf. D. Ussishkin, *Or.* xl (1971), 431 ff.; but see B. Landsberger, *Sam'al* (Ankara, 1948), pp. 35, 37. For Beth-Eden see also A. Malamat, in *Encyclopaedia Biblica*, ii (1954), pp. 94 f. (Hebrew); and *B.A.S.O.R.* cxxix (1953), 25 f. Unknown cities of Beth-Eden can now be seen on the recently published bronze strips from the Balawat gates of Ashur-naṣir-apli II—the earliest definite depiction of Aramaeans; see R. D. Barnett, *Qadmoniot* v (1972), 24 ff. (Hebrew).

32. Cf. the latest publication and treatment by J. A. Fitzmyer, *The Aramaic Inscriptions of Sefire* (Rome, 1967), and cf., for the diplomatic and legal terminology used there, J. C. Greenfield, *Ac.Or.* xxix (1965), 1 ff.

33. The Old Aramaic inscriptions, several of which are mentioned in this chapter, have conveniently been collected by Donner (and Röllig) in *K.A.I.* Several Aramaic inscriptions have been found recently in the Jordan valley: at Hazor (Y. Yadin *et al.*, *Hazor* iii–iv (Jerusalem, 1961), pl. ccclvii, 1); at 'Ein Gev (B. Mazar, *I.E.J.* xiv (1964), 27 f.); at Tel Dan (N. Avigad, *P.E.Q.* c (1968), 42 ff.); and a wall inscription in ink from Deir 'Alla, dated to the mid 8th century B.C. by J. Naveh, *I.E.J.* xvii (1967), 256 ff. In general, see also J. Naveh, 'The Development of the Aramaic Script', *Proceedings of the Israel Academy of Sciences and Humanities*, v. 1 (Jerusalem, 1970).

34. Cf. references in *C.A.D.* 1, Part ii, 293, s.v. *armû*; and J. Lewy, *H.U.C.A.* xxv (1954), 188 ff.; and for illustrations, see *A.N.E.P.*, nos. 235–6, 367 and pp. 276, 293. For the many Aramaic loan-words in neo-Assyrian and neo-Babylonian. see W. von Soden, *Or.* xxxv (1966), 1 ff.; xxxvii (1968), 261 ff. For another late eighth century reference to 'a sealed Aramaic document' sent from Tyre to the King of Assyria see H. W. F. Saggs, *Iraq* xvii (1955), 130, no. XIII, 3.

35. So as to ensure stability, the Aramaean exiles were provided by the Assyrian authorities with food, garments, and even wives; cf. H. W. F. Saggs, *Iraq* xviii (1956), 41 ff., 55.

36. See B. Porten, *Archives from Elephantine* (Berkeley & Los Angeles, 1968), 164 ff.; M. H. Silverman, *J.A.O.S.* lxxxix (1969), 698 ff.

37. On the cult of Adrammelech–Adad-milki cf. W. F. Albright, *A.R.I.* (Baltimore, 1946), pp. 163 f.; and now also K. Deller, *Or.* xxxiv (1965), 382 ff. For the Aramaic influence on Ahaz through Damascus see A. Malamat, *The Aramaeans*, p. 50.

38. Such a dating was recently restated by A. Moortgat, *Archäologie und altes Testament* (1970), 211 ff. For an earlier dating, in the second half of the 10th century B.C., see Albright, *Anat. Stud.* vi (1956), 75 ff. On the other hand, Albright there dates the Aramaic inscription on a limestone altar (*K.A.I.*, no. 231) to the 9th, rather than the 10th, century B.C. Incidentally, his proposal to find there the name Baḫyan (*bḥy*[*n*], pp. 82 f.), the name of the tribe or country of Gozan, was anticipated in my *The Aramaeans* (p. 52), where I suggested, however, that the *second* word should be read as *bʿyn*, i.e. the postulated Aramaic form of cuneiform Baḫyan (parallel to cuneiform Raḫyan for the name of Rezin, King of Damascus, Hebrew Reṣin, which would lead to an original Aramaic form Raʿyan); note also the significant cuneiform spelling *Raqyan*—L. D. Levine, *Two Neo-Assyrian Stelae from Iran* (Toronto, 1972), p. 18, l. 4.

39. On the material culture of the above-mentioned sites see H. Frankfort, *The Art and Architecture of the Ancient Orient*, 4th edn. (Harmondsworth, 1970), Ch. 11 and the supplementary bibliography on pp. 430 f. For an attempt to define Aramaean art at Zinjirli and other northern sites see E. Akurgal, *The Art of the Hittites* (London, 1962), pp. 136 ff. Cf. also G. Garbini, *R.S.O.* xxxiv (1959), 141 ff.

40. Quotation from a new passage in Sargon II's inscriptions from Nimrud; see C. J. Gadd, *Iraq* xvi (1954), 192. The expression *arame mār ḫabbāti*, 'a roving Aramaean' (ll. 59, 70), which occurs here for the first time, may be of significance for the biblical expression *ᵃrammī ʾōḇēḏ ʾābī* (see above, p. 140), especially in the light of the variant *ḫabātu/abātu*, 'to go astray', 'to move over', in Assyrian (cf. *C.A.D.* 1, Part i, 47b).

BIBLIOGRAPHY

ALBRIGHT, W. F., 'The Emergence of the Aramaeans', in *C.A.H.* rev. edn. ii (1966), Ch. xxxiii, pp. 46–53.

ALT, A., 'Die syrische Staatenwelt vor dem Einbruch der Assyrer', *Z.D.M.G.* lxxxviii (1934), 233 ff. (= *K.S.* iii. 214–32).

BOWMAN, R. A., 'Arameans, Aramaic and the Bible', *J.N.E.S.* vii (1948), 65–90.

BRINKMAN, J. A., *A Political History of Post-Kassite Babylonia* (Rome, 1968), pp. 267–85.

DEGEN, R., *Altaramäische Grammatik der Inschriften des 10–8 Jh. v. Chr.* (Wiesbaden, 1969).

DONNER, H. & RÖLLIG, W., *Kanaanäische und aramäische Inschriften*, 2nd edn., i–iii (Wiesbaden, 1966–9).

DUPONT-SOMMER, A., *Les Araméens* (Paris, 1949); 'Les Débuts de l'histoire araméenne', *V.T.* Supplement i (1953), 40–9.

EULER, K. F., 'Königtum und Götterwelt in den Altaram. Inschriften', *Z.A.W.* lvi (1938), 272–313.

FORRER, E., *R.L.A.* i. (1932), s.v. *Aramu*.

HOFTIJZER, J., *Religio Aramaica* (Leiden, 1968).

KITCHEN, K. A. in Douglas J. D. (ed.), *The New Bible Dictionary* (London, 1962), s.v. Aram.

KRAELING, E. G. H., *Aram and Israel* (New York, 1918).

KUPPER, J. R., *Les Nomades en Mésopotamie au temps des rois de Mari* (Brussels, 1957).

LANDSBERGER, B., *Sam'al I* (Ankara, 1948).

MALAMAT, A., *The Aramaeans in Aram Naharaim and the Rise of their States* (Jerusalem, 1952) (Hebrew); *Encycl. Biblica*, i (Jerusalem, 1950), s.v. Aram-Beth-Rehob, Aram-Damascus, Aram-Maacah, Aram-Zobah, pp. 577–83 (Hebrew).

MAZAR, B., 'The Aramean Empire and its Relations with Israel', *B.A.* xxv (1962), 98–120.

MOSCATI, S., *Ancient Semitic Civilizations* (London, 1957), Ch. vii; 'The Aramaean Ahlamu', *J.S.S.* iv (1959), 303–7.

NOTH, M., 'Beiträge zur Geschichte des Ostjordanlandes', *Beiträge zur biblischen Landes- und Altertumskunde*, lxviii (1949), 19–36.

O'CALLAGHAN, R. T., *Aram Naharaim* (Rome, 1948).

PARPOLA, S., *Neo-Assyrian Toponyms* (1970), s.v. *Ahlamu*, *Arumu*, etc.

ROSENTHAL, F., *Die aramäistische Forschung* (Leiden, 1939).

SACCHI, P., *Osservazioni sul Problema degli Aramei* (Accademia Toscana di Scienze e Lettere 'La Colombaria', 1960).

SCHIFFER, S., *Die Aramäer* (Leipzig, 1911).

UNGER, M. F., *Israel and the Aramaeans of Damascus* (London, 1957).

VATTIONI, F., 'Preliminari alle iscrizioni aramaiche', *Augustinianum* ix (1969), 305–61; 'Epigrafia Aramaica', ibid. x (1970), 493–532; 'I sigilli . . . aramaica', ibid. xi (1971), 47–87; 173–90.

VII

THE ASSYRIANS

H. W. F. SAGGS

(i) *Origins and History*

GENESIS 10: 10–12 attributes the origin of Assyrian civilization to the cultural influence of 'Shinar', a term representing the alluvial valley which today is South Iraq, known in cuneiform sources as Sumer.[1] Genesis 25: 3 makes the Aššurim the great-grandsons of Abraham, thereby implying Semitic ethnic affiliation.[2] The biblical implication, that the Assyrians were Semites with Sumerian cultural influence as primary, is substantially in accord with the evidence of archaeology and cuneiform texts, though ethnic and cultural influences from other groups, such as Hurrians and Indo-Aryans, are also discernible.

The primary strength of ancient Assyria lay in its being a rich agricultural state. Its heartland comprised the region along the Tigris and the adjacent plains, from Nineveh, controlling the fertile corn lands south of the foothills of the Hakkiari range, to Assur, south of which the precipitation is insufficient for agriculture based on rainfall.[3]

Assyrian tradition incorporated in a King List speaks of the first seventeen Assyrian rulers as being 'kings who lived in tents', indicating belief in nomadic origin, though of historical details of these alleged kings nothing is known.[4] The Assyrian area was under the direct cultural influence of the south at least from the time of the empire of Agade (twenty-fourth century B.C.), whose kings left inscriptions at Assur and Nineveh,[5] and was under the political control of the Sumerian Third Dynasty of Ur (twenty-first century B.C.).[6] It is in the period after the collapse of the latter dynasty that the first historically attested Assyrian kings, ruling at Assur, fall. Even at this time Assyrians were active outside their homeland, for merchant archives give evidence of an Assyrian trading colony in Cappadocia at Kültepe (near modern Kayseri in Turkey).[7] The most prominent ruler of the subsequent period was Šamši-Adad I, of Amorite origin, who, after conquering Assyria in about 1820 B.C. from the base of an earlier kingdom on the Habur, extended his control as far as Mari. After the reign of his son, Išme-Dagan, Assyria became subject to the increasing cultural influence of the Hurrians (Horites), who were expanding southwards from Armenia.[8] This had consequences upon subsequent Assyrian institutions and (indirectly) upon Israel.

By the Amarna period (*c.* 1400 B.C.) Assyria, lately a vassal successively of the Hurrian kingdom of Mitanni and of Babylonia, was beginning again to assert its independence. The foundations of the later power of Assyria were laid in the thirteenth century, the last independent Hurrian kingdom, Hanigalbat, being incorporated into Assyria. Assyria also secured dominance in the Zagros area and possibly beyond, since the presence at this time of pottery of Assyrian form at sites as far east as south of Lake Urmia possibly indicates deep Assyrian penetration into Iran, and certainly substantial Assyrian cultural influence in the area.[9]

Near the end of the thirteenth century B.C. King Tukulti-Ninurta I achieved a military defeat of Babylonia. Attempts have been made to see in this exploit the source of the tradition about the 'mighty hunter' Nimrod of Genesis 10: 9; yet, though the name Nimrod could indeed be philologically related to the divine element Ninurta, evidence for a more substantial connection is tenuous.[10] Tukulti-Ninurta's defeat of Babylonia had significant indirect consequences, in exposing Assyria, which geographically was peripheral to the main cultural area of the Tigris–Euphrates valley and had recently been much affected by the Hurrian factor, to more markedly Babylonian influences, particularly in religion. It is significant that the main sources for knowledge of Assyro-Babylonian religion in the first millennium are the texts from Nineveh and Assur, for whilst the bulk of these are of Babylonian (not native Assyrian) origin, their find-places emphasize the importance of the Assyrians as cultural transmitters.

A secondary indirect effect of Tukulti-Ninurta's success against Babylonia derived from the weakening of the administration of the southern kingdom, which left it subsequently less able to defend the trade routes from which Assyria also benefited. This time saw a period of marked unsettlement in the west, aspects of which were, on the one hand, the arrival of Philistines in the Palestinian littoral and attempts at settlement by their congeners in Egypt, and, on the other, Aramaean migration, to which the Patriarchal movements and those under Joshua may have been related.[11]

Aramaean pressure mounted to a climax around the turn of the millennium, with disastrous effects upon both Assyria and Babylonia; from this period we read of the sacking of cities by plundering Aramaeans,[12] the dislocation being so marked in Sippar and Babylon that there was a break in the regular temple-offerings and festivals. After 1000 B.C. the disruption eased, as the Aramaean tribes consolidated into settled kingdoms, amongst them Bît-Adini (Beth Eden of Amos 1: 5) and several encountered in connection with David (2 Sam. 8: 3–7).

The more settled conditions permitted fresh Assyrian expansion from the reign of Adad-nirari II (911–891 B.C.) onwards. He extended Assyrian control to the Euphrates and Habur, gaining suzerainty over Guzanu (the province Gozan of 2 Kings 17: 6). It was under Ashur-naṣir-apli II (883–859 B.C.) and Shalmaneser III (858–824 B.C.) that the major development took place. These two kings extended and consolidated control into the northern and eastern hills, in the direction of Babylonia, and in the west. In the west, Ashur-naṣir-apli broke the powerful kingdom of Bît-Adini, and reached the Syrian coast by way of Carchemish and the Orontes, receiving tribute from Syrian coastal states as far south as Tyre.

The reigns of Ashur-naṣir-apli and Shalmaneser were approximately contemporaneous with the Israelite period from Omri and Ahab to Jehu, and it is arguable that the expansion of Israel in the earlier part of this period, and its subsequent decline, had a direct relationship to Assyrian policy. Ashur-naṣir-apli's route to the Mediterranean through North Syria had the effect of cutting all the trade-routes of Damascus except those to the south, and could have been a factor in the attempt of Ben-Hadad of Damascus to take the Israelite capital (1 Kings 20: 1 ff.), after the earlier establishment of a trading colony there (1 Kings 20: 34). The dynastic alliance made between Israel and Sidon by Ahab's marriage (1 Kings 16: 31) could be another reflection of developments in the wider international field, in that Tyre and Sidon, although they had formally sent tribute to Ashur-naṣir-apli, were not under immediate Assyrian control as the ports further north were, and so were particularly desirable commercial allies for the more southerly states of Syria and Palestine.

Under Shalmaneser III Assyria's contacts with the Mediterranean were continued and extended, but in his reign the Assyrian forces entered Syria by a more southerly route, via Aleppo and Hamath. This made it explicit that the Assyrian threat affected all states of Syria and Palestine and drove them into a coalition to halt the aggressor, occasioning the first direct contact between Assyria and Israel. In 853 B.C. there was, according to the records of Shalmaneser, though unmentioned in the Bible, a major battle at Karkar on the Orontes, the forces opposed to Shalmaneser including '20,000 infantry of Hadadezer (Ben-Hadad) of Damascus, . . . and 2,000 chariots and 10,000 infantry of Ahab the Israelite'.[13] Shalmaneser claimed a victory. The justification for the claim has been questioned, on the ground that the subsequent war between Israel and Damascus (1 Kings 22) indicates that external pressures for coalition had been removed, implying success against Assyria.[14] But the supposed war is in fact presented in 1 Kings 22: 3 f. as a mere border dispute over one town. It is further to be noted that, either during or just after the reign of Ahab, Moab was able to regain independence[15]—a development which does not suggest that Israel was left in a strong position after the engagement at Karkar. Also, within less than ten years of the death of Ahab, there occurred in Israel a dynastic revolution (2 Kings 9) ushering in the Jehu dynasty, with a corresponding revolution against the Ben-Hadad dynasty in Damascus (2 Kings 8: 15). These revolutions would hardly have been successful against dynasties enjoying the prestige of having recently defeated Assyria, whilst there is the further point that within a few years Jehu himself was paying Shalmaneser tribute, a monument of the Assyrian king showing Jehu or his emissary doing homage (Plate VII).

These contacts affected not only the western states but also Assyria, in bringing the latter into contact with Syrian craftsmanship in ivory, of the kind known in the palaces of Ahab and his successors (1 Kings 22: 39; Amos 3: 15), and building styles. Some of the western building styles—for example, the design of a palace called a *bît ḫilāni*—were consciously copied by later Assyrian kings,[16] whilst carved ivory work found at Nimrud (the site of Calah of Genesis 10: 11) and other Assyrian cities, perhaps originating in some instances from as early as the late ninth century, shows Syrian influence and was probably the work of deported Syrian craftsmen.[17]

The earlier part of the eighth century saw a significant growth in the power of Assyria's northern neighbour, Urartu, and a corresponding recession in the position of Assyria. This adversely affected Assyrian control of North Syria and ultimately caused such pressures within Assyria itself as to bring about a revolt, in 746 B.C.

The king whom the revolt brought to the throne, mentioned in the Old Testament both under his personal name Pul and his throne-name Tiglath-pileser (III), was one of the most able of the long line of Assyrian rulers. An important feature of his reign was far-reaching administrative reforms involving a reorganization of the provincial system. It has been suggested that this was influenced by existing practice in Urartu,[18] though in assessment of this hypothesis it is relevant that, in administrative matters (such as communications) for which direct comparisons can be made during the succeeding quarter-century, Assyria seems to have been markedly superior to its northern neighbour and rival.

In the early part of his reign Tiglath-pileser faced a revolt in the west involving Menahem of Israel and a certain Azriyau of Yaudi.[19] There is an evident prima facie case, both philologically and chronologically, for identifying the latter with Azariah of Judah, though the alternative suggestion has been made that there is to be seen here a king of the state known in non-vocalized alphabetic inscriptions as Y'dy, centred on Zinjirli.[20] Whilst Menahem's encounter with Tiglath-pileser (Pul) is specifically mentioned in the Bible (2 Kings 15: 19–20), there is no corresponding account directly relating Azariah to the Assyrian king. But this negative evidence is not conclusive, as, in view of the favourable biblical judgement passed on Azariah, deliberate suppression may have been involved. It is also to be noted that 2 Chronicles 26: 6–15 does specifically mention vigorous military expansion under Uzziah (Azariah); and to this Assyria, exercising suzerainty over the area immediately to the north, would unquestionably have been sensitive. Furthermore, it is certain that within less than a decade, by the reign of Ahaz, Judah was an accepted vassal of Assyria (2 Kings 16: 7), a situation which makes it unlikely that there had been no contact between Tiglath-pileser and the predecessors of Ahaz. On this hypothesis, the encounter of Tiglath-pileser with Azriyau of Yaudi provides the probable point at which Judah irrevocably came into the Assyrian sphere.

Later, whilst Tiglath-pileser was engaged in the north-eastern part of his empire, further trouble broke out in Syria and Palestine, involving Ahaz. A coalition between Syria and Israel attempted to force the Judaean king into their camp (2 Kings 16: 5–6), Edom and the Philistine cities taking the opportunity of occupying or reoccupying border areas (2 Chron. 28: 17–18). It was Assyrian policy to defend loyal vassals, and when Ahaz turned to Tiglath-pileser for assistance in this emergency, it was duly forthcoming. Ahaz has been criticized for a panic reaction, but in fact his action represented strict protocol in the circumstances. Isaiah refers (7: 6) to a 'son of Tabeel' whom the Syro-Israelite coalition planned to set on the throne of Judah in place of Ahaz, and it has been suggested that an Assyrian royal letter refers to this person,[21] though other interpretations of the passage concerned are possible.[22] Tiglath-pileser's intervention culminated in his replacement of Pekah as King of Israel by Hoshea.[23]

Tiglath-pileser also faced difficulties in Babylonia, hitherto ruled by a pro-Assyrian native Babylonian. In 734 B.C. a chief of the Kaldu (Chaldaean) tribes usurped the throne, whereat another Chaldaean chieftain, later encountered in the Bible as Merodach-Baladan, sided with the Assyrians.[24] After putting down the revolt, Tiglath-pileser in person took the kingship of Babylonia.

In the brief reign of the next king, Shalmaneser V (727–722 B.C.), Egypt instigated anti-Assyrian intrigues in Palestine. The involvement of Hoshea in these led to the Assyrian invasion of Israel and a three-year siege of Samaria (2 Kings 17: 5), ending in its capture and the deportation of its inhabitants. This deportation was in accordance with normal Assyrian practice: it was a policy which had important consequences for later developments in the Near East, in that it served to accelerate ethnic and cultural mixing, so that it was one of the factors preparing the way for the eventual spread of Hellenism and Christianity.

The Bible implies that Samaria was taken by Shalmaneser; this attribution has been questioned, since Shalmaneser's successor Sargon II himself claims this feat in some of his inscriptions. It is significant, however, that in Sargon's earliest inscription, the so-called 'Ashur Charter', the capture of Samaria is not mentioned, though there is reference to action against a secondary insurrection in that area, shortly after Sargon had consolidated his succession.[25] This makes it likely that the Israelite capital was indeed taken under Shalmaneser, and that it was only later in Sargon's reign that his annalists conflated the major success against Samaria, actually due to his predecessor, with the secondary one under Sargon.

The main events of Sargon's reign related to defence against the north, where there existed not only the kingdom of Urartu, now at the apex of its power, but also Iranian tribes and the Cimmerians (Gomer of the Bible). Much of Sargon's strategy, including his creation of a new fortress-capital Dūr-Sharrukīn (i.e. 'Sargonsburg') north-east of Nineveh, commanding the principal pass from the northern mountains, was directed to controlling these threats. A major campaign into the heart of Urartu in 714 B.C., although it did not at once destroy that kingdom, crippled it as a challenge to Assyria.[26] The weakening of Urartu was, however, in the long term to the disadvantage of Assyria, since it left the northern kingdom less capable of acting as a buffer in holding off the migrating races pressing southwards from beyond the Caucasus.

After dealing with Urartu, Sargon was free to settle Babylonia, where Merodach-Baladan, no longer time-serving in the Assyrian camp, had followed the earlier Chaldaean rebel in seizing the kingship. Merodach-Baladan, though in 710 B.C. driven from Babylon, retained the chieftainship of his tribe, engaging in widespread diplomatic intrigue, of which the embassy to Hezekiah (2 Kings 20: 12) may have been a part, in preparation for some later opportunity. This came after Sargon's death in 705 B.C., probably in battle in the north-west in an attempt to check the advance of the Cimmerian hordes.

Sargon's son and successor, Sennacherib, for Byron the Assyrian who 'came down like a wolf on the fold', has more recently been denigrated by such phrases as 'a man of vastly less ability [than his father]'.[27] Such judgements, however, appear to have no more substantial basis than the subjective reaction of modern biblical scholars offended with this king for attacking Jerusalem. In fact Sennacherib was, at his accession, already an experienced soldier and administrator, and later not only proved himself a skilled strategist in dealing with the problems of his empire, and an outstanding tactician (a feature demonstrated in his building a fleet of Phoenician ships in Syria and Assyria to make possible a sea-borne attack on Elam from the Persian Gulf),[28] but also showed an interest in technological innovations (such as methods of metal casting and well construction), and considerable ability in town planning in connection with his redevelopment and extension of Nineveh. In the political sphere he also—if the interpretation proposed for a certain text (mentioned below) is correct—displayed considerable acumen in his use of religious propaganda against Babylon.

It was Babylonia which constituted the main problem of Sennacherib's reign. Within two years of Sennacherib's succession Merodach-Baladan had again seized the southern throne, with Elamite assistance bought with a massive bribe.[29] A major Assyrian campaign was needed to dispossess Merodach-Baladan and to cut at the source of his power in the tribal areas. This was scarcely completed when, in 701 B.C., a revolt broke out in Palestine, in which Hezekiah, who according to the biblical testimony had been in communication with Merodach-Baladan, was heavily implicated.[30] The anti-Assyrian forces received assistance from Egypt, as both Sennacherib's annals and the book of Isaiah (30: 1–5, 31: 1–3) indicate. Sennacherib dispatched an army, which defeated the Egyptians and, in the course of their action against the rebel cities, invested Jerusalem (Plate VI *b*). The siege is described in detail both in the inscriptions of Sennacherib and in the Bible.

Whilst the Assyrian account refers solely to the events of 701 B.C., the biblical narrative has been seen by some scholars as containing material dealing with two distinct attacks upon Jerusalem, one that of 701 B.C., and the other a much later siege not long before Sennacherib's death in 681 B.C., to which 2 Kings 19: 36–37 would (it is argued) be more apposite.[31] It appears more probable to the present writer that the apparent doublets in the biblical account either result from the composite literary structure of 2 Kings 18–19, or are to be seen as descriptions of two military movements against Jerusalem constituting successive stages in the tactical procedure of a single attack.

Sennacherib's settlement of Babylonia proved shortlived, inasmuch as Elam, vying with Assyria for control of the country, was giving support to Chaldaean insurgents. Finally, Sennacherib became convinced that the southern capital was a cancer to be destroyed. Babylon was besieged, taken, and sacked. It was probably as a theological justification of this impiety towards a great cult city that there was written a satirical trial and condemnation of Marduk, Babylon's tutelary deity, in the form of a cult commentary. This text was formerly taken as establishing the death and resurrection of Marduk at the New Year Festival, for which there exists no other conclusive evidence.[32]

Sennacherib's murder, according to the Bible (2 Kings 19: 37) by parricide, a situation likely enough, although not stated in the cuneiform sources,[33] opened the way to civil war. This was quickly checked by the energetic action of one of Sennacherib's sons, Esarhaddon, in whose favour the goddess Ishtar gave an oracle which brought his rivals' army over to his side.[34] Esarhaddon, who had already had experience as Governor of Babylonia, took action against recalcitrant Chaldaean leaders, replacing them by tribal rivals submissive to Assyria. By a diplomatically skilful and conciliatory policy, including the rebuilding of devastated Babylon, he produced stability in the southern kingdom.[35] In the north, however, Assyria was now less happily placed, as a result of the movement of Cimmerian and Scythian peoples, between whom and Assyria there was—now that Urartu was impotent—no effective buffer. There was a definite recession at this time in the area controlled by Assyria to the north, and although counterbalancing Assyrian expansion occurred in the south-west, where Esarhaddon (in a major departure from traditional policy) mounted an invasion of Egypt against the pharaoh Tirhakah, who had been fomenting insurrection in Palestine (2 Kings 19: 9), Assyrian decline may be considered to have begun. Recognizing the need for allies, Esarhaddon appears to have attempted to secure stability in the north by making a marriage alliance with the Scythians,[36] whilst a group of treaties has been found binding his Median vassals to support after his death the succession which he had decreed.[37]

The succession plan, by which Esarhaddon's son Ashurbanipal ruled as King in Assyria, and another son as sub-king in Babylonia, was duly carried into effect, and it was a mark of Esarhaddon's foresight that it worked satisfactorily for over fourteen years, giving, in continuation from Esarhaddon's reign, the longest period of peace and co-operation between Babylonia and Assyria for over a century.

Esarhaddon's invasion of Egypt had had only limited and temporary success. The favourable situation in Babylonia now gave Ashurbanipal the opportunity of making another attempt, from 667 B.C. onwards, at bringing Egypt under effective Assyrian control. The initial invasion was followed by the policy of using native princes in the administration. Prominent amongst these was a certain Necho, the grandfather of the pharaoh of that name mentioned in 2 Kings 23: 33. An attempt in 664–663 B.C., by the Nubian dynasty to which Tirhakah (now deceased) had belonged, to dispossess the Egyptian princes loyal to Assyria brought fresh Assyrian military action, in which Thebes (anciently known as No-Amon) was captured and looted, an incident recalled in Nahum 3: 8–10.

During this same period the protection of Assyria against Cimmerian invaders was sought by some of the states of Asia Minor. Amongst those concerned the most prominent was Gyges (Gugu) of Lydia, possibly the Gog of Ezekiel 38–39, who is mentioned in connection with the Cimmerians (Gomer of Ezek. 38: 6). Gugu, although initially supported by Assyria, was subsequently denounced by Ashurbanipal, with the implication that he was attempting independent expansion in Asia Minor; and the enigmatic references to Gog in Ezekiel may reflect the memory, over half a century later, of the fear aroused in Palestine by rumours of movements of Cimmerian hordes in Asia Minor, in a region where Gugu was the major independent ruler.[38] Alternatively, the chapters could refer to an otherwise unknown dynastic successor of the same name, contemporary with Ezekiel.[39]

In Egypt Necho's successor, Psammetichus, after achieving paramountcy amongst native princes by Assyrian assistance, subsequently set himself to expel the Assyrian garrisons, an objective accomplished by 651 B.C. The principal factor in his success was the outbreak of civil war in the Assyrian empire, where the Assyrian sub-king in Babylon rebelled against his brother. In consequence, Ashurbanipal was fully engaged in Babylonia from 652 until 648 B.C. Intermittent action against Elam, which had fostered the rebellion, continued for another nine years.

The annals of Ashurbanipal fail us after 639 B.C., and the events of the closing years of his long reign are not wholly clear. There is evidence, however, that Assyria was already facing serious difficulties, although these received no overt expression in the form of imperial disintegration until after the death of Ashurbanipal in 629 B.C. Details of the succession are not wholly beyond doubt, but recent evidence appears to favour discarding the previous view that rival kings divided the empire, the actual situation possibly being that there was from 629 B.C. to the fall of Nineveh in 612 B.C. a single ruler, known by the alternative names of Sin-shar-ishkun or Ashur-etil-ilāni.[40]

The death of Ashurbanipal was immediately followed by widespread outbreaks of unrest. Josiah's activities were probably an aspect of this, for, according to 2 Chronicles 34: 6, it was immediately afterwards, in his twelfth year (628 B.C.), that he assumed control of the Assyrian province comprising Samaria, Gilead, and Galilee. Such virtual rebellion would, under a strong Assyrian government, have evoked rigorous action. That this did not ensue was because Assyria faced more serious trouble in Babylonia, where by 626 B.C. a certain Nabopolassar, of Chaldaean descent, was able to assume the kingship. After achieving independence in Babylonia Nabopolassar began to move northwards against Assyria itself. Finally, after various successes, he attacked the capital Nineveh, in alliance with the Medes and a group called the Umman-manda, largely comprising Scythians (the Ashkenaz of Jer. 51: 27). At the fall of the city, probably facilitated by a flood,[41] a remnant of the army withdrew to Harran and Carchemish. Military assistance was sought from Egypt, and it was the Egyptian army on the way to Assyria's aid that Josiah intercepted at Megiddo, where he met his death (2 Kings 23: 29; 2 Chron. 35: 20–24) in 608 B.C. The joint Assyrian and Egyptian forces were defeated by Nabopolassar's son Nebuchadrezzar at Carchemish in 605 B.C., and the Assyrian empire was finally at an end.

(ii) *Religion and Influence*

The significance of the Assyrians in the context of Old Testament studies lies not only in their having been the predominant military and political force during the crucial centuries of the Hebrew monarchy, but also in the religious and general influences mediated by them, particularly from the time of Ahaz onwards. There were factors which made Assyria culturally intermediate between Babylonia and Israel. The peoples of Assyria and Babylonia spoke dialects of a common language, had a common literature, and (in broad terms) a common religious heritage. Yet there were respects in which Assyria was closer to Palestine than to Babylonia. Babylonia, a flat alluvial plain with its agriculture wholly dependent upon irrigation, had a concentration of great cities unparalleled in the ancient world, with much of the land in the ownership of temple estates. Assyria, on the other hand, was, like Palestine, a region of hills, characterized by small towns and villages rather than by great cities, Nineveh being exceptional.[12] The fact that much of Palestine and Assyria had the same limits of rainfall gave them a similar pattern of agriculture, with potential consequences for those aspects of life (including religion) dependent on agriculture. When Sennacherib's representative promised the men of Jerusalem deportation to 'a land like your own land' (2 Kings 18: 32), he was—if he had in mind Assyria itself—speaking no less than the truth.[13] The geographical and sociological similarity between Palestine and Assyria and the marked difference between Palestine and Babylonia may in part explain why, after deportation, the Israelites, most of whom went to Assyria, were assimilated without trace, whilst the Judaeans in Babylonia stubbornly retained their identity.

To the modern reader, approaching from the viewpoint of the Judaeo-Christian tradition, the most evident feature of Assyro-Babylonian religion is its polytheism. Inscriptions of Assyrian kings list long series of deities, such as 'Ashur the great lord, father of the gods, Anum, Enlil and Ea, Sin, Shamash, Adad, Marduk, Nabu, Nergal, Ishtar, the Seven, the great gods who stand at the side of the king', but such lists constituted only a small fraction of the total pantheon. As in Israel, so in Mesopotamia the form of deity was conceived as basically anthropomorphic, though a number of the major Assyro-Babylonian deities of the first millennium had an astral aspect, Ishtar being referred to in this form (represented by the planet Venus) as 'Queen of Heaven' in Jeremiah 44: 17, 25, the influence here being probably Babylonian rather than Assyrian; in Assyrian art deities were frequently depicted by non-anthropomorphic astral symbols.

It is possible formally to relate specific gods to specific functions in the cosmos, but more significant than the details of the pantheon is the concept of the nature of deity which prevailed. It is commonly held that there was a fundamental distinction between Israelite and Assyro-Babylonian religion in regard to the function of deity. The view has been maintained that whereas the Old Testament writers saw God as active primarily in history, other peoples of the ancient Near East recognized the activity of deity only in and through nature.[44] In fact, the Assyrians of the first millennium specifically claimed, in their statecraft, the intrusion of the divine into political activity. There was in connection with Assyrian imperial expansion what could almost be called a theology of holy war, of which the dominant theme was the universalistic one that the god Ashur made the claim to rule over all men. Thus Sargon II speaks of 'the great word of Ashur my lord who bestowed [on me] as a gift the bringing into submission of the princes of the mountains and the receiving of their presents'.[45] Another royal inscription, speaking of the death of an enemy king, attributes it specifically to divine intervention: 'At the command of my lord Ashur, Kudur-nahundu King of Elam did not fulfil another three months but quickly died unexpectedly.'[46]

A tendency to syncretism, operative since the third millennium, was very marked in the first millennium, and constituted a factor in an apparent movement (never completely realized) in the direction of monotheism in Assyro-Babylonian religion. The most specific evidence of this trend occurs in hymns containing the explicit statement that a number of the great gods are hypostases of one particular god, for instance Ninurta:

> Your two eyes, O Lord, are Enlil and Ninlil; . . .
> Anum and Antum are your two lips; . . .
> Your head is Adad, who made heaven and earth, . . .
> Your brow is Shala, his beloved spouse. . . .[47]

In the religion of Assyria there were various techniques purporting to give knowledge of the divine will, some comparable with means known from the Old Testament. One method by which the gods could communicate their wishes or intentions to mankind, employed in Assyria as well as in traditional (but not canonical) prophetic circles in Israel (Jer. 23: 25–28, 32), was oneiromancy (dream divination), and there were dream-diviners at the Assyrian court.[48] Other means included liver-divination and astrology. In the former technique, in Assyria in the first millennium, a question was put to the god, requiring a positive or negative answer, and a lamb then slaughtered.[49] The assumption was made that the god 'wrote' his response on the internal organs, principally the liver, of the sacrificial animal, and these organs were therefore scrutinized for markings of abnormalities giving positive or negative indications. At some periods the diviner was assisted by clay models of livers appropriately marked, and examples of these have been found from late second-millennium strata at Megiddo and Hazor, showing that this technique was not unknown in Palestine.[50] There is also a reference to it in Ezekiel 21: 21, though in a Babylonian rather than an Assyrian context. Astrological divination was of particular importance in first-millennium Assyria, observations of the moon and planets being reported to the king, with their prognoses bearing upon the well-being of the king himself or the state.[51]

A problem of some interest is whether the people of Assyria, or Mesopotamia in general, knew any phenomenon corresponding to the function of the Old Testament prophets. One type of evidence which comes into consideration from texts principally from first-millennium Assyrian sites, though ultimately deriving from Babylonia, is a literary genre designated 'Akkadian prophecies' by some scholars.[52] The following short extract shows the typical form: 'A prince will arise and exercise kingship for thirteen years; an attack by Elam upon Akkad will occur; . . . there will be confusion, distress, and misfortune in the land.' No sequence of these texts has been firmly related to a single historical context, and where historical references can be tentatively posited they give allusions to events of remote centuries. These texts may thus prove to be collections of omen apodoses given literary elaboration and arrangement.[53] They cannot be compared with Old

Testament prophecies in either phenomenology, content, or literary form.

There are, however, oracles extant from first-millennium Assyria for which a closer connection can be maintained with the type of prophetic utterance known from the Old Testament. Typically, these had relationship specifically to the king or state affairs. One text containing collections of such oracles attributes them by name to individuals, in most cases (but not all) to women. The form of the text indicates that these persons were considered to be vehicles for a message from a god. A typical section of the text reads: 'From the mouth of Rimute-allate of the town of Darahuya in the midst of the mountains. "Do not fear, Esarhaddon! I, Bel, speak with you. I watch over your innermost heart, like your mother, who gave you being. . . . Sixty great gods stand around about you, equipped for battle. Do not rely on mankind. Cast your eyes on me. . . . Do not fear, reverence me."'[54]

In the oracle quoted, the technical term for the woman through whom the oracle came is not given, though a number of terms for such persons are known, the commonest in Mesopotamia generally being *šā'iltu*, literally 'asker', with a male counterpart *šā'ilu*. In Assyria there also occurs the term *ragintu* for a woman who gave oracles. Letters report the words of such women to the king: in one there is quoted an oracle saying 'I shall conquer the enemies of my king. I shall not give a throne except for the king my lord.'[55] Clearly this is spoken in the name of the god. The fact that such oracles were reported to the king from a distance, in some cases from places not otherwise known and apparently of little political or cultic significance, suggests that in at least some instances the human vehicle of the oracle was not a formal cult functionary; this admits the possibility that oracles may on some occasions have been given through non-cultic persons in an ecstatic state.

An oracle could also be given by a manifestation called in Akkadian a *zaqīqu* (commonly translated 'phantom'), a term which when applied to a god appears to embrace a conception analogous to that of the 'angel of Yahweh'. Such an oracle, given to Ashurbanipal by 'a *zaqīqu* from before Nabu', said: 'Do not fear, Ashurbanipal. I shall give you long life. I shall appoint favourable winds for your life. My mouth . . . shall continually bless you in the assembly of the great gods.'[56] In the text, this oracle follows a passage in which Ashurbanipal squats in prayer before the god. The manner in which the *zaqīqu* gave the oracle—whether through an inspired person or by incubation—is not indicated.

More specific evidence for the giving of oracles through inspired persons comes from the Mari documents, which are outside the scope of this chapter.[57]

(iii) *Achievement and Character*

The conventional modern estimate of the Assyrians has been distorted by a combination of factors. In part there has been a tendency to read the history of the Near East in the Monarchy period from the Jerusalem-based Deuteronomist point of view, and in part judgement has been influenced by the anachronistic application of modern anti-imperialist sentiments. There has also been distorting over-emphasis upon the occasional atrocities of which the Assyrians, like all warring peoples ancient and modern, were guilty. Yet examination of the biblical attitude to Assyria shows that, even in its most aggressive and expansionist phase, it was by no means universally condemned in contemporary prophetic circles. For Isaiah, Assyria was the rod of God's anger, sent against nations as his instrument (Isa. 10: 5). Assyria did indeed incur condemnation, but for failing to recognize the source of its power, not for employing its power (Isa. 10: 12–15). Historically, Isaiah's judgement can (on the human level) be validated: Assyria did indeed have a function to perform. From the late second millennium until the fall of Assyria there were repeated threats upon the Near East from tribal hordes from the north—Mushku (Meshech, stopped by Tiglath-pileser I in about 1100 B.C. when pressing into the Upper Tigris region), the Medes (first encountered in the ninth century) and cognate Iranian tribes, the Cimmerians, and the Scythians. The circumstances of the Hyksos and Habiru, and Jeremiah's fear of the 'people from the north' (6: 22–26), give some idea of the havoc and terror that could be spread over the settled areas by an incursion of such hordes. It was a function of Assyria to safeguard the civilized world against such threats. Whilst Assyrian dominion may well have been harsh, it did prevent the breakdown of civil order which the incursion of nomads, or stateless warlike groups such as the Habiru had been, would have involved. Assyrian military activity was not wanton unpredictable invasion and plunder. A faithful vassal was secure from interference, whilst even against offending vassals action was subject to strict lines of procedure. Even an attack upon an enemy non-vassal state was not arbitrary; thus when Sargon invaded Urartu in 714 B.C. he was scrupulous in claiming theological justification.[58]

The success of Assyria, particularly in the century of its greatest extent, from Tiglath-pileser III to Ashurbanipal, was due, more than to any other factor, to administrative efficiency. A chain of command led from the court through the provincial governors to local officials, but the governors themselves, as well as those lower in the chain, were subject to investigation by inspectors reporting direct to the king, and inefficiency or corruption were rigorously punished.[59]

Concentration upon the military achievements of Assyrian rulers has tended to obscure other aspects of the Assyrian character. Though the evidence is limited, we are not wholly without indications as to these. One aspect of the Assyrian character seems to have been a feeling for landscape. The regions through which their kings passed on campaign are often vignetted in a telling phrase, as when Sargon II mentions that the branches of the trees in a certain pass were so thickly intertwined that the traveller could not see the gleam of the sun.[60] Sennacherib describes a mountain area of gullies, waterfalls, and cliffs, where he finally had to leave his chariot and proceed on foot, until his knees gave out and he sat on a boulder to drink cold water from a skin.[61] Esarhaddon sums up the god-forsaken land of Bazu as a region 'with soil of salt, a place of thirst, 800 miles of sand, a place where snakes and scorpions fill the terrain like ants'.[62] The kings clearly had a conscious appreciation of the more pleasing landscapes, for some of them attempted to recreate what they had seen, importing trees and herbaceous plants from foreign lands to establish parks.[63]

Assyrian kings (or the scribes who accompanied them on campaign) were also acute observers of the differing mannerisms and ways of life of other peoples whom they encountered. In one passage it is noted that the language of one of the mountain peoples sounded like the twittering of women,[64] whilst the rulers of the coastal Phoenician cities were described as 'kings who inhabit the sea, whose fortification walls are the sea, whose outer walls the waves, who ride a ship for a chariot, and have oarsmen harnessed in place of horses'.[65] It is in keeping with this characteristic of noticing the activities of other peoples that the Rabshakeh was aware of Hezekiah's destruction of provincial high places and of the opposition this aroused (2 Kings 18: 22).

Considerable attention has commonly been paid, in the discussion of Assyrian history, to individual kings. There is good justification for this. Pragmatically, state policy did effectively depend upon the personal qualities and preferences of the king (to some extent restricted by religious taboos to which the priesthood might subject him), and the sudden recovery of Assyria with the accession of Tiglath-pileser III is a striking instance of this. Also, from the theological point of view, the king was regarded as being the source and embodiment of the well-being of his land. A correspondent writing to one of the Assyrian kings says: 'The great gods of heaven and earth are venerated in the time of the king my lord. Old men dance, young men sing, women and maidens are glad with joy.'[66] Theologically the king was the shepherd in charge of the people who were the god's flock, and Sargon stigmatizes a cowardly Egyptian king as 'not a shepherd'.[67]

Although the Assyrian king was never a god, the whole of official religion centred upon him, the prosperity of the whole nation being tied up in his welfare. This is well exemplified in the rite of the 'substitute king', employed as late as the reign of Esarhaddon. By this, when an exceptional danger faced the king (according to the omens), a substitute was installed to take office over the period of danger, possibly being put to death if he survived that time.[68]

The converse of this centring of religion upon the king was the relatively limited claims of religion on private persons. Whilst there was some tendency, in Assyria as in Egypt, for religious concepts originally involving only the king to be disseminated to affect the ordinary man, this was limited in its effects. There is found nowhere in Assyrian sources anything comparable to the direct explicit claim of the prophets upon the whole life of every individual person.[69]

NOTES

1. A. Poebel, *J.N.E.S.* i (1942), 256, suggests that the mention of Assur (Assyria) in Gen. 10: 11 was in origin a marginal note calling attention to the fact that the cities built by Nimrod were in that land. For a suggestion that Shinar in Gen. 14: 1, 9 denoted not the Babylonian plain but a town on the middle Euphrates see F. M. Th. de L. Böhl, *J.E.O.L.* xvii (1963), 132. See also, for proposed identification of Shinar not with Sumer but with Shanḫar (supposedly) in North Syria, references in L. Matouš, *Ar.Or.* xxxvii (1969), p. 3 n. 11; but Shanḫar itself may be another name for Babylonia, as established by M. S. Drower in *C.A.H.* ii (1970), chap. x, fasc. 64 (i), p. 40 n. 3 and p. 45.

2. A. Poebel, *J.N.E.S.* i (1942), 255.

3. D. Oates, *Studies in the Ancient History of Northern Iraq* (O.U.P., London, 1968), p. 3 and fig. 1 on p. 2.

4. See most recently F. R. Kraus, 'Könige, die in Zelten wohnten', *Mededelingen der Koninklijke Nederlandse Akademie van Wetenschappen, Afd. Letterkunde,* Nieuwe Reeks xxviii/2 (1965), 123–42.

5. I. J. Gelb, *Hurrians and Subarians* (University of Chicago Press, 1944), p. 36 n. 100.

6. Sidney Smith, *Early History of Assyria* (Chatto and Windus, London, 1928), pp. 130 f.

7. A. Goetze, *Kleinasien,* 2nd edn. (C. H. Beck, München, 1957), pp. 64–81.

8. M. S. Drower, 'Syria *c.* 1550–1400 B.C.', *C.A.H.* 2nd edn., II, Part i, Ch. x (= fasc. 64 (i) (1970)), p. 6.

9. R. H. Dyson, 'Problems of Protohistoric Iran as seen from Hasanlu', *J.N.E.S.* xxiv (1965), 195.

10. For the proposed identification see E. A. Speiser, 'In Search of Nimrod', *Eretz-Israel* v (1958), 32*–36*, reprinted in J. J. Finkelstein and M. Greenberg (eds.), *Oriental and Biblical Studies; Collected Writings of E. A. Speiser* (Univ. of Pennsylvania Press, Philadelphia, 1967), pp. 41–52. For an alternative identification, as a corruption of MAR.TU, see A. Poebel, *J.N.E.S.* i (1942), 256 f.

11. For the view that there was no substantial Israelite immigration into Palestine under Joshua see G. E. Mendenhall, *B.A.* xxv, no. 3 (Sept. 1962), 66–87.

12. A. Goetze, 'An Inscription of Simbar-šiḫu', *J.C.S.* xix (1965), 121–35.

13. III R, Pl. 8, lines 90–2.

14. See e.g. J. Bright, *A History of Israel* (S.C.M. Press, London, 1960), pp. 224, 228.

15. 2 Kings 1: 1, 3: 4–27. The Moabite Stone, lines 4–7, 10–19; see most recently F. I. Andersen, 'Moabite Syntax', *Or.* xxxv (1966), 81–120.

16. See references in *C.A.D.* vi, 184 f., apud *ḫilānu*.

17. R. D. Barnett, *A Catalogue of the Nimrud Ivories* (B.M., London, 1957), p. 52.

18. E. Forrer, *Die Provinzeinteilung des assyrischen Reiches* (Hinrichs, Leipzig, 1920), p. 49.

19. P. Rost, *Die Keilschrifttexte Tiglat-Pilesers III* (Eduard Pfeiffer, Leipzig, 1893), ii, p. 10, Pl. XX, lines 4′, 5′ (= III R, Pl. 9, no. 2, lines 3, 4), and p. 13, Pl. XXI, line 2 (= III R, Pl. 9, no. 3, line 23).

20. C. H. Gordon, *J.N.E.S.* xiv (1955), 57. For the view identifying Azriyau of Yaudi with Azariah of Judah see H. Tadmor, 'Azriyau of Yaudi', *Scripta Hierosolymitana* viii (1961), 232–71.

21. W. F. Albright, *B.A.S.O.R.* cxl (Dec. 1955), 34 f.

22. H. Donner, *M.I.O.* v (1957), 171.

23. P. Rost, op. cit., ii, p. 15, Pl. XXV, lines 15–18.

24. H. W. F. Saggs, *Iraq* xvii (1955), 48 f. The hypothesis that Merodach-Baladan was negotiating with the Assyrians is confirmed by an unpublished letter, ND 2389, certainly written by Merodach-Baladan to the Assyrian king.

25. K. 1349, lines 16–20.

26. F. Thureau-Dangin, *Une Relation de la huitième campagne de Sargon* (Geuthner, Paris, 1912).

27. J. Bright, op. cit. 267.

28. I R, Pl. 43, lines 23 f., edited in D. D. Luckenbill, *The Annals of Sennacherib* (University of Chicago Press, 1924), pp. 86 f., lines 23 f.

29. J. A. Brinkman, *J.N.E.S.* xxiv (1965), 164.

30. For the placing of Merodach-Baladan's embassy to Hezekiah (2 Kings 20: 12–13 = Isa. 39: 1–2) at this period see J. Bright, op. cit. 267, n. 43; H. W. F. Saggs, *The Greatness that Was Babylon* (Sidgwick & Jackson, London, 1962), p. 119; J. A. Brinkman, 'Merodach-Baladan II', *Studies presented to A. Leo Oppenheim* (University of Chicago Press, 1964), p. 33. J. Gray, *I & II Kings: a Commentary*, 2nd edn. (S.C.M. Press, London, 1970), p. 701, puts the embassy earlier.

31. For an excellent detailed discussion of the problem see B. S. Childs, *Isaiah and the Assyrian Crisis* (= *Studies in Biblical Theology*, Second Series, 3; S.C.M. Press, London, 1967).

32. W. von Soden, 'Gibt es ein Zeugnis dafür, dass die Babylonier an die Wiederaufstehung Marduks geglaubt haben?', *Z.A.* N.F. xvii (1955), 130–66.

33. Ashurbanipal makes an allusion to the murder in V R, Pl. 4, lines 70–3, though without a specific accusation of parricide.

34. R. Borger, *Die Inschriften Asarhaddons Königs von Assyrien* (= *A.f.O.*, Beiheft 9; Biblio-Verlag, Osnabrück, 1967), p. 44, Episode 2, A, I 74–8.

35. For the theory that there were two parties in Assyria, one wishing to reduce Babylonia to an ordinary province and the other proposing to give it the greatest possible independence within the Assyrian Empire,

Sennacherib favouring the former party and Esarhaddon the latter, see W. von Soden, 'Die Unterweltsvision eines assyrischen Kronprinzen', *Z.A.* N.F. ix (1936), 6.

36. J. A. Knudtzon, *Assyrische Gebete an den Sonnengott* (Leipzig, 1893), no. 29. On the probable date see D. J. Wiseman, *Iraq* xx (1958), p. 10 n. 98.

37. D. J. Wiseman, 'The Vassal-Treaties of Esarhaddon', ibid. 1–99 and Pls. 1–32.

38. For a Cimmerian threat against Assyria in 657 B.C. see L. F. Hartman, *J.N.E.S.* xxi (1962), 25–37.

39. For a different interpretation of these chapters, in relation to Alexander the Great, see refs. in O. Eissfeldt, *The Old Testament: an Introduction* (Blackwell, Oxford, 1965), p. 371.

40. So R. Borger, *J.C.S.* xix (1965), 72. For different interpretations of the evidence see J. Reade, 'The Accession of Sinsharishkun', *J.C.S.* xxiii (1970), 1–9, and articles there mentioned on p. 1, n. 1. See also S. S. Ahmed, *Southern Mesopotamia in the Time of Ashurbanipal* (Mouton, The Hague & Paris, 1968), p. 126 n. 12.

41. H. W. F. Saggs, *J.T.S.* N.S. xx (1969), 225.

42. D. Oates, op. cit. 12.

43. The statement of J. Gray, op. cit. 620, that 'the promise of . . . olives could not apply to any part of the Assyrian Empire except the Mediterranean region, and certainly not to the Assyrian homeland' is not in accord with the ecological facts. A thriving olive orchard exists between Nebi Yunus and the Tigris, within Nineveh itself; there is also an olive plantation within a mile of Khorsabad (Sargon's new capital, Dūr-Sharrukīn), and one of 8,000 trees at the Yezidi village of Bashiqah, fourteen miles north-east of Nineveh.

44. See references and detailed discussion in B. Albrektson, *History and the Gods* (Gleerup, Lund, 1967), 11–15 *et passim.*

45. F. Thureau-Dangin, op. cit. 12, line 68.

46. D. D. Luckenbill, *The Annals of Sennacherib*, pp. 177–80 (v, 12–14).

47. Ebeling, *Keilschrifttexte aus Assur Religiösen Inhalts* (Leipzig, 1919), I, no. 102, lines 11, 16, 22 f.; German translation in A. Falkenstein and W. von Soden, *Sumerische und Akkadische Hymnen und Gebete* (Artemis-Verlag, Zürich/Stuttgart, 1953), pp. 258 f., no. 10.

48. A. L. Oppenheim, 'The Interpretation of Dreams in the Ancient Near East', *Transactions of the American Philosophical Society*, N.S. xlvi, no. 3 (1956), p. 238.

49. For a typical example of such a question to the god see J. A. Knudtzon, op. cit. no. 19.

50. B. Landsberger & H. Tadmor, 'Fragments of Clay Liver Models from Hazor', *I.E.J.* xiv (1964), 201–18.

51. Primary publication in R. Campbell Thompson, *The Reports of the Magicians and Astrologers of Nineveh and Babylon* (2 vols., Luzac, London, 1900). Most recent discussion in A. L. Oppenheim, 'Divination

and Celestial Observation in the last Assyrian Empire', *Centaurus* xiv (1969), 97–135.

52. A. K. Grayson & W. G. Lambert, 'Akkadian Prophecies', *J.C.S.* xviii (1964), 7–30.

53. R. D. Biggs, 'More Babylonian "Prophecies"', *Iraq* xxix (1967), 117.

54. IV R (2nd edn.), Pl. 61, col. ii, lines 13–21, 25–9.

55. *A.B.L.*, no. 149, rev. 7–11.

56. K. 1285, obv. 24–6, edited in M. Streck, *Assurbanipal und die letzten assyrischen Könige bis zum Untergange Niniveh's* (= *Vorderasiatische Bibleothek* 7, Hinrichs, Leipzig, 1916), 2. Teil, p. 346.

57. See A. Malamat, 'Prophetic Revelations in New Documents from Mari and the Bible', Supplements to *V.T.* xv (1966), 207–27; F. Ellermeier, *Prophetie in Mari und Israel* (Erwin Jungfer, Herzberg, 1968).

58. F. Thureau-Dangin, op. cit. 16, lines 92–5.

59. Implied by a number of Assyrian letters; e.g. *A.B.L.* 290, indicating that the recipient of the King's letter, who had been falsely denounced, faced execution if the King had believed the accusation. See also H. W. F. Saggs, *Iraq* xx (1958), 208, on Nimrud Letter XLI.

60. F. Thureau-Dangin, op. cit. 4, lines 15 f.

61. D. D. Luckenbill, op. cit. 175, col. iv, 2–9.

62. R. Borger, op. cit. 56, Episode 17, A, iv 54–6.

63. D. J. Wiseman, 'A new Stele of Aššur-naṣir-pal II', *Iraq* xiv (1952), 41 f., lines 39–52.

64. E. A. Wallis Budge & L. W. King (eds.), *Annals of the Kings of Assyria* (B.M., London, 1902), pp. 321 f., lines 75 f.

65. R. Borger, op. cit. 57, Episode 18, A, iv 82–4.

66. S. Parpola, *A.O.A.T.* v/1 (1970), no. 121, lines 14–18.

67. A. G. Lie, *The Inscriptions of Sargon II, King of Assyria*, Part I; *The Annals* (Geuthner, Paris, 1929), p. 8, line 55, reading the personal name as ^{m}*rē'û*^{u}; see also A. Goetze, *J.C.S.* xix (1965), 122, line 21, where a good ruler is called *re-'u pal-ḫu ša áš-rat* ^{d}*ellil ši-te-'a-a*, 'the reverent shepherd, who regularly sought the counsel of Ellil'.

68. W. von Soden, 'Beiträge zum Verständnis der neuassyrischen Briefe über die Ersatzkönigsriten', *Vorderasiatische Studien; Festschrift für Prof. Dr. Viktor Christian* (Wien, 1956), pp. 100, 103 f.

69. A. L. Oppenheim, *Ancient Mesopotamia* (University of Chicago Press, 1964), p. 176.

BIBLIOGRAPHY

ALBREKTSON, B., *History and the Gods* (Lund, 1967).

EBELING, E., MEISSNER, B., & WEIDNER, E. F., *Die Inschriften der altassyrischen Könige* (Altorientalische Bibliothek i, Quelle & Meyer, Leipzig, 1926).

FORRER, E., *Die Provinzeinteilung des assyrischen Reiches* (Hinrichs, Leipzig, 1920).

GARELLI, P., *Les Assyriens en Cappadoce* (Bibliothèque Archéologique et Historique de l'Institut Français d'Archéologie d'Istanbul xix, Adrien Maisonneuve, Paris, 1963).

LUCKENBILL, D. D., *Ancient Records of Assyria and Babylonia* (2 vols., Chicago U.P., 1926–7).

MALLOWAN, SIR MAX, *Nimrud and its Remains* (2 vols., Collins, London, 1966).

OATES, D., *Studies in the Ancient History of Northern Iraq* (O.U.P., London, 1968).

SAGGS, H. W. F., *The Greatness that Was Babylon* (Sidgwick & Jackson, London, 1962).

SMITH, SIDNEY, 'The Foundation of the Assyrian Empire', 'The Supremacy of Assyria', 'Sennacherib and Esarhaddon', 'The Age of Ashurbanipal', 'Ashurbanipal and the Fall of Assyria', = Chs. i–v in BURY, J. B., COOK, S. A., ADCOCK, F. E. (eds.), *The Cambridge Ancient History*, vol. iii (C.U.P., Cambridge, 1925).

—— *Early History of Assyria to 1000 B.C.* (Chatto & Windus, London, 1928).

THUREAU-DANGIN, F., *Une Relation de la huitième campagne de Sargon* (Geuthner, Paris, 1912).

WATERMAN, L., *Royal Correspondence of the Assyrian Empire* (4 vols., University of Michigan Press, Ann Arbor, 1930–6).

WISEMAN, D. J., 'The Vassal-Treaties of Esarhaddon', *Iraq* xx, part 1 (1958).

VIII

THE BABYLONIANS AND CHALDAEANS

W. G. LAMBERT

THE terms 'Babylonia' and 'Babylonian' are taken over in English from the ancient Greeks, and while they are altogether convenient and correspond with a reality, they were never used in this way by the relevant ancient peoples. 'Babylonia' is used here for the southern end of the Tigris–Euphrates plain, roughly from the modern Baghdad to Basra, an area to which some adjacent regions pertained at various periods of history. The convenience of the term is that the area in historical times usually had a common culture and language: Sumerian in the third millennium B.C., though a Semitic language, Akkadian, was also used, especially in the areas more distant from the Persian Gulf; Babylonian in the second millennium and on into the first, when it gradually gave way to Aramaic. In ancient Mesopotamia 'Babylon' meant the city. The whole area was referred to either as 'Sumer and Akkad' (a reflection of third-millennium conditions) or later as 'Akkad' alone. The Greek usage arose because after the great Hammurabi had made the city Babylon the political capital, its political, and later cultural, influence in the area was unchallenged, and the kings of the city of Babylon ruled the other cities as well.

Babylonia is a flat, alluvial plain some 300 miles long, watered by the two rivers, which flood in the spring and early summer. The winter is mild, but the summer extremely hot. There is so little rainfall as to be useless for agriculture, and the area is naturally desert, save for the luxuriant marshes, formerly more extensive, near the Persian Gulf. There are no trees yielding timber (even the date palm is probably an early import), and no sources of metal or stone, whether for jewellery or building. Thus human occupation depended on irrigation-agriculture, and barley was the staple. In the third millennium the Sumerians, living in city-states, developed the unpromising area into a dynamic centre of civilization, well ahead of the rest of the world, save for Egypt. From this time onwards southern Mesopotamia remained a leader in Near-Eastern culture until the Hellenistic age.

The Semitic Akkadians, who had probably migrated down the Euphrates valley into Babylonia, shared in the Sumerian civilization and no doubt contributed to it. By the end of the third millennium another group of Semitic migrants, the Amorites, entered Mesopotamia and went down the Euphrates valley, ultimately to overthrow the last Sumerian dynasty, the Third Dynasty of Ur. The land fell into city-states once more, with Amorite sheikhs imposing themselves on the Sumero-Akkadian city dwellers. Out of this amalgam the Babylonians first made their appearance in history. As a spoken language Sumerian died out, though it survived in the schools, and Babylonian, a Semitic language with substantial differences from Old Akkadian, became the language of the country. For a couple of centuries different cities tried vainly to control the rest, but only Babylon succeeded. The town was utterly unimportant until its first, Amorite, dynasty began to compete in the power struggles. The sixth ruler, Hammurabi (*c.* 1793–1750 B.C.), by a lifetime's skilful though unscrupulous diplomacy, coupled with appropriate military activity, emerged as the ruler of the whole of Babylonia and of some areas beyond. The town Babylon suddenly became the capital of an empire. While the succeeding kings of the dynasty failed to hold the full extent of Hammurabi's domain—the Sealand Dynasty near the Persian Gulf was in revolt for a number of centuries—the prestige of Hammurabi and his city continued.

The end of the First Dynasty was ignominious. The Hittite army from far-away Anatolia marched under King Muršili to Babylon and sacked it. The kingdom had already been weakened by a number of peoples, and among them were the Kassites, who probably came into Mesopotamia from the Zagros mountains in the north. They are first mentioned shortly after Hammurabi's death; they took over the ruined Babylon and formed the next dynasty, which lasted from about 1600 to 1150 B.C. Nothing is known of the first two and a half centuries, which silence is indicative of an impoverished, disorganized state. Documentation is abundant for the last two centuries, which cover the Amarna period and the Hebrew settlement. Under the Kassites the civilization changed by the normal processes of development. Art, architecture, and literature altered, but the Kassites themselves contributed almost nothing, except for a new social structure of the ruling class. Indeed, they were not assimilated like the earlier Amorites, and about 1170 the ruling dynasty was ousted.

The succeeding Second Dynasty of Isin (*c.* 1157–1025) had at least one successful king, Nebuchadnezzar I. He did something to restore Babylon's political fortunes, but the rising star of Assyria was to prevent any revival of Hammurabi's empire, and in any case another Semitic migration flooded the whole of Mesopotamia at this time. The Aramaeans arrived from the Syrian desert, disrupted agriculture and trade, and sacked cities. The south bore their full brunt, and the dynasties following the Second Isin are little known. Eventually the Aramaeans settled in the far south, adjacent to the Persian Gulf, and it is their tribes that the Babylonians called 'Chaldaeans'. In due course they mingled with the old-established city-dwelling Babylonians, and the Late Babylonian language, used before Aramaic, is largely characterized by Aramaic syntax with Babylonian words. As the Late Assyrian empire reached its height (*c.* 725–625 B.C.), the Babylonians were dominated from this quarter, but with the fall of Assyria Babylon was led by Nabopolassar and his son Nebuchadnezzar II to glory. At the height of its power the Neo-Babylonian empire, which lasted only from 626 to 539, ruled from Egypt and Cilicia in the west to the Persian Gulf in the east. Babylon, the city, as rebuilt by Nebuchadnezzar, became fabled among Greeks and Hebrews for its magnificence. It was this monarch who took the Hebrews into captivity. When Babylon fell to the Persians under Cyrus, the cultural and economic life was in no way interrupted, but a slow decay set in at the end of the Persian empire, and as the Near East was Hellenized under Alexander the Great and his successors, the millennia-old cities were gradually abandoned, so that by the first century A.D. only a handful of families survived in Babylon itself, keeping alive the old traditions.

(i) *Culture*

It is quite impossible to describe a highly complex culture like that of the Babylonians in a short compass: only a few points can be mentioned. Some aspects were inherited from the Sumerians: the Babylonian culture did not grow out of a vacuum. Babylonian civilization was urban. People lived in a relatively small number of old-established cities, while villages and smaller units played no important part. This urban character of life encouraged the development of specialist crafts and professions. Perhaps that of the scribe was one of the most distinctive Babylonian professions. It was probably the Sumerians who gave the world the first writing system. The Egyptian came a little later, it seems. Clay was the material, and cuneiform signs were impressed with a stylus while it was soft. It was first (*c.* 3000 B.C.) intended for administrative purposes connected with temple estates, and to the end (first century A.D.) most of these clay tablets were connected with economic or administrative affairs. Vast numbers of receipts, records of disbursements, etc. were being written at most periods.[1] With an urban society this produced a bureaucratic background stronger perhaps than in any other part of the ancient world. The economic arrangements were often highly sophisticated, merchant bankers playing a leading role. Credit in many forms was much used, and the lack of coinage proved no obstacle to commerce. Exports, of course, paid for imports, and a standard of value was set by silver, though internal transactions might be engaged in without its actual use, except as providing relative values of other commodities. Of the thousands of preserved cuneiform letters the majority are on commercial or administrative subjects. Since only a corps of professional scribes was literate, Babylonian letters contain little of personal interest, except for some royal correspondence. *Belles-lettres* had no place in this businesslike civilization.[2]

Quite early, *c.* 2700 B.C., writing was developed for literature, and right from the beginning scholarly lists were compiled. The first were simple lists of signs, perhaps for instructing apprentice scribes, and in time this genre was elaborated into what has been called a 'list science'.[3] That is, the attempt was made to write down the names of everything in the universe in list form: not only signs and words (lists of this kind could have up to five sub-columns of explanations), but also classes of men and women, objects natural and manufactured, animals, plants, rivers, stars, etc., etc. Difficult literary texts had commentaries explaining rare words. Sumerian texts were given Babylonian translations, and more philological help was given in lists of grammatical forms and other linguistic material. No other part of the ancient Near East could boast such a vast range of learned compilations, all of which have much helped the modern decipherers, of course.

Another text genre, more indicative of their concept of the universe, is omens. Certain conditions and natural events were held to portend consequences either private or public. Thus the positions of stars, the birth of physically abnormal creatures, features of the liver of sacrificial animals, and trivial happenings in everyday life were the 'causes' written down in list form on many hundreds of tablets, and opposite them were written the 'effects': the kingdom might fall, or a man might suffer loss. While eclipses have caused fear in many societies, it is doubtful if any other civilization has taken this 'science' to such lengths. Etruscan divination probably owed much to the Babylonians, even if through the Hittites rather than at first hand. The finding of an inscribed liver model at Hazor shows how this kind of material spread to Palestine during the Amarna period.[4]

Magic texts were also a speciality of Babylonian scribes. Incantations, in Sumerian, Babylonian, and (rarely) other languages, were regularly transmitted in written form. Some of the tablets also offer instructions for performance of the rituals in which the incantations were recited. Religious literature includes, of course, prayers and hymns, but the academic bent of the scribes manifested itself in the compilation of systematized lists of gods' names and other more complex theological expositions. Literature in the strict sense is represented by myths and legends and a small number of epics about historical events. It happens that those which appeal more to us, for example the *Gilgamesh Epic*, were less popular in the ancient world than those of more theological import, such as the Babylonian *Epic of Creation*. Sciences were also represented among the texts. A recipe for making glass and related material is more a witness to technology, but mathematics was a distinctively Babylonian science. Knowledge of the material contained in Euclid's *Elements*, but not the theoretical presentation, is now known to have originated in Babylonia in the early centuries of the second millennium B.C. The famous theorem of Pythagoras is used on a cuneiform tablet of this period.[5] Astronomy, however, was much later in its origin, and the Babylonians had nothing out of the ordinary to show until the Persian period, when a mathematical astronomy developed rapidly, based on observation by the unaided naked eye. For a couple of centuries this exceeded anything in the world, even the contemporary Greek learning, which in the early Christian centuries soon surpassed it.[6] Astrology, in the sense of omens based on the heavenly bodies, is a Babylonian art, but horoscope astrology only appeared in the Hellenistic age.[7]

It was not a misjudgement of the Hebrews to look on the Babylonian scholars as especially experts in magic lore. The large number of omens and incantations are indicative. Hence the use of the term 'Chaldaean' with 'magicians', 'enchanters', and 'sorcerers' in the book of Daniel (2: 2, etc.), but this is not a Babylonian use of the term.[8]

(ii) *Religion*

Of religion, the official city cults are the only well-known part. From the beginnings of civilization each city had its own patron god or goddess, who was present in the city in the form of a cult statue in a temple. This building was the largest in the city, a fact which reflects the theocentric view of the people. As time passed, religious establishments increased in number, size, and complexity of buildings and organization. A large Babylonian town had a number of temples, although only one deity was acknowledged as patron of the place. Also, each temple would have within it facilities for worship of various gods and goddesses in addition to the one whose temple it was. The various deities were mostly personifications of parts or aspects of nature. The moon, the sun, and Venus had their deities: Sin, Shamash, and Ishtar. This last was also goddess of love and war. The storm-god Adad was well known in Babylonia, but no major city professed him as patron. Anu was god of heaven, Nergal of the underworld, though Ereshkigal was queen in that place. Enki (Sumerian) or Ea (Babylonian) was god of the sweet water believed to lie under the earth. It is impossible to give here a complete list of all the Mesopotamian deities, some of which are little known. Despite their cosmic associations, the gods were conceived very much anthropomorphically. Most of them were represented in human form: they had parents, spouses, and children, and the sum total was organized by the theologians into a pantheon like a clan: the more senior headed it, their first generation of offspring followed in precedence, and the second generation still belonged to the 'great gods'. The lesser ones were often integrated in the pantheon by being made servants of the greater. The major deities had courts with attendants just like a human king. This systematic organization of the pantheon arose under the Sumerians, and the system was modified in some particulars by the Babylonians. Some of the changes were inevitable reflections of changed circumstances. For example, Anu and Enlil had been heads of the pantheon at the end of the third millennium, but with the rise of the city Babylon, Marduk, the city god, rose at once to the ranks of the 'great gods'. By about 1100 B.C. Marduk was officially considered head of the pantheon, the second and final step in his promotion. The well-known Babylonian *Epic of Creation*[9] is a mythical statement of this rise. Marduk (Hebrew: Merodach) became known as Bel, 'the lord', and is mentioned three times in the Hebrew prophets under this name: Isaiah 46: 1, Jeremiah 50: 2 and 51: 44. By the end of the first quarter of the first millennium B.C. Marduk's son, Nabû, who was by this time established as city god of Borsippa, close to Babylon, had similarly risen in power, so that under the Late Babylonian empire Bel and Nabû were co-equal rulers of the universe. They appear in Isaiah 46: 1 as Bel and Nebo. In this case historical changes brought about the elevation of new rulers of the gods. Other changes were entirely the work of scholarly theologians. As a result of the city origin of the various cults there was a great amount of duplication of deities when the whole land was considered together. Gods and goddesses of similar attributes were known and worshipped in a variety of cities, though often under different names. The theologians identified such deities and thereby brought order into what otherwise would have been a chaotic multiplicity of gods. But this process was pushed beyond the cases where close similarity was obvious, and in the first millennium a few scholars had gone so far as to identify all the major gods with Marduk, so creating a kind of monotheism.[10] It is doubtful if this view was ever widely held: polytheism remained normal to the end.

The cult consisted of seasonal festivals, of which very little is known, and more regular (often daily) rites. The latter included prayers addressed to the statue, and the putting of meals before it twice a day. This was merely feeding the god, and it is incorrect to speak of this as sacrifice. Mesopotamian religion had nothing that corresponded to sacrifice among the Hebrews and Canaanites. The buildings were of two main kinds: the temple (basically an oblong room with the entrance in the long side and the statue on a podium at one end), and the ziggurat (a kind of step pyramid of solid brick with a shrine on the top, though little is known of its function). The temples in all periods owned large estates, and were in consequence powerful economically. For such activities the temples owned buildings for what we would consider non-religious purposes.

It must not be imagined that the city temple was a centre of public city worship. Only certain priests and officials were allowed inside the temple buildings. No public worship ever took place there. All devotions were performed by the appropriate clergy alone. The populace was on hand at certain festivals and witnessed processions through the streets, and there is evidence that the whole city shared in the mood of particular celebrations, but that was the extent of popular participation. The ordinary people presumably went to the street-corner shrine, or had a private niche at home around which their devotions revolved, but little is known of this kind of religion.

Other aspects of Babylonian civilization are not so outstanding. Architecture was limited by the available materials, and sun-dried bricks were most commonly used. Stone and timber were expensive imports and never had much importance for building. The shortage of any readily available fuel meant that kiln-fired bricks were the exception. With such limitations it is a surprise that the temples and *ziggurat*s had a certain massive awe about them, but builders elsewhere in stone and wood had the advantage. Art, too, was not a field in which the Babylonians excelled. Cylinder seals[11] are one of the commonest and best-known forms of Babylonian art. They served the practical function of seals in other societies: to indicate consent and authorization, as is done in some other cultures by signing one's name. The cylinder seals vary in size; on average, they are from two to four centimetres high, and of varying diameter. They are bored through from top to bottom to be carried, usually on a string around the neck. The majority were made of stone, sometimes semiprecious, though other materials also occur. The curving outer surface was cut with designs which varied from period to period, and some seals bear in addition an inscription, usually the owner's name or religious phrases. The seals were rolled on the soft clay of a cuneiform tablet, or on clay used as a seal around a knot in string for security. Poor-quality seals were the work of hack artists, but the best, despite their small size, are real works of art. In the second millennium cylinder seals in the surrounding countries—Syria, Anatolia, Assyria, and Elam—were often based on Babylonian originals, but in the first millennium B.C. the prevailing styles had originated in northern Mesopotamia, and Babylonia then became the borrower. Other manufactured articles are not easy to assess, since some categories have largely perished in the wet soil, but what was outstanding was usually so for technological rather than artistic reasons.

(iii) *Babylonians and Hebrews*

There are three points at which Babylonian and Hebrew history meet. The first is Abraham's origin in 'Ur of the Chaldees' (Gen. 11: 27–31). Cyrus Gordon proposed that this Ur be sought in a place Ura, not certainly located, but known to have been somewhere in Syria.[12] Scholarly opinion still favours the well-known Ur, an originally Sumerian city near the Persian Gulf.[13] From a historical standpoint nothing precise can be said about the origin of Abraham's clan in Ur, since Genesis gives no indication of time, and very diverse opinions of the historical reliability of the Patriarchal narratives are held by competent scholars. What may be said generally is that Mesopotamian sources give abundant evidence of a migration of 'Amorites' down the Euphrates valley into Babylonia. They are often expressly so called, and in other cases Amorite personal names betray their presence. The language of the personal names may be described as a kind of early Hebrew, and some of the Patriarchs' names, though not, as it happens, Abraham's, are clearly Amorite. These people are first found in southern Mesopotamia under the Third Dynasty of Ur (*c.* 2100–2000 B.C.),[14] and a flood of them destroyed this dynasty. To the end of the First Dynasty of Babylon (*c.* 1600 B.C.) 'Amorites' were a distinguishable element in the population of Babylonia.[15] Hammurabi and his family belonged to this group. Thus there is no problem about locating an Amorite clan in Ur at whatever time one might assign to Abraham.

The second point of contact was much later, and of a very different kind. Merodach-baladan, King of Babylon, sent a diplomatic mission to Hezekiah (2 Kings 20 : 12 ff. = Isa. 39 : 1 ff.). This king is well known as an Aramaean who by sheer genius in diplomacy and intrigue proved himself a thorn in the Assyrian side over a number of years. He never won a military victory over an Assyrian army, but more than once he got other kings' troops to fight in his cause. As King of Babylon he reigned from 721 to 710 B.C., and again for nine months in 703. The episode with Hezekiah cannot be certainly dated, but it fits in with the known facts of the situation extremely well.[16] Ostensibly the mission was to congratulate Hezekiah on his recovery from a near-fatal illness. However, even the biblical narrative creates a suspicion that more was involved, since when Hezekiah had received the mission and shown its members his wealth, the prophet Isaiah confronted the king with two questions: 'What said these men? and from whence came they unto thee?' Hezekiah replied to the latter question only. The message from Babylon he chose to conceal. Merodach-baladan was, of course, concerned with anti-Assyrian intrigue, and was no doubt seeking to arrange simultaneous revolts against Assyria among Palestinian and other states.

The third point of contact is the Babylonian captivity under Nebuchadnezzar II, and a brief record of the events is offered in what is called the *Neo-Babylonian Chronicle Series* (Chronicle 5 rev. 11 ff.).[17] The capture of Jerusalem is dated to the second day of Adar of the seventh year of Nebuchadnezzar, which can be rendered into the Julian calendar as 16 March 597 B.C. In other respects the biblical account is more detailed.

There are three main periods during which Babylonian civilization may have influenced the Hebrews: (i) the Amarna period, which preceded the Hebrew settlement; (ii) the Exile; and (iii) the post-Exilic period.

(a) *The Amarna Period*

Whatever is thought of the historicity of the Patriarchal narratives, the relevance of this period to Babylono-Hebrew connections is not in doubt. Those who accept that Abraham came from Ur to Canaan, as described in Genesis, may hold that Babylonian ideas were passed down to the Hebrews by family tradition alone. Those who are more sceptical will still accept the veracity of the picture of nomadic clans, which, in view of the approximate date of the settlement, must be put somewhere about the Amarna period. No one disputes that the Hebrews emerged against a background of Canaanite culture, which they destroyed in the areas they took over. This culture, as best known in the Amarna period, was open to Mesopotamian influence. While a local alphabetic script was just beginning to appear, most writing was on clay in Babylonian cuneiform. Not only the script, but also the most commonly used language for writing was Babylonian, though in places influenced by the spoken dialects. Along with the techniques of writing and the Babylonian language went a certain amount of literary material and traditional Babylonian lists. Finds of this kind of material have been made at Amarna itself, at Megiddo and Hazor, but especially at Ugarit, the modern Ras Shamra on the Syrian coast, and at the Hittite capital in Anatolia, Boğazköy. The period was one in which cultural barriers from the Gulf of Suez to the Zagros mountains were broken down, and the whole area freely absorbed whatever cultural developments were available. There was, of course, native literature in Syria and Palestine, and best known are the texts from Ugarit, written in a kind of Amorite or Canaanite, with a specially developed cuneiform alphabet, on clay tablets.[18] Save for a few insignificant cases, these poetic texts show no Babylonian influence. Such local texts may have had a wide circulation in oral form, but the cuneiform copies of Babylonian texts would at first have been available only to the few professional scribes. However, in Anatolia Hittite and Hurrian translations of the Babylonian *Gilgamesh Epic* were created, and a Hittite version of the Babylonian Flood story,[19] and these could have been incorporated into the repertory of local story-tellers.

In Syria, at least, use of cuneiform antedates the Amarna period. There is a body of administrative documents from eighteenth-century Alalakh,[20] and letters from the King of Carchemish have been found in the Mari archives.[21] But by the Amarna period this use of Babylonian writing had spread. The relevance of these data to possible Babylonian influence on the Hebrews is that the early chapters of Genesis betray similarities to Babylonian texts which cannot be accidental. The over-all plan—Creation, ten long-lived worthies, Flood—is paralleled in the *Sumerian King List* and related material in Babylonian, where the giving of the arts of civilization results in a succession of eight, nine, or ten long-lived kings, after whom comes the Flood.[22] The seventh, when there are ten, received special revelations from certain gods, which parallels the Hebrew seventh, Enoch, who had a special relationship with God. Copies of the *Sumerian King List* survive from early in the second millennium, and a big edition of the Babylonian epic culminating in the Flood is preserved from *c.* 1630 B.C.[23] Thus priority in time certainly rests on the Mesopotamian side. The connection is indisputable, since in the Late Assyrian and Late Babylonian edition of the Flood story as given in Tablet XI of the *Gilgamesh Epic*[24] the episode of the sending out of three birds to ascertain if the waters were subsiding is undeniably very closely connected with the parallel verses in Genesis. The earliest preserved copies of this episode in cuneiform are from only the seventh century B.C., but, as will be demonstrated later, it is highly improbable that this episode reached the Hebrews after the time of the settlement, and equally improbable that the Babylonians borrowed it from the Hebrews. It is uncertain if this episode was contained in the Old Babylonian edition of *c.* 1630 B.C., though probably it was not, and there is no preserved version of this part of the story in any language from the Amarna period. The Babylonian background of Genesis 1–11 is not limited to the general plan and the Flood story. The world geography of Chapters 2–3 embraces the Tigris and Euphrates, but not the Nile. The Table of Nations (Ch. 10) has a long anecdote about Nimrod (vv. 8–12), whose kingdom is precisely described in terms of Mesopotamian towns. So far it has not proved possible to find a Mesopotamian king who fits the description. The story of the Tower of Babel in Chapter 11 is based on the ziggurat of Babylon. (Babel is simply the Hebrew form of that name.)

In estimating these similarities the differences are equally important. The *Sumerian King List* begins with the lowering of kingship from heaven, not with Creation, and its long-lived men are kings, not patriarchal figures in a single line of descent. The geography of Genesis 2–3 cannot be based on a purely Babylonian or Sumerian text as it now stands, since, quite apart from its being in Hebrew, only two of the four rivers would occur in a Mesopotamian cosmography. Nimrod, as already remarked, cannot be identified from cuneiform texts, though names of all important kings are known. The name might be the same as Ninurta, a Sumero-Babylonian god of war, also associated with hunting.

Whatever the differences, Babylonian material, or material based at some time on knowledge of Babylonia, is certainly conspicuous in the early chapters of Genesis, and this raises the question at what period this material reached the Hebrews. Criteria of judgement are available in the large number of datable cuneiform texts that can be compared. The Tower of Babel is important in this respect, since Babylon was utterly unimportant until the dynasty of Hammurabi, indeed among the tens of thousands of third-millennium cuneiform texts there are remarkably few mentions of the town, and none that attach any importance to it. When Hammurabi raised it to political supremacy, the fact was expressed theologically in the Prologue to the Laws of this king by saying that Marduk (the city god of Babylon) was exalted by Anu and Enlil (heads of the pantheon) to a place among the great gods.[25] This explicitly acknowledges that Marduk (and so his city also) was previously insignificant. The story of the Tower of Babel must come from a time when Babylon was an important city, so that myth and legend were clustering around it. This happened in Mesopotamia, but only some centuries after Hammurabi's time. An inscription of the Kassite king Kurigalzu II (*c.* 1335 B.C.) first attests the concept of Babylon as the 'first city'.[26] Religion was conservative in Babylonia and changes of status and concept came slowly. Thus it is improbable that a story such as the Tower of Babel would have arisen until a century or two after Hammurabi at the earliest. This is positive evidence for a *terminus a quo* of the Babylonian material in Genesis as not earlier than the middle of the second millennium, and the lack of knowledge of third-millennium Mesopotamia in these same chapters is also very striking. The Table of Nations has no name covering the Sumerians, though for a thousand years they were one of the most important peoples in the Near East, and the Table gives plenty of attention to the Babylonians and Assyrians. Thus on the available evidence it seems that the Babylonian traditions behind Genesis 1–11 date in their Mesopotamian context to a period not earlier than about 1500 B.C. The dating of the Hebrew form of these same traditions is, of course, difficult and complicated, but at the present time it will not be doubted that they are pre-Exilic. That they attained canonical status is evidence that loyal Yahwists respected and revered them. From the time of Solomon and onwards material of foreign origin would hardly have been acceptable in orthodox Hebrew circles, and its presence in the Pentateuch is therefore good evidence that it goes back among the Hebrews to pre-monarchical times. In all probability these traditions were part of Hebrew lore when the nation was establishing itself in its land. Thus the gap in time between the Mesopotamian material's *terminus a quo* and the Hebrews' adoption of it is not more than two or three centuries, and the Amarna period is the most likely time for the transmission of the traditions from Mesopotamia to Syria-Palestine. It is a fact that Babylonian myths and legends did circulate in Anatolia, Syria, Palestine, and Egypt at this time. The differences are explained in that the material reached the Hebrews orally, and was no doubt passed down among them first in this form. Any more precise suggestion as to how the material reached the Hebrews will depend on a theory of Hebrew origins.

Law is another case where Sumero-Babylonian texts are relevant. The oldest Hebrew civil code, the *Book of the Covenant* (Exod. 21–23), has some close parallels with the Laws of Hammurabi and the earlier Mesopotamian laws. For example, the section on the goring ox (Exod. 21: 28–32) is partly identical with the law on the same topic from Eshnunna (§§ 53–4).[27] This similarity remains in Deuteronomy, since this book takes over the laws of the *Book of the Covenant*, but the Priestly laws of Leviticus and other parts of the Pentateuch do not have any connection with Mesopotamian codes. This case, unlike the traditions in Genesis 1–11, is not one of borrowing, but rather of parallel development. The *lex talionis*, with its 'eye for an eye' and 'tooth for a tooth', is a revealing point. In the earliest Sumerian code, that of Ur-Nammu (*c.* 2100 B.C.),[28] bodily injury was compensated for with

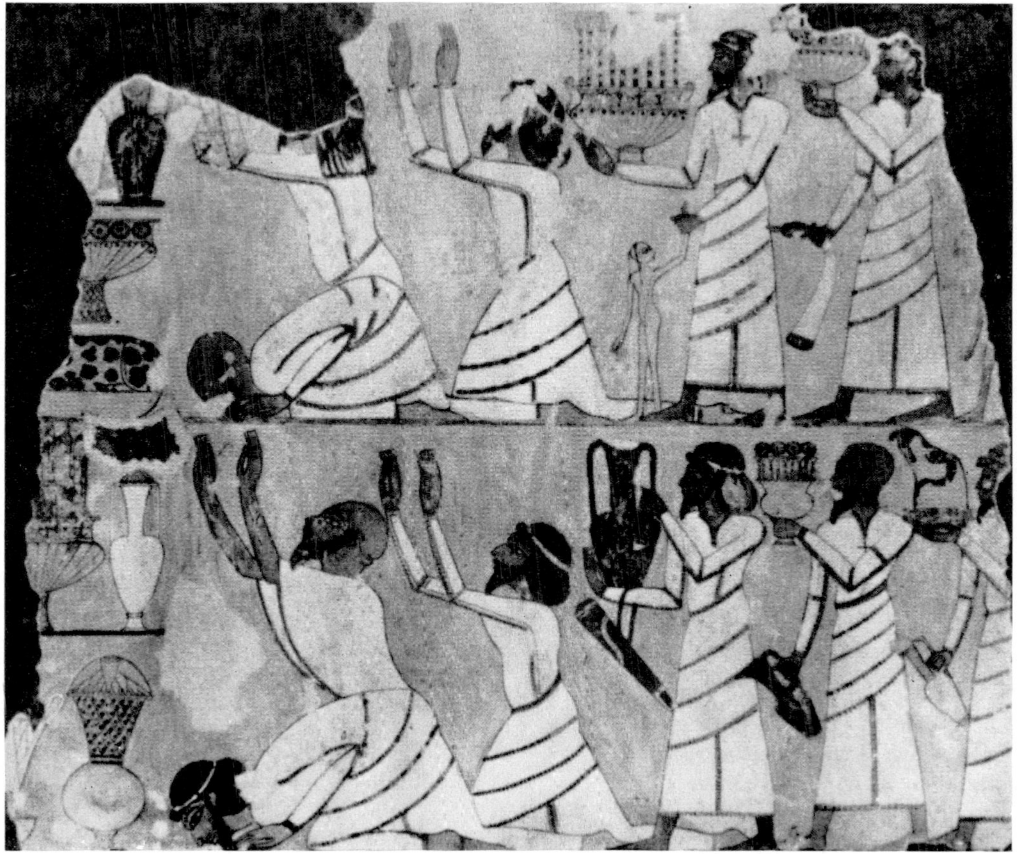

I. Syrian tribute bearers bringing a small girl and an ointment-horn (upper register), and various vessels including a bird-shaped rhyton. From a Theban tomb painting of the reign of Tuthmosis IV (1425–1417)

II. Philistines among the Sea-peoples captured by the Egyptians and led before Ramesses III (1198–1166 B.C.). From Medinet Habu

III. Abishai, 'the ruler of a foreign country', with thirty-seven Semitic tribesmen bringing stibium (used for eye-paint) into Egypt. An Egyptian scribe, Nefer-hotep, holds a tablet bearing the date (*c.* 1890 B.C.). From a wall painting in the tomb of Knumhotep at Beni-Hasan.

IV *a*. Akenaten and Nefertiti, the children of Amenophis III (*c*. 1380 B.C.)

b. Head from statue of a Sumerian lady. From Erech (Warka), *c*. 2900 B.C.

c. A woman from Ras Shamra, Ugarit

a. Syrian

b. Hittite

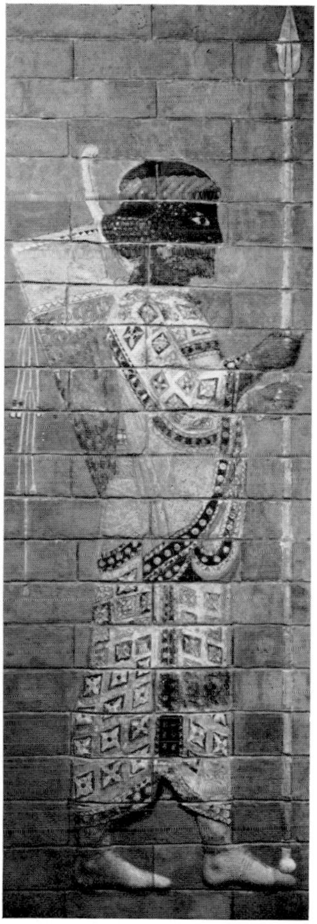

c. Persian soldier

V. Portraits on polychrome tiles

VI *a*. Syrian captives led by Egyptians before the pharaoh Harmhab (1348–1320 B.C.)

b. Judaeans leaving Lachish after its capture by Sennacherib in 701 B.C.

VII *a*. Jehu pays homage to Shalmaneser III in the presence of his officers

b. Continuation of the above panel: Israelite porters bringing in the tribute. From the Black Obelisk, Calah, *c*. 841 B.C.

VIII. Darius, King of Persia (521–486 B.C.), seated on his throne and attended by the Crown-Prince Xerxes and guards, receives a Median dignitary. From Persepolis

payment of silver by the guilty party, and this continued in the earliest Babylonian laws, those of Eshnunna (*c.* 1800 B.C.).[29] The *lex talionis* first appears in Mesopotamia in the Laws of Hammurabi, where it is enunciated explicitly for bodily injury, and the principle appears in a number of other laws: e.g., that if a house collapses and kills the owner's son, the builder's son shall be put to death.[30] There was no social change in Hammurabi's time to explain the sudden, and to us retrogressive, appearance of the *lex talionis*. On the contrary, Hammurabi was an excellent and just administrator of his empire. He was, however, an Amorite in origin, and the most plausible explanation of the facts is that the 'eye for an eye' and 'tooth for a tooth' was an old Amorite legal precept that reached Babylon and the Hebrews from a common origin. No society imperatively needs a tradition of a string of long-lived worthies followed by a Flood, but every society must have some customary law, even if it is never written down. A further reason for doubting whether the Hebrews had borrowed the Mesopotamian laws is lack of evidence that such material ever travelled in written form, unlike myths and legends. The Laws of Eshnunna were never, to our knowledge, copied like a work of literature. Hammurabi's laws were eventually treated in this way and became a text handed down by scribes (not, be it noted, a code observed as law), but so far nothing of this kind has been found in the west.

It isi mpossible to prove Babylonian influence on the Hebrews in non-literary matters at the time of the settlement, and such influence is not likely. In art the Canaanites did borrow Babylonian motifs and used them to better effect, but such things were despised by the Hebrews.

(*b*) *The Exile and the Post-Exilic Period*

The cultural interchange that had characterized the Amarna period was rudely shattered as the Hebrews settled down. First, the migrations of the so-called 'Sea Peoples' threw Syria and Palestine into chaos; then, from about 1100 to 900, the Aramaeans invaded Mesopotamia. With these events the cultural penetration of Syria and Palestine by Babylonian civilization came to an end. Thus, when Hebrew civilization was developing under the early monarchy it was free from any current Mesopotamian influence, except in so far as Phoenician and Aramaic neighbours mediated a little, but this was little indeed. It was only with the rise of the Assyrian empire that Mesopotamian influence began to be felt again in Palestine, and this trend continued after the fall of the Assyrians with the rise of the Neo-Babylonian empire. However, during these periods the Assyrians and Babylonians were the avowed enemies of the Hebrews, and this must have restricted the extent of cultural borrowing by the Hebrews. Even in exile, where they were exposed to the alien culture, a large number clung to their traditional beliefs and so resisted any absorption of Babylonian culture. For example, the writings of Deutero-Isaiah reveal no understanding of the complexity of the polytheism and idol worship that is denounced. An educated Babylonian would not have been impressed by the criticisms. However, in small matters the Hebrews were inevitably influenced. Their old pre-Exilic month names were replaced after the Exile by the standard Babylonian names. Also, so far as there was a Hebrew art, one may suspect that some Babylonian influence was apparent in it just before and after the Exile. The post-Exilic world was dominated more by the Aramaic language and culture, which were under Babylonian influence to some extent, as the Babylonian loan-words illustrate. Thus the post-Exilic world was more Aramaic than Babylonian, and the only real contribution of the Babylonians at this time was mathematical astronomy. The Hebrews had no competence at such forms of science and were therefore not influenced. While the Babylonians were dying out amid the rise and spread of Hellenism, the Hebrews were held together by their distinctive religion, and so survived.

NOTES

1. For a survey of cuneiform writing see G. R. Driver, *Semitic Writing* (1954), Ch. 1.

2. A selection of letters in translation, with an Introduction, is given by A. L. Oppenheim, *Letters from Mesopotamia* (1967).

3. See W. von Soden, *Die Welt als Geschichte*, ii (1936), pp. 418 ff.

4. B. Landsberger and H. Tadmor, *I.E.J.* xiv (1964), 201 ff.

5. Taha Baqir, *Sumer* vi (1950), 39 ff.

6. On this whole subject see the masterly survey of O. Neugebauer, *Proceedings of the American Philosophical Society*, cvii (1963), 528 ff.

7. A. J. Sachs, *J.C.S.* vi (1952), 49 ff.

8. 'Chaldaea' and 'Chaldaean' are used elsewhere in the O.T. to refer to Babylonia or Mesopotamia.

9. The best available English translations are by A. Heidel, *The Babylonian Genesis* (1951), and by E. A. Speiser, in *A.N.E.T.*, pp. 60 ff.

10. The major text on which this is based was published by T. G. Pinches in *Journal of the Transactions of the Victoria Institute*, xxviii (1896), 1 ff.; his conclusions are fully valid, and now supported by other evidence.

11. A recent publication of a big collection of seals, with appropriate comment, is Briggs Buchanan, *Catalogue of Ancient Near-Eastern Seals in the Ashmolean Museum*, i: *Cylinder Seals* (1966).

12. *J.N.E.S.* xvii (1958), 28 ff.

13. H. W. F. Saggs, *Iraq*, xxii (1960), 200 ff.

14. See G. Buccellati, *The Amorites of the Ur III Period* (1966).

15. A study of Amorite names is offered by H. B. Huffmon, *Amorite Personal Names in the Mari Texts* (1965). A document from the reign of Ammi-ṣaduqa distinguishes between 'Amorites' and 'Akkadians': F. R. Kraus, *Ein Edikt des Königs Ammi-ṣaduqa von Babylon* (1958).

16. A detailed study of this Merodach-baladan is given by J. A. Brinkman in *Studies Presented to A. Leo Oppenheim* (1964), pp. 6 ff.

17. See A. K. Grayson, *Assyrian and Babylonian Chronicles* (forthcoming); and for the present D. J. Wiseman, *Chronicles of Chaldaean Kings* (1956), p. 73.

18. English translations are available in *A.N.E.T.*, pp. 129 ff.

19. J. Siegelová, *Archiv Orientální*, xxxviii (1970), 135 ff.

20. D. J. Wiseman, *The Alalakh Tablets* (1953).

21. See G. Dossin, *R.A.* xxxv (1938), 115 ff.; idem, *Correspondance de Iasmaḫ-Addu* (Archives Royales de Mari 5, 1952), nos. 5–13.

22. See T. Jacobsen, *The Sumerian King List* (1939).

23. W. G. Lambert and A. R. Millard, *Atra-ḫasīs: The Babylonian Story of the Flood* (1969).

24. *A.N.E.T.*, pp. 93–6.

25. Ibid. 164.

26. A. Boissier, *R.A.* xxix (1932), p. 98, l. 4: *ip-pa-am-ba-li . . . a-li ṣa-a-ti*, 'In Babylon . . . the primeval city'.

27. *A.N.E.T.*, p. 163.

28. J. J. Finkelstein, *J.C.S.* xxii (1969), 70.

29. *A.N.E.T.*, p. 163, §§ 42–7.

30. Ibid. 175, §§ 196–7 (*lex talionis*) and 176, § 230. The reason that the *lex talionis* in the Laws of Hammurabi does not apply to the 'commoner' (actually a person in the king's service) and slaves is the same reason for which today a crime committed by a member of the armed forces is not dealt with by a civilian court. A tied legal status means that those under it are not strictly free, and so not responsible for their actions as free citizens are.

BIBLIOGRAPHY

Political and Cultural History:

CASSIN, E., BOTTÉRO, J., and VERCOUTTER, J. (eds.), *Fischer Weltgeschichte: Die altorientalischen Reiche*, ii–iv (Fischer, Frankfurt, 1965–7).

ROUX, G., *Ancient Iraq* (Allen & Unwin, London, 1964).

SAGGS, H. W. F., *The Greatness that Was Babylon* (Sidgwick & Jackson, London, 1962).

The Cambridge Ancient History (3 vols., C.U.P., Cambridge: vol. i, rev. edn., 1970; vol. ii, rev. edn., in press; vol. iii, 1925).

Religion:

BOTTÉRO, J., *La Religion babylonienne* (Presses universitaires de France, Paris, 1952).

JACOBSEN, T., 'Religion' in article 'Babylonia and Assyria', *Encyclopaedia Britannica* (1963).

For Babylonian Connections of Genesis 1–11:

LAMBERT, W. G., 'A New Look at the Babylonian Background of Genesis', *J.T.S.* N.S. xvi (1965), 287 ff.

For Oriental Connections with Hebrew Law:

MEEK, T. J., *Hebrew Origins* (Harper Torchbook, New York, 1960), Ch. 2.

IX

THE HITTITES AND HURRIANS

H. A. HOFFNER

A. THE HITTITES

EVERY treatise on the Hittites should begin with a warning to the reader about the pitfalls posed by the term 'Hittite', which often seems to connote something quite different to each scholar.[1] It is possible to identify at least four distinct ethnic groups in antiquity to whom the name 'Hittite' (Nesite LÚ URU *ḪATTI*, Egyptian *ḫt*, Ugaritic *ḫty*, Hebrew *ḥittî* = LXX *khettaios*, Akkadian *ḫattû*) has at some time been applied.

First in order of appearance were the Hattians,[2] whom the immigrant Indo-Europeans found inhabiting the central plateau of Asia Minor, when they arrived about 2000 B.C. This people in the course of time was completely assimilated into the culture of the immigrants. But far from being obscured by the culture of their conquerors, the Hattians left the stamp of their world-view and institutions indelibly on the fledgeling 'Hittite' state of the immigrants. So pervasive is Hattian influence in the civilization of the Hittite Old Kingdom, that the question has more than once been raised whether the nucleus of the Old Kingdom state was not in fact Hattian rather than Indo-European. The Hittite rulers from Hattušili I to Šuppiluliuma II with few exceptions bore Hattian throne names. Thus the names Hattušili, Muršili, and Hantili all exhibit the Hattic sufformative *-il*, to which a Nesite theme vowel *i* has been added. The stem of these names was probably a toponym (clearly so in Hattušili: *Ḫattuš*+*-il*). The dynastic titles of the king (*Labarna* or *Tabarna*) and queen (*Tawananna*) are non-Indo-European. It is most likely, although it remains to be proven, that they are Hattic. The principal deities in the state religion until well into the New Kingdom were Hattian deities: a storm-god named Taru; his consort, the sun-goddess of the city of Arinna, named Wurušemu; their daughter Mezzulla, and granddaughter Zintuhi; another daughter of the storm-god named Inara; a son of the storm-god named Telepinu; a warrior-god Wurunkatte; a moon-god Kašku; and a sun-god Eštan. All the local gods of the Hattians were properly venerated and their cults maintained. Native priests and priestesses presided over the cults, and the spoken language of the festivals continued to be Hattic. Hattian myths, which occasionally served as cult legends for particular festivals to be celebrated by the Hittite royalty, were committed to writing early in the Old Kingdom. Often they were written down on clay tablets in the form of bilinguals, with a Hittite (Nesite) translation in the column to the right of the Hattic transcription. In other cases no written record was made of the Hattic version, but a Hittite translation was drawn up.

The Hattian cultural legacy seems to have consisted chiefly of the religious (i.e. cult and mythology) and the artistic. No perceptible trace of Hattian precedents underlies the historical, administrative, legal, or diplomatic literature. Indeed, we have no reason to believe the Hattians were literate prior to their encounter with Old Assyrian merchant colonies and the subsequently literate Indo-European Hittites. Hittite interest in and practice of divination techniques may have been derived from the Assyrians and Babylonians to the east. The court life of the Hattians was well developed. In a pre-Šuppiluliuma text, which has been called the 'Protocol of the Gateman', we are informed that certain functionaries 'spent the night' (i.e. were permanently quartered) 'up in the palace' (i.e. on the acropolis or *büyükkale*). As they presented themselves at the gate for admittance to the acropolis, the gateman called out their professional designations in the Hattic language. The 'Protocol of the Gateman' tablet lists these Hattic titles, together with their translations into 'Hittite'. Thus we can identify what professions were included. Among them are cup-bearers, waiters ('tablemen'), couriers, cooks, jesters, singers, marshals, scouts, and 'tentmen'.[3] Another (unpublished) bilingual text has yielded the Hattic word for 'smith' (*ureš*). One can assess for oneself the level of Hattian craftsmanship by perusing any of the several lavishly illustrated volumes devoted to the art of ancient Asia Minor.[4]

A second ethnic group designated in antiquity as 'Hittite' was the Indo-European community which settled in Asia Minor about 2000 B.C., and rose to hegemony over the plateau's scattered urban centres about 1700 B.C. As noted above, this group only adopted the phrase 'men of Hatti' to identify themselves, after they had established their capital on the site of the old Hattian city of Hattuš. Before that time (*c.* 1650 B.C.) they identified themselves with the city of Neša and called their language *našili* or *nešumnili*. But after the establishment of the new capital at Hattuša, and the progressive assimilation of the Hattians into the Hittite state, the term 'Hittite' became increasingly common as a designation of the new Anatolian power, although the language of the Indo-Europeans continued to be called *našili* or *nešumnili*, in contradistinction to *ḫattili* ('in the language of the Hattians'). During that state's existence (*c.* 1700–1190 B.C.) the term 'Hittite' only had meaning as applied to the kingdom of Hattuša and its subjects.

The fall of Hattuša signalled the dissolution of the vast network of vassal states tied together by treaties with its ruler. Written historical records do not exist to inform us of the continuity or lack thereof in former Hittite possessions in Asia Minor proper. But to the south-east in North Syria certain Hittite centres remained. Until midway through the first millennium B.C. the rulers of these centres bore names resembling those of the kings of Hattuša (Saplulme and Lubarna), and had monumental inscriptions executed in a developed form of the hieroglyphic script employed by the kings of Hattuša on their monuments. Syria during the first half of the first millennium B.C. was ruled by kings of two ethnic groups, called 'Aramaeans' and 'Hittites'. To distinguish these kingdoms from the second-millennium Anatolian kingdom most scholars today refer to them as 'Neo-Hittites'.

A fourth group identified in antiquity as 'Hittites' is known almost exclusively from the Old Testament. Emil Forrer once suggested[5] that the same use of the term 'Hittite' (Assyrian *ḫattû*) to designate a people in southern Palestine is found in the annals of Sargon II of Assyria. There the citizens of the Philistine city of Ashdod are called 'Hittites'. More likely the term *ḫattû* was used in the annals of the Sargonids to designate anti-Assyrian rebels from all the kingdoms from the Euphrates to the border of Egypt. This was the 'land of Hatti' (*māt Ḫatti*), which included not only inland Syria but the Phoenician coastal cities as well. Sargon's application of the term to the Ashdodite rebels does not, therefore, constitute extra-biblical evidence for the 'Hittites' of southern Palestine. Yet the Old Testament evidence must be evaluated. An ethnic component did in fact exist in Palestine of sufficient importance to justify Ezekiel's statement (Ezek. 16: 3) that Jerusalem's dual parentage was Amorite and Hittite. We shall return to the subject of the Old Testament references to Hittites. For the present let us only note that they indicate the possibility of a fourth people identified by the same name.

Modern rediscovery of the Hittites of Asia Minor began with these biblical references. After the hieroglyphic script of the Egyptians was deciphered by Champollion in 1822, it was discovered that the pharaohs of the eighteenth dynasty had been in contact with a country called *Ḫt* (at the time the consonants were read 'Kheta'). In the Egyptian inscriptions the Kheta were always to be found in Syria. In the 1850s the cuneiform script of Mesopotamia was deciphered, and the study of the historical records of the Babylonian and Assyrian kingdoms commenced. From the Neo-Assyrian royal inscriptions it was learned that from *c.* 1100 B.C. Syria was known to the Assyrians as the 'land of Hatti'. In 1876 the British scholar A. H. Sayce proposed that the basalt blocks found at Hama and Aleppo, which were inscribed with hieroglyphic writing, should be ascribed to the Hittites. Similarly inscribed rocks were identified in subsequent years in central Asia Minor, especially near the Turkish villages of Boğazköy and Alaca Hüyük. In 1887 a cache of clay tablets inscribed with Babylonian cuneiform was recovered from the ruins of the Egyptian royal city at El Amarna. Among these tablets were two which, although inscribed in the pronounceable characters of Babylonian cuneiform, were composed in a previously unknown language. This language was called 'Arzawan', because the foreign correspondent of the Egyptian pharaoh in both letters was a king of Arzawa. In 1902 the Norwegian scholar J. A. Knudtzon published a brief study, in which he concluded that the new language had affinities with the Indo-European family. Knudtzon later gave up his views under the fire of heavy criticism which resulted. Yet scholars were fascinated by the fragments of clay tablets written in this same language found near Boğazköy in 1893. The concession to excavate the massive ruins near Boğazköy was obtained for the German Orient Society by Hugo Winckler, and the excavations began in 1906. In the first season of digging the site yielded thousands of tablets. Many were composed in the Akkadian language and could be read on the spot. They proved that this city had been the capital of a kingdom called 'Hatti'. Furthermore, the bulk of the tablets were written in the same language as the two 'Arzawan' letters from El Amarna, which was therefore the native language of the dynasty. Nine years were to pass until in 1915 a Czech Assyriologist entrusted with the task of copying the tablets published a decipherment. The Czech, named Hrozný, earned thereby the epithet 'father of Hittitology'.

The German Orient Society has retained the concession to excavate Boğazköy down through the years, in spite of interruptions caused by two world wars. Winckler worked with Theodore Makridi in 1907, 1911, and 1912. Then the Balkan War, the First World War, and the Graeco-Turkish War interrupted the work for many years. In 1931 the excavations were resumed under the joint auspices of the German Archaeological Institute and the German Orient Society. Nine consecutive annual campaigns (from 1931 to 1939) under the direction of Kurt Bittel were conducted on the site, until the outbreak of World War II. In 1952, seven years after the end of the war, the excavations were resumed. Since 1952 there have been no interruptions. The team has conducted excavations annually in the summer and early autumn. Since the resumption of the excavations in 1952 the epigraphic aspect of the operation has been under the direction of Heinrich Otten, at present a professor at the Philipps University in Marburg. Annual reports of the excavations and the cuneiform texts from the site have been published in several series.[6] The vast majority of the tablets were composed in the Hittite language. Smaller numbers were composed in Akkadian, Sumerian, Hurrian, Luwian, Hattic, or Palaic.

The main periods of the city of Hattuša which have been determined by the excavators are:[7]

(1) The transition from the Early to the Middle Bronze Age: attested on the *Büyükkale* by levels V f–c, on the area of the 'House on the Slope' by levels 9, 8c–8d, and on the Lower Terrace by level 5.

(2) Pre-Hittite city of Hattuš, the last phase of which can be correlated with the Assyrian merchant colonies: attested on the *Büyükkale* in levels V b–a, on the area of the 'House on the Slope' in levels 8a–8b, and on the Lower Terrace in level 4.
(3) The Old Hittite Period (*c.* 1700–1400 B.C.): attested on *Büyükkale* in level IV c, on the area of the 'House on the Slope' in level 7, and on the Lower Terrace in level 3.
(4) The Hittite Empire (*c.* 1400–1190 B.C.), subdivided into the early kings (Šuppiluliuma I to Muwattalli) and the later kings (Hattušili III to Šuppiluliuma II): early period attested on *Büyükkale* in levels IV b–a and III b, 'House on the Slope' level 6, Lower Terrace levels 2 and 1b; later half attested on *Büyükkale* level III a, 'House on the Slope' level 5, Lower Terrace level 1a.
(5) Post-Hittite or Phrygian Period: levels I–II of *Büyükkale*, levels 1–4 of 'House on the Slope'.

Within the perimeter of the city walls the excavators have examined the *Büyükkale* itself (which was the royal residence), Temple V in the Upper City, the 'House on the Slope', and Temple I in the Lower City (the great temple of the storm-god). In the last few seasons a building called the 'Südareal', which almost adjoins Temple I on the south-west but is separated from it by a roadway, has been explored. The structure measures *c.* 118 m. at its greatest length, 55 m. at its greatest width. The location of the 'Südareal' in relation to the Great Temple raised suspicions that it might have housed the artisans, priests, and cultic personnel of the temple, as similarly located structures served at Kahûn, El Amarna, and Deir el-Medîneh in Egypt. These suspicions were strengthened by the discovery (in complex 1, room-group XIV, room 12, in the upper stratum of debris of the upper half) of a single-columned tablet listing 205 members of the 'House of the Artisans' (DUMU.ḪÁ É GIŠ.KIN.TI), including priests (LÚ.MEŠ *ša-an-ku-ni-iš*), female cultic practitioners (MÍ.MEŠ *kat-ra-aš*), scribes (LÚ.MEŠ DUB.SAR), divination priests (LÚ.MEŠ ḪAL), and Hurrian singers.[8] Excavations were also carried out on the great rock *Büyükkaya* across the gorge from the main city. The building of a bridge across the gorge, and the extension of the city wall to enclose the *Büyükkaya* within the city's limits, were the work of one of the successors of Muwattalli: either Hattušili III, Tudhaliya

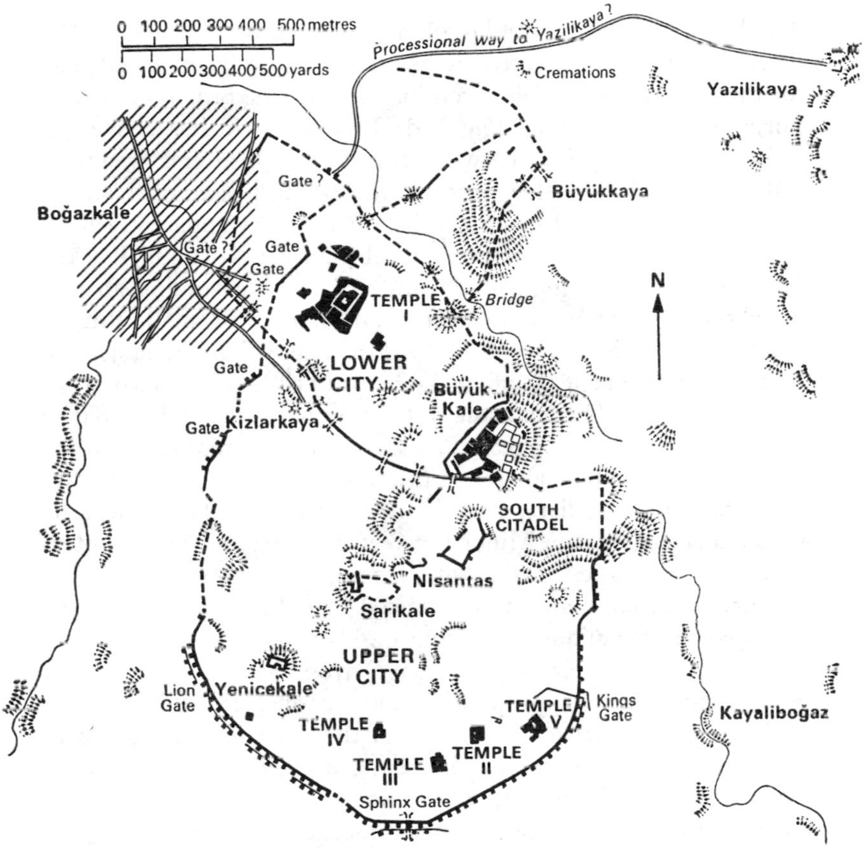

FIG. 5. Plan of Hattuša, the Hittite capital city (after K. Bittel, *Hattuša,* Fig. 3).

IV, or Šuppiluliuma II. It was during the reigns of these last three kings also that the buildings on the Upper City were completed, and the *Nişantaş*, with its hieroglyphic inscription, was finished. Also during these three reigns the famous rock sanctuary of *Yazılıkaya* and its attendant temple were inaugurated. The dual procession of deities carved there in low relief converges on the royal figure of Tudhaliya IV.

(i) *Origins and History*

The history of the Hittite kingdom has often been sketched. For details the reader is referred to monographs designed specifically for this purpose.[9] What is given here is only the broad outline for purposes of orientation. The Indo-European Hittites arrived in Asia Minor some time between the twenty-third and twentieth centuries B.C. Before they emerge into the full glare of 'history', as illumined by actual historical documents, they apparently lived in or around two cities of the central plateau: Neša and Kuššar. The earliest Hittite king whose name we know is a certain Labarna, of whose exploits we only hear: 'The land was small. But on whatever campaign he went, he held the enemy land in subjection by the neck. He kept ravaging the lands until he had utterly worn the lands out. And he made them [the conquered lands] boundaries of the [Mediterranean?] sea.' The same source names seven urban centres governed by Labarna and his sons: Hupišna, Tuwanuwa, Nenašša, Landa, Zallara, Paršuhanta, and Lušna. These cities lie within a sector of Asia Minor between Hattuša and the Mediterranean. The earliest texts date from the reign of Hattušili I (*c.* 1650–1620 B.C.), and it is surmised that the Hittites may have acquired the technique of writing on clay (first in Akkadian and then adapted to their own language) from scribal academies in Syria, which were appropriated on one of Hattušili's military raids. This first foreign conqueror of the dynasty campaigned in the land of Arzawa to the south-west, but most of his efforts were directed to the south-east, where he raided many Syrian cities over the course of ten years, and commenced a standing feud with the King of Aleppo. The outcome of this struggle with Syrian powers was not reached during Hattušili's own lifetime. But when he was succeeded by his grandson Muršili I, Hittite armies gained several decisive victories, including the defeat of Aleppo and the sack of Babylon, which brought to an end the reign of Samsuditana, the fifth successor of Hammurabi of Babylon (*c.* 1595 B.C.). When the conquering Muršili returned to his capital, he was assassinated by his brother-in-law Hantili. The period which ensued (*c.* 1590–1525 B.C.) was an unhappy one for all concerned. The succession of kings was unpredictable, since father was not succeeded by son, but by his murderer. The kingdom was assailed on all sides by its enemies, and matters were not improved by crop failures which occurred at this time. Our principal historical source, a text dating from the end of this seventy-year period, attributes the misfortunes of the kingdom to the assassinations and disorder in the ruling family. But one wonders if the author (a king named Telepinu) has not mistaken the effect for the cause. It was patently in the interest of this Telepinu (himself a usurper) to blame the failures of the preceding rulers on their own policies rather than on a combination of external conditions beyond their control, not the least of which was the over-extension of the kingdom's military powers by Muršili! Whatever the cause, Hittite political and economic fortunes deteriorated rapidly after the death of Hantili. Outlying provinces were lost, and a new dynasty of Hurrians invaded the coastal plain of Cilicia, which was known at that time as Kizzuwatna. The reformer chose the throne name Telepinu in order to stress the certainty that with his accession renewed prosperity was imminent. Telepinu (*c.* 1525–1500 B.C.) instituted many important legal reforms and entered into treaty relationship with the new kings of Kizzuwatna.

The period following the reign of Telepinu witnessed the rapid growth of the kingdom of Mitanni in Upper Mesopotamia and Syria. About 1450 B.C. a new dynasty came to power in Hattuša. The two royal names Tudhaliya and Arnuwanda recur among its rulers. Under these kings Hittite political fortunes took an upswing. One of them, a Tudhaliya, reconquered Aleppo. But the renewal of Hittite hegemony in Syria was the work of one of Tudhaliya's successors, Šuppiluliuma I (*c.* 1380–1346 B.C.), who defeated the Mitannian king, Tušratta, and reorganized Syria as a network of Hittite vassal states (Carchemish, Aleppo, Ugarit, Nuhašše, Kizzuwatna, and Mitanni) which endured for almost 200 years. The Hittites under Šuppiluliuma's dynasty dominated Syria as far south as the kingdom of Kadesh on the Orontes. The first serious challenge to this hegemony came in the year 1300 B.C., when the Egyptian pharaoh Ramesses II led four divisions of chariotry against the Hittite emperor Muwatalli and his allies. The battle, fought in the environs of Kadesh, was a stand-off, in that it failed to change the balance of power in Syra-Palestine. The Hittites maintained their borders in Syria. During the following years the tense relations between Egypt and Hatti relaxed, so that by the year 1284 B.C. a treaty of peace was concluded between Muwattalli's successor Hattušili III and Ramesses II. The boundary between the two spheres of influence was fixed just south of Damascus. The absence of formal annals belonging to Hattušili III and his successors suggests a relaxing in the military machine.[10] Whether this was a sign of weakness or of assurance may be debated. What is certain from the excavations of Hattuša is that Hattušili and his successors now devoted an enormous effort and expense to building-programmes. Four temples in the Upper City were constructed, one of them (Temple V) a double cella. The bridge over the *Büyükkaya-deresi* (the gorge separating the *Büyükkale* from the *Büyükkaya*) and the extension of the perimeter wall to enclose the *Büyükkaya* were constructed at this period. The famous rock sanctuary of *Yazılıkaya* and the attached festival house were finished by Hattušili's son, Tudhaliya IV. Yet enemies there were, both to the east in Assyria (Tukulti-Ninurta I) and to the west in the Arzawa and Lukka lands. The last Hittite military venture of which we have any certain knowledge was a sea battle which occurred off the coast of Alašiya (Cyprus) during the reign of the last Hittite emperor, Šuppiluliuma II (*c.* 1215–1190 B.C.). The battle was won by the Hittites, but the tide had turned decisively against them. Enemies who were quite unrelated to each other converged on the heartland. It is not known precisely which enemy deserves the credit for the sack of the capital city *c.* 1190 B.C. Quite probably it was the barbarian people called the Kaška, who had been a persistent foe over a period of centuries, always choosing intervals of weakness to attack and press their harried opponents. No written record of the final attack and siege has survived in the archives at Hattuša.

(ii) *Organization*

The economy of the Hittites, like that of all ancient peoples, was chiefly agricultural. Our documents tell us very little about the life of the average citizen. At the bottom of the social scale of free persons was the peasant who farmed his own plot. If he was fortunate enough to realize a surplus of production over personal consumption, he might take the surplus to the market. The Hittite word for 'city' (*ḫappiraš*) was evidently derived from the word for 'market' (*ḫappar*/*ḫappir*). In the Hittite laws, which date from the reign of the two earliest known rulers, Hattušili I and Muršili I, a table of prices is given for agricultural produce, a portion of which is reproduced below:

3 *parīsu* of wheat	1 shekel of silver
4 *parīsu* of barley	½ shekel
1 *parīsu* of wine	½ shekel
1 *zipattani* of lard	1 shekel
1 *zipattani* of butter	1 shekel
2 cheeses	1 shekel
1 *zipattani* of honey	1 shekel

If the citizen owned and bred livestock, he might market the meat and hide of a slaughtered animal. The same section of the laws lists prices for the meat and hides of adult and young animals—sheep, goats, and oxen. Some elements in the population were clearly breeders of livestock, for the prices of livestock are also given. These are listed below in order from the most to the least expensive:

mule	40 shekels
chariot horse	20 shekels
yearling filly	15 shekels
mature horse	14 shekels
plough ox	12 shekels
bull	10 shekels
yearling colt	10 shekels
cow with calf	8 shekels
cow	7 shekels
mare	7 shekels
ass mare	7 shekels
yearling calf	5 shekels
weaned calf, colt, filly	4 shekels
unweaned calf	3 shekels
sheep	1 shekel
goat	⅔ shekel
lamb	½ shekel
kid	¼ shekel

From this table it can easily be seen that the most expensive category embraces the harness (or draught) animals, which range in price from 40 to 12 shekels. Next come the breeding stock: the stud animals and the fertile females (10 to 7 shekels). Finally come the young of the large quadrupeds and the full-grown of the sheep and goats. Since only the wealthy and the military required riding animals, the most expensive animal required by the peasant would have been the plough ox (12 shekels). This was his 'tractor'. The table of prices also includes finished wares of the weaver and of the smith. There is ample evidence that the essentially agricultural economy produced the accompanying artisan skills. Among the professions explicitly mentioned in the texts are: potter, barber, physician, basket-weaver, saddler, lapidary, smith, cobbler, dairyman, weaver, carpenter, sculptor, bee-keeper, baker, gardener, fisherman, merchant, and scribe. Of these, several offered their services only to the nobility (especially barbers, cooks, and scribes).

Although there are vestiges of an earlier matrilineal society in Asia Minor, which survive in privileges granted to the Hittite queen, the laws reveal that Hittite society was thoroughly patriarchal in character. The husband negotiates for a bride with the girl's parents, pays the bride-price (*kušata*), and takes her to his home. The girl's parents confer a dowry upon her (*iwaru*), which is given to her in lieu of her share in her parents' estate. If the wife dies, leaving no children, her husband has sole claim to her dowry. If a man is displeased with his wife and wishes to divorce her, he may sell her and have custody of all the children. In another case described in the laws the husband is free and the wife a slave. It is admittedly, therefore, atypical. When the marriage is dissolved, they divide the household goods equally, but the man takes all the children but one. The parents of the bride are called her 'father and mother' rather than 'mother and father'. This sequence contrasts with that found in the Hittite translation of the pre-Hittite Anitta text ('I treated them like mothers and fathers'). And the bride's parents' home is 'her father's house' (*attaš-šaš per*).

Hittite society was thoroughly feudal in character. At the apex of the hierarchy was the king, who was the suzerain or lord's lord. In fact the king himself was only the deputy of the storm-god, the proprietor of the land. Nevertheless, among mortals the king occupied the highest rung in the social network of protection and dependence. Under him were his nobles, bound by the ties of homage and fealty. Under each of them in turn were their 'men', who owed them services. Each noble controlled his own manor, on which were settled peasants and artisans. Like the medieval manors, these were not always coterminous with the village in their vicinity. The feudatory (or socman) owed to his lord rents in kind (*šaḫḫan*) on the yield of his tenement, and services at request (*luzzi*) on the lord's demesne. It was in the power of the lord to exempt from rents and services, but if the socman refused or was unable to render what was demanded, he was evicted from his holding. A distinction was made between the socage of a peasant and that of a craftsman (or perhaps 'soldier'). The former obligated its holder to the payment of rent, while the latter required services appropriate to the holder's skill. If a holding was passed virtually intact to a single heir, the obligation to *luzzi* passed with it. If, on the other hand, the parental holding was subdivided, the obligation to *luzzi* lay with the holder of the larger portion. Thus the demands for services by the lord could not be inordinately multiplied. That there were independent small holdings ('allods') in the villages we may be sure. But the concern of the laws is for the interest of the king and the powerful feudal lords. As it has been observed with regard to medieval European feudalism, 'fields without lords are fields without a history'.[11] It was within the power of the socman to bequeath his holding to his son(s) without special approval from the liege lord. He could not, however, sell it to another man. The holding of the 'craftsman', however, could be sold with the obligation to services (*luzzi*) and land rent (*šaḫḫan*) passing to the buyer. In all cases but inheritance in which land changed hands it was the right of the lord to choose or approve the new holder and to invest him with the fief.

The Hittite king was the head of a great family (*šalli ḫašatar*) of nobles, feudal lords themselves dependent upon him and bound to him by homage and fealty. Originally they may all have resided at the palace and performed the duties corresponding to their titles: courtiers, bodyguard, grooms, cup-bearers, table-men, cooks, sceptre-men, and chamberlains. But in time, as the power and wealth of each increased, he lived on his own manor away from the capital or ruled a provincial city. His original title followed him, however, so that he was still 'cup-bearer' long after he had ceased to fulfil that role on a daily basis in the palace. Periodically (probably at least once a year) the king held court at the capital, and each vassal was required to be present. On such occasions he served in his old, but now chiefly honorific, position. On such occasions, too, the assembly of the king's liegemen (called the *pankuš*) fulfilled a judicial function. Complaints were heard, petitions filed, charges against individual members were weighed and acted upon. It was in a fashion the supreme court of the land. At all other times of the year, when the *pankuš* was not in session, critical decisions were made by the king personally. When a matter was of sufficient gravity, however, and could await the convention of the *pankuš*, it was considered at that time. Despite the literal meaning of the phrase applied to this body (*šalli ḫašatar*, 'great family'), membership therein was not conditioned by blood ties. The new admission placed himself in the hands of his lord by an initial act of homage and took an oath of fealty (*linkaiš*) which was renewed at regular intervals. The bond thus effected between liegeman and king was (as in medieval Europe) dissolved on the death of either party, although the surviving partner might choose to renew the relationship with the deceased's heir. Indeed, surviving records of such oaths of fealty anticipated these situations, and often bound the two parties to recognize each other's designated heir as automatic successor. Even so, a fresh act of homage and fealty was expected in such an event. The liegeman rendered to his lord aid (*warriš*) and protection (*paḫšanummar*). In time of military crisis his lord could expect from him a contingent of chariotry and infantry. At least once in the year, when the king held court, the liegeman's presence was required. At this time also it is likely that the liegeman would present whatever taxes on his own manor the king could lay claim to. This was the liegeman's 'tribute'.

The feudalistic structure pervaded all areas of Hittite life: diplomacy, domestic civil service, the priestly hierarchy, and life in the manors and villages. It has been observed that feudalism is the one necessary hermeneutic for the study of Hittite culture.

The king was at once both the commander-in-chief of the army and the highest priest of the realm. In pressing circumstances he might delegate tasks to his subordinate generals in the battlefield, but it was not considered advisable for him to absent himself from the task of presiding over the important festivals of the gods. If ever a military crisis demanded his presence in the field through the winter months, when the festivals were mostly celebrated, he was exposing himself to the risk that the gods' displeasure would bring calamity on him and his people. As the deputy of the storm-god and wielder of the gods' authority delegated to him, the Hittite king was endued with powers beyond those of the ordinary man. The native term for this enduement was *para ḫandantatar*. The expected corollary to this doctrine was the careful shielding of the king's person from all forms of defilement. During his lifetime, however, he was never considered to be divine. And when, at death, he was said to 'become a god', this probably meant little more than that he took his place among the other members of the ancestor cult and received a regular endowment of offerings.

The pantheon of the Hittites, as it is presented to the reader in lengthy lists of 'oath deities', or in lists of gods receiving offerings in rituals, presents an illusion of great complexity. This complexity actually existed only within the artificial construct of the national cultus, a creation of the latter part of the kingdom's history. Of the aggregate of divine names one can distinguish four classes: (1) those of Hattian origin, (2) those of Hurrian origin, (3) those of Hittite and Luwian origin, and (4) others which we will call Asianic. Those in categories 1, 3, and 4 were venerated during the Old Kingdom. Those in category 2 (Hurrian) were largely introduced by the dynasty of the Tudhaliyas and Arnuwandas (i.e. Šuppiluliuma I's ancestors). These do not appear in Old Kingdom literature. The king himself in the course of his duties as high priest worshipped all of these. The average citizen of the realm, on the contrary, venerated only a few. The temples in Hattuša housed a larger number of divine figures than did the modest temples in the outlying cities. In the following list a number of cities are correlated with the names of dieties who are known to have had shrines there:

Alanuwa	Hapantali
Ankuwa	Katahha
Arinna	Wurušemu, Mezzulla
Hahana	Telepinu, Ammamma
Hakm/piš	Hannahanna, Huzziya
Harpiš	Halmašuit
Hurma	Ammamma
Hurniya	Ištanu
Ištahara	Ištanu
Ištanuwa	Ištanu
Kakšat	Ištanu

Kapperi	Hatepuna
Karahna	Inara
Kaštama	Zašhapuna, Zaliyanu
Kiškilušša	Inara
Lawazzantiya	Lelwani, IŠTAR (= Šauška?)
Maliluha	Hatepiša
Malitaškuri	Ištanu
Nerik	Storm god of Nerik
Šahhaniya	Hannahanna
Šalampa	Kattahha
Šamuha	Lelwani, DINGIR.GE$_6$, IŠTAR (= Šauška?)
Šugziya	Zulima
Šulupašša	Mezzulla
Tahurpa	Ammamma, Tahurp-ištanu
Tamarmara	Šulinkatte
Tanipiya	Zašhapuna, Zaliyanu
Tarukka	Inara
Tawiniya	Telepinu, Kattahha
Tuhumiyara	Wurunkatte
Turmitta	Telepinu, Mezzulla
Uranna	Mezzulla
Zithara	Zithariya

The above list was compiled (with rare exceptions) from the known cult centres of Hattian deities, and so it contains mention of almost no Hurrian or Hittite-Luwian deities. It also does not contain the long roster of towns possessing a sanctuary to a storm-god (unnamed). Still, it serves its purpose to give an impression of the distribution of Hattian deities among the cities and towns of Central Asia Minor.

Thus it is clear that, when the citizen of Kapperi (for example) brought an offering to his local temple, he did not have the option of presenting it to seven or eight deities (much less the hundreds known from the state cult). He could offer it only to the goddess of his city, Hatepuna. Among the roster of divine names known from the state archives there are also deities for whom no temple is known. Some of these can be determined either from the etymologies of their names, or from hints in the texts, to be genii, or spirits, which indwell or embody familiar objects of daily life. In much the same manner as Janus was the Romans' genie of portals, so the Hittites recognized in Halmašuit the goddess of the throne, in Halki (Hattic: Kait) the grain deity, in Aškašepa the deity of gates, in Hilanzipa the deity of courtyards, in Ištamanašša the spirit of hearing, in Kamrušepa the genie of magical rites, in Miyatanzipa the genie of growth, in Pahhur the genie of fire, in Šakuwašša the spirit of the eyes, and in Daganzipa the earth spirit. It will be noted that a number of these names terminate in *-šepa* or *-zipa*. *Šepa-* (or *šipa-*) was the Luwian word for 'genius, spirit, daemon', which normally occurs only as the second element in compound nouns of the type listed above. Once, however, in an incantation for relief from evil forces the word *šipan* (accus. sg.) appears in a list of nouns denoting these evil forces, and must be translated as 'demon' or the like.[12] These genii were the objects of fear and respect, but they seldom enjoyed a cult in the strict sense of the term.

The leading figures in the state cult during the Old Kingdom were the sun-goddess of the city of Arinna and the storm-god of the land of Hatti. Their Hattic names were Wurušemu and Taru, respectively. From the mid fifteenth century and later the principal state deities were the Hurrian pair: the storm-god Teššup and his consort Hebat. Other Hurrian deities, who appear for the first time in the New Kingdom, were: the warrior-god Aštabi; Teššup's two divine bulls, Šeri and Hurri; the goddess of medicine, Išhara; the warrior-goddess Šauška, and her two hierodules, Ninatta and Kulitta; the Enlil-like figure Kumarbi ('he of the city Kumar' = *Kumar-we*); the moon-god Kušuh; and the sun-god Šimike.

(iii) *Old Testament Contacts*

It was noted above that the term 'Hittite' was applied to at least four groups in antiquity. It is not, therefore, a simple task to sort out the significance of the references to Hittites in the Old Testament.[13] It is my opinion that we never encounter Hittites of my first two categories (i.e. Hattians or Nesites) in the Old Testament. The 'kings of the Hittites' spoken of during the time of Solomon (2 Chr. 1: 17) and Jehoram son of Ahab (2 Kings 7: 6) were Syrians ('Hittites' of category three). But apart from the expression 'the land of Hittites', which sometimes denotes Syria, all other references to 'Hittites' in the Old Testament are to a small group living in the hills during the era of the Patriarchs and the later descendants of that group. In my opinion this fourth group is neither Hurrian (textual error *ḥty* for *ḥry*) nor the group of Kurushtameans which migrated into 'the land of Egypt' (anywhere south of Kadesh) during the era immediately preceding the reign of Šuppiluliuma I. The names of all 'Hittites' of this group in the Old Testament are good Semitic types: Ephron, Zohar, Judith, Beeri, Basemath, Elon, Adah, Ahimelech, and Uriah. This is particularly remarkable in view of the pronounced non-Semitic character of the names of Hivites and some Horites. Their customs cannot be shown to diverge markedly from those of their Palestinian neighbours. As I have sought to demonstrate elsewhere, the real-estate transaction between Abraham and 'Ephron, the Hittite' in Genesis 23 does not presuppose 'intimate knowledge of intricate subtleties of Hittite laws and customs', as has been claimed.[14] These 'Hittites' would seem to be natives in every sense of the word. The phonetic similarity of the name (it is not, incidentally, complete: LXX *khettaios* and Heb. *ḥēṯ* do not reflect primitive **ḫat*) could be due to chance conflation, as E. A. Speiser assumed for the conflation of two **ḥôrî* groups.

Hittite cultural influence, reaching the Israelites indirectly via the Canaanite and Aramaean kingdoms and only after the passage of time, can be detected in many instances. But it should not be assumed that the vehicle for such influence was a Hittite enclave existing in Palestine since the time of the Patriarchs. Assyriology as a discipline would have profound relevance to Old Testament studies, even if Abraham had not migrated from Ur or the Assyrian and Neo-Babylonian rulers had not led their armies westward into the land of Israel. The significance of Assyro-Babylonian literature (as of Hittite literature) to Old Testament scholars lies rather in its contribution to one's understanding of the way men lived and thought during the era of Old Testament revelation. When similarities are found between ancient Israelite laws and customs and those of the Sumerians, Babylonians, Egyptians, or Hittites, one does not always conclude that there has been direct influence of one society upon the other. If further evidence points in that direction, one may indeed be justified in seeking to determine precisely the time and manner of the transfer. But far more frequently scholars are left with the similarity alone. In the following paragraphs I shall attempt to summarize most of the parallels which have been drawn between Hittite and Israelite culture, grouping them in categories determined by subject-matter. Not all the parallels are equally convincing. Some I have criticized in print in other articles; others I have advocated or defended. For the sake of brevity I have refrained from extensive criticism here.

Direct influence of one culture upon another is often measured by the number of vocabulary items from the influencing culture which have entered the language of the influenced. One acknowledges the debt of Rome to Greece in the stock of Greek words in Latin. Similarly one finds many words of Sumerian in Akkadian, of Akkadian in Aramaic, and of Hurrian in Hittite. Measured by this standard it would appear that there was no appreciable direct influence of Hittites on Hebrews. For, although one scholar has compiled a list of twenty-two Hittite words in Hebrew,[15] few Hittitologists will agree that more than three or four out of the list could be valid. And of the list most are of the order of 'culture words', old substratum terms whose linguistic origin is long forgotten: Hittite *wiyanaš*, 'wine' (Heb. *yayin* from **wayn-*); *kubaḫiš*, 'headgear' (Heb. *kōḇaʿ*); *šapšama*, 'sesame' (Heb. *šumšōm*, Akkad. *šamaššammu*); *allan*, 'oak', in *allan-taru-* (Heb. *'allōn*); *zapzigi*, 'glaze' (Heb. *sip̱sīḡī-m* in Prov. 26: 23, Akkad. *zabgû* and *zabzabgû*, Ugar. *spsg*); *a-a-bi*, 'ritual pit, mundus' (Heb. *'ôḇ*, Neo-Assyrian *apu*, Ugar. *'eb* in *'el'eb*); *tarpiš*, 'demon' (Heb. *t^erāp̱îm*); and *taluppi-*, 'furrow' (Heb. *telem* from **talm-*, Akkad. *talūmu*). The conclusion prompted by this evidence is not direct influence by the one people on the other, but that both peoples drew upon the common fund of 'culture words', as indeed they drew upon the common fund of customs and techniques. Partially related to the question of linguistic transfer is the case of a borrowed *topos*. One such is the phrase employed in Hittite prayers and rituals to describe the preparation of nature for the advent of the deity: *nu-šmaš kalmareš peran takšatniyantaru*, 'Let the mountains be levelled before you (O gods)!' (K.U.B. XV 34, i 45; iii 52). The same *topos* in fuller form is found in the incantation ritual for the goddess Wišuriyanza: 'Eat, you awesome deity! Before (you) let the rivers be bridged! Before (you) let the valleys be levelled! Let the mountains betake themselves down to the vegetation!' (K.Bo. XV 25, obv 13–15). The Old Testament parallel is the well-known poem of Second Isaiah: 'In the desert prepare the road of Yahweh! In the Arabah make a straight highway for our God! Every valley shall be elevated; every mountain and hill shall be brought low. The crooked shall become straight, and the rough places a plain' (Isa. 40: 3–4).

According to 1 Samuel 28: 6, in the days of King Saul there were three 'approved' channels of communication between God and man, three approved forms of divination: dreams, *'ûrîm*, and prophets. If these failed, however, there were additional methods available to the less scrupulous. These were the *'ōḇôṯ* and the *yiddeʿōnîm* (1 Sam. 28: 3) and the *terāp̄îm* (Ezek. 21: 21; Hos. 3: 4; Zech. 10: 2). Both the *'ôḇ* and the *terāp̄îm* have been greatly clarified by the Hittite religious texts, in particular the incantations. The *'ôḇ* (= Hitt. *a-a-bi*, pronounced **ayabi* or **aybi*)[16] was a pit dug in the ground, which served as a means of access between infernal spirits of gods or deceased persons and the upper world. Among the Hittites rituals were carried out which involved the opening up of such pits in places selected by oracle, the lowering of offerings into the pits, and the luring up of spirits out of the pit to eat the sacrifices and drink the blood libations and show their favour and superior knowledge to the sacrificers. A similar practice is known from Babylonia and Assyria at both an early (Gilgamesh) and a late (Neo-Assyrian) period. The Sumerian term for such a pit is AB.LÀL, the Neo-Assyrian term *apu*. It has been suggested that the Hebrew *'ôḇ* also originally designated a pit of this type, out of which the spirit was solicited, as perhaps still in 1 Samuel 28. In time *'ôḇ* was extended to cover also the spirit which emerged from the pit. In a similar way in Hittite texts *a-a-bi* is the pit, while *ᵈA-a-bi* is the deity who personifies the pit. The primitive sense 'pit, well' may still be found in the name of the desert station *'ōḇôṯ*, 'Wells' (Num. 21: 10–11, 33: 43–44). In the sense 'deceased ancestor' one finds the word in the Mari tribal name *Ub-rapi*, in the Byblian personal names *Ib-dādī* and *Ib-addī*, and in the Luwian personal name *Uba-ziti* ('man of Uba', cf. *Ḫuḫḫa-ziti* 'man of the deceased ancestor'). The solicited spirit 'rises' out of the ground (1 Sam. 28: 8, 11, 13–14), or its voice issues from the open hole in the ground (Isa. 29: 4) in a form which can be described as either whispering (Isa. 29: 4) or a bird-like chirping (Isa. 8: 19, 29: 4).

Like the old substratum word **ab/*ayab* which underlies Hebrew *'ôḇ* and Hittite *a-a-bi*, one finds also a common denominator between the source of Hebrew *tᵉrāp̱îm* (singular **tarp-*) and Hittite *tarpi-*, 'spirit, demon'.[17] The Hittite (or Luwian) pair *tarpiš annariš*, like the Babylonian *šēdu lamassu*, represent protective spirits of a benevolent type. As such they (*tarpiš annariš*) appear in Hittite incantations or prayers among benevolent and desirable forces. When, however, *tarpiš* appears without *annariš*, it seems to denote a baneful force, which together with other baneful forces must be banished to the nether world by incantations and kept there by enchantments. Along with other netherworld forces, however, it is conceivable (not yet attested in a text) that the *tarpiš* might be solicited through the *a-a-bi* pit. In the Old Testament the *tᵉrāp̱îm* can be used as mantic devices to inquire of the future: *š'l btrpym* (Ezek. 21: 21), *htrpym dbrw 'wn* (Zech. 10: 2). As such they are often paired with the ephod (Hos. 3: 4; Jud. 17: 5), which also was a mantic device. It is not clear what form the *tᵉrāp̱îm* assumed. Traditionally scholars have assumed that they were 'household gods' like the Roman *di penates*, and there is reason to believe that on occasion *tᵉrap̱îm* were anthropomorphic, even life-size (1 Sam. 19: 16). Yet in other passages they were small enough to conceal under a camel's saddle (Gen. 31: 34–35).

Since divination, magic, and incantation were illicit activities in ancient Israel, we owe our limited knowledge of them from Hebrew sources to their description in connection with prohibition in legal sources, or ridicule in historical or prophetic literature. We know of transvestism from its prohibition in Deuteronomy 22: 5. That transvestism was practised among the Hittites in the course of magic rituals to ensure the worshipper's sexual potency, or to destroy that of the worshipper's enemy, has suggested a similar role for it among the Canaanites.[18] In 1 Samuel 6 a ritual of the Philistines is described, which is intended to pacify a hostile deity from a neighbouring land. In its essentials the ritual closely resembles similar rituals known from the Hittite archives, which likewise have as their purpose the pacifying of hostile deities from neighbouring lands. In Zechariah 5: 7–8 a figure representing wickedness is confined in an ephah-sized container by a lid made of lead. The significance of the lead lid as a magical force impenetrable by evil is illuminated by a series of Hittite incantations, which depict evils as confined in bronze cauldrons in the nether world with lids of lead.[19]

Occasionally one finds elements of earlier magic rituals, which have penetrated the national cult of Israel and are no longer felt to be magic acts. Such is the ritual of the scapegoat on the Day of Atonement (Lev. 16). Similar scapegoat rituals are to be found in Hittite texts, where the scapegoat is designated by the Hurrian loan-word *nakkuššī-*.[20]

Among the people of Israel it is well known that both priests and kings were inaugurated by a ceremony of anointing. Consequently either king or priest could be called *māšîaḥ*, 'anointed one'. In Assyria and Babylonia a certain class of priests bore the name *pašīšu* ('anointed'), attesting to the custom of initiatory anointing of religious functionaries. But it does not appear that kings were anointed as a necessary step in the coronation rites. Among the Hittites both kings and priests were anointed. The priest class *tazzelli-* (= Sum. GUDÚ, = Akkad. *pašīšu*) was by its very name the class of the 'anointed ones'. As to the kings, we possess rituals for the coronation and installation of the 'substitute king', which faithfully reproduce the rites employed in genuine coronations. Here it is stated 'they anointed the prisoner-of-war ('substitute king') with the fine oil of kingship' (K.U.B. XXIV 5; IX 31, i 19).

In the area of law and legal procedures a number of parallels have been noted. The parallel which has most occupied Old Testament scholars is the format for the international treaties. The pioneering studies were those of Viktor Korošec (1931)[21] and George Mendenhall (1954),[22] who were followed by K. Baltzer (1960)[23] and D. J. McCarthy (1963).[24] What has been recognized is that from earliest times in Mesopotamia there was a rudimentary format for treaties. This simplest format was elaborated into a relatively consistent pattern of five or six parts by the Hittite chancery: (1) the king's titulature, (2) the historical background of the pact, (3) the stipulations of the pact, (4) the clause requiring preservation of the tablet in the sanctuary of the deity and its periodic public reading (this portion occasionally omitted), (5) the list of divine witnesses to the pact, and (6) the curses for violating and the blessings for obeying the stipulations. Individual sections were occasionally omitted, or the order was different. Thus out of a group of fourteen datable treaties studied by McCarthy, three lack a historical prologue. Out of that same selection five lack the 'tablet clause'. In the earliest treaties from the Old and Middle Hittite periods (Zidanza–Pilliya and Kaška treaties) the sequence blessings+cursings was observed, while from Šuppiluliuma I to the end of the empire the sequence cursings+blessings was preferred. Traces of this treaty format have been found in several places in the Old Testament, principally in the form of God's covenant with Israel (the Decalogue, and the Book of Deuteronomy).[25]

One may even compare legal content in the Old Testament with the Hittite laws. Accordingly, Exodus 21: 18–19 has been compared with Hittite law § 10; Deuteronomy 21: 1–9 with Hittite law § 6; Deuteronomy 22: 23–27 with Hittite laws §§ 197–8.

A very interesting comparison can be drawn between the custom of removing the shoe of a man who has been judged remiss in discharging a responsibility, a form of public humiliation, as it is found in Deuteronomy 25: 5–10 (and Ruth 4: 7 ff.), and the formulation in the Hittite 'Mešedi Protocol': 'If a guard deserts [his post] and carries off a lance from the postern, and the gateman catches him in the sin, he [the gateman] shall remove his [the guard's] shoe' (I.Bo.T. I 36, i 53–4). The sandal removed in Deuteronomy 25, therefore, is probably not *only* a symbolic attestation of transferred or ceded (property) rights, but also more generally a stigmatization, as the act of spitting also suggests.[26]

It has recently been suggested by J. Milgrom that the shared custody of the Israelite tabernacle, as depicted in 'P', also represents a very ancient practice attested among the Hittites.[27] Basing his claim for the Hittite cult on the 'Instructions for Priests and Temple Officials' (K.U.B. XIII 4 and duplicates), Milgrom draws the parallel between the Hittite 'keepers' (*ḫaliyattalleš*), who patrol a beat outside the gate leading into the temple courtyard, but can be summoned by the priests within the enclosure in order to evict an unauthorized person, and 'P's Levites, who serve the same purpose. He then compares the Hittite 'temple servants' (*karimnaleš*, Sum. LÚ.MEŠ É.DINGIR-*LIM*) with 'P's priests. The analogy is close, and many of the minor discrepancies can be explained as due to the different designs of temple and courtyard. One point—that the 'temple servants' exercise authority over the 'keepers'—he does not adequately support. The subject deserves further study.

In the realm of the concept of divine wrath two key passages in Hebrew and Hittite religious texts should be juxtaposed. In Exodus 34: 6 we read of 'Yahweh, a merciful and gracious God, slow to anger and having abundant mercy and faithfulness'. This passage depicts a characteristic of Israel's God which a modern might call his 'high threshold of anger'. That is, it requires a great deal of provocation over a great deal of time to arouse God's anger. Once it has been aroused, however, it is violent and long-lasting, continuing to work in the third and fourth generations of the transgressor's family. In the Hittite 'Instructions for Priests and Temple Officials' (K.U.B. XIII 4, ii 27 ff.) the following theological statement is made: 'The temper of the gods is massive. It does not quickly take hold. But when it does take hold, it will not let go.' The word 'temper' translates Hittite *ištanza* (Sum. ZI), while the word 'massive' renders the Hittite adjective *daššuš*, 'heavy, massive, strong'. The depiction of the god is exactly the same in the two passages—a temperament which is not easily disturbed, but which is capable of extreme violence when it is aroused.

A final area of cultural comparison is historiography. The Hittites made significant contributions in this realm. The genre of royal annals in particular was developed most fully prior to the Neo-Assyrian period among the Hittites. So far we have annals for Hattušili I, Šuppiluliuma I, Muršili, and by an Arnuwanda and a Tudhaliya who are probably ancestors of Šuppiluliuma I. It is possible that we have fragments of annals by Hattušili III. But it seems clear that the popularity of the genre declined rapidly after Muršili II, since we possess no annals for Muwattalli or for Hattušili III's three successors. A second type of historical composition attested among the Hittites is the edict or proclamation. The best-known example is the so-called Telepinu Proclamation, but variant types may include the Testament of Hattušili I and the Apology of Hattušili III. The Telepinu Proclamation and the Apology of Hattušili III may also, in view of their historical function, have served as political justifications of *coups d'état*. In this latter function the Apology of Hattušili III has been compared by H. M. Wolf with the 'succession narrative' of 1 Samuel 15 to 2 Samuel 8, which relates the divine choice of David as king, and traces the stages of his rise to power over an incompetent king.[28] The doctrines of causality in Hittite and Hebrew historiography have been analysed by A. Malamat, who draws on historical material in the Hittite royal prayers, principally the so-called 'Plague Prayers of Muršili II'.[29]

Not all of the examples cited above will be equally convincing to any Old Testament scholar. They are assembled here as a convenience to the biblical scholar, who may not have mastered the Hittite sources personally. Critical evaluation has been kept to a minimum. Further criticism of many of the parallels can be found in the articles cited in the notes.

It is not my contention that the Hittite civilization centred in Asia Minor which came to an end *c.* 1190 B.C. made direct contacts with the people of Israel. Extra-biblical evidence would seem rather to suggest that the Hittites never penetrated south of the kingdom of Kadesh on the Orontes. But through the many years of sustained contact with cities in Syria and Phoenicia (Carchemish, Aleppo, Ugarit) Hittite civilization left its marks there (Plate V *b*). These influences may have filtered southward over the years and found their way into Israel just prior to the beginning of the kingdom of David. It is becoming ever clearer that the first period of intensive scholarly writing in Israel coincided with the kingdoms of David and Solomon. Both kings possessed highly cosmopolitan courts. Certain elements of Hittite culture in their 'Neo-Hittite' after-life may have been brought into David's court by North Syrian immigrants. This might account for those parallels which are best explained as transfers. As mentioned above, however, many of the other parallels can be adequately explained as outgrowths of a cultural continuum spanning southern Asia Minor and the Levantine coast. What cannot be doubted is that our understanding of the people of Israel is extended the more we come to know about its neighbours. The contribution of the Hittites in this regard is not negligible.

B. THE HURRIANS

Although very little outside the biblical allusions to the Horites was known about the Hurrians until the 1920s, it is now believed that they and another group known as the Subarians were an important component of the population of Mesopotamia during the late third and early second millennia B.C. Since the Hurrians are known to date only as influential minorities in non-Hurrian centres, one can but speculate about Hurrian law, religion, and art by abstracting what seem to be foreign elements in the literature, art, and architecture of these centres. If the Mitannian capital city of Waššukkanni is ever located and excavated, we may discover Hurrian civilization in its purest form. The history of the Hurrians is reconstructed on the basis of onomastic data. The assumption is made that where Hurrian names are found, one can identify Hurrian presence.[30]

(i) *History*

Hurrians first appear in the written records of Mesopotamia during the last two centuries of the third millennium B.C. Hurrian princes were the authors of two inscriptions dating from the beginning of the Third Dynasty of Ur (*c.* 2150 B.C.): the foundation lion inscription of Tišatal of Urkiš, and the dedicatory tablet of Arišen prince of Urkiš, which was found at Samarra. Other evidence from onomastics indicates that Hurrians infiltrated the region to the east of the Tigris during the Sargonic period (*c.* 2400–2200 B.C.). Many more names occur during the ensuing Ur III period (*c.* 2150–2000 B.C.) and the Isin–Larsa hegemony (*c.* 2000–1800 B.C.). During the age of Hammurabi of Babylon and his successors (*c.* 1792–1595 B.C.) the evidence becomes more varied, and the settlement pattern more extended. Among the Old Babylonian texts from Mari seven Hurrian texts dating from the beginning of the eighteenth century B.C. were found. Their contents are of a religious nature, except for the seventh, which is a portion of a letter from one king to another. One of the two may even have been Zimri-Lim of Mari (*c.* 1779–1761 B.C.). A contract from the city of Hana recovered in the Mari archives mentions for the first time the Hurrians as a people. Hurrian names are found in documents from Alalakh in the far west, Chagar Bazar in the north, and Dilbat in the south, dating to the period of the last four kings of the Hammurabi Dynasty (*c.* 1750–1595 B.C.). The intensification of Hurrian penetration of Upper Mesopotamia and North Syria must have been rapid during these years. By *c.* 1635 B.C., the middle of the reign of Hattušili I of Hatti, the first recorded Hurrian military incursion of Asia Minor took place. It was repulsed, but indicated the trend of things to come. In 1595 B.C., when Muršili I led his army through Syria on his way to Babylon, he encountered Hurrian armies, which fought with him. The semi-legendary account of the siege of Ursum in the time of Hattušili I mentions a 'battering ram of the Hurrian type'. Between the reign of Telepinu (*c.* 1525–1500 B.C.) and that of Zidanza II (*c.* 1480–1470 B.C.) a change of dynasty in Kizzuwatna (Cilicia) brought Hurrians to power. At about the same time (*c.* 1490 B.C.) we first hear of the dynasty of Mitannian kings, who ruled continuously at Waššukkanni in Upper Mesopotamia until about 1370, when the Hittite emperor Šuppiluliuma I destroyed their kingdom and installed his own vassal ruler Kurtiwaza in their place. These Mitannian rulers dominated Upper Mesopotamia and Assyria for over a century and corresponded with the Egyptian pharaohs as equals. We are fortunate to possess some of this correspondence in the archives of El Amarna (*c.* 1400–1350 B.C.). The official language of the kingdom was Hurrian, in which one of its kings, a certain Tušratta, composed a long diplomatic letter to the Egyptian pharaoh Amenophis IV. But the rulers of Mitanni took names which are non-Hurrian. Authorities on the ancient languages of India have recognized as of an Indo-Aryan type the royal names Paratarna, Saušatar, Artatama, Šuttarna, Tušratta. It is almost certain that it was these Mitannians who were responsible for the introduction into the Near East of scientific techniques for the breeding and training of chariot horses. A manual of these techniques by a Hurrian named Kikkuli was found at Hattuša. The kingdom of Mitanni, which dominated the kingdoms of Arrapha in the east, Assyria in the central area, and Mukiš in Syria, probably reached the zenith of its power under Saušatar *c.* 1450 B.C. Saušatar came into conflict with Thutmose III of Egypt over the possession of Syria, and was defeated by him, losing much of his territory west of the Euphrates. But under that pharaoh or his successor Thutmose IV the two countries concluded a treaty of alliance, under the terms of which Mitanni regained control of Aleppo and North Syria. Artatama I, who succeeded Saušatar, gave his daughter in marriage to Thutmose IV. This procedure was followed by Šuttarna and his successor Tušratta, both of whom gave their daughters in marriage to Amenophis III and IV. Because the Hurrian kingdom of Kizzuwatna (Cilicia) was in league with Mitanni, Šuppiluliuma I's advance into Syria by the usual route through the Taurus mountain passes was blocked. Circling round to the north through the kingdom of Išuwa, and marching rapidly southward along the upper course of the Euphrates, the Hittite conqueror caught his Mitannian foes off guard and routed all opposition. He claimed the principal centres of North Syria for the Hittite empire, and even installed Tušratta's own son, Kurtiwaza, as his vassal over a much reduced kingdom of Mitanni. Kurtiwaza held his own until late in the reign of the Assyrian king Aššur-uballiṭ I (1365–1330 B.C.). Shortly after the death of Šuppiluliuma I in 1346 the Assyrian overcame the hapless kingdom of Mitanni and incorporated it into his realm.

But if Mitanni had fallen, Hurrians had not thereby vanished from positions of political power all over the Near East. Šuppiluliuma I himself and his dynasty were Hurrians, and it is known that each of the kings of the New Kingdom in Hatti had a Hurrian personal name as well as a 'Hittite' (actually Hattic) throne name. The Hittite state cult was well populated with Hurrian deities. Religious documents were composed in Hurrian. In Syria and along the Phoenician coast Hurrians made up a large proportion of the population. During the fourteenth and thirteenth centuries B.C. several of the royal names of cities like Ugarit (Ar-Halpa), Carchemish (Šarri-kušuh, Ini-teššup, Talmi-teššup), and Amurru (DU-teššup, Tuppi-teššup, Bentešina) were Hurrian. Hurrian religious texts have been found in significant numbers at Ugarit, including those written in both the syllabic and the alphabetic texts. Bilingual and trilingual texts of which one version was Hurrian have been recovered.

(ii) *Old Testament Contacts*

Further to the south in Palestine enclaves of Hurrians had long been established. Among the names of the Hyksos invaders of the period *c.* 1700–1580 B.C. have been found a number which are Hurrian. When the last Hyksos ruler was driven out of the Delta *c.* 1570, enclaves of 'Hyksos' settled in Palestine. In Egyptian documents from the New Kingdom (*c.* 1580 and following) a common designation of Palestine is 'the Land of Ḫuru'. During the Amarna Age (*c.* 1400–1350 B.C.) princes with Hurrian names ruled at Jerusalem, Shechem, and Taanach.

In the Old Testament itself there are two ethnic terms which may at times identify Hurrians: Horite and Hivite. E. A. Speiser deserves the credit for pointing out that the LXX reading 'Horite', in passages like Genesis 36: 2 and Joshua 9: 7, for the M.T.'s 'Hivite' indicates that an early confusion of the Hebrew consonants *w* and *r* may have given rise to the 'Hivites' as a separate group from the 'Horites'.[31] Speiser further claimed that most of the references to Horites in the Old Testament are to ancient inhabitants of Edom or Mt. Seir, who were probably not Hurrians. Thus in the Old Testament one should seek Hurrians under the name 'Hivite', and the following 'Hivites' in the Old Testament are probably Hurrians: Hamor of Shechem (Gen. 34) and his clan, and the Gibeonites (Josh. 9: 7 and 11: 19). Another group which might be Hurrian is the Jebusites. They are associated with pre-Israelite Jerusalem, which, as we saw above, was ruled by a Hurrian dynast (named 'Servant of Hepa') during the Amarna period. In 2 Samuel 24: 16 the Jebusite ruler of Jerusalem in David's day is called Araunah. The parallel account in 1 Chronicles 21: 14–30, as well as the LXX translation of both accounts, suggests that the M.T. consonants *'rwnh* in 2 Samuel 24 have resulted from a transposition of the consonants *'wrnh*. The 'name' (if it be not rather a title) of this Jebusite was the Hurrian word *ewri-ne*, 'the lord'. The same name (spelled *'wrn*) occurs in a text from Ugarit.

Hurrian cultural influence on the people of Israel has often been documented by E. A. Speiser[32] and C. H. Gordon.[33] Particularly rich in parallels to the documents of the Hurrian-dominated community of Nuzi are the Patriarchal narratives. Before the birth of his sons Abraham had adopted a slave named Eliezer as his heir (Gen. 15: 2–3). At Nuzi it was a custom for childless people to adopt a son to serve them as long as they lived, to bury and mourn for them when they died. As compensation the adopted son was made heir to the possessions of the childless couple. If, however, the couple should have a son of their own after the adoption, the actual son would assume the right of heir. Similarly explained from almost identical cases at Nuzi are Sarah's giving Hagar to Abraham as his second wife, Esau's sale of his birthright, Jacob's dealings with Laban, the importance attached to his idols (*t^erāp̱îm*) by Laban (Gen. 31), and the binding character of the oral death-bed blessings of Isaac (Gen. 27) and Jacob (Gen. 49).

Data from the Nuzi tablets have also been used to elucidate the institution of fratriarchy in the Old Testament (1 Chr. 26: 10, 5: 12; 1 Sam. 8: 2, 17: 13), the right of daughters to a share in the father's estate (Num. 27: 8), and the institution of levirate marriage (Deut. 25: 5–7, 38; Ruth).

NOTES

1. H. G. Guterbock, 'Towards a definition of the term "Hittite"', *Oriens* x (1957), 233 ff.

2. For a scholarly assessment of this people see A. Goetze, *Kleinasien*, 2nd edn., pp. 45–7; O. R. Gurney, *The Hittites*, pp. 15 ff.; E. Akurgal, *The Art of the Hittites*, pp. 13–29.

3. The Hittite text is copied in K.Bo. V 11, i 5–20.

4. Especially recommended is E. Akurgal, *The Art of the Hittites*.

5. E. Forrer, *P.E.Q.* (1937), 114.

6. In the *M.D.O.G.* Definitive excavation publications have appeared in the *Wissenschaftliche Veröffentlichungen der Deutschen Orient-Gesellschaft* (= *W.V.D.O.G.* below) under the title *Boğazköy-Hattuša* (*Ergebnisse der Ausgrabungen des Deutschen Archaeologischen Instituts und der Deutschen Orient-Gesellschaft*) (6 vols., 1952–69). The first volume publishing the cuneiform texts, entitled *Keilschrifttexte aus Boghazköi*, forms a part of the larger *W.V.D.O.G.* series mentioned above. Nineteen volumes in this series have appeared up to the present time (vols. 1–20). The second series is entitled *Keilschrifturkunden aus Boghazköi*. It has enjoyed the sponsorship of the German Academy of Sciences in Berlin, and now comprises 42 vols. Other tablets from Boğazköy have been published in smaller series.

7. K. Bittel, *Hattuša: the Capital of the Hittites* (1970).

8. The small fragment is now published as K.Bo. xix 28.

9. H. Otten, 'Hethiter, Hurriter und Mitanni', in *Fischer Weltgeschichte: Die Altorientalischen Reiche*, ii. 102 ff., E. Cassin *et al.* (eds.); even more complete is *C.A.H.* ii, rev. edn. (see Bibliography below).

10. This presentation assumes the position advocated by H. Otten, O. R. Gurney, O. Carruba, and Houwink ten Cate, that the famous Madduwatta and Mita of Paḫḫuwa texts, together with the annals formerly attributed to Tudḫaliya IV and Arnuwanda III, are to be dated

to the period immediately prior to the accession of Šuppiluliuma I. See P. H. J. Houwink ten Cate, *The Records of the Early Hittite Empire* (*c. 1450–1380 B.C.*), pp. 57–79. This position is strenuously opposed by A. Kammenhuber, *Zeitschrift für vergleichende Sprachforschung* lxxxiii (1969), 256 ff.

11. Marc Bloc, *Feudal Society* (Routledge & Kegan Paul, London, 1961), i. 242. The feudalism of medieval Europe is well described in this two-volume work of Bloc's. In essentials the structure of Hittite society, which antedates Frankish feudalism by 2000 years, is identical.

12. I have interpreted this passage in my article, 'Hittite *Tarpiš* and Hebrew *Terāphîm*', *J.N.E.S.* xxvii (1968), p. 65 and n. 31. In the footnote I failed to recognize the identity of *ši-pa-an*, and sought to read it *lúm-pa-an*, 'grief'. *Šipa-*, 'demon', as an independent word is still not recognized by the Hittite dictionaries.

13. For a detailed analysis of the problem see H. A. Hoffner, *Tyndale Bulletin* xx (1969), 28 ff.

14. Ibid. 33 ff.

15. Ch. Rabin, 'Hittite Words in Hebrew', *Or.* N.S. xxxii (1963), 113–39; see also P. Fronzaroli, 'Rapporti lessicali dell'ittita con le lingue semitiche', *Archivo Glottologico Italiano* xli (1956), 32–45.

16. See H. A. Hoffner, Jr., 'Second Millennium Antecedents to the Hebrew *'Ôbh*', *J.B.L.* lxxxvi (1967), 385–401; and the same author in *Theologisches Wörterbuch zum Alten Testament*, i. 141–5.

17. See H. A. Hoffner, Jr., 'Hittite *Tarpiš* and Hebrew *Terāphîm*', *J.N.E.S.* xxvii (1968), 61–8.

18. See H. A. Hoffner, Jr., 'Symbols for Masculinity and Femininity', *J.B.L.* lxxxv (1966), 326–34.

19. Hoffner, *J.N.E.S.* xxvii (1968), 65.

20. Nadia van Brock, 'Substitution rituelle', *R.H.A.* xvii, fasc. 65 (1959), 117–46. Cf. now Hoffner, *A.G.A.T.* xx (1973).

21. *Hethitische Staatsverträge* (Leipzig, 1931).

22. 'Law and Covenant in Israel', *B.A.* xvii (1954).

23. *Das Bundesformular* (Neukirchen, 1960).

24. *Treaty and Covenant* (Rome, 1963).

25. Ibid. 109 ff.; M. Kline, *Treaty of the Great King* (Grand Rapids, Minn., 1963).

26. Hoffner, *Tyndale Bulletin* xx (1969), 42–4.

27. J. Milgrom, 'The Shared Custody of the Tabernacle and a Hittite Analogy', *J.A.O.S.* xc (1970), 204–9.

28. H. M. Wolf, *The Apology of Hattusilis Compared with Other Political Self-justifications of the Ancient Near East* (Ann Arbor, Mich., 1967).

29. A. Malamat, *V.T.* v (1955), 1–12.

30. Though now badly in need of revision, the fundamental sketch of Hurrian (and Subarian) history is still I. J. Gelb's *Hurrians and Subarians* (Chicago, 1944).

31. E. A. Speiser, 'Hurrians', *I.D.B.* ii. 664–6.

32. Speiser's most significant articles (many on the Nuzi tablets) can now be found conveniently collected in *Oriental and Biblical Studies: Collected Writings of E. A. Speiser*, J. J. Finkelstein & Moshe Greenberg (eds.) (Philadelphia, 1967).

33. 'Biblical Customs and the Nuzu Tablets', *B.A.* iii (1940), 1–12.

BIBLIOGRAPHY

(i) *Hittites*

AKURGAL, E., *The Art of the Hittites* (Munich, 1962).

BITTEL, K., *Hattuša: the Capital of the Hittites* (New York, 1970).

Cambridge Ancient History, ii, rev. edn. (in press).

GOETZE, A., *Kleinasien*, 2nd edn. (Munich, 1956).

—— in *A.N.E.T.* (1952).

GURNEY, O. R., *The Hittites*, rev. edn. (Harmondsworth, 1966).

GÜTERBOCK, H. G., 'Hittite Religion', in *Forgotten Religions*, V. Ferm (ed.) (1949).

—— 'Hittite Mythology', in *Mythologies of the Ancient World*, S. N. Kramer (ed.) (New York, 1961).

HOFFNER, H. A., 'Some Contributions of Hittitology to Old Testament Study', *Tyndale Bulletin* xx (1969).

LAROCHE, E., 'Recherches sur les noms des dieux hittites', *R.H.A.* vii, fasc. 46 (1946–7).

OTTEN, H., 'Das Hethiterreich', in *Kulturgeschichte des alten Orient*, H. Schmökel (ed.) (Stuttgart, 1961).

WALSER, G. (ed.), *Neuere Hethiterforschung* (Wiesbaden, 1964).

(ii) *Hurrians*

GELB, I. J., *Hurrians and Subarians* (Chicago, 1944).

GÖTZE, A., *Hethiter, Churriter und Assyrer* (London, 1936).

GÜTERBOCK, H. G., 'The Hurrian Element in the Hittite Empire', *Journal of World History* ii (1954), 383 ff.

O'CALLAGHAN, R. T., *Aram Naharaim* (Rome, 1948).

SPEISER, E. A., 'Ethnic Movements in the Near East', *A.A.S.O.R.* xiii (1933), 13–54.

X

THE MOABITES AND EDOMITES

J. R. BARTLETT

(i) *Territory*

It is unfortunate for the student of the Moabites and Edomites that the Israelites seem to have known comparatively little about these neighbours and their territory. True, the Old Testament (and King Mesha's inscription) tells us much about the Moabites and their cities north of the river Arnon (Seil el-Mōjib), but south of it we hear for certain only of Kir-hareseth (Kerak).[1] In Edom, whose northern border with Moab was the Wādi el-Ḥeṣā, we have certain knowledge only of Ezion-geber (which was not in origin an Edomite city),[2] Punon,[3] Bozrah,[4] the land of the Temanites,[5] and the fort which Amaziah renamed Joktheel (2 Kings 14: 7). We are also told of Masrekah and Rehoboth by the River, whose sites are virtually unknown, and Me-zahab, Dinhabah, Avith, and Pau, which may, with the Tophel and Laban of Deuteronomy 1: 1, belong to Moab rather than to Edom.[6] The borders of these countries are equally difficult to determine from the biblical records; Edom was probably restricted to the high land between the Wādi ʿArabah in the west and the desert to the east, the Wādi el-Ḥeṣā in the north and the Wādi Hismeh in the south. Certain texts, however, show that in its later history Edom extended west across the Wādi ʿArabah.[7] Moab's northern border seems to have fluctuated as Israelites and Moabites and others competed for the plains north of the Arnon, but perhaps one should think of Moab not as the land between the Seil el-Mōjib and the Wādi el-Ḥeṣā but as the land of the former river's basin and its surrounding hills.[8]

(ii) *Origins and History*

Who the Edomites and Moabites were by origin is not clear. The designation of the Moabites as 'the sons of Seth' (Num. 24:

17, R.S.V.; R.V., 'sons of tumult') does not help us much. The Israelites thought of the Moabites as closely connected with the Ammonites (Gen. 19: 30 ff., cf. Deut. 23: 3; Neh. 13: 1), and these peoples probably belonged to the 'Aramaean migration' of the end of the Bronze Age and the beginning of the Iron Age.[9] But Edom is always thought of apart from Moab and Ammon, and is described as a 'brother' to Israel. This 'brotherhood', however, does not seem to refer to a close blood relationship between the early Edomites and Israelites; it may mean rather that Edom became a brother to the northern kingdom of Israel in the sense of being a covenanted ally, and to the kingdom of Judah by being associated with Esau of Seir, brother of Jacob, whose clans lived in the wilderness on the southern borders of Judah.[10] Thus Edom was not necessarily a part of the Aramaean migration, perhaps being linked rather with the Arabian world. Edom's god, Qaus, has an Arabian background (see below, p. 246), and J. A. Montgomery remarks that 'Edom was always Arabian in race and sympathy'.[11]

The settlement of these two peoples in their respective homes again raises many questions. The Moabites called their predecessors Emim (Deut. 2: 10 f.; cf. Gen. 14: 5 f.), and the Deuteronomist classes them as Rephaim, i.e., as pre-Israelites of giant stature.[12] Alt, linking the Emim with the stele from Baluʿah, whose inscription (partly erased by a later relief) is perhaps related in script to the Linear B script, suggested that the Emim entered Transjordan from the west.[13] According to Genesis 36: 20 ff.; Deuteronomy 2: 12, 22; Genesis 14: 6, the Edomites' predecessors were the Horites, but 'Les Horites de la Bible ne sont pas davantage les Ḫurrites de l'histoire; ils habitent une région où les Ḫurrites n'ont pas pénétré et ils se portent des noms sémitiques.' De Vaux thinks that the Israelites took the name 'Horites' from the Egyptian name for Canaan, Ḫuru, and applied it to the southern Transjordan because no other name was available; so they said that Horites had lived there.[14] The list of Horite clans in Genesis 36: 20 ff. contains names which appear to belong originally to the clans of Judah and the other peoples of the Negeb,[15] and are uncertain witnesses for the existence of the pre-Edomite Horites east of the Wādi ʿArabah.[16]

Unfortunately we are as yet unable to learn much about the arrival of the Moabites and Edomites, and their effect on any previous inhabitants, from archaeological evidence, for not enough sites have been dug. Tell el-Kheleifeh is not representative; at Tawilân traces of a large Edomite town of the eighth to sixth centuries B.C. have recently been uncovered;[17] at Aroer on the north bank of the Arnon excavation has revealed a ninth-century B.C. fortress built on the ruins of earlier buildings, and pottery mainly from the eleventh to ninth centuries B.C.;[18] at Dibon there seems to be nothing earlier than the twelfth century;[19] at Medeba was found a tomb dating from perhaps the beginning of the twelfth century B.C.;[20] and at Heshbon an initial sounding has revealed 'three or four LB painted pieces of pottery, of which one is clear bichrome LB I ware'.[21] A little further north near Amman various Late Bronze Age finds, including a sanctuary, have been made,[22] and it is as yet an open question how far these finds modify Glueck's view, based on a surface survey of pottery fragments, of a gap in sedentary occupation between the eighteenth and the thirteenth centuries B.C. The precise date of the Iron Age buildings—e.g. the border fortresses—found in Edom and Moab[23] awaits elucidation from careful archaeological study; in view of 2 Samuel 8: 14 it is not impossible that David was responsible for some of these buildings. The Balu'ah stele in its final form has been shown, from the details of the clothing on the relief, to be no earlier than the beginning of the twelfth century B.C.;[24] according to Albright, this relief, showing a god extending to a king the sign of life, 'proves that there was already a well organised monarchy of some kind in Moab'.[25] From a reinvestigation of evidence at Luxor K. A. Kitchen has recently suggested that Ramesses II invaded the Moabite region *c.* 1280–1270 B.C., plundering Dibon and an unknown town '*in (the) land of Moab*: B(w)trt', possibly the Raba-batna of the *Tabula Peutingeriana*, 62 Roman miles south of Amman.[26] This gives us an early thirteenth-century B.C. date for knowledge of the 'land of Moab',[27] but we lack archaeological confirmation of Dibon's existence at this time. 'The lands of Seir' are mentioned in Amarna Letter No. 288,[28] and there are Egyptian references to the Shasu peoples of mount Seir (not necessarily identical with Edom) from Ramesses II's reign.[29] The Shasu tribes of the land of Edom are mentioned as crossing the border into Egypt in Sethos II's reign (1214–1208 B.C.),[30] and the nomadic Shasu of Seir in Ramesses III's reign (1198–1166 B.C.).[31]

We can probably conclude that in the thirteenth century B.C. the population of Moab and Edom was mainly semi-nomadic, with some more permanent settlements beginning to come into existence. Glueck's surface findings show further that, at least in the height of the Iron Age, there were border fortresses of varying sizes, a few larger settlements, and some small 'farm centers in which the Edomite *fellāḥîn* lived and stored their crops'.[32] In the Wādi 'Arabah there were settlements devoted to copper mining, e.g. at Timna', where B. Rothenberg claims that the mines functioned in the twelfth and eleventh centuries B.C., but not in the tenth or later centuries.[33]

Biblical evidence for the early Moabites and Edomites is sparse and debatable. The Song of Moses (Exod. 15: 15) refers to the *'allûpîm* of Edom and the *'êlîm* of Moab, who with the Canaanites and Philistines are afraid at Yahweh's action on Israel's behalf. The *'allūpîm* appear elsewhere only in Genesis 36: 15 ff., 21, 29 f., 40 ff. (cf. 1 Chr. 1: 51 ff.) and Zechariah 9: 7, 12: 5 f.; Moab's *'êlîm* (rams) may be a nickname reflecting Moab's fame as a land of sheep and rams (cf. 2 Kings 3: 4), or a title. But whether Israelite tradition has preserved Edomite and Moabite titles correctly or not, we need not doubt that such pre-monarchic leaders existed, presumably as clan-chiefs; the *'allūpîm* of Genesis 36: 16 f. appear to be Edomite clans (cf. *'elep*, thousand),[34] of which Genesis 36: 10–14 lists twelve, together with the concubine's son Amalek.[35] Unfortunately we know nothing of the clans of Moab.

Traditionally, Edom had kings before Israel had them. According to Numbers 20: 14 'Moses sent messengers from Kadesh unto the king of Edom'; but other details in this passage, such as Edom's brotherhood with Israel and Kadesh's situation on the border of Edom, may reflect a later period than the thirteenth century B.C., and the king of Edom, who is unnamed, is a very shadowy figure who has disappeared from the narrative by verse 18. The list of Genesis 36: 31–39 (cf. 1 Chr. 1: 43–50) has often been taken to refer to nearly two centuries of Edomite monarchy prior to Saul or David's monarchy, but examination of this list suggests that it may be compiled from two sources, one from Moab and one from Edom, and that each king rules a region rather than the whole land of Edom. Thus, for example, Jobab ruled the region of

Bozrah in the northern half of Edom's mountains, and Husham ruled 'the land of the Temanites' in the southern half.[36] Bela the son of Beor, the name of whose city was Dinhabah, Hadad the son of Bedad, the name of whose city was Avith, and Hadar, the name of whose city was Pau, however, perhaps belonged to Moab rather than to Edom.[37] It is in fact unlikely that Edom and Moab were political entities very much earlier than Israel, for they were large in area, and their peoples faced pressures similar to those met by the Israelite tribes. North of the Arnon the kingdom of Heshbon, early Israelite settlers, and perhaps also the Ammonites were forces to be reckoned with, while to the east and south there was pressure from the Midianites (cf. Gen. 36: 35),[38] and from the west there were perhaps attacks from Israelite groups.[39] But Israel's contact with Edom and Moab in this period was not great. Whatever route Israel followed through the wilderness, she clearly did not defeat Edom south of the Wādi el-Ḥeṣā, or Moab south of the Arnon, as she defeated the Midianites and Amorites elsewhere. Our difficulties lie in establishing what happened in the region north of the Arnon.

Noth has argued that the Moabites settled north of the Arnon from the first, as is evidenced by the name *'arḇôṯ mô'āḇ* for the plains to the north-east of the Dead Sea, a name which, though appearing only in Priestly material, was coined, Noth thinks, at the time of the Moabite settlement by Israelite neighbours. The Deuteronomistic tradition of Moses' grave outside the Promised Land in Moab, conflicting with the Deuteronomistic tribal geography, according to which Moses' grave is in the area inhabited by Israelite tribes, again suggests that the 'valley . . . over against Beth-peor' (Deut. 34: 6) was actually in Moabite territory. The Balaam story shows that the region of Pisgah and the sanctuary of Baal-peor lay in Moabite territory. Noth argues that Beth-peor was a border sanctuary where Moabite, Midianite, and Israelite met, and that the Israelite tribes Reuben and Gad settled to its north and north-east in the land of Jazer and Gilead (Num. 32: 1). Sihon conquered Moabite cities southwards to the Arnon, and the Reuben–Gad group conquered his territory, at least as far as Medeba, on the western edge of the hills. Thus by Solomon's time Israelite territory reached as far as the Arnon (2 Sam. 24: 5; cf. 1 Kings 4: 7–19).[40] This is persuasive, but it has its difficulties.

The Priestly writer's *'arḇôṯ mô'āḇ* and Deuteronomy's setting of Moses' death 'in the land of Moab' are hardly surprising, when we recall that for most of the monarchic period Moab held territory north of the Arnon, and are uncertain evidence for thirteenth-century B.C. Moabite control of this area. The evidence of the song in Numbers 21: 27–30 is also uncertain: was Heshbon the destroyer or the destroyed, Amorite or Moabite? To what date can we assign the events of this song?[41] To what date can we assign the tradition that the Arnon was the border of Moab (Num. 21: 13 ff., 22: 36; Jud. 11: 18, 22; cf. Deut. 2: 24)? The first clear evidence of Moabite control north of the Arnon comes from the story of Ehud (Jud. 3: 12–30), and presumably this Moabite occupation deprived the Reuben–Gad group of some at least of their cities. Saul 'vexed' Moab (1 Sam. 14: 47); David conquered Moab and reduced her to vassaldom (2 Sam. 8: 2, 12), and made the Arnon the border between Israel and Moab (2 Sam. 24: 5).

Of internal events in Moab in this early period we can only guess. We hear of Balak, son of Zippor, King of Moab, in the region north of the Arnon; 'it is possible that Balak was not actually "king of Moab" but some petty king or other in the early period who was neighbour to the Israelites who lived in that southern region of Transjordan.'[42] Perhaps the later Eglon (Jud. 3: 12–30) was a similar, but more powerful, figure, though where his kingdom was based we do not know. Elsewhere in Moab we may similarly have to think of city or regional kings such as Bela and others (see above, p. 233); one Hadad defeated the Midianites 'in the field of Moab' (a unique phrase; cf. 'the field of Edom', Gen. 32: 3, Jud. 5: 4), and this event, impossible to date, is perhaps comparable with Gideon's exploit (Jud. 7 and 8).[43] Towards the end of Saul's reign David left his parents for safety at Mizpeh of Moab, with the King of Moab (1 Sam. 22: 3 f.); but where this place—not necessarily the royal residence—was we do not know. It is quite clear that the Israelites knew virtually nothing of events and persons and places south of the Arnon, until the campaigns of Saul and David explored Moab and Edom.

David reduced Moab and Edom to vassaldom (2 Sam. 8: 2, 12 ff.; cf. 23: 20, Num. 24: 17 f.); apparently Edom, at least, by this time had a hereditary monarchy (cf. 1 Kings 11: 14 f.). Edom's king, presumably, was killed, and his son Hadad escaped to exile in

Egypt. Moab and Edom were probably conquered not so much because they constituted a serious threat to David as because they offered the prospect of wealth. Both lay on a famous highway; Moab was rich in sheep, Edom in copper. Thus we are not surprised to find Solomon (whose use of copper is attested by 1 Kings 7: 13 f., 46) exploiting these resources by establishing Ezion-geber on the Gulf of Aqaba (1 Kings 9: 26 f., 10: 11 ff.) as a port and trading centre.[44] However, towards the end of Solomon's reign the Edomite crown-prince Hadad returned from Egypt, and, if 1 Kings 11: 25b is rightly to be emended and restored to a place after verse 22, 'reigned over Edom'.[45] Ezion-geber was soon destroyed—perhaps by Sheshonk of Egypt, however, rather than by Hadad and his Edomites.[46] At all events, Sheshonk's invasion and Judah's troubles with Israel gave Edom the chance to regain her independence. Solomon's control over Moab, too, was probably far from strong. His nearest provincial capital in Transjordan was at Mahanaim (1 Kings 4: 14),[47] and soon after his reign Moab seems to have gained control of Aroer and Dibon, just north of the Arnon. Mesha, born *c.* 880 B.C.(?), was himself a Dibonite, the son of *kmšyt* the king of Moab,[48] and was thus presumably born in a period of Moabite occupation of Dibon. Medeba also probably belonged to Moab soon after Solomon's death, for Mesha refers to the land of Medeba as Moabite territory which had in his own time or shortly before passed into Omri's hands. We may compare the implication of lines 5 f. of Mesha's inscription, that until Omri took the country, it was not subject to Israelite rule. Moab may have taken the opportunity to grasp land north of the Arnon at Solomon's death, or when Israel, in Baasha's reign, was under pressure from Syria (1 Kings 15: 16 ff.), or even a little later under the leadership of Mesha's father himself.

The course of subsequent events, however, is exceptionally difficult to follow.[49] Mesha's father ruled Moab for thirty years (stele, line 2) and was succeeded by Mesha. Israel took the land of Medeba and held it for forty years, a period surprisingly equated with the reign of Omri (885–874 B.C.) and half that of Ahab (874–853 B.C.) (stele, lines 7 f.). 2 Kings 1: 1 and 3: 5 say that Mesha rebelled after the death of Ahab. Possibly Mesha rebelled *c.* 853 B.C., while Ahab and Israel were occupied with the coalition against the Assyrians. Jehoshaphat of Judah (870–848 B.C.) joined with the King of Edom and the King of Israel in an attack on Moab from the south or south-east (an attack followed, some think, by the campaign related in 2 Chr. 20).[50] But according to 1 Kings 22: 47 'there was no king in Edom', and it was not until Joram's reign that 'Edom revolted from under the hand of Judah, and made a king over themselves' (2 Kings 8: 20). One can suppose that 'the king of Edom' in 2 Kings 3 is in fact Jehoshaphat's 'deputy' (1 Kings 22: 47), or one can follow Lucian's revision of the LXX and read 'Ahaziah' for 'Jehoshaphat' in 2 Kings 3: 7, but neither proposal is very satisfying, and the problem is not easily answered. One further wonders whether Edom campaigned as Judah's vassal or as Israel's ally, for the war was primarily the war of Israel against Moab, and Edom and Israel were natural allies against Moab (or Judah); the common interests of Israel and Edom are clear on several occasions.[51] Thus when Jehoshaphat tried to revive Ezion-geber as a port, it is not surprising that Ahab's son Ahaziah should immediately ask for a share in the venture (1 Kings 22: 49). According to 2 Chronicles 20: 35 ff. the venture failed precisely because Jehoshaphat undertook it in co-operation with the King of Israel, who may indeed have had reason to be pleased with the result. According to 1 Kings 22: 48 it failed because the ships were broken at Ezion-geber, and it is tempting to ascribe this disaster not to the winds of the Gulf of Aqaba but to Edomite or even Israelite action. The fact that Edom threw off Judah's rule in Joram's reign (2 Kings 8: 20 ff.) may well owe something to Israelite support.[52]

This difficult period is also notable for the arrival of the Assyrians in the west. The battle of Karkar in 853 B.C. involved the Syrian states, Israel, and Ammon in alliance against Shalmaneser III (859–824 B.C.), who in a subsequent campaign finally gained tribute in 841 B.C. from Tyre, Sidon, and Israel.[53] We do not hear of any Assyrian contact with Edom or Moab until *c.* 800 B.C., when Adad-nirari III (810–782 B.C.) conquered 'the country of the Hittites, Amurru-country in its full extent, Tyre, Sidon, Israel, Edom, Palestine, as far as the shore of the Great Sea of the Setting Sun [i.e. Mediterranean Sea]' and 'made them submit all to my feet, imposing upon them tribute'.[54] Assyria's hold over Edom, however, was hardly strong; Amaziah of Judah (796–767 B.C.)

attacked Edom, defeated an army of 10,000 in the Valley of Salt, captured Sela, and renamed it Joktheel (2 Kings 14: 7).[55] 2 Chronicles 25: 6 ff. says that Amaziah originally enlisted Israelite mercenaries for the campaign, but later sent them home on the advice of a prophet. Perhaps the Israelite soldiers were regarded as unreliable allies in a campaign against Edom, and perhaps, too, the subsequent war of Amaziah with Jehoash of Israel (2 Kings 14: 8 ff.) is to be understood in the light of an Edomite–Israelite *entente*. It is hard to believe that Amaziah made any lasting conquest of Edom. We hear nothing further of Joktheel, even if its name did remain in use (cf. 2 Kings 14: 7), and the historian has already remarked (2 Kings 8: 22) that 'Edom revolted from under the hand of Judah, unto this day'. The fact that in Uzziah's reign (767–740 B.C.) Elath was built and restored to Judah (2 Kings 14: 22)[56] need not imply that Judah controlled Edom—Elath was not really in Edomite territory—but only that Judah controlled the Negeb and the roads south (cf. 2 Chr. 26: 1–15). Uzziah's reign marks the third great period of Tell el-Kheleifeh's activity and prosperity; from this period comes the signet ring inscribed 'belonging to Jotham', perhaps bearing a representation of a pair of bellows, indicating the continued importance of the copper industry.[57] But *c*. 735 B.C. this profitable outpost was lost to Judah; according to 2 Kings 16: 6 'Rezin king of Syria recovered Elath to Syria, and drave the Jews from Elath: and the Syrians came to Elath, and dwelt there, unto this day.' For 'Syrians' we should probably read 'Edomites', and possibly Rezin's name was added when an original 'Edom' in verse 6a became 'Aram' under the influence of verse 5.[58] We have no other evidence that Damascus ever claimed possession of Elath. It seems most likely that the Edomites took Elath as their contribution to Judah's difficulties at the time of the Syro-Ephraimite war; again one notices how Israel and Edom can act in concert against Judah. The Chronicler has no reference to the loss of Elath, but he says that 'again the Edomites had come and smitten Judah, and carried away captives. The Philistines also had invaded the cities of the lowland, and of the south of Judah . . .' (2 Chr. 28: 17 f). 'It now appears that Ahaz's appeal for help was against Edom and Philistia rather than against Aram and Israel . . . though the rebellions were put down, the states involved were not returned to Judah but organised into

Assyrian provinces.'[59] The fire which destroyed Period III of Tell el-Kheleifeh probably belongs to its capture by the Edomites, who now for the first time occupied the town as its masters, rebuilt it with a new type of brick, and used it as a trading centre until its destruction in the late sixth century B.C.[60]

In the century following Mesha's death (perhaps *c.* 840 B.C.) we hear very little of Moab. 2 Kings 10: 32 f. (cf. Amos 1: 3), which says that Hazael of Syria captured from Israel the Transjordan as far south as Aroer, perhaps suggests that Israel (under Jehu?) had previously recaptured the cities north of the Arnon from Moab; van Zyl thinks that this happened in a period of confusion after Mesha's death.[61] 2 Kings 13: 20 f., however, shows that in the reign of Joash of Israel (798–782 B.C.) the Moabites were able to raid the area where Elisha was buried (Gilead?). 2 Kings 13: 25 tells us that 'Jehoash the son of Jehoahaz took again out of the hand of Ben-hadad the son of Hazael the cities which he had taken out of the hand of Jehoahaz his father by war', which probably refers to Transjordanian cities among others (cf. 2 Kings 10: 32 f.). We may doubt that changing ownership of this region brought about much alteration in basic population, which probably remained much as Mesha left it. Adad-nirari III, who exacted tribute from Edom, is not known to have exacted tribute from Moab—perhaps Moab was weak and insignificant at the time.[62] Joash's son Jeroboam II (782–753 B.C.) 'restored the border of Israel from the entering in of Hamath unto the sea of Arabah' (2 Kings 14: 25), presumably enlarging on his father's work. Just how far south Israel's border in Transjordan lay as a result of Jeroboam's work is hard to say,[63] but however far south it was, we may not simply 'assume that at the least Moabites and Ammonites were ejected from Israelite territory and held severely in check'[64] without further evidence. Probably the kingdom of Moab south of the Arnon remained independent.

(iii) *Assyrian contacts*

Assyrian contact with Moab and Edom helps the historian considerably, because we have Assyrian as well as biblical records to inform us. Thus in 734 B.C. Tiglath-pileser III received the tribute of various kings, including 'Sanipu of Bit-Ammon, Salamanu of Moab, . . . Mitinti of Ashkelon, Jehoahaz (*Ia-ú-ḫa-zi*) of

Judah (*Ia-ú-da-a-a*), Kaushmalaku of Edom (*Ú-du-mu-a-a*), Muzr[i . . .], Hanno (*Ha-a-nu-ú-nu*) of Gaza'.[65] Edom was being punished for her attack on Judah, and Moab, just conceivably, chastised for the attack by Salamanu (= Shalman, Hos. 10: 14?) on Beth-arbel (= Irbid, in north Gilead?);[66] but Assyria hardly needed such pretexts. This period also saw the beginnings of pressure on Moab and Edom from the peoples of the North Arabian desert, and a letter found at Nimrud, datable to the period 740–705 B.C., refers to 'the people of the Moabite city, those whom the men of Gidir-land, when they crossed over to the land of Moab and went away, slaughtered'. The attackers have been connected with Kedar, Gederoth in southern Palestine (2 Chr. 28: 18), or with semi-nomads east of Moab, who used stone-walled enclosures for their animals, and the attack has been connected with the incident recorded in 2 Chronicles 28: 18 (*c.* 735 B.C.) or with that which lies behind the elegy on Moab in Isaiah 15, 16 (*c.* 715 B.C.).[67] The destruction of Edom, Moab, and Ammon at the hands of the people of the east is prophesied in Isaiah 11: 14 and Ezekiel 25: 8 ff.; one feels that the peoples east of Moab had more motive for such an attack than the men of an obscure city on the borders of Judah and Philistia. It is interesting, however, to see that Edom and Moab were drawn into the revolt of Ashdod in 713 B.C.; Sargon records that Ashdod appealed to 'the rulers of Palestine (*Pi-liš-te*), Judah (*Ia-ú-di*), [Ed]om, Moab', and others,[68] but these seem to have avoided Assyria's vengeance by paying their tribute. Perhaps Nimrud Letter XVI, which refers to the delivery of horses, presumably tribute, to Calah by officials from Egypt, Gaza, Judah, Moab, and Ammon, and mentions the Edomites with two other peoples, one of which could be the people of Ekron, throws light on this situation.[69] Similarly Hezekiah probably canvassed the support of Edom and Moab for his revolt—unsuccessfully, it seems, for Sennacherib tells us that 'Kammusunabdi from Moab [and] Ayarammu from Edom, they brought sumptuous gifts (*igisû*) and—fourfold—their heavy *tâmartu*-presents to me and kissed my feet.'[70] From some time in this period—from the reign of Sennacherib or his successor—we have an Assyrian receipt of tribute brought from Palestine, listing 'two minas of gold from the inhabitants of Bit-Ammon ($^{m\bar{a}t}$*Bît-Am-man-na-a-a*); one mina of gold from the inhabitants of Moab ($^{m\bar{a}t}$*Mu-'-ba-a-a*);

ten minas of silver from the inhabitants of Judah (^{māt}*Ia-ú-da-a-a*); [. . . mi]nas of silver from the inhabitants of [Edom] (^{māt}[*U-du-ma*]-*a-a*) . . .'. Unfortunately, the text is partly lost; the reading 'Edom' is likely, but uncertain. The amount of tribute she paid was probably less than Judah's.[71]

Sennacherib may have campaigned in Transjordan and Arabia *c.* 690 B.C.,[72] and possibly for a short time Moab (though not Edom) may have lost its vassal status and become an Assyrian province.[73] Esarhaddon (681–669 B.C.) employed Qausgabri, King of Edom, Musuri, King of Moab, Puduil, King of Beth-Ammon, and nineteen other kings of 'Hatti, the seashore, and the islands' on transporting 'under terrible difficulties, to Nineveh, the town (where I exercise) my rulership, as building material for my palace', various heavy materials from the Lebanon and elsewhere.[74] Labour, as well as tribute, was now demanded from Moab and Edom, and in Ashurbanipal's reign (669–627 B.C.) military service; Qausgabri of Edom, Musuri of Moab, Manasseh of Judah, and Amminabdi of Beth-Ammon are listed among twenty-two kings who helped Ashurbanipal in his wars against Egypt.[75] He also campaigned against the Arabian king Uate', and fighting took place in Edom and Moab; '[I] defeated him in bloody battles, inflicted countless routs upon him (to wit) in the *girû* of the towns of Azaril (and) Hirata(-)kasaia, in Edom, in the pass of Iabrudu, in Beth-Ammon, in the district of Haurina, in Moab, in Sa'arri. . . . Uate' had misgivings and he fled, alone, to the country Nabate.'[76] Ashurbanipal's wars against the Arabs were wide-ranging, and Edom and Moab were deeply involved, probably providing bases, supplies, and troops. King Kamashaltu of Moab was apparently primarily responsible for defeating and capturing Ammuladi, King of Kedar.[77] Moab and Edom, both vulnerable to attack from the east, had good reason to support Assyria in these wars. Moab appears to have been the richer, stronger nation, and, preoccupied with wars against the Arabs, probably did not get involved in affairs west of the Jordan for most of the seventh century B.C. (though see below, p. 242). Edom, however, with poorer land and perhaps under greater pressure from the Arabs, was already infiltrating and settling parts of the Negeb, a process whose beginnings may be discerned as early as *c.* 735 B.C. (cf. 2 Chr. 28: 17).[78] From that date Ezion-geber/Elath was apparently in Edomite hands, and a seal-impression has been found there with the reading 'belonging to Qaus-'anal, the servant of the king'.[79] The name is theophoric, Qaus being the Edomite deity (see below, pp. 245 f.); the king referred to could be Qausgabri. Glueck found evidence from this period of trade with southern Arabia,[80] and perhaps the profits of this trade helped subsidize the Assyrian campaigns. But Glueck also notes, on the evidence of surface pottery finds, that from the eighth century B.C. Edom entered a period of decline and disintegration.[81]

In the Assyrian period, then, from *c.* 733 B.C. to the end of the Assyrian empire, Edom under Qausmalaku, Ayarammu, and Qausgabri and Moab under Salamanu, Kammusunabdi, Musuri, and Kamashaltu (and perhaps in each case under other kings, of whom we hear nothing) were vassal kingdoms paying tribute. On the whole they seemed content to remain so, in the face of pressure from the east, and were not over-ready to share in revolts planned by Judah and Philistia in the west. Moab and Edom probably followed the same policy under the Babylonians. 2 Kings 24: 2 suggests that in 598 B.C. the Moabites, at least, were ready to be used as troops in Babylon's employ.[82] In 594 B.C. Moab, Edom, Ammon, Tyre, and Sidon are discussing rebellion (Jer. 27), but Ezekiel 21: 18 ff. and 26, where attacks by Nebuchadnezzar on Ammon and Tyre, but not on Edom and Moab, are contemplated, perhaps allow us to infer that Moab and Edom followed Jeremiah's advice and paid tribute. Such withdrawal of support would not have pleased Judah, and we must expect, for this and other reasons, to find some exaggeration in Judaean accounts of Edomite and Moabite action at this time. 1 Esdras 4: 45 says that the Edomites actually burned the Jerusalem temple; but this is not supported by the earlier witness of 2 Kings and Jeremiah, or even by 2 Chronicles, and Edom's behaviour from 594 to 587 B.C. suggests that her chief motive was not enmity with Judah but a desire for self-preservation. In 587 B.C. Edom probably remained officially neutral; according to Jeremiah 40: 11, Edom (with Moab and Ammon) offered a home to Jewish refugees. Obadiah castigates Edom not for assisting at the destruction of Jerusalem but for standing aloof (Obad. 11, R.V.marg.), rejoicing, speaking proudly, looking on, taking advantage of the calamity to raid Judah, and handing over captives to Babylon—some fugitives, it seems, were not as lucky as others. Ezekiel 35: 5, 15 makes similar complaints, and even Psalm 137 represents the Edomites as encouraging rather than actually assisting the Babylonians in the destruction of Jerusalem. In Lamentations 4: 21 f. Edom's iniquity is not specified. However, there was a long history of enmity between Judah and Edom, and Edomite encroachment on the Negeb from the eighth century onwards inevitably led to the sort of complaint made in Ezekiel 35: 10, 12, 36: 5. The picture of Edom as an enemy was given greater colour by the identification of Edom with the figure of Esau of Seir, the brother of Jacob, an identification we believe closely connected with the Edomite occupation, from the eighth century onwards, of the ancient land of Seir.[83] It is hardly surprising to find other prophetic complaints against Edom, often referring to events difficult to elucidate (cf. Amos 1: 11; Ezek. 25: 12 f.), and finally to see Edom destined for judgement in Israel's eschatological expectations (cf. Joel 3: 19; Isa. 11: 14, 34: 5 f., 63: 1 f.; Ezek. 32: 29; Dan. 11: 41). Amos 9: 11 f. sees Edom 'on that day' as part of the restored kingdom of David. Malachi 1: 4 speaks of the Lord's perpetual indignation against Edom.

Moab does not incur as much prophetic anger as Edom. Micah 6: 5 urges Israel to recall what Balak, King of Moab, consulted (R.S.V. 'devised'); Amos 2: 1 ff. threatens fire on Moab and its capital Kerioth 'because he burned the bones of the king of Edom into lime'.[84] Isaiah 15, 16 (apart from the prose ending, 16: 12 f.) actually laments a disaster that has overtaken Moab,[85] and the theme of Moab's military pride recurs several times (cf. Isa. 16: 6, 25: 11 f.; Jer. 48: 7, 14, 42; Zeph. 2: 8). Ezekiel 25: 8 ff. threatens that Moab will be given to the children of the east, because Moab said 'the house of Judah is like unto all the nations' —a taunting reference to Judah's humiliation by Assyria or Babylon? Further threats to Moab appear in Jeremiah 9: 25 f., 25: 21, and Daniel 11: 41. Thus the major complaints against Moab are Judaean, and stem from the end of the seventh century B.C. or the beginning of the sixth, when Moab appears to have taunted Judah and even attacked her (cf. Jer. 48: 27; 2 Kings 24: 2).[86] Jeremiah 48 is an interesting chapter, using earlier poetic material (cf. Num. 21: 27 ff.; Isa. 15, 16) to describe something about to happen. It is possible that Nebuchadnezzar invaded Moab in 582 B.C. on his way to Egypt (in which case he perhaps visited Edom as well), and van Zyl takes this as the beginning of the end of the state of Moab, some Moabites being taken into exile (cf. Jer. 48: 7), some escaping to Egypt, and some finding homes in Judah, leaving the land open to new arrivals from the desert to the east.[87]

The sixth century was for Edom also a period of decline. We have no certain Babylonian references to the country, though probably Nabonidus' stay at Taima affected Edom.[88] Tell el-Kheleifeh appears to have flourished again; the second phase of town IV would then presumably represent the last Edomite occupation of the site, perhaps in the time of Nabonidus' mercantile activity in N. W. Arabia *c.* 552–545.[89] But Glueck remarks (see above, p. 241) on the decline of Edomite pottery in the second half of Iron Age II, and Albright notes that 'Glueck's explorations do not suggest that the Edomites became semi-nomadic again after the eighth century B.C., but simply that they became weaker, and were forced to abandon many of their towns (which we know from the inscription of Ashurbanipal to have been a fact).'[90] The Edomite settlement in southern Judah is confirmed by later Jewish literature. Thus 1 Maccabees 5: 65 finds children of Esau in the Hebron district (cf. Jub. 38: 8 f.). Josephus (*Ant.* xiii. 9. 1, 15. 4; *Bell. Iud.* i. 2. 6) mentions Adorea and Marisa west of Hebron as Edomite towns, and the Zenon papyri[91] mention the same towns as towns of Idumaea, the Hellenistic name for Edom and southern Judaea, whose use can be traced back to the end of the fourth century B.C.[92] Albright believes that the Edomite 'occupation of the southern hill country of Judah centring round Hebron, Adoraim and Marisa . . . must have been substantially completed by the end of the sixth century, since the Jewish province of the fifth century extended south only as far as Beth-zur, north of Hebron.'[93] Passages such as Obadiah 1–9; Malachi 1: 2 ff.; Ezekiel 25: 12 ff., 35: 1 ff.; Jeremiah 49: 7 ff. perhaps also witness to the decline of Edom east of the Wādi 'Arabah. Obadiah 9 suggests that Edom owed her downfall to neighbours and allies—possibly her trading partners from Arabia and the south, such as Teima and Dedan. In Ezekiel 25: 12 ff. the destruction of Edom (as of Moab, Ezek. 25: 8 ff.) from Teman to Dedan suggests a similar cause, though an appendix to the original oracle threatens 'vengeance upon Edom by the hand of my people Israel' (v. 14).

The fifth period of Tell el-Kheleifeh's occupation 'undoubtedly covered much of the Persian period, between the later sixth and fourth centuries. . . . The population of Ezion-geber was now predominantly Arab; in the fifth century the town was probably controlled by Geshem the Arabian, one of Nehemiah's enemies.'[94] Nehemiah does not mention the Edomites (though there is reference to Moabites probably resident in Judah intermarrying with Israelites, Ezra 9: 1 ff.; Neh. 13: 1 ff.), and his memoirs suggest that the Arabians, not the Edomites, are the foes of Judah in the south. So too Herodotus in the mid fifth century B.C. refers to those Arabs who lived between Syria and Egypt south of Gaza.[95] Diodorus refers to a late-fourth-century B.C. attack on Arab-held Petra from the eparchy of Idumaea.[96] The eparchy of Idumaea seems to be the descendant of the Persian province of Edom, with an administrative centre at Lachish.[97] The Edomites, by settlement in this area, have gained an interest in the preservation of the land from incoming Arabs, and thus are not to be included among Nehemiah's Arabians; they are now under the control of Nehemiah's colleague, the Governor of Lachish. The Edomite occupation of the Negeb and the Arab occupation of land bordering on the Negeb are related but distinct movements. By settlement in southern Judah the Edomites survived as a distinct group, while the Moabites were absorbed into other elements. The Idumaeans of the south were always suspect—witness the Herodian family—in the eyes of the Jews.

(iv) *Religion and Culture*

About the religious and cultural life of Edom and Moab there is little certain knowledge and much speculation. In the case of Moab, for example, the Balu'ah stele may portray a god and a goddess with a human being in an attitude of worship, but we do not know how to interpret these figures.[98] Various Iron Age figurines of men on horseback and of a mother-goddess,[99] and place-names such as Bamoth-ba'al, Beth-ba'al-peor, Beth-ba'al-meon, all indicate that the religious cult of Moab had its similarities with the cult of Canaan.[100] Excavation at Dibon in 1955 is said to have revealed the foundations of a possible sanctuary with an incense stand,[101] and the inscription of Mesha (line 3) tells of the building of a high place for Chemosh in *qrḥh*, but where this place was is still debated;[102] Solomon also made a high place for Chemosh outside Jerusalem (1 Kings 11: 7, 33; cf. 2 Kings 23: 13). Booty and prisoners could be devoted to Chemosh (Mesha's inscription, lines 12 f., 17 f.), and to Chemosh also, perhaps, the King's son was sacrificed (2 Kings 3: 27). Jeremiah 48: 7 refers to Chemosh's priests and princes, and Numbers 21: 29, Jeremiah 48: 46 to the Moabites as sons and daughters of Chemosh. Chemosh appears as an element in Moabite personal names.[103] Seers such as Balaam were known and used (cf. Jer. 27: 9, which mentions the prophets, diviners, dreams, soothsayers, and sorcerers of the nations conspiring against Nebuchadnezzar). In all this there are obvious similarities to Israel's religious practices and beliefs.

The Edomite religion is barely mentioned in the O.T. 2 Chronicles 25: 14 f. says that Amaziah worshipped the gods of the children of Seir, i.e., Edomite gods, and 1 Samuel 21: 7 that Doeg the Edomite was 'detained before the Lord' at Nob. It is unlikely that the Edomites were any more irreligious or primitive than the Moabites. Glueck notes various female figurines and an animal figurine from Edom,[104] while from Tell el-Kheleifeh come a crude pottery plaque representing the pregnant mother-goddess, a figurine of the same type of fertility goddess with what may be an incense cup, and evidence of foundation offerings.[105] Possibly the deities *šlm* and *'ēl* are known at Elath in the fifth century B.C.[106] But the deity peculiar to Edom was Qaus.[107] Twelve seventh-century B.C. stamped jar handles found at Tell el-Kheleifeh bear an inscription which has been read as *lqwsʿnl* (or *ʿml*) *ʿbd hmlk*,[108] and on Ostracon 6043, probably a list of names, from the same place, Albright finds the names *Qwsb[nh]*, *Pgʿqws* (twice), and *Qwsny*.[109] These names appear to come from the period of Edomite occupation of the site. A seal recently found on Umm el-Biyāra reads *lqws g** mlk '***, probably to be restored as *lqws gbr mlk 'dm*;[110] Qausgabri is known to us from the records of Esarhaddon and Ashurbanipal in the seventh century B.C., and from the records of Tiglath-pileser III we know of Qausmalaku. Qaus is found in personal names from the reigns of Darius and Artaxerxes I; one Galti-qôs was Governor of el-ʿUlā in the early third century B.C. The name perhaps also appears in Barkos (Ezra 2: 53; Neh. 7: 55), Kushaiah (1 Chr. 15: 17), and in

Proverbs 30: 31 (emended). Qosnatan, Qosallah, and Qosmelek are found as Nabataean names, and Josephus refers to Herod's sister Salome's husband Kostabaros as 'an Idumaean by birth, . . . one of whose ancestors had been priest to Koze, whom the Nabataeans had formerly worshipped as a god'.[111] The god's name continued to appear in the pre-Islamic Arabian world, though Vriezen notes that apparently it has not been found in the northern Semitic world.[112]

The origin of Qaus, as of the Edomites themselves, may lie in Arabia. Albright, commenting on the phrase *qaus Quzah*, 'bow of (the North Arabian storm-god) Quzah', thinks that Josephus confused the Edomite Qaus with the similar Arabian god Quzah, and sees no reason 'not to identify the Edomite name of the storm god with the Arabic *qaus*, "bow"'.[113] Vriezen argues that Qaus, as the god of the bow, must primarily have been a god of hunting and war, and that he only secondarily became a storm-god.[114]

Another divine name perhaps known in Edom was Eloah, used in the book of Job, and in the words of Agur the son of Jakeh, of Massa (Prov. 30: 1, R.V.marg.), and spoken of by Habakkuk as coming from Teman (Hab. 3: 3). Eloah is identified in the Hebrew tradition with Yahweh, who was said to have marched from Edom, among other places in the south (Jud. 5: 4; cf. Isa. 63: 1). The characteristics of Yahweh and Qaus are similar, and it is not impossible that the Edomites and the Israelites were aware of the similarities. If so, we can understand the almost complete absence of O.T. reference to the god of the Edomites, the case of Doeg, detained before the Lord at Nob, and the provision of Deuteronomy 23: 8 allowing Edomites (though not Moabites or Ammonites) to worship (after a few generations of integration) in the assembly of the Lord.

Edom was known for her 'wisdom' (cf. Jer. 49: 7; Obad. 8; Baruch 3: 22), presumably the same kind as that known elsewhere in the O.T. world. R. H. Pfeiffer attempted to show that the book of Job, Proverbs 30–31: 9, Psalms 88, 89, and his 'S' document in Genesis are of Edomite origin, and reflect the outlook of Edomite wisdom, which he takes to be agnostic and pessimistic in character.[115] The book of Job and the words of Agur and Lemuel may well have a North Arabian origin, and perhaps a common outlook (though we may note Pedersen's opinion that 'the psychology of the Book of Job is from first to last typically Israelitic. The Arabians would not be able to produce a writing of this kind, because a fate like that of Job would offer no problems to them').[116] Psalms 88 and 89, however, show more in common with Ugaritic literature than with anything recognizably Edomite, and their theology is not as close to that of the book of Job as Pfeiffer maintains. Pfeiffer's case for an Edomite 'S' source is unconvincing; even if we can agree to find a unifying philosophic viewpoint in the material Pfeiffer ascribes to 'S' in Genesis 1–12, there is no indication that Edom was interested in this kind of legend and mythology and Israel less so, apart from a presupposition based on Pfeiffer's conclusions about the book of Job and the words of Agur and Lemuel; and in the case of material ascribed to 'S' from Genesis 14, 19, 34, 35, 36, 38, one must object that Edom's alleged geographic centrality is questionable, and stories told to the discredit of Ammon and Moab, and various Israelite tribes of the south, do not necessarily suggest that the people most interested in repeating them were the Edomites. Genesis 36 is neither hostile nor friendly to Edom, and is probably not an Edomite work. In short, a pessimistic wisdom school in Edom is not proven, and we need some undoubted Edomite evidence before further judgement can be passed.

Written material from Edom and Moab is indeed scant. From Moab we have the Baluʿah stele (undeciphered), Mesha's stele, a fragment of an inscription from Kerak,[117] and another inscription fragment from Dibon,[118] and perhaps some seals.[119] From Edom we have a mid-seventh-century ostracon from Umm el-Biyāra, referring, perhaps, to a delivery of oil; a seal from the same place bearing the name of Qausgabri;[120] an eighth- or seventh-century seal from Tawilân, showing Assyrian features;[121] a seal from Petra datable only to the ninth–sixth centuries B.C., with the legend 'belonging to bᵉ-ʿēzer-'ēl son of ʿaḇdi-baʿal';[122] and another seal, acquired in Tafīleh but of uncertain origin, reading *šmʿʾl*, perhaps from the ninth century B.C.[123] Tell el-Kheleifeh has yielded the famous 'Jotham' signet ring,[124] twelve seventh- or sixth-century stamped jar-handles reading 'belonging to Qausʿanal, servant of the king',[125] and a seventh- or sixth-century B.C. juglet, incised 'belonging to ʿAmīrû' or (ʿAmīrân".[126] From the same site also come several ostraca bearing personal names,[127] a fifth- or fourth-century ostracon referring to some wine transaction,[128] and two jar fragments from the eighth century B.C., with inscriptions in what is perhaps a South Arabic script.[129] All this is little enough, and relates for the most part (in Edom's case) to a cosmopolitan trading centre unrepresentative of life in Edom, and to 'a domesticated settlement with a busy weaving industry',[130] surprisingly situated on top of a huge natural fortress. For the Edomite language we have hardly enough to go on, though perhaps we may assume that it was not very different from the Moabite.[131]

Study of the scripts suggests that earlier Moabite and Edomite script 'did not differ from that of the Hebrews', but that 'in the seventh to sixth centuries we already find clear signs of the intrusion of Aramaic elements into these two scripts'—an intrusion possibly connected with the influence of Damascus in the ninth century, or with Assyria's use of Aramaic for diplomatic purposes in the eighth and seventh centuries.[132] Glueck remarks that 'the orientation of Edom, Moab, Ammon and Gilead, because of cultural, topographical and geographical reasons, may be said to be directed more from north to south than from east to west, that is, mainly from Syria to Arabia rather than from the Mediterranean to the eastern desert.'[133] The evidence of the epigraphic material bears this out, and Glueck thinks that Moabite and Edomite pottery has also been influenced by this factor.[134] However, the references of Amos 1: 6, 9 to slave-trading between Edom and Gaza and Tyre, the finding of black-glazed Greek pottery at Tell el-Kheleifeh,[135] and Judaean weights at Umm el-Biyāra,[136] remind us that there was influence from the west as well as from the north and the south. From Egypt and Sinai came to Tell el-Kheleifeh 'such varied objects as carnelian, agate, amethyst and crystal beads, cartouche-like seal impressions, a tiny faience amulet head of the god Bes, a small Egyptian amulet of a cat, fragments of alabaster cups and plates and buttons, and part of a scaraboid bead . . .'.[137] We perhaps have a reference to Edom's trade in Ezekiel 27: 16, where either Syria or Edom—the reading is unsure—'was thy trafficker by reason of the multitude of thy handyworks; they traded for thy wares with emeralds, purple and broidered work, and fine linen, and coral, and rubies.'

However, as we can perhaps see from the tribute list mentioned above (p. 239), Edom, in spite of the trade attracted through Tell el-Kheleifeh and the King's Highway, was probably a poorer country than Moab; and Moab, in spite of her wealth from her sheep-rearing, and sometimes from the rich agricultural land north of the Arnon, was poorer than Judah and Israel. Whether this comparative material poverty had any effect on the spiritual heights attained by Moab and Edom is hard to say. Edom was known for her wisdom; but any religious insights peculiar to Edom and Moab have survived, if at all, only through the medium of the Hebrew tradition, and are no longer discernible.

NOTES

1. 2 Kings 3: 25; Isa. 15: 1, 16: 7, 11; Jer. 48: 31 ff. J. Simons, *The Geographical and Topographical Texts of the Old Testament* (1959), section 447 f., suggests that in Num. 22: 39 Kiriath-huzoth is an error for an original Kir-hareseth.

2. 1 Kings 9: 26, 22: 48; Deut. 2: 8. For this site and its relationship with Eloth/Elath see the articles by N. Glueck in *B.A.S.O.R.* lxxi (1938), 3 ff.; lxxii (1938), 2 ff.; lxxv (1939), 8 ff.; lxxix (1940), 2 ff.; and more recently his 'Ezion-geber', *B.A.* xxviii (1965), 70 ff., and chapter 'Transjordan' in *A.O.T.S.*, 428 ff. See also note 56 below.

3. Num. 33: 42 f.; cf. Gen. 36: 41, 'duke Pinon'; identified with modern Feinan (cf. Y. Aharoni, *The Land of the Bible* (1966), p. 382; N. Glueck, *The Other Side of the Jordan* (1940), pp. 27, 66 ff.).

4. Gen. 36: 33; Isa. 34: 6, 63: 1; Jer. 49: 13, 22; Amos 1: 12 (cf. Pss. 60: 9, 108: 10).

5. Gen. 36: 34; Jer. 49: 7, 20; Ezek. 25: 12 f.; Amos 1: 12; Obad. 9; Hab. 3: 3; Baruch 3: 22 f. Possibly Rishathaim (Jud. 3: 10) is a corruption of an original *rôʾš hatêmānî* (cf. J. Gray, *Joshua, Judges and Ruth* (1967), pp. 260 f. and pp. 214 f.). Compare also Eliphaz the Temanite, Job 2: 11 etc., and Gen. 36: 11, 15, 42. See R. de Vaux, 'Téman, ville ou région d'Édom?', *R.B.* lxxvi (1969), 379 ff.

6. See J. R. Bartlett, 'The Edomite King-List of Gen. xxxvi. 31–39 and I Chron. i. 43–50', *J.T.S.* N.S. xvi (1965), 301 ff.

7. See N. Glueck, *H.U.C.A.* xi (1938), 141 ff., 'The Boundaries of Edom'; id., *A.O.T.S.*, p. 436. Glueck quotes Deut. 1: 2, 44, 33: 2; Josh. 11: 17, 12: 7; Jud. 5: 4 f.; 1 Chr. 4: 42 f.; Hab. 3: 3, dating them in their present form to the Exilic age or later. The question is complicated, however, by the relationship of 'Edom' and 'Seir'; see J. R. Bartlett, 'The Land of Seir and the Brotherhood of Edom', *J.T.S.* N.S. xx (1969), 1 ff.

8. Cf. Aharoni, op. cit. 36.

9. Cf. M. Noth, *The History of Israel*, 2nd English edn. (1960), p. 83.

10. See J. R. Bartlett, *J.T.S.* N.S. xx (1969), 1 ff. and M. Fishbane, *J.B.L.* lxxxix (1970), 313 ff.

11. *Arabia and the Bible* (1934), p. 175. Connection between Edomite and early Arabic names is shown by B. Moritz, 'Edomitische Genealogien', *Z.A.W.* xliv (1926), 81 ff.; 'Die Könige von Edom', *Muséon* l (1937), 101 ff.; 'Ergänzungen zu meinem Aufsatz, "Die Könige von Edom"', *Z.A.W.* lvii (1939–40), 148 ff.

12. For the use of 'Rephaim' to describe early Transjordanian peoples see J. R. Bartlett, 'Sihon and Og, Kings of the Amorites', *V.T.* xxi (1971), 1 ff., especially 12 ff.

13. A. Alt, 'Emiter und Moabiter', *P.J.B.* xxxv (1940), 29 ff. The use of Mycenaean ware at the Late Bronze Age shrine outside 'Ammān (see J. B. Hennessy, 'Excavation of a Late Bronze Age Temple at Amman', *P.E.Q.* xcviii (1966), 155 ff.), and the finding of Mycenaean imports at Medeba in a tomb datable to *c.* 1250–1150 B.C. (cf. G. L. Harding & B. S. J. Isserlin, 'Four Tomb Groups from Jordan', *A.P.E.F.* vi (1953), 27 ff.), show contact between the Transjordan and the Mediterranean world. But more evidence is needed before we can posit any settlement of Mediterranean immigrants.

14. R. de Vaux, 'Les Hurrites de l'histoire et les Horites de la Bible', *R.B.* lxxiv (1967), 481 ff.; see 501 f.

15. See E. Meyer, *Die Israeliten und ihre Nachbarstämme* (1906), pp. 328–54.

16. E. A. Speiser, *Genesis* (1964), p. 283, while agreeing that the Horites of Seir–Edom can no longer be equated with the Hurrians, thinks that 'the Hebrew *Ḥōrī* . . . designated two unrelated groups: the non-Semitic Hurrians, who had spread to Syria and North-Central Palestine; and the Semitic group that bore by coincidence the same name and was centered in Seir.' This name *Ḥōrī* 'was apparently of Semitic origin, perhaps even "cave dweller" as tradition has suspected all along'.

17. C. M. Bennett, 'Ṭawilan, Jordanie', *R.B.* lxxvi (1969), 386 ff.

18. E. Olavarri, 'Sondages à *ʿarôʿer* sur l'Arnon', *R.B.* lxxii (1965), 77–94. Olavarri describes two, or perhaps three, sherds as Late Bronze, but in a private communication Mr. P. Parr cites parallels for all of them in post-1200 B.C. contexts in Palestine, e.g., at Beth-Shan Level VI and in the Medeba tomb.

19. 'The Excavations at Dibon (Dhiban) in Moab', I: 'The First Campaign, 1950–1951', by F. V. Winnett; II: 'The Second Campaign, 1952', by W. L. Reed (*A.A.S.O.R.* xxxvi–xxxvii (1964)). W. H. Morton (*B.A.S.O.R.* cxl (1955), 6) notes that 'An MB–LB occupational gap on the site now seems definitely established.'

20. See G. L. Harding & B. S. J. Isserlin, *A.P.E.F.* vi (1953), 27 ff.

21. *A.S.O.R. Newsletter* (Oct. 1968), kindly communicated to me by Professor S. H. Horn; see id., 'The 1968 Heshbon Expedition', *B.A.* xxxii (1969), 26 ff.

22. Cf. J. B. Hennessy, *P.E.Q.* xcviii (1966), 155 ff.

23. See Glueck, *Explorations in Eastern Palestine, I, II, III* (*A.A.S.O.R.* xiv (1933–4), xv (1934–5), xviii–xix (1937–9)).

24. Cf. E. Drioton, 'A propos de la Stèle du Balou'a', *R.B.* xlii (1933), 353 ff. See also M. G. Horsfield & R. L. Vincent, 'Une Stèle égypto-moabite au Balou'a', *R.B.* xli (1932), 417 ff.; A. Alt, 'Emiter und Moabiter', *P.J.B.* xxxv (1940), 29 ff.

25. 'The Oracles of Balaam', *J.B.L.* lxiii (1944), 207 ff.; see 227.

26. K. A. Kitchen, 'Some New Light on the Asiatic Wars of Ramesses II', *J.E.A.* l (1964), 47 ff., especially 63 ff.

27. Compare the possible mention of Moab on a list of Ramesses II at Luxor, in J. Simons, *Handbook for the Study of Egyptian Topographical Lists Relating to Western Asia* (1937), pp. 155 f., List XXII, d, 10, and p. 205. But see also *A.N.E.T.*, p. 242.

28. See *A.N.E.T.*, p. 488.

29. Albright, *J.B.L.* lxiii (1944), 207 ff.; see 228 ff.

30. *A.N.E.T.*, p. 259; R. A. Caminos, *Late-Egyptian Miscellanies* (1954), p. 293.

31. *A.N.E.T.*, p. 262.

32. See Glueck, op. cit., *A.A.S.O.R.* xiv (1933–4), xv (1934–5), xviii–xix (1939); for a farm centre see *A.A.S.O.R.* xv, 67.

33. 'Ceci nous oblige à reconsidérer l'interprétation historique admise qui voyait dans les industries du cuivre de la 'Arabah "les Mines du Roi Salomon" et à regarder les Édomites, peut-être conjointement avec les Kénites–Madianites, comme les anciens mineurs et fondeurs de cuivre de la 'Arabah' (B. Rothenberg, *R.B.* lxxiv (1967), 80–5). See, however, Glueck, 'Some Edomite Pottery from Tell el-Kheleifeh', *B.A.S.O.R.* clxxxviii (1967), 8 ff., p. 18 n. 40; G. E. Wright, 'More on King Solomon's Mines', *B.A.* xxiv (1961), 59 ff.; and Glueck, 'Ezion-geber', *B.A.* xxviii (1965), 70 ff. See further 'Notes and News', *P.E.Q.* ci (1969), 57 ff.

34. Cf. E. A. Speiser, *Genesis* (1964), p. 282.

35. See M. D. Johnson, *The Purpose of the Biblical Genealogies* (1969), p. 24 nn. 3 and 4.

36. See R. de Vaux, 'Téman, ville ou région d'Édom?', *R.B.* lxxvi (1969), 379 ff.

37. See J. R. Bartlett, *J.T.S.* N.S. xvi (1965), 301 ff.

38. See O. Eissfeldt, 'Protektorat der Midianiter über ihre Nachbarn im letzten Viertel des 2 Jahrtausends v. Chr.', *J.B.L.* lxxvii (1968), 383 ff.

39. e.g., possibly by Othniel of Debir, Jud. 3: 8 ff.; see J. Gray, *Joshua, Judges and Ruth* (1967), 213 ff.

40. See Noth, 'Israelitische Stämme zwischen Ammon und Moab', *Z.A.W.* lx (1944), 11 ff.

41. For discussion of some of the possibilities see J. R. Bartlett, 'The Historical Reference of Numbers xxi. 27–30', *P.E.Q.* ci (1969), 94 ff.

42. Noth, *Numbers* (1968), p. 172.

43. See J. R. Bartlett, *J.T.S.* N.S. xvi (1965), 301 ff.

44. See Glueck, *B.A.* xxviii (1965), 70 ff. For a location at Jazirat Fara'un *c.* 10 m. S. of Ezion-Geber see B. Rothenberg, *P.E.Q.*, cii (1970), 4 ff.

45. See J. Gray, *I and II Kings*, 2nd edn. (1970), p. 283.

46. Glueck, *B.A.* xxviii (1965), 82. For Sheshonk's interest in the Negeb see Noth, 'Die Schoschenkliste', *Z.D.P.V.* lxi (1938), 277 ff.; Albright, *A.f.O.* xii (1939), 385 f. (review of J. Simons, *Handbook for the Study of Egyptian Topographical Lists Relating to Western Asia*); B. Maisler, 'The Campaign of Pharaoh Shishak to Palestine', *V.T.* Supplement iv (1956), 57 ff.; Y. Aharoni, op. cit. 283 ff.

47. Mahanaim appears in Gen. 32: 2; Josh. 13: 26, 30, 21: 38; 2 Sam. 2: 8, 12, 29, 17: 24, 19: 32; 1 Kings 2: 8, 4: 14; 1 Chr. 6: 80. Simons, *The Geographical and Topographical Texts of the Old Testament* (1959), section 848, finds it in 1 Chr. 11: 46 by a textual change. J. Gray, *I and II Kings* (1964), p. 134, identifies Mahanaim with *khirbet maḥneh* well north of the river Jabbok; Aharoni, op. cit. 381, identifies it with *tell eḏ-ḏahab el-gharbi* on the north bank of the Jabbok. Simons, op. cit., sections 415, 848, 1006, following de Vaux, 'Notes d'histoire et de topographie transjordaniennes', *Vivre et penser* i (1941), 16 ff., 31, prefers *tell ḥajjāj* south of *tulul eḏ-ḏahab* in the Jabbok valley. J. Gray, *Joshua, Judges and Ruth* (1967), p. 134, follows this identification, as in his *I and II Kings*, 2nd edn. (1970), p. 139.

48. For this name, see W. L. Reed & F. V. Winnett, 'A Fragment of an Early Moabite Inscription from Kerak', *B.A.S.O.R.* clxxii (1963), 1 ff., and I. Schiffmann, 'Eine neue moabitische Inschrift aus Karcha', *Z.A.W.* lxxvii (1965), 324 f.

49. See J. Liver, 'The Wars of Mesha, King of Moab', *P.E.Q.* xcix (1967), 14 ff.; J. Gray, *I and II Kings*, 2nd edn. (1970), pp. 66 f.; J. D. Shenkel, *Chronology and Recensional Development in the Greek Text of Kings* (1968), pp. 93–108; and J. R. Bartlett, 'The Rise and Fall of the Kingdom of Edom', *P.E.Q.* civ (1972), 26 ff. for recent discussion of this problem.

50. On this chapter, however, see M. Noth, 'Eine palästinische Lokalüberlieferung in 2 Chr. 20', *Z.D.P.V.* lxvii (1945), 45 ff.

51. See J. R. Bartlett, *J.T.S.* N.S. xx (1969), 1 ff., 12 ff.

52. For the text of this passage see B. Stade, 'König Joram und der Text von 2 Kön. 8. 21–24', *Z.A.W.* xxi (1901), 337 ff.

53. *A.N.E.T.*, pp. 280 f. H. N. Wiener, 'The Historical Background of Psalm 83', *J.P.O.S.* ix (1929), 180 ff., suggested that the situation of these years is reflected in Psalm 83, where we find Edom, the Ishmaelites, Moab, the Hagarenes, Gebal, Ammon, Amalek, Philistia, and Tyre allied against Israel, supported by Assyria.

54. *A.N.E.T.*, p. 281.

55. The Valley of Salt is usually taken to be the plain just south of the Dead Sea; Simons, *Geographical and Topographical Texts*, section 221, identifies it with the *wādi el-milḥ* near Beersheba, while Noth, *The History of Israel*, 2nd English edn. (1960), p. 196 n. 4, thinks it was 'probably east of the *wādi el-ʿaraba*'. For Sela compare Num. 24: 21; Jud. 1: 36; 2 Chr. 25: 12; Isa. 16: 1, 42: 11; Obad. 3, though it is not always clear that 'the rock' in these verses is a proper name, or if it is, that it is the place referred to in 2 Kings 14: 7. Glueck observes that 'there must have existed during the Early Iron Age in Eastern Palestine

numerous sites built on more or less isolated prominences and known by the name "Sela'" (*A.A.S.O.R.* xviii–xix (1937–9), 26; see also G. F. Buhl, *Geschichte der Edomiter* (1893), pp. 34 f.). Thus for Sela, of 2 Kings 14: 7, Khirbet Ṣilʻ, a few kms. north-west of Buseirah, with the remains of a small Iron Age fort, has been suggested (cf. Glueck, ibid.). Recently Mrs. Crystal M. Bennett has shown by her excavations on Umm el-Biyāra at Petra that there is no positive evidence for the commonly accepted equation of the site with the biblical Sela (cf. 'Fouilles d'Umm el-biyara: rapport préliminaire', *R.B.* lxxiii (1966), 372 ff.; 'A Cosmetic Palette from Umm el-Biyara', *Antiquity* xli (1967), 197 ff.; 'Exploring Umm el Biyara, the Edomite Fortress Rock which Dominates Petra', *I.L.N.* 30 Apr. 1966).

56. Why Ezion-geber became Elath is not clear. Glueck ('The Topography and History of Ezion-geber and Elath', *B.A.S.O.R.* lxxii (1938), 2 ff.; cf. 'Ezion-geber', *B.A.* xxviii (1965), 70 ff.) argues that Ezion-geber was built in Solomon's time west of the original Eloth (1 Kings ix. 26), and that both cities stood side by side until the destruction of Ezion-geber in Jehoram's reign, leaving Elath alone at the head of the gulf. When Uzziah 'restored Elath', he rebuilt the ruins of Ezion-geber, which had meantime acquired the name 'Elath' from the near-by town now fallen into decay. Until archaeological traces of a second IA town in the area are discovered, it seems simpler to suppose that the two names referred to the one place, 'Eloth' or 'Elath' perhaps being its native name, and 'Ezion-geber' the name given by Solomon. The Edomites would use 'Elath' or 'Eloth', and after the town's destruction in Jehoram's reign the Solomonic name passed out of use. The Deuteronomist knew both names, and made the natural error of thinking two towns were meant (cf. Deut. 2: 8; 1 Kings 9: 26).

57. See N. Avigad, 'The Jotham Seal from Elath', *B.A.S.O.R.* clxiii (1961), 18 ff.

58. Cf. J. Gray, *I and II Kings*, 2nd edn. (1970), p. 632.

59. J. L. Myers, *II Chronicles* (1965), p. 163; see also J. Gray, 'The Period and Office of the Prophet Isaiah in the Light of a New Assyrian Tablet', *E.T.* (1952), 263 ff.

60. See Glueck, 'Ezion-geber', *B.A.* xxviii (1963), 70 ff., 86 f.

61. A. van Zyl, *The Moabites* (1960), p. 145.

62. Cf. *A.N.E.T.*, p. 281; van Zyl, op. cit. 146 f.

63. If the reference of Amos 6: 14 to 'the brook of the Arabah' and of Isa. 15: 7 to 'the brook of the willows' (*naḥal haʻarāḇîm*) have the same boundary in mind, then possibly Jeroboam's conquest reached southern Moab. G. B. Gray, *A Critical and Exegetical Commentary on the Book of Isaiah, i–xxvii* (1929), p. 284, thinks the watercourse of Isa. 15: 7 may reasonably be identified with the Wādi el-Ḥeṣā; Aharoni (op. cit. 313), however, thinks tentatively of the Wādi ʻArabah, while van Zyl, op. cit. 147 f., thinks that 'the brook of the Arabah' of Amos 6: 14 'must be located in the vicinity of the northern end of the Dead Sea, and not at the southern end of it', and he suggests identifying it with the Wādi el-Kefrein. See also E. Power, 'The Prophecy of Esaias against Moab', *Biblica* xiii (1932), 435 ff., and especially 445 f.

64. J. Bright, *A History of Israel* (1960), p. 239.

65. *A.N.E.T.*, p. 282.

66. For these identifications see van Zyl, op. cit. 23 f., 149; Aharoni, op. cit. 373.

67. See H. W. F. Saggs, 'The Nimrud Letters, 1952—Part II', *Iraq* xvii (1955), 126 ff., especially 132 f., 151 f.; H. Donner, 'Neue Quellen zur Geschichte des Staates Moab in der zweiten Hälfte des 8. Jahrh. v. Chr.', *M.I.O.* v (1957), 155 ff.; and van Zyl, op. cit. 36 ff., 150.

68. *A.N.E.T.*, p. 287.

69. H. W. F. Saggs, loc. cit. 152 f.; H. Donner, loc. cit. 178 ff.

70. *A.N.E.T.*, p. 287.

71. *A.N.E.T.*, p. 301; cf. R. H. Pfeiffer, 'Judah's Tribute to Assyria', *J.B.L.* xlvii (1928), 185 f.

72. Cf. W. F. Albright, 'New Light from Egypt on the Chronology and History of Israel and Judah', *B.A.S.O.R.* cxxx (1953), 4 ff.

73. E. Forrer, *Die Provinzeinteilung des Assyrischen Reiches* (1921), pp. 64, 70.

74. *A.N.E.T.*, 291.

75. Ibid. 294.

76. Ibid. 297 f.

77. Ibid. 298.

78. See J. R. Bartlett, *J.T.S.* N.S. xx (1969), 1 ff., especially 15 ff.

79. See N. Glueck, 'The First Campaign at Tell el-Kheleifeh', *B.A.S.O.R.* lxxi (1938), 3 ff., 17, and 'The Topography and History of Ezion-geber and Elath', *B.A.S.O.R.* lxxii (1938), 2 ff., 12 f.

80. Glueck, *B.A.S.O.R.* lxxi (1938), 16 f.; cf. Glueck, *The Other Side of the Jordan* (1940), pp. 105 ff.

81. 'Explorations in Eastern Palestine, II', *A.A.S.O.R.* xv (1934–5), 137 ff.

82. Possibly 'Edomites' should be read in this verse for 'Aramaeans', but cf. Jer. 35: 11, and J. Gray, *I and II Kings* (1964), p. 689. 2 Kings 24: 2 may be illuminated by an ostracon found at Arad, referring to an expected Edomite attack; see Y. Aharoni, 'Three Hebrew Ostraca from Arad'. *B.A.S.O.R.* cxcvii (1970), 16 ff.

83. See J. R. Bartlett, *J.T.S.* N.S. xx (1969), 1 ff.

84. It is possible that the Massoretic pointing represents a misunderstanding of an original *mōleḵ 'āḏām*; the reference would then be to a human sacrifice, and Mesha's action (2 Kings 3: 27) may have been in mind. See N. H. Torczyner, *hallāšôn wᵉhassēp̱er*, ii (1948), p. 66; O. Eissfeldt, *Molk als Opferbegriff* (1935), pp. 13 ff.

85. See G. B. Gray, op. cit. 271 ff.; J. Mauchline, *Isaiah 1–39: Introduction and Commentary* (1962), p. 150; E. Power, *Biblica* xiii (1932), 435 ff., 448, where he argues that the raiders mentioned in Isa. 15 and 16 come from the south and are Edomites, not Assyrians.

86. Van Zyl, op. cit. 153 f., argues that in the seventh century B.C. Moab was flourishing and expanding; her tribute to Assyria was small, not because Moab was poor, but because she was loyal. This loyalty,

however, meant that Moab put a good deal of her energy and resources into the war against the Arabs.

87. Op. cit. 157 ff.

88. The Nabonidus Chronicle, col. 1, line 17 (see *A.N.E.T.*, pp. 305 ff.), refers to the Babylonian siege and capture of a place *-dummu*. This is probably not Edom, but a city, which S. Smith finds near modern ʿAzraq. See S. Smith, *Babylonian Historical Texts* (1924), p. 77; 'Assyriological Notes; Adumu, Adummatu', *J.R.A.S.* (1925), 508 ff.; *Isaiah, Chapters xl–lv: Literary Criticism and History* (1944), pp. 37 f., cf. p. 137 n. 80, and pp. 138 f.

89. W. F. Albright, *B.A.S.O.R.* lxxxii (1941), 14.

90. *J.B.L.* lv (1936), 322, in a review of *H.U.C.A.* xi (1936). C. M. Bennett, 'Ṭawilân, Jordanie', *R.B.* lxxvi (1969), 386 ff., found no trace of Edomite occupation there after the sixth century B.C.

91. C. C. Edgar, *Zenon Papyri*, i (1925), nos. 59006, 59015.

92. From the work of Hieronymus of Kardia, preserved in Diodorus, *Bibliotheca Historica* xix. 95, 98.

93. *B.A.S.O.R.* lxxxii (1941), 14.

94. Albright, ibid.

95. *Histories* ii. 8, 12; iii. 5; vii. 89; cf. also 2 Chr. 17: 11, 21: 16, 26: 7, where Arabians are mentioned alongside the Philistines. For Gur-baal in 2 Chr. 26: 7 see G. F. Buhl, *Geschichte der Edomiter* (1893), p. 41, and J. Simons, *Geographical and Topographical Texts*, section 1000.

96. *Bibliotheca Historica* xix. 95; cf. xix. 98, where the Dead Sea is said to lie in the middle of the satrapy of Idumaea.

97. Cf. M. Noth, *The History of Israel*, 2nd English edn. (1960), p. 345, and for details his article, cited above, in *Z.D.P.V.* lxvii (1944–5), 45 ff., 62 f.

98. See notes 24 and 25.

99. N. Glueck, 'Explorations in Eastern Palestine, I', *A.A.S.O.R.* xiv (1933–4), 22 ff.

100. See van Zyl, op. cit. 193 ff.; 'mais ces noms sont groupés dans l'ancien royaume de Siḥôn l'Amorite et l'absence de noms ainsi formés avec Baal dans tout le territoire proprement moabite indique que Baal n'y était pas considéré comme un dieu national' (R. de Vaux, reviewing van Zyl's work, *R.B.* lxix (1962), 472).

101. W. H. Morton, *B.A.S.O.R.* cxl (1955), 6.

102. See R. de Vaux, *R.B.* lxxiii (1966), 472 ff.

103. See van Zyl, op. cit. 40, for Moabitic names found in Egypt, and compare the name of Mesha's father given by W. L. Reed & F. V. Winnett, 'A Fragment of an Early Moabite Inscription from Kerak', *B.A.S.O.R.* clxxii (1963), 1 ff., especially 7 f.

104. See N. Glueck, op. cit. *A.A.S.O.R.* xv (1934–5), 136; xviii–xix (1939), 32 ff.; 'The Early History of a Nabataean Temple', *B.A.S.O.R.* lxix (1938), 7 ff.; *The Other Side of the Jordan* (1940), pp. 150 ff.

105. N. Glueck, 'The Third Season of Excavation at Tell el-Kheleifeh', *B.A.S.O.R.* lxxix (1940), 2 ff., 16.

106. See G. R. Driver, 'Notes on Some Recently Discovered Proper Names', *B.A.S.O.R.* xc (1943), 34 f. (cf. the eighth-century B.C. Moabite king Salamanu); for *'ēl* cf. compound names from Tell el-Kheleifeh and on a seal acquired in *eṭ-ṭafīleh* (see Glueck, 'Ostraca from Elath, continued', *B.A.S.O.R.* lxxxii (1941), 3 ff., and G. L. Harding, 'Some Objects from Transjordan', *P.E.Q.* lxix (1937), 253 ff., 255).

107. For a full study of this deity, see Th. C. Vriezen, 'The Edomitic Deity Qaus', in *Oudtestamentische Studiën* xiv (1965), 330 ff.

108. N. Glueck, 'The Topography and History of Ezion-geber and Elath', *B.A.S.O.R.* lxxii (1938), 2 ff., 11 ff.

109. N. Glueck, 'Ostraca from Elath, continued', *B.A.S.O.R.* lxxxii (1941), 3 ff., and W. F. Albright, ibid., 11 ff.

110. C. M. Bennett, 'Fouilles d'Umm el-biyara: rapport préliminaire', *R.B.* lxxiii (1966), 372 ff., 399 ff.

111. For references and discussion see Vriezen, loc. cit. See also R. D. Biggs, 'A Chaldaean Inscription from Nippur', *B.A.S.O.R.* clxxix (1965), 36 ff.

112. Vriezen, ibid. 334.

113. W. F. Albright, 'Islam and the Religions of the Ancient Orient', *J.A.O.S.* lx (1940), 283 ff., 295 n. 29.

114. Vriezen, loc. cit. 334 ff.

115. R. H. Pfeiffer, 'Edomitic Wisdom', *Z.A.W.* xliv (1926), 13 ff.; 'A Non-Israelite Source of the Book of Genesis', *Z.A.W.* xlviii (1930), 66 ff.; *Introduction to the Old Testament* (1941), p. 21.

116. J. Pedersen, *Israel*, ii (1926), p. 367.

117. W. L. Reed & F. V. Winnett, *B.A.S.O.R.* clxxii (1963), 1 ff.

118. R. E. Murphy, 'A Fragment of an Early Moabite Inscription from Dibon', *B.A.S.O.R.* cxxv (1952), 20 ff.

119. See E. J. Pilcher, 'A Moabite Seal', *P.E.Q.* xlvii (1915), 42; van Zyl, op. cit. 31.

120. C. M. Bennett, *R.B.* lxxiii (1966), 372 ff., 398 ff.

121. C. M. Bennett, 'Ṭawilân, Jordanie', *R.B.* lxxvi (1969), 386 ff.

122. G. R. Driver, 'Seals from ʿAmman and Petra', *Quarterly of the Department of Antiquities of Palestine* xi (1944), 81 f.

123. G. L. Harding, 'Some Objects from Transjordan', *P.E.Q.* lxix (1937), pp. 253 ff., 255; K. Galling, 'Beschriftete Bildsiegel des ersten Jahrtausends v. Chr. vornehmlich aus Syrien und Palästina', *Z.D.P.V.* lxiv (1941), 121 ff., 150, 171, 198.

124. *D.O.T.T.*, p. 224, and references there given; N. Avigad, 'The Jotham Seal from Elath', *B.A.S.O.R.* clxiii (1961), 18 ff.

125. See note 107.

126. N. Glueck, 'The First Campaign at Tell el-Kheleifeh', *B.A.S.O.R.* lxxi (1938), 3 ff., 17 f.; and more recently, id., 'Some Edomite Pottery from Tell el-Kheleifeh, Part I', *B.A.S.O.R.* clxxxviii (1967), 8 ff.

127. N. Glueck, 'Ostraca from Elath', *B.A.S.O.R.* lxxx (1940), 3 ff.; id., 'Ostraca from Elath, continued', *B.A.S.O.R.* lxxxii (1941), 3 ff.;

J. Naveh, 'The Scripts of Two Ostraca from Elath', *B.A.S.O.R.* clxxxiii (1966), 27 ff.

128. Glueck, *B.A.S.O.R.* lxxx (1940), 3 ff.; lxxxii (1941), 3 ff., 15.

129. Glueck, 'The First Campaign at Tell el-Kheleifeh', *B.A.S.O.R.* lxxi (1938), 3 ff., 16 f.; 'The Second Campaign at Tell el-Kheleifeh', *B.A.S.O.R.* lxxv (1939), 8 ff., 19.

130. C. M. Bennett, *I.L.N.* 30 Apr. 1966, p. 29; cf. Bennett, *Antiquity* xli (1967), 197 ff.

131. See van Zyl, op. cit. 188; S. Segert, 'Die Sprache der moabitischen Königsinschriften', *Ar.Or.* xxix (1961), 197–267.

132. J. Naveh, *B.A.S.O.R.* clxxxiii (1966), 27 ff., 30.

133. In *A.O.T.S.*, p. 435.

134. For Moabite and Edomite pottery see Glueck, *A.A.S.O.R.* xiv (1933–4), Pl. 20 ff.; xv (1934–5), pp. 123 ff., Pl. 23 ff.; xviii–xix (1939), pp. 251 ff., Pl. 1 ff.; 'Some Edomite Pottery from Tell el-Kheleifeh, Part I', *B.A.S.O.R.* clxxxviii (1967), 8 ff. For the recent discovery of pottery in north-western Saudi Arabia, identical with some found at Tell el-Kheleifeh and Timna, see P. J. Parr, 'Exploration archéologique du Hedjaz et du Madian', *R.B.* lxxvi (1969), 390 ff.

135. Glueck, 'Ezion-geber', *B.A.* xxviii (1965), 70 ff., 87.

136. C. M. Bennett, *R.B.* lxxiii (1966), 372 ff., 395 f.

137. Glueck, *The Other Side of the Jordan* (1940), p. 108.

BIBLIOGRAPHY

AHARONI, Y., *The Land of the Bible* (London, 1966).

ALBRIGHT, W. F., 'The Oracles of Balaam', *J.B.L.* lxiii (1944), 207 ff.

ALT, A., 'Emiter und Moabiter', *P.J.B.* xxxv (1940), 29 ff.

AVIGAD, N., 'The Jotham Seal from Elath', *B.A.S.O.R.* clxiii (1961), 18 ff.

BARTLETT, J. R., 'The Edomite King-List of Genesis xxxvi. 31–39 and 1 Chron. i. 43–50', *J.T.S.* N.S. xvi (1965), 301 ff.

—— 'The Land of Seir and the Brotherhood of Edom', *J.T.S.* N.S. xx (1969), 1 ff.

—— 'The Historical Reference of Numbers xxi. 27–30', *P.E.Q.* ci (1969), 94 ff.

—— 'Sihon and Og, Kings of the Amorites', *V.T.* xxi (1971), 1 ff.

—— 'The Rise and Fall of the Kingdom of Edom', *P.E.Q.* civ (1972), 26 ff.

BENNETT, C. M., 'Fouilles d'Umm el-biyara: rapport préliminaire', *R.B.* lxxiii (1966), 372 ff.

—— 'A Brief Note on Excavations at Tawilân, Jordan, 1968–70', *Levant* iii (1971), v–vii, Pl. 1, 11.

BUHL, G. F., *Geschichte der Edomiter* (Leipzig, 1893).

DE VAUX, R. 'Notes d'histoire et de topographie transjordaniennes', *Vivre et penser* i (1941), 16 ff.

DONNER, H., 'Neue Quellen zur Geschichte des Staates Moab in der zweiten Hälfte des 8 Jahrh. v. Chr.', *M.I.O.* v (1957), 155 ff.

DRIOTON, 'A propos de la Stèle du Balou'a', *R.B.* xlii (1933), 353 ff.

Glueck, N., *The Other Side of the Jordan* (New Haven, Conn., 1940).
—— *Explorations in Eastern Palestine* I–IV, *A.A.S.O.R.* xiv (1933–4); xv (1934–5); xviii–xix (1937–9); xxv–xxviii (1951).
—— 'Ezion-geber', *B.A.* xxviii (1965), 70 ff.
—— 'Some Edomite Pottery from Tell el-Kheleifeh', *B.A.S.O.R.* clxxxviii (1967), 8 ff.
—— 'Transjordan', *A.O.T.S.*, pp. 429 ff.
Harding, G. L. & Isserlin, B. S. J., 'Four Tomb Groups from Jordan', *Annual of the Palestine Exploration Fund* vi (1953).
Kitchen, K. A., 'Some New Light on the Asiatic Wars of Ramesses II', *J.E.A.* l (1964), 47 ff.
Liver, J., 'The Wars of Mesha, King of Moab', *P.E.Q.* (1967), 14 ff.
Moritz, B., 'Edomitische Genealogien', *Z.A.W.* xliv (1926), 81 ff.
—— 'Die Könige von Edom', *Muséon* l (1937), 101 ff.
Murphy, R., 'A Fragment of an Early Moabite Inscription from Dibon', *B.A.S.O.R.* cxxv (1952), 20 ff.
Myers, J. M. 'Edom and Judah in the Sixth–Fifth centuries B.C.', *Near Eastern Studies in honor of W. F. Albright*, ed. H. Goetze (Johns Hopkins Press, Baltimore, 1971), pp. 377 ff.
Naveh, J., 'The Scripts of Two Ostraca from Elath', *B.A.S.O.R.* clxxxiii (1966), 27 ff.
Noth, M., 'Israelitische Stämme zwischen Ammon und Moab', *Z.A.W.* lx (1944), 11 ff.
—— 'Eine palästinische Lokalüberlieferung in 2 Chr. 20', *Z.D.P.V.* lxvii (1945), 45 ff.
Oded, B., 'Egyptian references to the Edomite deity Qaus', *Andrews University Seminary Studies*, ix (1971), 47 ff.
Olavarri, E., 'Sondages à *ʿarôʿer* sur l'Arnon', *R.B.* lxxii (1965), 77 ff.
Pfeiffer, R. H., 'Edomitic Wisdom', *Z.A.W.* xliv (1926), 13 ff.
—— 'A Non-Israelite Source of the Book Genesis', *Z.A.W.* xlviii (1930), 66 ff.
Power, E., 'The Prophecy of Esaias against Moab', *Biblica* xiii (1932), 435 ff.
Rothenberg, B., 'Ancient Copper Industries in the Western Arabah', *P.E.Q.* xciv (1962), 5 ff.
Saggs, H. W. F., 'The Nimrud Letters, 1952—Part II', *Iraq* xvii (1955), 126 ff.
Simons, J., *The Geographical and Topographical Texts of the Old Testament* (Leiden, 1959).
van Zyl, A. H., *The Moabites* (Leiden, 1960).
Vriezen, Th. C., 'The Edomitic Deity Qaus', *Oudtestamentische Studiën* xiv (1965), 330 ff.
Winnett, F. V. & Reed, W. L., *The Excavations at Dibon*, I and II, *A.A.S.O.R.* xxxvi–xxxvii (1964).
—— 'A Fragment of an Early Moabite Inscription from Kerak', *B.A.S.O.R.* clxxii (1963), 1 ff.
Wright, G. E., 'More on King Solomon's Mines', *B.A.* xxiv (1961), 59 ff.

XI

THE PHOENICIANS

D. R. AP-THOMAS

In free association the word 'Phoenician' probably suggests to most people some or all of the following: Tyrian purple for dyeing wool, the invention of the alphabet, and the development of seafaring—an impressive list, but woefully incomplete. Nor will the average person recall the names of many persons in Phoenician history, apart from Hiram, the ally of Solomon, and probably Jezebel, the wife of Ahab and the bane of the prophet Elijah (1 Kings 5; 16: 31 ff.). Of recent years, however, our knowledge of the Phoenicians has rapidly increased and has been made reasonably accessible.[1]

The homeland of the historical Phoenicians lay along the eastern Mediterranean coast. So much is common knowledge; but where exactly were its frontiers? Only the coastal limit is static. Inland the eastern boundary tended to run along the watershed in the mountains parallel to the coast—probably less than thirty miles from the sea at its furthest, while the lowland strip along the edge of the sea varies from four miles to nothing. Greatest vagueness and variation, however, plague the attempt to draw the short northern and southern frontiers of this narrow land. The maximum length given is about 500 miles, which includes the whole east Mediterranean seaboard, from Myriandrus near Iskanderun/Alexandretta in the north, down to Rhinocolura at el-'Arish on the Egyptian border in the south.[2] The minimum north to south extent is probably under 200 miles, centring roughly on modern Jubeil, ancient Gebal (Ps. 83: 7; Ezek. 27: 9; Josh. 13: 5), classical Byblos. On this minimal reckoning ancient Phoenicia would approximate in size to the present-day state of Lebanon, or slightly more, particularly to the south. In this geographical assessment no account is taken of possible overseas possessions,

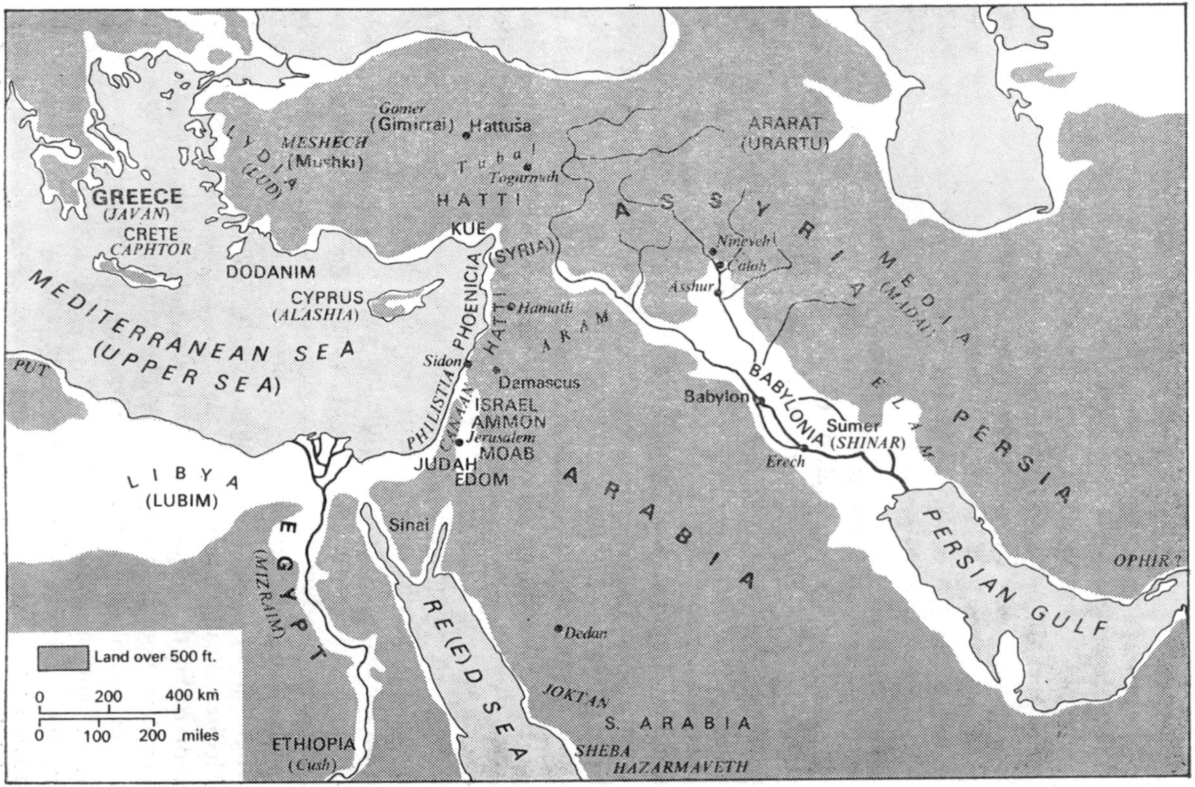

FIG. 6 The ancient Near East in Old Testament times.

because, except in the case of Carthage, very little is known about their extent; but the general impression given is that Phoenician communities overseas for the most part formed not so much self-supporting landed populations as trading outposts and civic boroughs planted at commercially strategic points, with little attempt at integration with the native populations.

(i) *History*

Even the history of Phoenicia proper is the history of its towns, and, still more narrowly, that means its coast towns. The inland area, though fertile in parts, was too mountainous to be more than self-supporting in agricultural produce, and the bulk of the population gathered in the string of towns sited on the coast, wherever a river mouth or small bay or off-shore islet offered some sort of haven for small ships and enough land for the necessary crops. The best-known of these settlements, from north to south, are Aradus/Arvad, Simyra/Zemara, Tripolis, Gebal/Byblos, Beeroth/Berytos/Beirut, Sidon, Zarephath, and Tyre.[3] Tripolis does not figure in the records before the Persian period, but the others are all referred to in the Old Testament, as well as in other early, particularly Egyptian, sources, such as the campaign records of Pharaoh Thutmose III, *c.* 1504–1450 B.C.[4] Although some of the earliest known human remains have been found in Phoenicia, going back over 400,000 years to the Old Stone Age, this is scarcely relevant to the Phoenicians themselves, especially as a people of the Old Testament. Phoenicia becomes distinctive only after the rise of civilization in Egypt and Mesopotamia, for the first Phoenician cities deserving the name seem to have come into being at the beginning of the Early Bronze Age, *c.* 3000 B.C. They were never very big, and were probably unhealthy because of malaria and contaminated water; they were subject to attack from outside enemies, and, eventually, forced to look seawards under pressure of hostile neighbours.[5]

But the Phoenicians—or maybe their racial predecessors—took to the sea, apparently, very early in history. Contact between Egypt and Dorak, a site on the coast of the Sea of Marmara, is known to have existed during the Early Bronze Age; and the drawing of a line of ships on a silver dagger blade found there[6] suggests that travel might have been by sea, in which case the ships would almost certainly have had to put in at some Phoenician ports. In many ways sea travel was easier than travel overland, not least in Phoenicia itself. The divisive nature of their geography is reflected in their history. One Phoenician city might become dominant for a period, but it never succeeded in creating a really united people. That is largely the reason why a definitive northern and southern border cannot properly be drawn. The concept 'Phoenicia' as understood by us, as by the Romans and the Greeks, scarcely seems to have existed for the Phoenicians themselves, any more than it did for the Old Testament, which speaks of 'the Giblites' (i.e. people of Gebal), 'the Sidonians', or 'the king of Tyre' (Josh. 13: 5; 1 Kings 5: 6; Jer. 25: 22). One passage (Obad. 20), however, does seem to use the term Canaanites to refer to Phoenicia as a unit.

It was, in fact, the Greeks who coined the name 'Phoenicia' and gave currency to the concept. Just as they named the Aramaeans 'Assyrians' (and then shortened it to Syrians), because they were the subjects of the Assyrian empire nearest and best known to them, so they appear to have translated the name Canaanite by 'Phoenician', and then restricted it to those Canaanites most familiar to them.

There is no doubt that the Phoenicians of the historical period were Canaanites culturally,[7] and indeed racially also. Even as late as the fifth century A.D. St. Augustine remarks that the country folk near Carthage in North Africa, a colony of Tyre, referred to themselves as Canaanites.[8]

The so-called Table of Nations (Gen. 10) includes four known Phoenician cities or city-states, Sidon, Arka, Arvad, and Zemar,[9] as 'children of Canaan' (Gen. 10: 15–18; cf. 1 Chr. 1: 13–16), i.e. Canaanites.

It is true that the genealogy describes Canaan there as belonging to Ham rather than to Shem, but there is no evidence for reversing the obvious racial affiliation of the Phoenicians. Probably, indeed, that is not intended by the Table, which indicates political at least as much as ethnic affiliation.[10] Byblos, which is not mentioned here, may indeed have been officially a colony of Egypt during the Old Kingdom, for its ruler refers to himself as 'the son of Re, beloved of the gods of his land'.[11] Moreover, during the Eighteenth Dynasty, pharaoh Thutmose III (1504–1450) maintained Egyptian garrisons in Tyre, Arvad, and Simyra, and took their crown princes to the Egyptian court for education, and, of course, incidentally as hostages. By blood, however, the true Phoenicians were and remained basically Semitic and Canaanite—or possibly Amorite, if we prefer the Assyrian nomenclature, as used, for example, by Ashur-naṣir-apli II (883–859), who claims, 'I seized the entire extent of the Lebanon mountain and reached the Great Sea of the Amurru country. . . . The tribute of the sea coast—from the inhabitants of Tyre, Sidon, Byblos, Mahallata, Maiza, Kaiza, Amurru,[12] and Arvad which is in the sea . . . I received.'[13]

The Old Testament knows no distinction between the inhabitants of the coastal strip and those who occupied inland Canaan or Palestine before and during the Israelite conquest. They are all Canaanites (see Gen. 10: 15–18; Josh. 5: 1; 2 Sam. 24: 6–7; Isa. 23: 11). The Greeks apparently did make such a distinction, by naming the coast-dwellers *Phoinikoi*, which is taken to mean 'Purple-folk'. Is this a translation of 'Canaanites'? In Akkadian transcription the latter sometimes appears (e.g. Amarna Letter 8: 13 ff.) as (*māt*) *kinaḫḫi*, and a Hurrian derivation yielding the meaning '(land of) purple-folk' was suggested. But now that the spelling *knʿn* can be traced back in Egypt to the reign of Amenophis II (*c.* 1430), and in Ugarit to roughly the same period, an original Semitic derivation seems preferable.[14] The root *knʿ* in Hebrew has the meaning 'to sink, be low', and, if it applied to the sun in this context, the Canaanites would be the 'Sundowners, Westerners', and so possibly an exact parallel in meaning to 'Amorites'. But if Greek *phoinikos* is not a translation of *knʿny*, it may be their rendering of the Semitic word for the madder plant (*Rubia tinctorum* L.), which provided a commonly-used purple dye. Its Arabic name is *fuwwa*, corresponding to a Hebrew *puwwâ* and found in the Old Testament as Puvah (Gen. 46: 13), a clan of the tribe of Issachar and associated there with Tola (*tōlaʿ*, 'crimson worm'). Its gentilic form *pûnî* (Num. 26: 23) brings it still nearer to Greek *phoinikos*, Latin *poenus*, *puniceus*. A connection has also been found with *ponika*, used in the Linear B texts, possibly for some imported goods.[15] Many have sought to link the Greek *Phoinikoi* with the similar-sounding Egyptian *Fenkhu*, which is used in Fifth Dynasty texts for the inhabitants of the Syrian coast.[16]

It is not known what the Canaanites were called before they were given or adopted the appellation Canaanite. Once settled on the coast, there is archaeological evidence that they spread south-west into Palestine before 1800 B.C.[17] The name 'purple-folk' must refer to their exploitation of the local sea snails which yielded the famous purple dye.

Apart from its ethnic use the word *k*^{e}*naʿanî* occurs in the Old Testament as a common noun with the meaning 'merchant' or 'pedlar' (Job 41: 6; Prov. 31: 24; Zech. 14: 21), and, in the historical period, that is exactly what the Phoenicians were—the middlemen, trading goods between the two great riverine civilizations, Egypt to the south of them and Mesopotamia east across the desert, or, indeed, between any two centres open to traffic.[18]

Without the impetus given to the development of civilized life by the emergence of political organization in the rich lands of the Nile and Euphrates valleys Phoenicia would probably never have risen very far up the ladder of culture, or have deserved more than a footnote in a history of civilization. But, as it happened, she was strategically placed on the only natural line of communication between centres of more advanced culture, and, by a process of absorption, transmitted the goods of one to the other, enriching and civilizing herself in the process, and, indeed, making her own not insignificant contribution to the sum of world advancement. This she did not so much by direct invention as by refinement and development, with a flair for exploitation which was very widely recognized even in ancient times. Napoleon's contemptuously-intended remark about 'a nation of shopkeepers' might well have been anticipated and applied to the Phoenicians by a Roman consul, a Greek historian, or even an Assyrian ruler or Egyptian pharaoh.

There is reference to Phoenician maritime enterprise on the Palermo Stone inscription (*c.* 2200 B.C.). This records the arrival in Egypt during the reign of the pharaoh Snefru, *c.* 2600 B.C., of forty timber-carrying ships from Byblos,[19] and suggests that, by this time, commercial sea-going traffic had long been established; in fact, alabaster vases bearing Egyptian royal cartouches of the Second Dynasty have been found in Byblos.[20] Nor were these Fourth Dynasty ships mere boats; the Palermo Stone reveals that the wood carried was for the construction of three ships each

170 feet long. The actual ship which was built of Phoenician cedar for Khufu, the Cheops of pyramid fame who followed Snefru, was found in 1954.[21] The wood was probably exported from Byblos, which seems to have been the earliest of the Phoenician cities to have developed, and, from early dynastic times, to have had very close links with Egypt.[22] The rulers of Mesopotamia were as interested in cedar-wood as were the Egyptians, but their source of supply was usually not Lebanon proper but the more northerly Amanus range of mountains, which was nearer the headwaters of the Euphrates, along which river the logs could be floated to their destinations. Naram-Sin of Agade (2159–2123 B.C.) states that 'Nergal . . . presented him with the Amanus, the Cedar Mountain, and the Upper Sea'; and Gudea of Lagash, roughly his contemporary, is more explicit: he 'made a path into the Cedar Mountain which nobody had entered before; he cut its cedars with great axes . . ., cedar rafts were floating down the water [of the river] from the Cedar Mountain, pine rafts from the Pine Mountain.'[23] Later, Esarhaddon (681–669) names twenty-two rulers of Syrian, Phoenician, Palestinian, and Cyprian petty kingdoms (including Baal of Tyre and Manasseh of Judah) whom he conquered, and states, 'all these I sent out and made them transport under terrible difficulties to Nineveh . . . as building material for my palace: big logs, long beams, and [thin] boards from cedar and pine trees, products of the Sirara and Lebanon mountains.'[24] Even pharaoh Thutmose III, when he invaded the middle Euphrates area, 'had many ships of cedar built on the mountains of God's Land near the Lady of Byblos. They were placed on chariots with cattle drawing [them] . . . in order to cross that great river which lies between this foreign country and Naharin.'[25]

For the sea journey from Byblos to Egypt, and up the Nile, the logs seem to have been carried as cargo.[26] Presumably a raft would have proved unmanageable on the high sea, though for the shorter voyage down the coast from Byblos to Jerusalem's most convenient port (probably Jaffa) Hiram made the logs up into rafts which were broken apart again on landing (1 Kings 5: 9).

Byblos has been more fully excavated than any of the other Phoenician cities, but, even here, there remain very many gaps in its history. The excavations have yielded many finds from the

Bronze Age, but only very few from the main biblical period, the Iron Age. The reason probably is that the Iron Age city lies beneath the present town of Jubeil.

Other cities, such as Tyre, Sidon, and Beirut, have yielded finds which, conversely, belong largely to the later, Graeco-Roman period. At these sites, too, it seems that the present settlements are built over the Iron Age cities. The exception is Ras Shamra, the deserted site of the once flourishing ancient city-kingdom of Ugarit, lying a few miles inland from its still-used port, now called Minet el-Beidha.

(ii) *Language and Literature*

In the extended sense, Ugarit could be reckoned Phoenician,[27] but, since this centre has been described elsewhere, only some of the evidence from the rich finds made there needs to be cited here.[28] The most astounding discovery was the library of clay tablets written in an alphabetic cuneiform script, in contrast to the, also early, alphabetic hieroglyphic writing, of which examples have been found in more southerly Phoenicia and in Palestine.[29] This dichotomy reflects the divergent orientation and ambivalent political necessities of this entrepreneurial region.

Some inscriptions in a syllabic hieroglyphic writing have been discovered at Byblos, dating to the early second millennium. Presumably this was a system inspired directly by the two other syllabic scripts already known to them from their trading contacts with the great powers of Egypt and Mesopotamia.[30] Phoenicia has provided the earliest attested normative use of alphabetic signs for writing—signs earlier than those of the Sinaitic inscriptions;[31] it is therefore only reasonable to conclude that the invention of exclusively alphabetic writing may be credited to these Canaanites, as tradition asserts; this, however, does not imply that they invented the art of writing as such, or even that they were the first to express a single sound (phoneme) by a separate sign (grapheme).

A further advantage of alphabetic over syllabic writing, besides bringing the number of signs needed to below thirty, is that fairly elemental graphemes suffice for each one of these, so cutting down still further the drudgery of learning to read and write. This systematization and rationalization carried through by the Phoenicians underlies every other alphabet in use throughout the world ever since. The only really basic improvement on the original has been the Greek decision to express all the vowel sounds on a par with the consonants.[32]

The Phoenician language is basically the same as that of the other Semitic-speaking peoples of the Levant, but it reflects dialectal variations of a historical and geographical nature within itself, as well as being distinguishable from even Hebrew and Aramaic, its nearest neighbours in time and place, by still more obvious grammatical and consonantal variations. If we may judge from the narrative of Elijah and the widow of Zarephath (1 Kings 17: 8–24), the differences were no insuperable barrier to communication in the ninth century, even in colloquial speech; they would be still less in the period represented by the earlier inscriptions from Byblos. The tablets from Ras Shamra show the language of Ugarit in the mid second millennium as an even more archaic and less differentiated form of North-west Semitic.

Some features which Phoenician had in common with the contemporary Hebrew, apart from script, were a close general similarity in verb and sentence structure, and the absence of the article, as in the tenth-century Ahiram sarcophagus inscription and the Gezer Calendar—though both languages gradually brought it into common use. Both languages also indicate the definite direct object by an almost identical particle, *'eṯ* (in Phoenician sometimes *'iyyaṯ*). But there are obvious differences of usage, vocabulary, and pronunciation. The common Phoenician negatives are *'i* and *bal*, not *lō'* as in Hebrew. Where Phoenician has *pā'al* for 'to do, make', and *ḥārōṣ* for 'gold', Hebrew prefers *'āsâ* and *zāhāḇ* (though it sometimes uses the others, too). Transliterations show that Phoenician was inclined, even more than Hebrew, to turn *ā* into *ō*: e.g. *lābōn* 'white' for Hebrew *lāḇān*.[33] As is not unexpected, the branch of Phoenician Canaanite which developed in the west-Mediterranean colonies diverged still more strikingly from the parent language in its different environment, especially after Carthage had developed independent status. Punic, as it is called to distinguish it from the mother Phoenician, has itself two forms, which are referred to as Punic and Neo-Punic respectively.

H. Donner and W. Röllig recently listed twenty-nine inscriptions from the Phoenician homeland, Syria, and Asia Minor.[34]

Some are admittedly of a few words, but others run to a score or so of lines. Cyprus has yielded fourteen inscriptions, Rhodes two, Sardinia one, and Malta one; five have been found in Egypt and two in Greece. Fifty-six Punic inscriptions are recorded by these authors, and another fifty-seven in Neo-Punic. Most of these inscriptions are of a votive or sepulchral nature, though not all;[35] and some of them are of prime importance for the history, geography, and economics of the Phoenicians.

It is ironical that the people who apparently invented and certainly were the first to exploit the alphabet have, with the notable exception of the clay tablets from Ugarit, left us so little in the way of literature or indeed of any written material. This does not mean that the Phoenicians made little use of writing; the reverse is probably the case—the needs of commerce are still one of the most potent forces in the development of communication techniques. Presumably the normal writing substance of the Phoenicians was papyrus, which is so perishable that it needs specially dry conditions if it is to be preserved for any length of time; and these conditions do not exist along the humid coast of Phoenicia. The fact that the Greeks called Gebal 'Byblos' is often adduced as proof that papyrus was extensively used there, because *byblos* is the Greek word for papyrus. It would have been normal for the material to be given the name of the place, rather than vice versa. Papyrus was commonly used for making sails and cordage[36] but also provided paper for books,[37] in Greek *biblia*, hence our word Bible.

Apart from the inscriptions mentioned above, several literary works in Phoenician are known to have existed. Josephus (*Ant.* VIII. ii. 8) speaks of 'the public records of Tyre' being available for perusal in his own day,[38] and says that they had been translated into Greek by Menander of Ephesus (ibid. v. 3; *Contra Ap.* i. 18). Josephus also mentions a certain 'Dius, one that is believed to have written the Phoenician History after an accurate manner' (*Contra Ap.* i. 17). Unfortunately, all that has come down to us is the little that Josephus himself quotes in confirmation of the biblical account of the transactions between Solomon and Hiram (1 Kings 5); though he does go on to list the rulers of Tyre, from Hiram's father Abibalus (Abibaʿal) down to Pygmalion (Pumayyaton), whose sister founded Carthage *c.* 814 B.C., according to tradition. The close ties between Phoenicia and Israel from the days of David make it possible that the Hebrew historians were prompted to undertake their literary labours by the example of their Phoenician contemporaries. The Old Testament refers frequently to writing in connection with legal, political, commercial, and social transactions (1 Sam. 10: 25; 2 Sam. 11: 14 f.; 1 Kings 21: 8 f.; Isa. 8: 1; 10: 1, 19; 30: 8, etc.), and the almost complete loss of these documents is certainly as regrettable as the even greater scarcity from Phoenician quarters.

Sanchuniaton of Beirut wrote an account of the Creation, and this 'Phoenician Genesis' of the eleventh century was translated into Greek in the first century A.D. by Philo of Byblos. Fragments of it are quoted by the fourth-century Church historian Eusebius of Caesarea in his *Praeparatio Evangelica*,[39] taken from the Neo-Platonist Porphyry. It is doubtful how much is authentic and how much colouring of Greek philosophic thought has been added in what Eusebius reports. He quotes 'that a gloomy, windy air, and a thick, turbid chaos were the first principle of all things' (cf. Gen. 1: 2). Desire then arose and, from the interaction of these, 'was begotten *Môt*, some call it mud; others decayed aqueous vegetable matter. . . . Môt also developed into light, moon, stars, and the great constellations.' Elsewhere Eusebius states that 'male and female life on land and sea' developed from egg-like creatures, who were called by the Phoenician name *Zophasemim*, 'skygazers', and who were woken into life by the clash of aerial elements and the crash of thunder caused by the heat of the sun.[40] A Phoenician cosmogony is claimed to have existed, written by an author whom the Neo-Platonist Damascius calls Mochus; the same Mochus is also credited with having written a history of Phoenicia.

The loss of virtually all this literature, and maybe much more, and the brevity and often mangled nature of what has survived by quotation in Greek authors, are an irreparable loss, in spite of numerous references to matters Phoenician in both Greek and Latin authors, and the very reliable though restricted information given in the pages of the Old Testament.

(iii) *Religion*

Had Sanchuniaton's history of Creation been more fully preserved, it would have been easier to write of Phoenician theology; as it is, apart from the dedicatory inscriptions, the best contemporary evidence comes from the Ugaritic tablets, eked out by the divine element in personal names (as found also in Old Testament nomenclature), the discoveries of the archaeologists, and also what is said in the Old Testament about Canaanite religion. There were probably certain specific differences and variations of emphasis between Canaanite religion in general and the religious beliefs of Phoenicia, but the common ground was probably much greater than such differences.

From the proper names found in the Egyptian Execration Texts of the eighteenth century B.C.[41] it may be inferred that deities worshipped in Canaan included El, Hadad, ʻAmm, Anat, Horon, Shamash, Shahar, and Rapha.[42] From Ugarit and the Old Testament might be added Baʻal, Dagan, Asherah, Astarte, Elyon, and Mot.

Turning to Phoenician territory proper, Byblos provides most details of its pantheon. The main deities there were El, Baʻalat, and Adonis—an apparent triad. But El is becoming past his prime, a *deus otiosus*, yielding precedence to Eliun. The latter is mentioned as a god in the eighth-century Aramaic Sefire inscriptions, but in the Old Testament his name has been combined with El to give El Elyon, rendered as 'God Most High' (R.S.V., N.E.B. at Gen. 14: 19 etc.). Other instances of such conjunctions are known, e.g. Hadad-Rimmon (Zech. 12: 11) in which the names of two well-known Syrian weather-gods are united.

The most celebrated deity at Byblos was undoubtedly Baʻalat, 'Lady' or 'Mistress', and dedications to her are more numerous than to any other Byblian deity. The Yehawmilk inscription is a long dedication to her by a fifth- or fourth-century king of Byblos.[43] 'Baʻalat' is a title, not a name. Since Sanchuniaton gives Astarte and Ashera as the two other wives of El,[44] maybe she was Anath; but there were other goddesses, and, since they change their names and characters so confusingly (at least in the incomplete records available), she might even have been Asherah, who, as Asherat-yam, 'She who walks the sea', would obviously have a high claim on the veneration of a sailor community—not to mention some of her other characteristics.

Adonis, the third member of the Byblian triad, was the young, active male deity. His name is an adaptation of Semitic Adon, 'Lord'; and he seems to be referred to also as Baʻal, 'Master'. Both names are appellatives and not personal names, and it is interesting to note that the Old Testament accepted Adon as an orthodox epithet for Yahweh (especially in the form Adonai), but eventually decidedly rejected the use of Ba'al, which preponderantly refers to Yahweh's Canaanite rival.

Rather than to multiply references to individual deities of whom only few facts are known, it appears best to give now a short description of Phoenician religion in its main features, so far as is possible.[45] Like the Canaanite religion found in Palestine by the Hebrews, and condemned by their prophets (e.g. Lev. 19: 26–31; Hos. 2), Phoenician religion seems to have been primarily nature-adoration, the quest for fertility leading to flagrant sexuality in worship, and other practices, which seem to have continued down to classical times and earned the condemnation of Greek and Latin authors.[46] Along with this licentiousness went the practice of human sacrifice, which the Judaeans seem to have adopted from the Canaanites, and continued until Josiah 'defiled Topheth, which is in the valley of the children of Hinnom, that no man might make his son or his daughter to pass through the fire to Molech' (2 Kings 23: 10; cf. Jer. 7: 31; 19: 5). Sacrificial precincts of the 'topheth' type have not been certainly identified in Phoenicia itself, but are known from Sardinia and North Africa; and in the precinct of the goddess Tanit (who may be equivalent to Astarte) at Salammbo, Carthage, 'thousands of urns containing the cremated remains of small children . . . have been found'.[47] These were apparently the sacrifices described as *mlk 'dm* in Punic, the *humana victima* of Pliny.[48]

But not only were human beings sacrificed to appease the gods, Phoenician theology also posited sacrifice of gods by gods. According to U. Oldenburg,[49] Ba'al and Anat were Amorite deities who overthrew and mutilated the Canaanite deity El; in subsequent battles both Ba'al Hadad and El were killed, but Hadad came to life again when Anat slew his murderer Mot. It must be admitted that the Old Testament prophets had a strong case for condemning what may inclusively be called Ba'alism! This is so, even though some allowance should be made for the fact that most accounts have come down to us—whether in the Old Testament or in classical authors—through commentators who are unsympathetic for religious or political reasons, or both.

No mention of Phoenician religion in connection with the Bible would be complete without reference to the conflict between Yahwism and Ba'alism in the days of Elijah (1 Kings 16: 31 ff.). When Jezebel, daughter of Ethba'al, King of the Sidonians (1 Kings 16: 31), left her palace home at Tyre to become the wife of Ahab, she brought with her the worship of Melqart, literally 'King of the City', equated by Greek writers with Herakles. The 'city' could quite well refer to Tyre, but in the view of some scholars[50] it is more than likely that it refers to the underworld. Others, not necessarily inconsistently—such is the fluidity of conception—would identify him with Ba'al Shamem, 'Lord of Heaven', a solar deity.[51] The missionary zeal of Jezebel *c.* 874 B.C. may reflect some outburst of national energy reflected in the dominating position of Ethbaal, King of the Sidonians (1 Kings 16: 31), and the establishment of Carthage as a Tyrian colony in 814. This would make more possible still the equation of Melqart with the favourite god of other princedoms. Indeed, of the many divine names which are invoked to buttress the curses in the treaty of Esarhaddon with his vassal, a seventh-century king of Tyre,[52] most seem to be hypostases of Melqart and his consort Astarte, rather than distinct gods in their own right. Anat and Eshmun, who also occur in the list, are, of course, independent deities who were amongst the best-known all over the Levant; maybe the god Pumay was less widely recognized, but he is named in the Nora inscription from Sardinia, and appears in the name of Pumayyaton (Greek form, Pygmalion), King of Tyre. He is thought to have been originally a Cyprian deity.

The question how far the Phoenicians took over pre-Phoenician deities is not easy to answer satisfactorily. Even the existence of pre-Phoenician place-names is a very vexed question.[53] It appears, however, that the Philistines, their neighbours and possibly successors in the southern areas of once-Phoenician territory, took over from them the worship of the corn-god Dagan (biblical Dagon, Jud. 16: 23; 1 Sam. 5: 1–5), who is known from several other sources. The Philistines also seem to have taken over from the Phoenicians the god of fire, lightning, and pestilence, who was called Resheph (Hab. 3: 5). He has sometimes been identified with Mekal, Lord of Beth-Shan, following the discovery of a votive stele to the latter in a Canaanite sacred area at Beth-Shan, in which the god seems to have the attributes normally linked with figures of Resheph.[54] From two parallel lists in Ugarit it appears that Resheph was identified with Mesopotamian Nergal, a god associated in the same way with pestilence, war, death, and the underworld. Both had as their sacred emblem the gazelle, and, when Resheph was adopted by the Egyptians, he became very popular there during the New Kingdom; as the victory-bringing warrior god, he is often depicted with a gazelle head mounted on his helmet. Furthermore, we learn from Egyptian magical texts that Resheph had a consort named Atum or Adum, maybe meaning 'red earth' and indicating a goddess of the underworld. Although her presence has not yet been verified in Phoenicia or Israel, Albright has suggested that Obed-edom (2 Sam. 6: 10–12; 1 Chr. 15: 24 f.) was a convert from her worship.[55] The Greeks called Resheph 'Apollo' because of his similar characteristics.

Several temples and simpler sanctuaries to various gods have been excavated in and near the cities of Phoenicia, one of the oldest being at Aphka, at the source of the river Adonis (Nahr Ibrahim), which runs into the Mediterranean near Byblos. At a certain season of the year the river ran red; this was taken to be due to the killing of Adonis, and was a cue for the annual mourning rites, which, apparently, were efficacious in bringing about his resuscitation. The theme of the dying-and-rising god is, of course, known elsewhere, e.g. at Ugarit, and similar lamentations seem to be referred to in Zechariah 12: 11, the relevant god being Hadad-Rimmon.[56] On the slopes of Mt. Lebanon it is not surprising that trees were venerated, and a grove sacred to Astarte grew near the Aphka sanctuary. Elsewhere, too, a symbolic pole, the biblical Asherah (2 Kings 23: 6 etc.), was often used to represent the goddess. It stood near the open-air altar of the 'high place' (*bāmâ*), together with the stone pillar called a *maṣṣeḇâ* (Gen. 28: 18–19), also known as a *baitulos* or 'house of god', which represented the male deity. These symbols are depicted on coins of the late period, and one from the reign of the Roman emperor Macrinus (A.D. 217) shows not only such a baetyl but, in addition, a roofed temple and an open-air precinct.[57] But the best description of a Phoenician temple is undoubtedly the account in 1 Kings 6–7 of the temple which Hiram of Tyre built for Solomon in Jerusalem, with its typically Phoenician decoration, based largely on Egyptian motifs.[58]

In the realm of art, more examples of Phoenician arts and crafts have come to light outside the bounds of Phoenicia than within them. Byblos and Ugarit—the two most fully excavated cities of this coast—have certainly yielded noteworthy buildings and objects from the Bronze Ages,[59] but Iron Age finds are scarce from any sites in Phoenicia, and after a long gap it is only in the Graeco-Roman period that a significant increase in the number of noteworthy artefacts is recorded.

(iv) *Trade and Influence*

As stated earlier, the Phoenicians were above all else middlemen. They accepted ideas, methods, and processes from every quarter. Egyptian influence is particularly evident in their ivory carving; they show more affinity with Mycenaean and other Aegean types where pottery is concerned; in seal-cutting on the other hand, especially cylinder seals, Mesopotamian prototypes are fairly closely copied. Lastly, Asia Minor, probably their earliest rich source of metallic ores, provided the pattern for their metalwork.

These four examples of sources from which Phoenicia derived inspiration and was an obvious borrower all concern comparatively small and easily transportable objects. Furthermore, with the exception of pottery, the exercise of Phoenician workmanship was directed to finishing processes on imported materials. This tendency may be attributed to the fact that Phoenicia possessed only a very limited range of raw materials, the main ones being cedar and other hardwoods from her mountains, and two types of sea snail from along her coasts, *Murex brandaris* and *Murex trunculus*, from which the famous Tyrian purple (really a range of colours from reddish-brown to deep purple) was distilled, and then used to dye those woollen goods that possibly gave the Phoenicians/Canaanites not only their stock-in-trade but their very name. The poet Browning remarks:

> Who has not heard how Tyrian shells
>   Enclosed the blue, that dye of dyes
> Whereof one drop worked miracles,
>   And coloured like Astarte's eyes

Raw silk the merchant sells?

. . .

. . . Who fished the murex up?[60]

Mounds of waste shells left over from this malodorous industrial process may still be found along the Phoenician coast, though over-exploitation or some other cause has made the living murex a much rarer creature there than on neighbouring shores. The wool for dyeing was presumably obtained from the hinterland's nomadic shepherds. Amos may have traded his wool to some Tyrian factor (Amos 7: 14; 6: 1–2; 1: 9–10); Mesha, King of Moab, at least, was a wool producer in a big way of business, whose rebellion against the successors of Ahab and Jezebel might have been an attempt to cut out the middleman and deal directly with Tyre (2 Kings 3: 4–5). Tiglath-pileser III (745–727) mentions 'garments of their native [industries being made of] dark purple wool' amongst the tribute he exacted from rulers in the west, including Sibitti-baʿali of Byblos and Matan-baʿal of Arvad.[61]

Phoenicia's other main native product, and, apparently, its only heavy industry, cedarwood lumbering, has also become extinct because of exhaustion of supplies. For centuries the Phoenicians supplied the rulers of Egypt and Mesopotamia with massive timbers, either for payment,[62] or as tribute,[63] and Solomon too obtained his building timber from the same source (1 Kings 5: 8 ff.). But the Phoenicians were not content to treat their priceless heritage as mere lumber to be shipped out as bulk cargo. Solomon's temple had its inner sanctuary lined with cedar panelling; and wooden coffins were used in Phoenicia, and may have provided the models for stone sarcophagi. Possibly indeed some of the wooden coffins found in Lower Egypt were fashioned by Phoenician joiners.[64] Their expertise in ivory work demands a flourishing wood-carving tradition already in being, and that delicately carved cedar panels should have figured in export orders, along with ivory inlays and reliefs, such as those found in the remains of Esarhaddon's palace at Calah/Nimrud. The Phoenician provenance of these ivory panels is proved by the discovery of Phoenician tally marks inscribed on the back to make sure that they were fitted together in the right sequence. Some idea of the variety of goods available in Phoenicia may be gathered from the lists of spoil and tribute taken by various invaders. The Egyptians seem to have concentrated on horses, chariots, and precious metals as such,[65] but the Assyrian monarchs are often more detailed in their descriptions: e.g., Tiglath-pileser III, on one of his raids to the west, took home 'gold, silver, tin, iron, elephant-hides, ivory, linen garments with multicoloured trimmings, blue-dyed wool, purple-dyed wool, ebony-wood, boxwood-wood, whatever was precious enough for a royal treasure; also lambs whose stretched hides were dyed purple, [and] wild birds whose spread-out wings were dyed blue'.[66]

The presence of suitable timber near at hand meant that Phoenicia became famous for ship-building as well as seafaring. The evidence, from Assyrian monuments mainly, suggests that the Phoenicians built three main types of ship. Largest was the long 'Tarshish ship', so called either because it sailed to and fro from one of the cities called Tarshish (e.g. Tarsus, later St. Paul's home town in Asia Minor, or Tartessus in Spain, or even a Tarsisi in Sardinia),[67] or because it was a carrier of metallic ores or copper ingots,[68] since 'Tarshish' is said to mean 'smelting plant', 'refinery'.[69] Solomon and Hiram joined to build a fleet of Tarshish ships at Ezion-geber at the head of the Gulf of Aqaba, and, using that as their home port, sent out trading missions which might be away from base for up to three years at a time (1 Kings 9: 26–8, 10: 11–12, 22). The advantage to Hiram apparently would be that his agreement with Solomon enabled him to bypass Egypt and so save on tolls. The Tarshish ships illustrated on the monuments were obviously armed; they are hung around with a row of shields and have armed warriors on the top deck. Propulsion was by two banks of oars, and there was also a short mast; the stern curves up and then in, like a crescent, whereas the prow drops straight down until it meets an obviously offensive forward-projecting keelson ending in a pointed ram.[70]

Another type of sea-going ship looks quite different; both bow and stern posts curve up to the vertical and end in a sort of flat capital, so that, in side elevation, the ship looks like a deepish bowl. These ships have no mast, but, like the Tarshish ships, have two banks of oars and were steered by two sweeps projecting astern; also they carried a complement of marines on the top deck, which was hung around with shields. It has been suggested that these were the ships called *gauloi* in Greek and *golah* in Phoenician,[71] and that they were used for local coastal trips. The Greeks called one type of boat used by the Phoenicians *hippos*, 'horse', and the name obviously derives from the carved bowpost of these boats, which are illustrated on a wall relief from the palace of Sargon II at Khorsabad,[72] and on the famous Balawat gate of Shalmaneser III.[73] The two *hippoi* on the Balawat bronze are particularly interesting, because they seem to be double-ended ferry boats. Not only do they have a horse's head bow and stern, but they appear to be running a shuttle service between island and mainland Tyre, the boatmen pulling the loaded boats across by means of a rope stretched from shore to shore. The superscription reads, 'I received the tribute (brought) on ships from the inhabitants of Tyre and Sidon.'[74]

Since the Phoenicians were traders, and since they had developed a fleet—in the first place possibly to avoid the arduous land route to Egypt—it is not surprising that they carried their wares overseas to the major coastal and island settlements to the west. Until the downfall of the Minoan and Mycenaean powers under the hammer-blows of northern invaders around 1200 B.C., it is possible that lack of naval supremacy kept the Phoenicians from going far afield.[75] After this date the route west was more open—pirates were an occupational hazard anyway—and some would suggest that the Phoenicians received substantial co-operation from scattered groups of Mycenaeans, who now joined forces with the less harried Phoenicians, and let them into some of the secrets of navigating remunerative trade routes. At all events their fleet soon circled the entire Mediterranean.

Phoenician sailing expertise is well indicated by the feat whereby, at the command of pharaoh Necho, they circumnavigated the whole of Africa *c.* 600 B.C., travelling clockwise from the Red Sea and taking three years for the voyage.[76] Later, *c.* 450, sailors from the Tyrian colony of Carthage sailed as far as Britain under admiral Hamilco, probably testing the practicability of a sea route to come by Cornish tin.[77] A little later again, Hanno sailed from Carthage down the west coast of Africa, maybe as far as the Niger, and when he got back he wrote an account of his voyage which was inscribed in the temple of Ba'al Hammon. A somewhat garbled Greek version is still extant.[78] Madeira and the Azores may have been discovered by accident,[79] but the alleged discovery of an authentic Phoenician inscription at Paraibo in Brazil is still regarded with scepticism.[80]

Settlements on the Levant coast, both north and south of their own land, would almost certainly have been the earliest foreign bases for the Phoenicians. Since their ships depended for their progress on rowing rather than on sailing, and since it was the practice to travel by daylight and to anchor or run their vessels ashore overnight, during storms, and for the duration of the winter season, friendly stopping-places at fairly close intervals along their established trade routes were clearly necessary.[81] What more likely, therefore, than that they would seek to establish chains of such shelter-cum-trading posts, in the first place, on the route to their earliest customer, Egypt? South of Tyre, Achzib and Acco could be regarded as within Phoenicia's territorial limits. Even south of Mt. Carmel the little ports of Dor and Joppa are claimed for Sidon by Eshmunazar *c.* 450, which suggests that previously they may have had not a wholly Phoenician affiliation but perhaps a Phoenician quarter.[82] Such could well have been true also of Ascalon and Gaza, and of other smaller places such as Retabe in the Nile delta where typical Phoenician pottery has been discovered. Gaza, it might be noted, was ruled in the eighth century by a certain Hanno,[83] a good Phoenician name.

A more striking demonstration of Phoenician influence was the discovery of eighth-century inscriptions in Phoenician script and language at Zinjirli (Sam'al) and Karatepe (Azitawanda) in Asia Minor. The inscriptions in Old Phoenician, besides being the longest discovered in that language, were also the key to the decipherment of Hittite hieroglyphic writing, the language of Azitawandas, the local ruler who set up the series of bilinguals, not apparently from any colonizing efforts of the Phoenicians themselves, but rather because it had become a lingua franca for purposes of trade.[84]

Once the idea of establishing Phoenician nuclei or cells abroad showed its worth, it cannot have been long before the possibilities of Cyprus would strike the mainlanders. This island is regarded by most as being the Alashia mentioned in Egyptian records of the second millennium B.C., in the Amarna Letters, and also by the Hittites.[85]

Cyprus possessed much to attract the Phoenician—good harbours and natural resources, pastoral, agricultural, and above all mineral.

It was so rich in copper[86] that *Kupros* the island gave the Greeks their name for the metal. Though the island had been inhabited since at least Neolithic times, perhaps the first, and certainly the foremost, Phoenician settlement seems to have been Kition on the south coast at Larnaka. This was founded *c.* 1000 B.C., but there is as yet no agreement whether it was a Phoenician colony before 700. Mycenaeans also inhabited the island in some force, as either colleagues or competitors, but it is not easy to distinguish between their respective settlements, owing to their influence on one another's artefacts.[87]

The name 'Kition' does not occur in the Assyrian records of conquest, but it has been supposed that Qartihadasti ('Newtown') may be another name for it, and if so then its King Damusi was among the ten rulers of Cyprus (Assyrian *Yadnana*) who submitted to Esarhaddon.[88]

The Old Testament seems to use the word 'Kittim', which apparently is the same as Kition, for Cypriotes as such (Isa. 23: 1, 12) and even for the inhabitants of other islands too (Jer. 2: 10; Ezek. 27: 6). The inhabitants of Cyprus are referred to as Kitti by the Phoenicians themselves.[89] The biblical genealogy (Gen. 10: 4; 1 Chr. 1: 7) calls the Kittim 'sons of Javan', i.e. Ionians (Greeks), and maybe stresses the Mycenaean element in the island populace from early times. Equally, though, it might reflect the growing southward penetration of the later Greeks, who competed vigorously with the Phoenicians for Mediterranean trade, e.g. in Cyprus itself the Greeks colonized Salamis on the opposite side of the island as a rival to Kition.

A detailed account of Phoenician colonization further afield is not particularly relevant for the Phoenicians as a people of the Old Testament, except that the number of sites at which Phoenician remains have been found is constantly growing. In 1965 there were thirteen known sites on Cyprus, only a few in the Aegean (because of rivalry from the Greeks), but sixteen on the foot and ankle of Italy, twenty on Sicily, ten on Sardinia, and twenty-one along the North African coast; another nine sites are spread over Corsica, southern France, southern Spain, and the Balearics.[90] Even if several of these prove to be little more than casual deposits, indicating a temporary rather than a permanent settlement, the total is remarkable.

Traditionally the earliest settlement in the west was at Gades (Cadiz) on the Atlantic coast of southern Spain, founded in the twelfth century[91] on what was then a small islet at the mouth of the Guadalete, an excellent spot from which to ship the ores mined at Spanish Tarshish or Tartessus some miles inland.

Utica was founded in Tunisia *c.* 1100, B.C. but the most famous Phoenician colony is undoubtedly Carthage, which is also the best known from literature (mostly Latin) and from archaeology. Eusebius quotes a Sicilian historian named Philistus, to the effect that Carthage was founded before 1200 by 'Zor and Carchedon' (Tyre and Carthage), but little credence is given to what appears to be an aetiological fable. Some scholars even doubt the much better authenticated tradition which gives the year 814 as the year when Jezebel's grand-niece Elissa or Elisha, later called Dido, brought a group of sympathizers from her native Tyre, and a band of hierodules from Cyprus, to found a *Qartihadasti* (Newtown) at this spot, with the support of neighbouring Utica. Carthage eventually eclipsed not only other Phoenician colonies but even the cities of the motherland itself, until the commercial and territorial jealousy of Rome, after considerable uncertainty as to the outcome, finally led to the complete destruction of the city and its hegemony in 146 B.C., after the third and last Punic, i.e. Phoenician, war.

Many of the remains of Phoenician occupation found on the islands of the western Mediterranean, and even on the mainland of Spain, leave the question open, whether they were colonized from the motherland or were secondary foundations established by Carthage. Sardinia, once thought to be one of the later scenes of colonization, has already yielded the Nora inscription, which may be as early as the ninth century, though other evidence from the same site appears to be slightly later. In either event, these early dates suggest that in Sardinia, and perhaps elsewhere, Carthage in due course took over from Tyre colonies founded considerably earlier.

It causes some surprise that Phoenicia, after enjoying such a wide-reaching superiority at sea, and controlling the Mediterranean trade routes for so long, never became an empire. There may be other reasons, but one of them must be the low moral fibre indicated by, if not also in part induced by, a religion of fierce and unethical selfishness; then there was the lack of a sufficiently productive home base—Carthage, it may be remembered, soon eclipsed the home country for this very reason—and lastly, Phoenicia was too open to attack. Egypt, Assyria, Babylonia, Persia, and Greece, one after another, bled her white. Even lesser nations, such as the Aramaeans and the Hebrews, and possibly the Sea Peoples,[92] could embarrass the Phoenicians by being astride the land routes used by them.

However, had the literature of the Phoenician people been less inadequately preserved, we might the more readily appreciate many of their excellences. Even as it is, their contribution to the development of civilization, most notably on its practical side, leaves us all in their debt—were it only that they made it possible for those who are not professional scribes to write and to read this volume! Perhaps more than any other people before them, they made the world a more easily known, and a better-looking place.

NOTES

1. See below, Bibliography.

2. e.g. M. Dunand, 'Phénicie', *Supplément au Dictionnaire de la Bible*, ed. L. Pirot *et al.*, fasc. 40 (Letouzey et Ané, Paris, 1965), cols. 1141 ff.

3. One biblical list (Jud. 1: 31) adds Acco, Ahlab/Helba, Achzib, Aphik, and Rehob; another (Josh. 19: 28–30) is less straightforward but adds at least Achzib and Ummah. The Mehebel or Mahalab mentioned here was probably the same as Ahlab and Helba in Jud. 1: 31, and has been identified with Khirbet el-Mahālib, about 8 km. north-east of Tyre, mentioned as Mahalliba or Mahalab in several Akkadian lists. (See D. J. Wiseman, 'A Fragmentary Inscription of Tiglath-pileser III from Nimrud', *Iraq* xviii (1956), 129.)

4. Translated in part in *A.N.E.T.*, pp. 234 ff.

5. Dunand, op. cit. col. 1155.

6. *The Dawn of Civilization*, ed. S. Piggott, pp. 168, 188 (see n. 20).

7. K. M. Kenyon, *Amorites and Canaanites*, Schweich Lectures 1963 (Oxford University Press, London, 1966), p. 59.

8. D. Harden, *The Phoenicians*, pp. 22, 219, quoting Augustine, 'Ep. ad Romanos', from Migne, *Pat. Lat.*, vol. 35, col. 2096 (see n. 40). It might be noted also that in Matt. 15: 22 'Canaanite' is used for the 'Syro-Phoenician' of Mark 7: 26.

9. On Zemar see A. van Selms in *Oudtestamentische Studiën* xii. 187.

10. See S. R. Driver, *The Book of Genesis*, Westminster Commentary (Methuen, London, 1904), pp. 113 f.; H. G. May & B. M. Metzger, *The Oxford Annotated Bible* (Oxford University Press, 1962), p. 12.

J. Skinner, *A Critical and Exegetical Commentary on Genesis*, I.C. Comm. (Clark, Edinburgh, 1912), p. 193, argues for a geographical arrangement.

11. G. Steindorff & K. C. Seele, *When Egypt Ruled the East* (University of Chicago Press, 1942), p. 21.

12. S. Moscati, *The World of the Phoenicians*, p. 16, accepts the emendation 'Simyra' here, though R. de Vaux, 'La Phénicie et les Peuples de la Mer', *Mélanges de l'Université Saint-Joseph* xlv (Beirut, 1969), 484, speaks of an Amurru which lay north of the Egyptian province of Canaan. Originally Amorite meant simply 'Westerner', and was a loan-word from Sumerian (see pp. 102 ff). See Albright, *B.A.N.E.*, p. 353 n. 17.

13. *A.N.E.T.*, p. 276.

14. Albright, *B.A.N.E.*, p. 356 n. 50.

15. See the interesting treatment by M. C. Astour, 'The Origin of the Terms "Canaan", "Phoenician", and "Purple"', *J.N.E.S.* xxiv (1965), 346–50.

16. *A.N.E.T.*, p. 21 n. 34; p. 234 n. 18. Kenyon, op. cit. 59, suggests that the Greeks adopted the Egyptian name 'Fenkhu'—which means 'woodworker'—but assimilated it to their own word *phoinix*, 'purple'.

17. So Kenyon, op. cit. 57 ff. Albright, *B.A.N.E.*, p. 332, however, claims that the Canaanites 'may well have been settled in Palestine and southern Syria as early as the fourth millennium'.

18. This may be the best place to draw attention to the view of B. Mazar, in *B.A.S.O.R.* cii (1946), 7–12, who argues that *k^ena'ani* meant first 'trader', then 'trader in purple', and lastly 'Canaanite' (ethnically).

19. *A.N.E.T.*, p. 227. A. Gardiner, *Egypt of the Pharaohs* (Oxford, 1964), p. 89, seems to interpret the text differently.

20. W. Cullican, 'The First Merchant Venturers: The Sea Peoples of the Levant', in *The Dawn of Civilization*, ed. S. Piggott, p. 151.

21. The site is illustrated in G. Daniel, *The First Civilizations* (Penguin Books, Harmondsworth, 1971), Pl. 19. An artist's impression of how the boat originally looked occurs in the reconstruction of Khufu's funeral procession in L. Casson, *Ancient Egypt* (Time–Life International, 1966), p. 138.

22. Cf. J. A. Wilson, 'Egyptian Culture and Religion', in *B.A.N.E.*, p. 303.

23. *A.N.E.T.*, p. 268. An interesting account of temporary Assyrian control of the Phoenician timber trade—forbidding export to Egypt and Philistia—and other affairs is found in two letters from the Assyrian Governor of Tyre to Tiglath-pileser III, written between 738 and 734. (See Letters XII and XIII in H. W. F. Saggs, 'The Nimrud Letters, 1952—Part II', *Iraq* xvii (1955), 127 ff.)

24. *A.N.E.T.*, p. 291; *D.O.T.T.*, pp. 73 f. Sennacherib made the Phoenicians actually build him a flotilla at Nineveh and Til Barsip, to hunt down Merodach-Baladan (2 Kings 20: 12–19; Isa. 39); see A. T. Olmstead, *History of Assyria* (Chicago, 1951), p. 290.

25. *A.N.E.T.*, p. 240.

26. *A.N.E.T.*, p. 28.

27. See, e.g., Albright, *B.A.N.E.*, p. 354 n. 25.

28. See *A.O.T.S.*, pp. 145–67.

29. Cf. *B.A.N.E.*, pp. 339 f.

30. Dunand, op. cit. col. 1176.

31. So *B.A.N.E.*, p. 340.

32. Two well-known works which deal at length with the history of writing are D. Diringer, *The Alphabet*, 3rd edn. (2 vols., Hutchinson, London, 1968); and G. R. Driver, *Semitic Writing: From Pictograph to Alphabet*, 3rd edn. (Oxford University Press, 1966). A useful outline is given in M. Noth, *The Old Testament World* (A. & C. Black, 1966), pp. 202–23.

33. Further examples may be culled from J. Friedrich, *Phönizisch-Punische Grammatik* (Analecta Orientalia 32, Rome, 1951).

34. *K.A.I.*, pp. 1–32.

35. The more important ones are translated in *A.N.E.T.*, pp. 501–5 and 653–62.

36. Herodotus, ii. 96.

37. See L. Casson, *Ancient Egypt*, p. 143, for a short description of the process.

38. Cf. how Wenamun speaks of Zakar-baʿal of Byblos producing and reading before him 'the journal rolls of his fathers', *A.N.E.T.*, p. 27.

39. I. ix. 20–x. 54; IV. xvi. 6; X. ix. 11–12. See O. Eissfeldt, *Sanchunjaton von Berut und Ilumilku von Ugarit* (Halle, 1952); id., *Taautos und Sanchunjaton* (Berlin, 1952).

40. The quotations are taken from J. E. Hirsch-Davies, *Eusebius' Praeparatio Evangelica* (Lampeter, 1904). The Greek text may be found in J. P. Migne, *Pat. Gr.*, vol. 21 (Paris, 1857), col. 75. The relevant passages are in Bk. I, Ch. x (ll. 31 ff.).

41. *A.N.E.T.*, pp. 328–9; *A.N.E.P.*, no. 593.

42. R. Dussaud, *Les Religions des Hittites et des Hourrites, des Phéniciens et des Syriens* (Paris, 1945), p. 358.

43. *A.N.E.T.*, p. 656.

44. *A.R.I.*, p. 73.

45. Most works dealing with Phoenician religion draw on the whole Near Eastern area, especially Ugarit, for details, e.g. *A.R.I.*, Dussaud, Harden, and Moscati. This is justifiable, but has been avoided as far as possible here.

46. Some instances and references may be found in W. R. Smith, *Lectures on the Religion of the Semites*, 3rd edn. (A. and C. Black, London, 1927), pp. 329, 611 ff.

47. Harden, op. cit. 95.

48. For a good treatment of the evidence for Israel and Carthage see R. de Vaux, *Studies in Old Testament Sacrifice* (University of Wales Press, Cardiff, 1964), pp. 52–90.

49. 'The Conflict between El and Baʿal in Canaanite Religion', Suppl. ad *Numen*, Ser. II, vol. iii (Brill, Leiden, 1969).

50. e.g., *A.R.I.*, p. 196 n. 29.

51. See further the present writer, 'Elijah on Mount Carmel', *P.E.Q.* xcii (1960), 146 ff.

52. *A.N.E.T.*, p. 534.

53. Albright, *B.A.N.E.*, p. 352 n. 7; Kenyon, 'Syria and Palestine, *c.* 2160–1780 B.C.', *C.A.H.* I, Part ii, 568 f. (= fasc. 29 (1965), p. 36).

54. So G. M. Fitzgerald, *A.O.T.S.*, p. 189, following L. H. Vincent in *R.B.* xxxvii (1938), 512–43.

55. *Y.G.C.*, pp. 121 ff.

56. *A.R.I.*, p. 80.

57. Illustrated in Moscati, op. cit. 48, fig. 4.

58. Cf. Harden, op. cit. 91 ff., and Eissfeldt, 'The Hebrew Kingdom', *C.A.H.* II, Ch. xxxiv (= fasc. 32 (1965), pp. 24–33).

59. Finds from both sites are usually published in *Syria*; the excavations at Byblos are published in M. Dunand, *Fouilles de Byblos*, and those at Ugarit in the series *Mission de Ras Shamra* (1939–).

60. 'Popularity'. I am indebted to my colleague the Revd. D. Eirwyn Morgan for reminding me of this example, among many instances, of this poet's obvious interest in biblical and classical antiquities.

61. *A.N.E.T.*, p. 282.

62. Cf. Tale of Wenamun, ii. 3–9, *A.N.E.T.*, p. 27.

63. e.g., Esarhaddon, *A.N.E.T.*, p. 291.

64. Harden, op. cit. 141.

65. e.g., the Asiatic campaigns of Thutmose III, *A.N.E.T.*, pp. 237 ff.

66. *A.N.E.T.*, p. 283.

67. Albright, *B.A.N.E.*, p. 361 n. 103.

68. A number of smelted hide-shaped ingots of copper were recovered from a Late Bronze Age wreck off the south coast of Asia Minor in 1959—the oldest shipwrecked cargo ever found—and illustrated in the *National Geographic Magazine* (May 1960).

69. Albright, *B.A.N.E.*, p. 347.

70. *A.N.E.P.*, no. 106; Harden, op. cit., Pl. 50.

71. Harden, op. cit. 169, referring to R. D. Barnett in *Antiquity* xxxii (1958), 227.

72. Harden, op. cit., Pl. 48, 49; *A.N.E.P.*, no. 107.

73. *A.N.E.P.*, no. 356, taken from L. W. King, *Bronze Reliefs from the Gates of Shalmaneser* (B.M., London, 1915), Pl. 13. Layard in his *Popular Account of Discoveries at Nineveh* (John Murray, London, 1852), pp. 326–9, gives drawings of each of the three types of ship, and suggests that the sternpost of the *hippos*, of equal height with the bow, ends in a fishtail in order to give it 'the shape of a seamonster'. He also suggests that the tulip-shaped mast included a crow's nest to accommodate an archer, as on certain Egyptian sculptures.

74. *A.N.E.P.*, no. 356, p. 291; *A.N.E.T.*, p. 281.

75. But cf. Albright, *B.A.N.E.*, pp. 337, 344.

76. Herodotus iv. 42; for Solomon's three-year voyages, see above p. 276.

77. Daniel & Evans, 'The Western Mediterranean', *C.A.H.* II, Ch. xxxvii (= fasc. 57 (1967), p. 55).

78. Moscati, pp. 182 f., gives an English translation.

79. Moscati, p. 184.

80. See O. Eissfeldt in *J.S.S.* xv (1970), 102, reviewing L. Delekat, *Phönizier in Amerika*.

81. Though tents were normally carried, too, on longer voyages, see J. P. Brown, 'Peace Symbolism', *V.T.* xxi (1971), 22, citing Skylax, *Periplus*, the 4th-cent. admiralty guide.

82. Cf. the position between Samaria and Damascus, regarding land trade, in 1 Kings 20: 34.

83. *A.N.E.T.*, pp. 282–5.

84. Translation in *A.N.E.T.*, pp. 653–5. For a good popular account see C. W. Ceram, *Narrow Pass, Black Mountain* (London, 1956).

85. Catling, 'Cyprus in the Early Bronze Age Periods', *C.A.H.* I, Part ii, Ch. xxvi (*b*) (= fasc. 43 (1966), pp. 58–62). For a dissenting view see R. S. Merrilees in *P.E.Q.* c (1968), 66.

86. Catling, ibid., pp. 70–2.

87. Cf. Desborough & Hammond, 'The End of Mycenean Civilization and the Ark Age', *C.A.H.* II, Ch. xxxvi (= fasc. 13 (1962), pp. 12 f.); Catling, loc. cit. 67 ff.

88. *A.N.E.T.*, p. 291. A similar claim is made by Ashurbanipal, ibid., p. 294. Sargon, ibid., p. 284, claims that he was the first Assyrian monarch to receive tribute from Cyprus, 'an island in the Western Sea at a distance of seven days'.

89. *K.A.I.*, 14: 18–19.

90. As shown on the maps in Moscati, op. cit. 245–50.

91. So Velleius Paterculus, *Historia Romana* i. 2. 4; supported by Strabo i. 3. 2. Both are cited by Harden, op. cit., p. 222 n. 36.

92. R. de Vaux, op. cit., p. 489, considers that relations between the Sea People settled in Palestine and the Phoenicians were mainly cordial.

BIBLIOGRAPHY

ALBRIGHT, W. F., *Archaeology and the Religion of Israel*, 3rd edn. (Johns Hopkins Press, Baltimore, 1953).

—— 'The Role of the Canaanites in the History of Civilization', *The Bible and the Ancient Near East*, ed. G. E. Wright (Routlege & Kegan Paul, London, 1961), pp. 328–62.

—— 'Syria, the Philistines and Phoenicia', *Cambridge Ancient History*, vol. II, rev. edn., Ch. xxxiii, fasc. 51 (Cambridge, 1968).

—— *Yahweh and the Gods of Canaan: a Historical Analysis of Two Contrasting Faiths*, Jordan Lectures 1965, University of London (Athlone Press, London, 1968).

AP-THOMAS, D. R., 'Elijah on Mount Carmel', *P.E.Q.* xcii (1960), 146 ff.

BARAMKI, D., *Phoenicia and the Phoenicians* (Khayat, Beirut, 1961).

BOTTÉRO, J., 'Syria and Palestine *c.* 2160–1780 B.C.', *Cambridge Ancient History*, vol. I., rev. edn., Ch. xxi, fasc. 29 (Cambridge, 1965).

BROWN, J. P., *The Lebanon and Phoenicia: Ancient Texts Illustrating their Physical Geography and Native Industries*, vol. i (American University of Beirut Centennial Publications, Beirut, 1969).

CATLING, H. W., 'Cyprus in the Neolithic and Bronze Age Periods', *Cambridge Ancient History*, vol. II, rev. edn., Ch. xxii (*b*), fasc. 43, (Cambridge, 1966).

CULLICAN, W., 'The First Merchant Venturers: The Sea Peoples of the Levant', *The Dawn of Civilization*, ed. S. Piggott (Thames & Hudson, London, 1961), pp. 133–60.

DANIEL, G. and EVANS, J. D., 'The Western Mediterranean', *Cambridge Ancient History*, vol. II, rev. edn., Ch. xxxvii, fasc. 57 (Cambridge, 1967).

DESBOROUGH, V. R. D'A. & HAMMOND, N. G. L., 'The End of the Mycenaean Civilizations and the Dark Age', *Cambridge Ancient History*, vol. II, rev. edn., Ch. xxxvi, fasc. 13 (Cambridge, 1962).

DE VAUX, R., 'La Phénicie et les Peuples de la Mer', *Mélanges de l'Université Saint-Joseph* xlv, fasc. 29 (Beirut, 1969).

DIRINGER, D., *The Alphabet*, 3rd edn. (2 vols., Hutchinson, London, 1968).

DRIVER, G. R., *Semitic Writing: From Pictograph to Alphabet*, Schweich Lectures 1944, British Academy, 3rd edn. (London, 1966).

DROWER, M. S., 'Ugarit', *Cambridge Ancient History*, vol. II, rev. edn., Ch. xxi, fasc. 63 (Cambridge, 1968).

DUNAND, M., 'Phénicie', *Supplément au Dictionnaire de la Bible*, ed. L. Pirot *et al.*, fasc. 40 (Paris, 1965), cols. 1141–1204.

DUSSAUD, R., *Les religions des Hittites et des Hourrites, des Phéniciens et des Syriens* (Paris, 1945).

EISSFELDT, O., 'The Hebrew Kingdom', *Cambridge Ancient History*, vol. II, rev. edn., Ch. xxxiv, fasc. 32 (Cambridge, 1965).

HARDEN, D., *The Phoenicians* (Ancient Peoples and Places, Thames & Hudson, London, 1962).

KENYON, K. M., *Amorites and Canaanites*, Schweich Lectures 1963, British Academy (London, 1966).

MOSCATI, S., *The World of the Phoenicians*, Eng. trans. by A. Hamilton (Weidenfeld & Nicolson, London, 1968).

NOTH, M., *The Old Testament World*, Eng. trans. by V. I. Gruhn (A. & C. Black, London, 1966).

PRITCHARD, J. B., *A.N.E.P.*, 2nd edn. (University Press, Princeton, N.J., 1969).

—— *A.N.E.T.*, 3rd edn. (University Press, Princeton, N.J., 1969).

WARD, W. A. (ed.), *The Role of the Phoenicians in the Interaction of Mediterranean Civilizations* (American University of Beirut Centennial Publications, Beirut, 1968).

XII

THE ARABS AND ETHIOPIANS

A. K. IRVINE

To the casual reader the impact of the outside world on the early history of Israel is most strikingly felt in terms of her mighty neighbours, the Assyrians, Babylonians, Egyptians, Phoenicians, and Hittites, the more so in the light of the impressive material results of a century and a half of intensive excavation in the Near East and the ever-increasing understanding of their literary remains. Yet it could scarcely be argued that this is any more than an accident of the Holy Land's geographical situation in antiquity. When we turn our attention to her closest neighbour, Arabia, the picture alters significantly. Although references to the Arabs are not infrequent in the Old Testament, particularly in the later books, yet with a handful of notable exceptions they are vague and imprecise, betraying no more than a superficial acquaintance with the nomadic hordes and the inhabitants of the oases of Northern Arabia, Syria, and Mesopotamia with whom the Jews inevitably came into contact through their trading interests. The real legacy of the Arabs to the Jews must be sought, not in anything material, of which the bedouin had precious little to give, but in the psychological values, the mores, rites, and customs which, transplanted into the settled milieu of the Fertile Crescent, made of the Jews a nation in the spiritual sense which could survive every attempt to crush them. The Arabs have been described as Semites biologically, psychologically, socially, and linguistically,[1] and the isolation and uniformity of desert life has made of the Arabian Peninsula a store-house of almost every spiritual value which is now looked on as typically Semitic, so that it comes as no surprise that almost any page of the Old Testament can bring to the reader's mind the picture of the typical bedouin.[2] No one has brought this out more forcibly than J. H. Montgomery, whose *Arabia and the Bible*, albeit published in 1934, when our knowledge of ancient Arabian history and chronology was somewhat defective, can still maintain a position of authority in the literature on the subject, at least when dealing with the tangible impact of bedouin life on the Jews.

It appears that even in antiquity it was not possible to look on Arabia as a composite whole, politically or culturally. In fact the peoples of the Peninsula could be divided into at least two distinct groups. In the south-west, where the high coastal mountain chain serves with the monsoon to bring to the region a plentiful supply of rain, which makes it a land of singular fertility, there dwelt a settled, politically highly organized community, whose successful manipulation of the overland trade from India and East Africa up the western part of Arabia to the Mediterranean[3] excited the envy of more than one of the great powers to the north. A comparable society may have existed in eastern Arabia as well. The rest of the Peninsula, as far as the Syro-Mesopotamian desert, consisted largely of stony wilderness, broken up by sandy wastes and occasional outcrops of lava (*ḥarra*). These flowered with a scant vegetation when the rare rainfalls occurred, and could provide a livelihood only for nomadic pastoralists, with their herds of camels and sheep and their fiercely independent ways of life. Possessing an intense feeling of blood relationship and family responsibility, they were at one and the same time democratic and aristocratic, looking upon their settled neighbours with undisguised contempt. The uniformity and isolation of desert life so conditioned their outlook that we may assume that their society in early biblical times can scarcely have differed from the picture of their existence which we may derive from their own rock inscriptions,[4] or indeed from the observations of travellers in more recent times. These characterize them as tenacious, enduring, fatalistic, and individualist, yet respecting the right of the individual to make his voice heard and placing much reliance on the guidance of elders. Rarely submitting to conquest, they invested their concept of heroism in the organized raiding of caravans or neighbouring tribes, and in hunting. Their intimate knowledge of wells and routes across the desert rendered them indispensable to the caravaneer, yet they despised the artisans of the oasis and constituted a threat to the life of the community. Nevertheless, hospitality and generosity to the stranger were desirable qualities to complement their strong interest in the common good of the clan. It was otherwise in the oases, such as Taymā' or Dedan or Dūma, where the presence of water and cultivable land, and the dictates of the passing caravan trade, made it possible to lead a settled—the bedouin would have said 'effete'—life, and it was against such that the Hebrew prophets inveighed with particular vehemence (Jer. 25: 24; Ezek. 27: 21). It is of these too that one can most fluently write the history, for their trading monopolies inevitably brought them into sharp contact with the world powers to the north. It is understandable, therefore, that no precise information about them should be available till the time of the Assyrian empire, when the rulers of that country were attempting to establish a foothold on the Mediterranean coast at the expense of the Aramaean and Syrian city-states.[5] Trading interests alone were sufficient to bring the princes of Arabia to the assistance of the threatened cities. They cannot, however, have constituted the sole reason for the establishment of such political units, and it is probable that, as emerges rather clearly in South Arabia, it was the organization behind irrigation procedures, dependent upon unpredictable flash-floods, or wells which brought about the cohesion necessary for the establishment of well-run societies. One of them, Taymā', may also have been responsible for the elaboration of a system of writing some time before the early sixth century.[6] This gradually spread to other communities as well, reaching its full flowering in the monumental script of South Arabia. But for these scripts, one would hardly be in a position to write this chapter.

(i) *Contacts with the North*

Such are the peoples whom the Jews termed *'ara^b*, a word which, it must be stressed, did not certainly acquire the modern sense of 'Arab' till the advent of Islam in A.D. 622 gave all the peoples of the Arabian Peninsula a common goal.[7] *'Ara^b* in the Old Testament should rather be understood in the collective sense of 'nomads', that is, the bedouin of North Arabia, Syria, and Sinai, just as Old South Arabian *"rb* denotes the bedouin elements living alongside the settled population. The word is thus probably connected with Hebrew *'^{a}rā^{b}āh*, 'wilderness, desert', and hence 'the Jordan Depression'. A comparable situation probably exists for the Assyrian term *aribi*. Whether there ever was an actual tribe, the ʿArab, is unknown, and the designation of the land as 'Arabia' is an innovation of the Greeks. These peoples, who were such a plague on their neighbours, felt political cohesion only in family terms, and the further this feeling was carried outside the immediate environment of the clan, the weaker it became. They could and did unite against external threats, but their very remoteness made such circumstances exceptional, and instead their impact on 'World History' was exercised rather in their capacity as pawns in rivalries between powers such as the Assyrians and the Babylonians, or later the Seleucids and the Lagids. It is in such a situation that we find the earliest known explicit reference to an Arab. When Shalmaneser III (859–824) in his sixth year made a thrust into Syria to reach the Mediterranean, he encountered an Aramaean coalition of twelve kings, including Ahab of Israel (874–853) and the princes of Damascus and Hamath. At the indecisive battle of Qarqar on the Orontes a certain Gindibu' from Arabia supplied 1000 camel-riders to the allies.[8] Beyond that, nothing is known of him. References to the Arabs or their country become increasingly frequent from the reign of Tiglath-pileser III (745–727), when the Assyrian rulers were engaged in constant campaigning in Syria and Palestine. The Arab peoples reveal themselves as a constant thorn in the side of Assyria. Tiglath-pileser records the reception of rich tribute in gold, silver, precious woods, garments, and livestock, from Zabibe,[9] Queen of Arabia, while in 736 a second queen, Samsi,[10] who had rebelled against the king, was soundly defeated, and had to flee to Bazu[11] in eastern Arabia, whence she later returned and submitted. Seven further cities and tribes also undertook to pay tribute: the Massā', Taymā', Saba', Haiappa, Badana, Hattia, and the Idiba'lu.[12] Their tribute consisted of camels, aromatics, spices, gold, silver, and other goods associated with the Arabian trade route. Sargon II (722–705) claims in his seventh year to have crushed far distant desert tribes in the west and to have settled the survivors in Samaria.[13] One of the tribes, the Thamud,[14] was to become particularly prominent in post-biblical times, so that Sargon may be guilty of some exaggeration in estimating his success. Under Sennacherib (705–681) Arab mercenaries appear in the service of the King's rebel brother in Babylon. A King of the Arabs, Haza'el, is also mentioned for the first time.[15] Sennacherib attacked the Arabs and their king fled with Queen Te'elhunu to Adumatu (Dūma).[16] After a siege the city fell and Queen Iskallatu was captured, while the gods of Adumatu were carried off to Nineveh. Haza'el, however, succeeded in obtaining their return in the reign of Esarhaddon (681–669),[17] who placed a certain Ta(r)bua alongside Haza'el as queen. After Haza'el's death his son Yata' (Yathaʿ) became King of the Arabs, subject to increased tribute, and a few years later the Arabs revolted against him under a certain Uabu (Wahb). Assyrian troops crushed the revolt but did not stop Yata' from rebelling himself. Consequently he had to flee and the Arab gods were again taken to Nineveh. In the reign of Ashurbanipal (669–627)[18] Uabu recovered them and peace was restored. Later, however, he went over to the side of Ashurbanipal's brother, Shamash-shum-ukīn, the King of Babylon. Arab troops were sent to Babylon under a Qedarite prince, Abiate' (Abyathaʿ), whilst the Arabs laid waste the Assyrian territories in the west. This led to their defeat, and Yata' fled to the Nabaiati,[19] whose king, Natnu, preferred to declare his allegiance to Ashurbanipal. The King of Qedar, Ammuladi, continued the attack on the west, but was checked by the King of Moab, while Yata''s wife, Adiya, Queen of the Arabs, became Ashurbanipal's prisoner. Meanwhile, Babylon's Arab mercenaries were also crushed, but Abiate' became reconciled with the Assyrian king and was himself proclaimed King of the Arabs in place of Yata'. His allegiance was not of long duration, and, obtaining help from Natnu, he allied himself with Uate', son of Birdadda, who had proclaimed himself King of Arabia. The Arabs camped near Damascus. In the course of a long campaign from the north-east, however, Ashurbanipal was able to drive off the Nabaiati and trap the Qedar, though their king escaped. At Khulkhuliti, on the Lajāh, Ashurbanipal attacked and captured Abiate', and compelled the Qedar to surrender by occupying the local wells. Finally Uate' too surrendered and his son was set up as King of the Arabs. The final defeat of the Qedar is recorded in the time of Nebuchadrezzar (605–562) by Jeremiah (49: 28).

So far the Assyrian annals. Largely political, they tell us little of the Arab peoples, beyond the names of several tribes and gods, some verifiable from other sources, a list of typical merchandise offered as tribute, and a number of personal names of characteristically Arabic formation. A comparison of these records with the epigraphic remains of those peoples, however, makes it possible to fill in some detail. Of the tribes explicitly mentioned in the Old Testament, the Qedar seem to be particularly prominent, though otherwise we learn only that they were pastoralists (Isa. 60: 7), employed archers (Isa. 21: 17), and traded with Tyre in lambs, rams, and goats. It is, however, reasonably certain that the oasis of Dūma[20] in the Jawf region of the Wādī Sirḥān was associated with them, for Haza'el's son was the King of Qedar[21] (cf. also Isa. 21: 11–17). Dūma was, moreover, the seat of a line of Arab queens or high priestesses.[22] Zabibe and Samsi probably belonged there, whilst Te'elhunu is known to have been the priestess (*kumirtu*) of Dilbat, or Atarsamain/Ishtar. That they probably also played an important social and political role is suggested by Samsi's being placed on the same level as the pharaoh of Egypt, with whom she paid tribute to Assyria. Their status is most probably to be explained in terms of the predominance of the cult of Atarsamain, to whom Esarhaddon presented an ornate gold star.[23] The gods whose images were removed from Dūma by Sennacherib are given as Atarsamain, Dai, Nuhai, Ruldaiu, Abirillu, and Atarquruma. Later Thamudic graffiti from the region attest to the persistence of the worship of Ruḍā, the Evening Star, Nuhay, the sun-god, and Atarsamain. Of the other gods we know nothing.

The later history of Dūma is uncertain, though Minaean and Nabataean inscriptions have been found there, whilst the nearby site of Sakākah has yielded Taymānite, Thamudic, and Nabataean texts. The Qedar, however, apparently continued to flourish after Nebuchadrezzar's attack, for Nabonidus (556–539) is recorded as having laid siege to a place called [-]*dummu* in 552.[24] During the Achaemenid period it is uncertain to what extent North Arabia became subject to the Persians, but the Arabs do seem to have sent tribute to Cyrus (539–530)[25] and certainly assisted Cambyses (530–522) on his campaign to Egypt. Finally, the Egyptian site of Tell el-Maskhūṭa recently yielded an interesting find of several fragmentary vessels bearing dedicatory inscriptions in Aramaic.[26] One explicitly mentions Qaynū bar Geshem, King of Qedar, and all are offerings to the goddess Han-Ilāt, who is probably the

Ἀλιλατ of Herodotus iii. 3, and to be equated with the sky-goddess Urania. Since old-style Athenian tetradrachms were found in association, it is tempting to compare Geshem or Gashmu the Arabian, the adversary of Nehemiah in 444 B.C. (Neh. 2: 19, 6: 1–6).

(ii) *The Arab Kingdoms*

One of the key cities on the Arabian trade route in antiquity was certainly the walled centre of Taymā' (Taima), with its well, al-Haddāj, and the nearby high place at Jabal Ghunaym.[27] It is first mentioned as a source of tribute by Tiglath-pileser III,[28] and occurs in the Old Testament as early as the sixth century as forming part of Edom (Jer. 49: 7; Ezek. 25: 13, etc.), though once more with scant detail. It was to this city that in 552 the Chaldaean king Nabonidus betook himself, perhaps to escape the hostility of the priesthood towards his unpopular favour of the moon-god Sīn of Ḥarrān.[29] After killing the King of Taymā', he had his palace built there, and the town was beautified and provided with a wall. The texts of the period make it clear that Nabonidus' unorthodoxy was indeed a primary motive for his action, yet one must allow that he could have foreseen the gradual rise of Cyrus, and hoped by this step to win the Arab tribes to his support and also gain some control over Arabian trade. He indulged in a far-reaching campaign amongst the Arab tribes, and probably attacked Dadānu, Padakku, Hibra, Yadihu, and Yatribu,[30] the last four being oases in the Ḥijāz region of Central Arabia. It is perhaps no coincidence that a group of proto-Arabic texts from Jabal Ghunaym alludes to wars against Dedan, the Nabayāt, and the Massā'. They form a homogeneous group and may belong to the time of Nabonidus' residence in Taymā'.[31] His stay would undoubtedly attract foreign artisans and workers, and may help to explain the presence in the city of a number of remarkable Aramaic inscriptions of the sixth century and later. One of them[32] tells of the entry into Taymā' of the god Ṣalm of Hagam, and his incorporation amongst the gods of the city, Ṣalm of Maḥram, Sangalā, and Ashīrah. The stele further lists the revenues of the temple and names the priest, Ṣalmshezib, who bears a Babylonian name, as the son of an Egyptian, Peṭosiri. It has been pointed out that the stele shares features in common with other stelae from Ḥarrān.[33] Taymānite texts from Jabal Ghunaym attest the persistence of the worship of Ṣalm of Hagam by the people, and an interesting stone plaque was also found there depicting a goddess sitting on a four-legged stool, holding a vessel and a sceptre over an incense-burner. The lack of facial features suggests the influence of the evil eye, whose presence is well attested in South Arabia, but the identity of the goddess is still undecided.[34] Local inscriptions also mention the presence of a tribe, *sm'l*. The annals of Ashurbanipal record that Uate' was the king of Sumu'il[35] as well as king of Qedar. It may thus be assumed that the city lay within the lands of the Qedar.

Some 150 kilometres south-west of Taymā' lies the hill-encompassed oasis of al-'Ulā, where there are extensive ruins.[36] This is known to have been a centre of the kingdom of Dedan, which was already flourishing in the sixth century, according to Isaiah (21: 13), and was regarded with Taymā' as part of Edom (Ezek. 25: 13). Ezekiel (27: 20) speaks of her trading with Tyre in saddle-cloths for riding, and we have already seen that she was visited by Nabonidus. Neither the ruins at al-'Ulā nor the handful of inscriptions of meagre content which can be classified as Dedanite tell much about the people. There are documents relating to proprietary rights on tombs or pasturage, as one might expect, but little of a political nature. The only known king was Kabir'il bin Mata''il, whose funerary text alludes to the deity Gadd, or Fortune.[37] Little is known of the local religion and no gods are explicitly mentioned. Theophoric names, however, yield such deities as *h̲rg*, which etymologically refers to the first rains, the moon-god Wadd or 'Amm, and Manāt, 'destiny'. Archaeological information seems limited to the fact that the dead were buried in vaults at the foot of the hills. Even the date of the inscriptions is uncertain, though their range must have been short. One, however, mentions a certain 'Abd, Governor of Dedan. The word for 'governor', *fḥt*, being Persian, a date in the Persian period or shortly thereafter is to be preferred.[38]

The kingdom of Dedan seems to have been followed, as a result of some dynastic change, by that of Liḥyān.[39] Of this people the Old Testament has no knowledge but the local inscriptions are fortunately plentiful and informative, being drafted in a script derived from Dedanite. Eight kings of Liḥyān are known, suggesting that the kingdom may have lasted upwards of 150 years, and the fact that amongst their names is found the Egyptian Tulmay suggests that they belong to the Ptolemaic period. This is supported by the Hellenistic features of some of the statuary found there. The function of the kings is unknown, but may have been advisory, to judge by the phrase *b-r'y*. For political discussion there was a popular assembly in which doubtless only Liḥyānites could participate, though many foreigners resided in the town, including Nabataeans, Taymānites, Greeks, and Jews. Several inscriptions record building activities; for example, of a shrine which apparently was shared by several gods, and of such objects as cisterns. Though the society seems to have been patriarchal, women too could indulge in building. A priesthood is mentioned (*'fkl*, feminine *'fklt*). The principal deity was called Dhū Ghābat, 'He of the thicket', though other gods such as al-ʿUzzā, the Morning Star, Wadd, and Baʿalsamīn from Ḥarrān also occur.[40] Human beings might be dedicated to a god, and in the ruins of the temple, to which the inscriptions ascribe houses and herds, there have been found stone altars for food and drink offerings to Dhū Ghābat. One inscription also alludes to burnt offerings to atone for murder, suggesting the absence of vendetta. The belief in a life after death is indicated here as elsewhere in the south by the term *nfs*, denoting 'a funerary stele'.

A major element in the foreign population of the oasis consisted of a Minaean trading colony organized under a *kabīr*, who seems to have controlled such matters as taxation. The independence of this group, who owed allegiance to the Minaean kings in South Arabia, suggests that good relations were maintained with the Liḥyānite kings. Their inscriptions, which are numerous, are mainly concerned with public building works and matters of cult.

The close of the Liḥyānite kingdom, which, to judge by the inscriptions, was probably brought about by force, is perhaps to be connected with a certain Masʿudū, King of Liḥyān, of whom three texts are known, all drafted in the Nabataean script. It seems likely that he was a usurper, presumably a Nabataean, though not of the royal house, which had a very restricted nomenclature. At any rate, his reign was probably brought to an end by the incorporation of al-ʿUlā into the Nabataean dominions in the late second or early first century B.C. The decline of Dedan presumably was accompanied by the rise of the neighbouring city of al-Hijr, now Madā'in Ṣāliḥ,[41] though seven monumental Minaean texts and several Liḥyānite graffiti suggest that the site had a history even before then. It became particularly prominent under the Nabataeans, who were in control of the town by 24 B.C. and probably favoured it at the expense of non-Nabataean Dedan.

None of the Arab peoples of the Bible is so well documented as the Nabataeans, though they are relatively late in appearance. The later books of the Old Testament and the writings of Josephus provide us with adequate testimony to their dealings with the Judaean kingdom. They are first mentioned by Diodorus Siculus[42] in connection with the Syrian ruler Antiochus Monophthalmus, against whom they apparently posed a threat. An army sent against them located their centre at Petra, and captured stocks of incense, spices, and silver, so one may assume that already by 312 B.C. the Nabataeans participated in the trade from South and East Arabia. Since at this time the route via the Persian Gulf and the Euphrates was threatened by Parthia, while the Red Sea trade was in decline, the overland caravan trade must have been particularly lucrative. Probably still few in numbers, the Nabataeans dwelt in the Sharā mountains south of Petra, whence came their chief god, Dusares, 'He of Sharā'. In the course of the third century they seem to have expanded southwards to the Gulf of Aqaba, where they took to piracy. The Maccabean uprisings and the internal quarrels of the Seleucids enabled them to prosper to the point where Aretas III, in 85 B.C., could capture Damascus and Coele-Syria, albeit only for a short while, though long enough to justify the issue of a coinage.[43] The Auranitis, however, was retained and Bostra founded as a commercial capital, while the southwards expansion was maintained towards Egra (al-Hijr), where Nabataean rock tombs have been found, and subsequently Taymā', and Dūma. Coastal ports too were occupied as far as Leuke Kome, and finally by 24 B.C. Dedan itself was Nabataean. The consequent reduction in transit tolls enabled this mighty empire to survive for over a century, and it was the scene of a particularly brilliant Hellenistic culture whose impressive ruins still survive in centres such as Petra and Madā'in Ṣāliḥ, while their skilled irrigation techniques in such districts as the Negev have excited the admiration of modern engineers. The demands of Rome for the luxury goods of the East doubtless helped their success, but at the same time brought about their downfall. In A.D. 105 the Syrian portion of the kingdom was annexed to Rome as Provincia Arabia and the remainder apparently went into decline.

Already in 312 B.C. the Nabataeans seem to have written Aramaic, and this remained the language of their numerous inscriptions. It is clear, however, that their real language was Arabic, which has left marked traces in the written medium. Their proper names too were Arab. The splendid tombs for which the Nabataeans are renowned find an echo in many inscriptions recording their construction or delimiting the rights of usage. Otherwise information from this source is somewhat limited, but a full pantheon of gods emerges, with Dusares at the top. Also attested are al-ʿUzzā, Baʿalshamīn, Allāt, Shayʿ al-Qawm, Manāt, Hubal, and Aʿrā. One text alludes to an apparently deified King ʿObodat, who was served by a confraternity.

Eastern Arabia has long posed a mystery to the archaeologist. Bahrain, for example, was famed as the site of an enormous complex of stone tumuli, which occasioned much speculation as to authorship and date.[44] Such are, of course, commonplace all over Arabia, but nowhere in such concentrations as in the eastern part generally. The trade route via the Persian Gulf to ancient Gerrha and thence to Taymāʾ was well known, but the location of Gerrha itself, a very prosperous city, to judge by classical sources, was totally unknown. The land also featured in Sumerian and Akkadian records as a source of trade and occasionally too as a region of conquest,[45] but the location of Dilmun, the fabled market for wood, copper, and ivory, could only be guessed at. Recent Danish archaeological work, however, has radically altered the situation, and several sites have received attention which the historian of North or South Arabia might justly envy.[46] The identity of Dilmun with Bahrain has now been established with reasonable certainty, though unfortunately practically nothing can be said of the ethnic or social constitution of the region, native records being very rare. It appears, however, that in prehistoric times eastern Arabia generally was quite densely populated. The most spectacular results were achieved on the island of Bahrain (Baḥrayn), where excavation of the site of Qalʿat Baḥrayn revealed a succession of no less than five cities over the period from about

2500 B.C. to the Seleucid era. On the island of Faylaka in Kuwait a comparable range of sites was unearthed, including a temple dedicated to the god Inzak, who in Sumerian records is exclusively associated with Dilmun. The role of this ancient civilization can now be explained in terms of the suitability of Bahrain as a watering-place and transit post in the luxury-goods trade with India; and, indeed, a number of seals of Indus Valley type were found there, together with a set of stone weights of Indus type and weight-standard. Much of the trade, however, was financed from Ur. It appears that the Dilmun civilization stretched some 250 miles along the coast between Kuwait and Bahrain and up to 60 miles inland, whilst a contemporary culture was discovered in Oman (ʿUmān), which can plausibly be identified with Magan, the ancient source of copper.[47] The religion of Dilmun seems to have involved a fertility cult, to judge from the discovery of a number of snake sacrifices. It was also established that the Bahrain tumuli spanned the entire first three millennia B.C.

It is known that Alexander the Great had an interest in eastern Arabia, and a fine Greek temple dedicated to Artemis was uncovered on Faylaka, probably Arrian's island of Ikaros. Nearby was a contemporary township. But of Gerrha no trace could be found, and we must content ourselves with the notices of later Latin and Greek authors.[48] According to Strabo it was a Chaldaean colony, and Eratosthenes comments on its role in the spice trade. Aristobulus adds that goods were carried thence on rafts up the Euphrates to Thapsacus. Artemidorus makes the inhabitants the wealthiest of all tribes, possessing large quantities of wrought gold and silver articles, and Pliny adds that the city was large and had great towers built of square blocks of 'salt'. But although information as to its location is fairly explicit, so far it has defied all attempts to find it.

In South-West Arabia some thousands of inscriptions, both monumental and graffiti, have survived as evidence for the ancient kingdoms of Saba', Maʿīn, Qatabān, and Ḥaḍramawt. A number of smaller kingdoms are also known.[49] Saba' and Ḥaḍramawt alone were known to the Old Testament writers (Gen. 10: 26; Ezek. 27: 22), whilst the Assyrians mention only Saba'.[50] The languages of these peoples divide neatly into two groups, Sabaean showing some affinities with Canaanite, the others rather with features characteristic of Mesopotamia. Since the vast fund of inscriptions has bequeathed to posterity the names of very many rulers, and the texts themselves, where adequately interpreted, contain abundant information on social, political, and religious matters, it is possible to elaborate fairly detailed historical sketches of the South Arabian civilization. Differing interpretations of texts do, of course, lead to much disagreement over detail. But where the inscriptions perhaps let us down most severely is in the almost total absence of fixed synchronisms with outside events. Greek and Roman writers describe the land rather generally, and not till Strabo is any personage named. Serious lack of agreement still centres upon the date of the earliest texts. Some authorities, influenced by comparison of artistic styles and palaeographic considerations, would place them around 500 B.C.[51] Others again reject any foreign influence in the script, and appeal in preference to Sabaean rulers mentioned in the annals of Sargon II (It'amra) and Sennacherib (Karibilu), whom they would equate with a pair of Mukarrib rulers known from Sabaean sources.[52] This discrepancy has yet to be resolved, but it might be noted that, whoever It'amra and Karibilu were, the Assyrian texts do not seem to regard them as coming from anywhere other than North Arabia. The apparent relationships of the South Arabian languages may suggest that while Minaean, Qatabanian, and Ḥaḍrami could have a north-eastern origin, Sabaean came rather from Central or North Arabia. Since, moreover, the Sabaeans give the appearance of having been a warrior people who, at some as yet unknown date, infiltrated South Arabia and gradually let their influence spread throughout the existing peoples, it cannot be excluded that in the eighth and seventh centuries at least part of Saba' still lay in North Arabia. This assumption gains significance when one recalls the story of the Queen of Sheba's visit to Solomon (1 Kings 10: 1–13; 2 Chr. 9: 1–12). The extant Sabaean records contain not one single mention of a queen, let alone the journey of a ruler to the far north. It will be recalled, however, that queens played a not insignificant religious and political role amongst the Qedar. Would it be too far-fetched to suppose that it was from this northern Saba' that the unnamed Queen set out on her fabled journey to Solomon's court?[53]

The extreme conservatism and impersonality of all South Arabian texts make the writing of the history of that region very hazardous, and many of our assertions and hypotheses are founded on philologically-based probabilities rather than verifiable facts. Though these texts are rather better understood than, say, Liḥyānite, there is very little vocabulary of whose meaning one can be absolutely certain. Nevertheless, it seems that the political development of Saba', Qatabān, and Ḥaḍramawt proceeded along comparable lines.[54] Saba', however, is the only state which provides continuous documentation. Basically the country people were organized into communes of peasants and herdsmen, while the inhabitants of towns dwelt in quarters allotted to specific 'tribes', which in turn were subdivided into clans. Initially all three states were probably ruled by functionaries called Mukarribs, though some scholars argue that they were actually contemporary with kings. Their exalted role is ill defined, but may have included sacerdotal functions. They belong to a time when Saba' was still a relatively small community centred in and around the fertile regions of Mārib and Ṣirwāḥ, and in a sense they personified the true Sabaean people as opposed to the client peoples. They led such activities as temple or wall building and negotiated decrees affecting the peoples. They were assisted by a kind of senate (*mśwd*), probably consisting of privileged landowners. These were organized into three tribes, each with a subordinate client clan, and from them were drawn, on a triple seven-year rota, 'eponymate' officials whose duties were connected with an annual irrigation rite.[55] It is to this tripartite division of the state that certain texts relate which apparently describe an act of *συνοικισμός*. The Mukarribs also engaged in military activities, for example, against Qatabān to the south. About 400 B.C. one of them, Karib'il Watar bin Dhamarʿalīy, appears to have extended his conquests, in alliance with Qatabān, as far as Najrān in the north and the Indian Ocean in the south, and to have settled Sabaean colonists on the conquered territory of Maʿīn. Probably in consequence, he abandoned the title Mukarrib in favour of King (*mlk*), and initiated the true kingdom of Saba', which endured some 500 years. Throughout, the king's powers appear to increase in the civil sphere. Royal participation in or initiation of building projects, irrigation schemes, and the like, continues, but on a lesser scale and rather as a personal act. More effective control over the enlarged Sabaean dominions led to increased centralization of authority, particularly in the religious centre of Mārib. The people seem to have been constituted as before, but by the advent of the Christian era, there is evidence of increased tribalism with consequent decentralization, and rival dynasties arose. The situation was probably a result of the decline in the overland transit trade in favour of the sea route.

Qatabān,[56] which lay to the south-east in the Wādī Bayḥān, also was governed by Mukarribs in the earliest period, but it was a distinctly more theocratic state than Saba'. The community was regarded as consisting of ʿAmm, the moon-god, the Mukarrib or King, and the Qatabanian people, who were also styled 'children of ʿAmm'. Here too the privileged land-holding tribes acted in conjunction with the ruler in issuing decrees or promulgating laws from their capital at Timnaʿ, and it would appear that the landowners were required to furnish to the state corvée-labour for fixed periods every month. Qatabān emerges as a much more tightly-knit community than Saba', so it is natural that many Qatabanian texts are of a legal, prescriptive nature. A sort of temple-feudalism prevailed there, where the land belonged to ʿAmm and the tribes were theocratically organized under a god or a patron. Her history is mostly known from Sabaean sources, for there seems to have been fairly constant warfare between the two states. Around the turn of the era, in fact, there arose a section of Qatabān, Ḥimyar, which was destined to overthrow the rival Sabaean dynasties and rule a united South Arabia.[57]

Maʿīn was basically a group of city-states in the South Arabian Jawf, to the north of Saba'. Minaean texts unfortunately tend to be rather fragmentary, but reveal that the nation did not pass through a Mukarrib period. For this reason it is usually assumed that they were late in organizing themselves. Their kings, as elsewhere, functioned alongside a council of magistrates, probably of a religious nature. Minaean texts are mostly limited in content to recording the construction of temples and public buildings, or the issuance of decrees relating, for example, to levies or taxes, no doubt to finance public works. The state thus was also theocratic, but with one major difference, that it was a trading community *par excellence*, and probably achieved political independence only for limited periods. We have already seen how Minaean colonists lived as a self-contained community in Dedan, and their texts have been found as far away as Egypt and Delos. Maʿīn disappeared from history for unknown reasons some time in the first century B.C.

Finally, of the kingdom of Ḥaḍramawt[58] little is known for the most ancient period. Her inscriptions are none too numerous, and do not permit much speculation on her ethnic or political constitution. On the whole the community seems to have been largely bedouin and was grouped around religious centre at Shabwa. The foundations of the state economy must have lain in the cultivation of incense, which grew in the Ḥaḍrami colony of Sumhurām in Dhofar,[59] and myrrh. It was also in the Ḥaḍramawt that the principal port of access to Arabia from the Indian Ocean, Qana', was situated, and from there a trade route ran up through Shabwa and Timnaʿ to the main northern road from Mārib.

The place of the South Arabian kingdoms on the incense route has frequently been alluded to. Apart from exporting incense, myrrh, and balsam, however, the country also received luxury goods from India, China, and Africa for forward shipment by caravan to the Mediterranean ports, and this trade was promoted to the extent that the Romans obtained the impression that the Sabaeans were singularly wealthy.[60] In fact, their wealth seems to have been rather elusive, for archaeology has not revealed a civilization of great complexity or richness.[61] The inscriptions themselves describe the frequent use of gold, probably locally washed or mined, silver, and copper, and there is evidence of extensive cultivation of dates, corn, vegetables, vines, and the like. Oxen, sheep, and camels also were of importance in the economy, and the over-all impression one receives is of a moderately prosperous agricultural community, where the more refined metallurgical and architectural skills were mainly at the service of the temples and larger towns. It certainly should not be considered a predominantly urban culture, even though building technique had reached a high degree of excellence. Several ancient building complexes are known, but the more impressive ruins are limited to a relatively small number of sites which were in any case significant in their day. The artistic achievements of the ordinary South Arabians, their funerary statuettes and stelae, are usually crude and featureless, and in the finer work or architectural decoration foreign influences are usually to be detected. Where the South Arabians really excelled was in the utilization of land and water.[62] Surveys of ancient irrigation complexes and the associated inscriptions demonstrate that a superbly efficient system of irrigation, based on the use of wells or cisterns or flash-floods, was linked to a skill in land terracing which can hardly be matched in the present day. Several inscriptions show that a complicated, if imperfectly understood, system of land tenure prevailed. Boundary disputes were common then as now, to judge from the clauses of delimitation appended to many agricultural texts. It is probably in the social organization which emerged from this that the real genius of South Arabia should be sought, rather than in the impressive excavations at Mārib or Timnaʿ.

There is an over-all unity in the religious systems of the various South Arabian kingdoms, in that a pantheon was worshipped which, though varying from one state to another in its nomenclature, contained the same basic triad: the Morning Star, the moon-god, and the sun-goddess. ʿAthtar, the male Venus star, was accorded particular veneration under that name at shrines throughout all South Arabia. The moon-god, however, was called Ilmuqah or Hawbas in Saba', ʿAmm or Anbay in Qatabān, Wadd in Maʿīn, and Sīn or Ḥawl in Ḥaḍramawt. The sun-goddess is nowhere explicitly named, but occurs under a variety of local designations, notably Dhāt Baʿadān and Dhāt Ḥimyam. Beyond these a large number of purely local divinities, water-gods and house-gods, are attested, often of very uncertain identification. It is a striking fact that many of the greatest shrines of these gods are sited at key cities on the trade route, such as Shabwa, Timnaʿ, Mārib, and Maʿīn. Of religious practice we are not too well informed. Gods were not usually represented in any form other than by symbols or associated animals,[63] and in the latter connection it is interesting to find evidence in the inscriptions of the persistence of the sacred hunt.[64] Temples, which seem to have been places of asylum, and sometimes were centres of pilgrimage, were served by priests (*ršw* or *šwʿ*) and, in some cases, hierodules. The domain of the priests may have extended beyond cultic matters, and no doubt involved the maintenance of the temple properties, including the herds of sacred animals, and the safekeeping of official documents placed in their care. Many dedicatory inscriptions record the fulfilment of actions called for in oracular responses, in return for which statuettes might be dedicated to the god. From a homogeneous group of texts from the ruined temple at Jār al-Labbā in the Jawf it has been possible to derive a coherent picture of the procedures followed there.[65] The temple probably consisted of a shrine with an image of ʿAthtar, the whole surrounded by a low wall. There was at least one altar, perhaps two, where burnt offerings and blood sacrifices were made. Oracles were sought over the altar in the name of ʿAthtar. An oblation was brought and the inquiry made of a priest. When the response was given, a thanksgiving offering was made. There seem to have been specific times reserved for the rite. Another group of texts from the site of Madīnat Haram in the north of Saba', although obscure in detail, demonstrates clearly the importance laid on ritual purity, and that penitence and public confession might play a part in worship.[66] The offences described in these texts include sins of commission in the sexual sphere as well as ritual omissions.

Before concluding this chapter some mention must be made of the situation in contemporary Ethiopia.[67] This name is used here rather guardedly, since, as the Greek translation of Biblical 'Kush', it seems in every case in the Old Testament to refer rather generally to the region of the Sudan and Nubia.[68] Of the land immediately across the Red Sea from the Yemen, modern Ethiopia, we learn but little in the ancient sources, presumably because of the difficulty of access, but the northern part is known archaeologically as the site of a culture deriving from South Arabia during the fifth century B.C. This was centred on a number of inland sites, such as Melazo, Maṭarā, and Kaskassē. Inscriptions of South Arabian type and palaeographically belonging to the time of Karib'il Watar have been found there, alongside others which betray slight linguistic peculiarities. Culturally too there is little to distinguish them from genuine South Arabian texts. The same gods occur and the same civil titles were employed. It has, moreover, been observed that there were several place-names in Eritrea and northern Ethiopia in classical antiquity which seem to have been borrowed from the South Arabian mainland.[69] The explanation is generally thought to be as follows. At some indeterminate date, perhaps about 1000 B.C., waves of South Arabian immigrants entered Ethiopia, mingled with the local Cushitic population, and, by means of their superior culture, produced a civilization similar to that of their homeland. In the course of Karib'il Watar's conquests, further bands of military colonists arrived. To the latter belong the purely South Arabian texts, to the indigenous inhabitants the derivative ones. The colonies presumably were not of long duration, and in any case Ethiopia was soon to be cut off from the Yemen by the Ptolemaic presence in the Red Sea. The indigenous brand of South Arabian culture developed in isolation, finally to flower as the later civilization of Aksum. The older inscriptions are so few in number and so uninformative that little can be said about the early culture. Most of them are dedications to such gods as Ilmuqah, ʿAthtar, Dhāt Ḥimyam, and Dhāt Baʿadān, and the title *mlk* occurs alongside *mkrb*. It is an interesting commentary on the persistence of the worship of the South Arabian gods that the name of ʿAthtar should survive into the modern Tigre language as the word for 'sky', *ʿästär*.

NOTES

1. P. K. Hitti, *History of the Arabs from the Earliest Times to the Present*, 7th edn. (London, 1960), p. 8.

2. The language of the Old Testament and the culture and practices of the Jewish people were of considerable assistance in earlier attempts to interpret the inscriptional remains of the pre-Islamic Arabians, though in more recent research the emphasis has tended to shift away from this approach. Conversely, in elucidating the more obscure portions of the Old Testament, such as the book of Job, it is not uncommon for philologists to have recourse to the immense linguistic and cultural resources of the Arabic language. There is, of course, justification for this procedure, provided that the materials adduced by the researcher are properly understood in their context. Regrettably, this is not always the case. See James Barr, *Comparative Philology and the Text of the Old Testament* (Oxford, 1968), where the dangers inherent in lexical pillaging are amply demonstrated.

3. On the Arabian trade routes see Carl Rathjens, 'Die alten Welthandelsstraßen und die Offenbarungsreligionen', *Oriens* xv (1962), 115–29; R. L. Bowen, 'Ancient Trade Routes in South Arabia', in R. L. Bowen and F. P. Albright, *Archaeological Discoveries in South Arabia* (Baltimore, 1958), pp. 35–42; W. W. Müller, 'Alt-Südarabien als Weihrauchland', *Theologische Quartalschrift* cxlix/4 (1969), 350–68.

4. The graffiti of the early bedouin Arabs are conventionally termed 'Thamudic', since they share palaeographical features which distinguish them from other Arabian script forms. They are heavily concentrated along the ancient trade routes, but are so meagre in content as hardly to permit the reconstruction of a coherent history. Their geographical

distribution militates against the assumption that they are the work of one tribe, or even a confederation of tribes. However, taken in conjunction with the rock drawings which so frequently accompany them, they do provide an interesting sidelight on ancient bedouin life. On the rock drawings see E. Anati, *Rock-Art in Central Arabia* (2 vols., Louvain, 1968).

5. Peoples and places to be located in Arabia do, of course, occur in earlier records, but little can be said of them. See, for example, Sidney Smith, *Early History of Assyria to 1000 B.C.* (London, 1928), Index, under 'Aḫlamu', 'Sutu', and 'Ḫabiru'.

6. There is much disagreement on the history and development of the Old Arabian scripts, largely because the relative chronologies of the peoples using them have not yet been adequately established. On the problem generally see most recently Winnett & Reed, *Ancient Records*, *passim*.

7. Dietrich, 'Geschichte Arabiens', p. 294. The earliest biblical references to the Arabs seem to be Isa. 13: 20 and Jer. 3: 2, 25: 24.

8. *A.N.E.T.*, p. 279 (*A.R.A.B.* i, § 611).

9. *A.N.E.T.*, p. 283 (*A.R.A.B.* i, § 772).

10. *A.N.E.T.*, pp. 283–4 (*A.R.A.B.* i, §§ 778–9).

11. Probably near Dilmun; see the description in *A.R.A.B.* ii, § 520.

12. On Taymā' and Saba' see below. Idiba'lu is the Adbe'el of Gen. 25: 13. On the Massā', biblical Massa (Prov. 31), opinions vary. W. F. Albright thinks they were Aramaeans living just south-east of Damascus ('The Biblical Tribe of Massa' and some Congeners', *Studi Orientalistici in onore di Georgio Levi Della Vida*, i (Rome, 1956), pp. 1–14). Winnett, on the other hand, locates them, on topographical grounds, near the north-west tip of the Nafūd (*Ancient Records*, pp. 101–2).

13. *A.N.E.T.*, p. 286 (*A.R.A.B.* ii, § 17).

14. See note 4 above. Classical sources associate the Thamud with the coastal regions of Midian.

15. *A.N.E.T.*, p. 291 (Esarhaddon) (*A.R.A.B.* ii, § 518 *a*).

16. *A.N.E.T.*, p. 301 (*A.R.A.B.* ii, §§ 358, 940, 943).

17. *A.N.E.T.*, pp. 291–2 (*A.R.A.B.* ii, § 518 *a*).

18. *A.N.E.T.*, pp. 297–300 (*A.R.A.B.* ii, §§ 817–31).

19. Biblical Nebaioth. This people, whom the Old Testament places with the Qedar (Isa. 60: 7), is mentioned in early graffiti from Jabal Ghunaym near Taymā', but no source specifies their location. According to Winnett the most natural direction for Yata''s flight would be south-east across the sand-dunes of the Nafūd towards present-day Ḥā'il (*Ancient Records*, pp. 99–100). Certainly there is no foundation for the equation of the Nebaioth (*nbyt*) with the Nabataeans (*nbṭw*).

20. Winnett & Reed, op. cit. 71–3.

21. *A.R.A.B.* ii, § 869.

22. See N. Abbot, 'Pre-Islamic Arab Queens', *A.J.S.L.* lviii (1941), 1–22.

23. *A.N.E.T.*, p. 301 (*A.R.A.B.* ii, § 943).

24. *A.N.E.T.*, p. 305, and cf. W. F. Albright in *J.R.A.S.* (1925), 293–4.

25. Xenophon, *Cyrop.* VII. iv. 16, *A.N.E.T.*, p. 316, as against Herodotus iii. 97.

26. See I. Rabinowitz, 'Aramaic Inscriptions of the Fifth Century B.C.E., from a North-Arab Shrine in Egypt', *J.N.E.S.* xv (1956), 1–9.

27. See Winnett & Reed, op. cit. 22–34, 88–112.

28. *A.N.E.T.*, pp. 283, 284 (*A.R.A.B.* i, §§ 799, 818).

29. *A.N.E.T.*, pp. 313, 562–3. See also C. J. Gadd, 'The Harran Inscriptions of Nabonidus', *Anat. Stud.* viii (1958), 35–92; W. Röllig, 'Nabonid und Tēmā', *Compte Rendue de l'onzième Rencontre Assyriologique Internationale* (Leiden, 1964), 21–32; and H. Tadmor, 'The Inscriptions of Nabonaid: Historical Arrangement', *Assyr. Stud.* xvi (1965), 351–64.

30. Hibra is probably the oasis of Khaybar; Padakku is Fadak, now al-Ḥuwayyiṭ; Yadihu is Yadīʿ, now al-Ḥāyiṭ; and Yatribu is Yathrib, the former name of Madīna.

31. Winnett & Reed, op. cit. 99–103.

32. See H. Donner & W. Röllig, *Kanaanäische und aramäische Inschriften* (3 vols., Wiesbaden, 1962–4), no. 228.

33. See Gadd, op. cit.

34. Winnett & Reed, op. cit. 167–71.

35. *A.N.E.T.*, p. 300.

36. Winnett & Reed, op. cit. 38–42, 113–20.

37. Van Den Branden, *Inscriptions dédanites* (1962), p. 58, no. 24. Cf. Winnett & Reed, op. cit. 114–15.

38. Winnett & Reed, op. cit. 115–16.

39. Winnett & Reed, op. cit. 116–20.

40. See Ryckmans, *Religions*, pp. 19–20.

41. Winnett & Reed, op. cit. 42–53, 130–1.

42. xix. 94.

43. See G. F. Hill, *Catalogue of the Greek Coins of Arabia, Mesopotamia, and Persia* (B.M., London, 1922), pp. xi–xii. According to 2 Cor. 11: 32 there was a governor of King Aretas [IV] in Damascus at the time of Paul's escape from the city. Since Imperial Roman coins were struck there from the reign of Augustus onwards, it is possible that the city had been temporarily ceded to the Nabataeans at that particular time.

44. See, generally, R. L. Bowen, *The Early Arabian Necropolis of Ain Jawan*, *B.A.S.O.R.* Supplementary Studies nos. 7–9 (Newhaven, Conn., 1950), and Grohmann, *Arabien*, pp. 51–4, 258–64.

45. See R. P. Dougherty, *The Sealand of Ancient Arabia* (Newhaven, Conn., 1932).

46. The excavations generally are described in Bibby, *Looking for Dilmun* (1970), and ably summarized by Grohmann, *Arabien*, pp. 255–69.

47. The problem of the identification of Magan and Meluhha is adequately rehearsed by Bibby, op. cit., 219–22. Magan was known in the late third millennium as the producer of Dilmun's copper, and also as a source for diorite and palm trees. It is usually mentioned along with Dilmun, and sometimes with Meluhha too. The arguments of

those who would identify Magan with Oman are based on considerations of ease of communications and the chemical analysis of copper samples from Oman. However, it is clear that to the Assyrians of the first millennium Magan and Meluhha were located in Upper Egypt, albeit as somewhat legendary regions. It appears that the later references have misplaced the two lands, and one must bear in mind that commercial allusions to Magan and Meluhha cease about 1800 B.C. According to Bibby, the carnelian of Meluhha can only have come from Rajputana in India. See also I. J. Gelb, *R.A.* lxiv (1970), 1–8.

48. For a recent discussion of the location of Gerrha see W. E. James, 'On the Location of Gerra', in F. Altheim & R. Stiehl, *Die Araber in der alten Welt* V. ii (Berlin, 1969), pp. 36–57. Full references to classical and modern sources are given there.

49. Only Awsān seems to have survived for any appreciable time during the epigraphic period. Its inscriptions are not numerous, though it was well known to classical authors, and its culture shows marked similarities to that of Qatabān. See von Wissmann & Höfner, 'Beiträge', pp. 56–9, 69–75.

50. *A.N.E.T.*, pp. 283, 284; 285, 286 for It'amra in the reign of Sargon II (*A.R.A.B.* i, §§ 778, 799, 818; ii, §§ 18, 55). For Karibilu in the reign of Sennacherib see *A.R.A.B.* ii, § 440.

51. The classic statement of this viewpoint is contained in J. Pirenne, 'La Grèce et Saba' and *Paléographie des inscriptions sud-arabes*, i (Brussels, 1956).

52. For example, Jamme, *Sabaean Inscriptions*, and von Wissmann, 'Zur Geschichte . . .'.

53. The story of the Queen of Sheba's visit to Solomon in search of wisdom is retailed fairly simply in the Old Testament versions, but has undergone considerable elaboration in later Jewish, Arab, and, above all, Ethiopian tradition. In the latter, indeed, it has become central to the national saga as embodied in the *Kəbrä nägäst* ('Glory of the Kings'). See E. A. W. Budge, *The Queen of Sheba and her Only Son Menyelek (I)* (London, 1932). The most recent discussion of the historicity of the event is that of E. Ullendorff, *Ethiopia and the Bible* (London, 1968), pp. 131–45, where a full bibliography is given. Ullendorff is inclined to treat with respect the view that her realms may have included Ethiopia.

54. On this aspect see J. Ryckmans, *L'Institution monarchique*, and the recent works of A. G. Lundin in the Russian periodicals *Epigrafika Vostoka*, *Vestnik Drevnei Istorii*, and *Palestinskii Sbornik*. Some of this work has been summarized by J. Ryckmans, 'Études d'épigraphie sud-arabe en russie', *B.O.* xxiv (1967), et seq.

55. See A. G. Lundin, 'Die Eponymenliste von Saba (aus dem Stamme Ḫalīl) (Sammlung Eduard Glaser V), *Sitzungsb. Öst. Akad. Wiss.*, Phil.-hist. Klasse, 248/1 (1965).

56. See Pirenne, *Royaume sud-arabe*, and von Wissmann, *Zur Archäologie*.

57. See von Wissmann, 'Ḥimyar, Ancient History', *Le Muséon* lxxvii (1964), 429–99.

58. See von Wissmann, *Zur Archäologie*.

59. See F. P. Albright, 'The Himyaritic Temple at Khor Rory (Dhofar, Oman)', *Or.* xxii (1953), 284–7, and, generally, Wendell Phillips, *Unknown Oman* (London, 1966).

60. Hence the abortive expedition to Arabia Felix under Aelius Gallus recorded by Strabo, XVI. iv. 22–4.

61. So far South Arabia has not been extensively excavated, but for representative surveys see C. Rathjens & H. von Wissmann, *Vorislamische Altertümer* (Hamburg, 1932); G. Caton Thompson, *The Tombs and Moon Temple of Hureidha* (Oxford, 1944); R. L. Bowen & F. P. Albright, *Archaeological Discoveries in South Arabia*; G. Van Beek, *Hajar Bin Ḥumeid* (Baltimore, 1969); Wendell Phillips, *Qataban and Sheba* (London, 1955); and B. Doe, *Southern Arabia* (London, 1971).

62. For a description of an irrigation complex in the Wādī Bayḥān see R. L. Bowen, 'Irrigation in Ancient Qatabân (Beiḥân)', in *Archaeological Discoveries in South Arabia*, pp. 43–88.

63. These have been classified by A. Grohmann, 'Göttersymbole und Symboltiere auf südarabischen Denkmälern', *Denkschr. Akad. Wiss. Wien*, Phil.-hist. Kl. 58, i (1914).

64. See A. F. L. Beeston, 'The Ritual Hunt: A Study in Old South Arabian Religious Practice', *Le Muséon* lxi (1948), 183–96.

65. See A. F. L. Beeston, 'The Oracle Sanctuary of Jār al-Labbā', *Le Muséon* lxii (1949), 207–28.

66. See G. Ryckmans, 'La Confession publique des péchés en Arabie Méridionale préislamique', *Le Muséon* lviii (1945), 1–14.

67. See, generally, H. de Contenson, 'Les Principales Étapes de l'Éthiopie antique', *Cahiers d'Études africaines* II. i (5) (1961), 12–23; A. J. Drewes, *Inscriptions de l'Éthiopie antique* (Leiden, 1962); most of the relevant inscriptions are published in *Annales d'Éthiopie* and *Rassegna di Studi Etiopici*.

68. Biblical references to Ethiopia (O.T. Cush, LXX Αἰθιοπία) are discussed in full by Ullendorff, op. cit. 5–15, who notes the lack of any precise connotation in the usage of the name there or in classical writers. Originally Αἰθιόπες seem to have been the inhabitants of Egypt, Nubia, and India, but were specified by some writers, such as Herodotus, to Meroe. In the Old Testament Cush was apparently limited to the Nile Valley south of Egypt, perhaps including Abyssinia, though more by default than through any clear knowledge of the country.

69. See C. Conti Rossini, *Storia d'Etiopia* (Bergamo, 1928), 103–4.

BIBLIOGRAPHY

General

DIETRICH, A., 'Geschichte Arabiens vor dem Islam', *Handbuch der Orientalistik* Abt. 1, Bd. II, Abschn. 4, Lief. 2 (Leiden 1966), 291–336.

GABRIELI, F. (ed.), *L'antica società beduina* (Università di Roma, Centro di Studi Semitici: Studi Semitici 2, Rome, 1959).

GROHMANN, A. 'Arabien', *Handbuch der Altertumswissenschaft*, 3. 1. 3. 3. 4, (München, 1963).

IBN AL-KALBĪ: *Das Götzenbuch Kitâb al-Aṣnâm des Ibn al-Kalbî*, ed. Rosa Klinke-Rosenberger (Sammlung Orientalistischer Arbeiten, 8, Leipzig, 1941).

LUCKENBILL, D. D., *Ancient Records of Assyria and Babylonia* (2 vols., Chicago, 1926–7).

MONTGOMERY, J. A., *Arabia and the Bible* (Philadelphia, 1934).

MÜLLER, D. H., 'Arabia', in Pauly-Wissowa's *Realencyclopädie*.

PRITCHARD, J. B., *Ancient Near Eastern Texts Relating to the Old Testament*, 3rd edn. (Princeton, N.J., 1969).

RYCKMANS, G., *Les Religions arabes préislamiques* (Bibliothèque du Muséon 26, Louvain, 1951).

SIMONS, J., *The Geographical and Topographical Texts of the Old Testament* (Leiden, 1959).

WEISS ROSMARIN, T., *Aribi und Arabien in den babylonisch-assyrischen Quellen* (New York, 1932).

WINNETT, F. V. & REED, W. L., *Ancient Records from North Arabia* (Toronto, 1970).

Thamud

VAN DEN BRANDEN, A., *Histoire de Thamoud*, 2nd edn. (Publications de l'Université Libanaise, Section des Études Historiques, 6, Beyrouth, 1966).

—— *Les Inscriptions thamoudéennes* (Bibliothèque du Muséon 25, Louvain, 1950).

—— *Les Textes thamoudéens de Philby* (2 vols., Bibliothèque du Muséon 40–1, Louvain, 1956).

LITTMANN, E., 'Thamūd und Ṣafā', *Abhandlungen für die Kunde des Morgenlandes*, Bd. 25, Nr. 1 (Leipzig, 1940).

WINNETT, F. V., *A Study of the Lihyanite and Thamudic Inscriptions* (Toronto, 1937).

The North Arabian Cities

EUTING, J., *Tagbuch einer Reise in Inner-Arabien* (2 vols., Leiden, 1896–1914).

JAUSSEN, A. & SAVIGNAC, R. *Mission archéologique en Arabie* (3 vols., Paris, 1909–22).

MUSIL, A., *Arabia Deserta* (New York, 1927).

—— *The Northern Ḥeğâz* (New York, 1926).

—— *Northern Neğd* (New York, 1928).

Dedan and Liḥyān

CASKEL, W., *Das altarabische Königreich Lihjan* (Crefeld, 1950).

—— 'Lihyan und Lihyanisch', *Arbeitsgemeinschaft für Forschung des Landes Nordrhein-Westfalen: Geisteswissenschaften*, Heft 4 (Köln and Opladen, 1954).

VAN DEN BRANDEN, A., *Les Inscriptions dédanites* (Publications de l'Université Libanaise, Section des Études Historiques, 8, Beyrouth, 1962).

Nabataea

CANTINEAU, J., *Le Nabatéen* (2 vols., Paris, 1930–2).

GLUECK, N., *Deities and Dolphins* (London, 1966).

—— *Rivers in the Desert* (London, 1959).

GROHMANN, A., 'Nabataioi', in Pauly-Wissowa's *Realencyclopädie*.

KAMMERER, A., *Pétra et la Nabatène* (2 vols., Paris, 1929).

LANKESTER HARDING, G., *The Antiquities of Jordan*, 2nd edn. (London, 1967).

Eastern Arabia

BIBBY, G., *Looking for Dilmun* (London, 1970).

Southern Arabia

BEESTON, A. F. L., *A Descriptive Grammar of Epigraphic South Arabian* (London, 1962).

CONTI ROSSINI, C., *Chrestomathia Arabica Meridionalis Epigraphica* (Rome, 1931). (Latin and Greek sources cited in full, pp. 1–37.)

DOE, B., *Southern Arabia* (London, 1971).

HÖFNER, M., *Altsüdarabische Grammatik* (Porta Linguarum Orientalium 24, Leipzig, 1943).

JAMME, A., 'Le Panthéon sud-arabe préislamique d'après les sources épigraphiques', *Le Muséon* lx (1947), 57–147.

—— *Sabaean Inscriptions from Maḥram Bilqîs (Mârib)* (Baltimore, 1962).

NIELSEN, D., *Handbuch der altarabischen Altertumskunde*, i: *Die altarabische Kultur* (Copenhagen, 1927).

PIRENNE, J., 'La Grèce et Saba', *Mém. Acad. Inscr. et Belles-Lettres, Paris*, xv (1955), 89–196.

—— *Le Royaume sud-arabe de Qatabân et sa datation* (Bibliothèque du Muséon 48, Louvain, 1961).

RATHJENS, C., 'Kulturelle Einflüsse in Südwest-Arabien von den ältesten Zeiten bis zum Islam unter besonderer Berücksichtigung des Hellenismus', *Jahrb. für Kleinasiat. Forschung* i (1950), 1–42.

RYCKMANS, J., *L'Institution monarchique en Arabie Méridionale avant l'Islam (Ma'în et Saba)* (Bibliothèque du Muséon 28, Louvain, 1951).

TKAČ, J., 'Saba', in Pauly-Wissowa's *Realencyclopädie*.

VON WISSMANN, H. & HÖFNER, M., 'Beiträge zur historischen Geographie des vorislamischen Südarabien', *Akad. der Wiss. und der Lit., Mainz, Abh. der Geistes- und Sozialwiss. Klasse* Jg. 1952, Nr. 4 (Wiesbaden, 1953).

—— 'De Mari Erythraeo', Stuttgarter Geographische Studien 69 (1957), 289–324.

—— *Zur Archäologie und antiken Geographie von Südarabien* (Uitgaven van het Nederlands Historisch-Archaeologisch Instituut te İstanbul 24, Istanbul, 1968).

—— 'Zur Geschichte und Landeskunde von Alt-Südarabien', *Sitzungsb. der Österreichischen Akad. der Wiss.*, Bd. 246 (Wien, 1964).

XIII

THE PERSIANS

GEO WIDENGREN

(i) *History*

TRACES of Indo-European influences are found in the Near East from about 1700 B.C. A new and stronger influence makes itself felt in the kingdom of Mitanni after 1500 B.C.[1] The military successes of Mitanni were won chiefly thanks to their excellent chariotry and their use of weapons made of iron. The horse, the chariot, and iron were distinctive in the military equipment of Indo-European peoples. The chariot-fighters were great feudal lords, possessing large domains, for chariotry was an expensive weapon, presupposing a costly breeding and training of horses.[2] These feudal lords were called *maryanni*, a word attested also in the Ugaritic texts. Many of these *maryanni* bore Aryan, i.e. Indo-Iranian, names, and they may be looked upon as the precursors of the later Iranian and Indian tribes, both because of their (theophoric) proper names and because of their otherwise attested Indo-Iranian deities.[3] The traditions of the Mitannian kingdom were to some extent inherited by the Assyrians, and there is in the epic poem glorifying Tukulti-Ninurta a warlike, heroic spirit, seldom expressed in older Semitic poetry.[4] Moreover, the description of the Assyrian warriors reveals close agreement with what we know from later times of the organization and behaviour of warrior societies in ancient Iran. The Assyrian warriors are called *ardāni*, corresponding with the Old Persian (OP) term *bandaka*. But these *ardāni*, 'servants', are also *mutu*, 'men', in the heroic sense of the word (they are *uršannu*, 'heroes'), corresponding with *marīka* (**maryaka*), the OP form of the *maryanni* (*maryān-ni*). Their behaviour is characterized by some distinctive features: the ecstatic rage (*tēšū* and *labbu*), dancing into battle (*sāru* and *melēlu*), special hair-dress and the arrangement of their hair (*qaṣāru pirēti*), and fighting without protection (*balū taḫlipi*, 'naked', at any rate without *saryamāti*, 'armour'). All these traits are found later in Iranian society as special characteristics of the warrior societies from which feudal institutions were developed.

It is important to observe that Israel in its heroic age, the period of the Judges and the first kings, shows much both of feudal institutions and of the distinctive traits so typical of the Mitanni and Assyrian warriors. For example, we may cite the special hair-dressing of the warriors in Judges 5: 2 and in the Samson stories.[5]

The immigration of Iranian tribes is observable first in an archaeological context, as in the excavations at Sialk in Media.[6] Here we meet with traces of the immigrating Iranians, with their brachycephalic skulls, and find weapons of iron mixed with those of bronze. In particular, there were reins made of both iron and bronze, and pictures of horses painted on ceramic wares. The warrior painted on these wares carried a sword at his belt, and one seal also shows a horseman. It is a characteristic of the religion of this Iranian people that they buried their dead in a special place in the ground, with many and varied utensils and pieces of jewellery. It is difficult to date this Iranian structure at Sialk with certainty, but it must be earlier than the first millennium B.C.

It is to be assumed that these western Iranian tribes made their way into Iran from the Caucasus, and then settled around Lake Urmia, to spread later into adjacent regions. They were divided into two tribes, the Medes and the Persians.

In written sources, these western Iranian tribes first appear in the annals of Shalmaneser III, which state that in 836 B.C. the Assyrian king received tribute from kings of Parsuaš.[7] This country is located west of Lake Urmia. He then reached the lands of the Mada, situated south-east of Urmia. In 820 Shamshi-Adad V came in contact with Iranians in Parsuaš, which was by now, however, the designation of a more southerly region in the vicinity of Kermanshah. In 737 Tiglath-pileser III invaded the original Parsuaš. He was able to receive tribute—or perhaps rather gifts—from Median chieftains living at Mount Bikni, which is to be identified with Demavand. Both Persians and Medes were independent of Assyria, as the frequent Assyrian raids testify.

In 715 a local Median chieftain, Daiaukku, called 'King', was taken captive and deported to Syria. It is assumed that he is the Deiokes who, according to Herodotus (i. 96 ff.), founded the united Median kingdom. This achievement is, however, difficult to reconcile with his failure against the Assyrians. In the following year, 714, Sargon II is said to have received tribute from U(a)k-satar (Cyaxares). This Assyrian king made several raids into the Iranian lands and was in contact with many Median and Persian chieftains. By this time horse-breeding in Media had already produced the Nisaean chargers, which were later to be famous, for Sargon received such horses as tribute, a welcome addition to his cavalry. The word for lucerne (*aspast*), used as fodder for the grazing horses, entered the Assyrian language as an Iranian loanword (*aspastu*). The Medes were respected enemies, for the Assyrian Sargon calls them 'the mighty Medes' (*madaia dannūti*; Eighth Campaign, line 75).

Sargon II made several expeditions to the east, but he scarcely penetrated Median territory. In contrast, during the reign of Sennacherib, Cyaxares I (Huvakhshathra) attacked an Assyrian province (702). The same Assyrian king in the battle of Halule was opposed by troops from Parsuash and Anshan. It is possible that their leader was Achaemenes (Hakhamanish), founder of the famous Persian dynasty. Teispes (Khišpiš), his son, was actually King of Anshan, but was also called 'Great King', so he must have extended his territory. In this period the Persians had moved southward and occupied territories not far from Elam. Presumably they had been pushed in that direction by the Medes, who for nearly 200 years dominated the history of Iranian peoples in the west.

After the invasion by Cimmerians and Scythians (hordes coming from Central Asia, and, at least as far as the Scythians are concerned, of Iranian origin) Phraortes (Fravartish) ruled Media *c.* 675–653. He formed a coalition of Medes and Cimmerians against Assyria, and, supported by the Persians, attacked Assyria in 653, but was defeated and died on the battlefield.

After the Median defeat Persia became independent. In 651 Cyrus I of Persia, belonging to the family of the Achaemenians, sent help to Shamash-shum-ukin, King of Babylonia, who had rebelled against his brother Ashurbanipal, as had Elam. Ashurbanipal crushed the revolt and marched against Elam, conquering the country and destroying its capital. Cyrus I, the King of Parsuaš, terrified by these events, then sent his eldest son Arukku (Aryavaka) to Nineveh to present his submission and tribute.

In Media Phraortes had been succeeded by his son Cyaxares II, who reorganized the Median kingdom and its army. He regained the position of overlord of Persia. When planning to attack Assyria, Cyaxares was himself menaced by a new Scythian invasion, and was forced to pay tribute to the invading tribes—for 28 years according to Herodotus (i. 106). Ultimately, about 620, he regained his independence. Herodotus (i. 106) says that he killed the Scythian chieftains at a banquet. If the story is true, it was not the last time in Iranian history that undesirable persons were eliminated in this way.

Cyaxares, in alliance with Nabopolassar of Babylonia, now attacked and crushed the Assyrians, first by conquering and destroying Nineveh in 612, and then by defeating the last remnants of the Assyrian army under King Ashur-uballiṭ at Harran in 610. These events, recorded in the Babylonian Chronicles, mark the end of a series of attacks by the Medes against Assyria over a hundred years. Cyaxares then extended the boundaries of his kingdom in Asia Minor, until, after a prolonged war with the Lydians, he had to agree that the river Halys should be the definite boundary between the two kingdoms. This decision followed an indecisive battle between Medes and Lydians on 28th May 585 B.C., the day of a solar eclipse. The peace was negotiated by the intervention of Syennesis, King of Cilicia, and Nebuchadrezzar.

Cyaxares was succeeded by his son Astyages (Arshtivaiga), known in the Babylonian texts as Ishtuwegu. His was a long reign —from 585 to 550. Astyages gave his daughter Mandane to the Persian king of Anshan, Cambyses I (Kanbujiya). Of this marriage a son was born, Kuraš, called by posterity 'Cyrus the Great'.[8] The stories told by Herodotus and Ctesias about the birth, exposure, and remarkable deliverance of the young prince reflect the traditional royal birth-legend among Iranian peoples, and lack all historical value.[9]

Cyrus succeeded in uniting all Persian tribes under his sceptre, and established friendly relations with Nabonidus, King of Babylonia. This ruler was obviously afraid of his former ally Media and its imperial aspirations. Cyrus then began a revolt against his overlord Astyages, who sent against him an army under the command of Harpagus. This general, however, dissatisfied with his monarch (whether for personal reasons or not we do not know, for what Herodotus and others have to say is legend, based on well-known folklore motifs), deserted the Median cause and brought his army over to Cyrus. Only the barest outline of historical facts is known, including the fact that the Median capital Ecbatana (Agmatana) was conquered and looted in either 553 or 550 B.C. Astyages was either conquered in battle or captured in his capital, according to the Nabonidus Chronicle (ii. 1–4) which relates these events.

Media lost its position as an independent kingdom and was turned into the first satrapy of the Persian empire. Medes were used along with Persians in the army and administration, and occupied a position in the empire equal to that of the Persians. Both Medes and Persians were often called simply 'Medes' by the Greeks, and this usage evidently dates from the first contact between Greeks in Ionia and Iranians of the west.

Cyrus resumed the Median policy and turned against the Lydian kingdom, ruled by Croesus. On the way he conquered Armenia, Cappadocia, and Cilicia, which he organized as satrapies. A first battle against the Lydians was inconclusive, but Croesus retired to his capital, Sardes. According to Herodotus, he intended to summon his allies Amasis of Egypt, Nabonidus, and the Spartans, but the reliability of this report is doubtful.[10] He seems to have disbanded his provincial levies, not expecting a winter campaign. Cyrus, however, attacked just before winter set in. The Lydians were forced back to the citadel of Sardis, which was invested and taken in 547 B.C., after only fourteen days. The fate of Croesus offered excellent opportunity for legendary traditions, stressing the magnanimity of Cyrus toward his royal prisoner.[11] The Nabonidus Chronicle (ii. 17), however, states that the king was killed.

Of the Greek cities in Asia Minor only Miletus accepted Cyrus as overlord. It was necessary to fight and conquer the other Ionian city-states, but they were overcome easily, since they made war separately. The Lycians also were conquered, but only after a heroic resistance. The Greek islands, on the other hand, showed no fighting spirit and were subjugated without any difficulty. The coastland then formed the satrapy of Ionia. Internal strife, caused by struggle between the various classes, and reluctance to co-operate with other Greek city-states were the chief reasons that the Ionian city-states were so easily conquered.[12]

While these operations were going on in the west, Cyrus had turned his attention to the east. He secured the whole of the Iranian plateau for his new empire, incorporating also what was later known as the satrapy of Gandara, territory partly belonging to north-west India.[13] In this way Cyrus paved the way for war with Babylonia. He had by now all the military resources of Iran (in its geographical sense) behind him, thereby gaining an overwhelming superiority in cavalry, the most important arm at this time. Nabonidus, the last King of Babylonia and an enigmatic personality, found himself placed in a difficult situation, not least because of internal dissension, caused in part by the powerful priesthood of Marduk, since Nabonidus was probably in conflict with the priests of Babylon on account of his religious policy. Nabonidus tried to elevate the moon-god Sin, who had a major sanctuary at Harran in northern Mesopotamia, at the cost of Marduk, the city-god of Babylon and the supreme deity of the Babylonian pantheon.

The Jewish exiles in Babylonia (and probably also those deported from northern Israel by the Assyrians) would be among the enemies of Nabonidus and secret supporters of Cyrus. Though not very numerous, they possibly possessed some financial resources. The anonymous prophet 'Deutero-Isaiah' glorifies Cyrus in his oracles as the promised saviour of the Jewish people, the Messiah, the Anointed of Yahweh. This underground propaganda from both Babylonian and Jewish quarters must have considerably weakened Nabonidus' position.[14] The King, moreover, was very old.[15] His political and military measures—above all the reason for his ten-year stay in the oasis of Taima—are the subject of much discussion, and not easily explained.[16]

In this situation Cyrus—who obviously had prepared his campaign well—had little more to do than to undertake a display of military force. He started his offensive by striking from the mountains in a westerly direction straight towards Babylon. At Upi (Ophis) his general Gobryas (Gubaruva) crushed all resistance of the Babylonian army, which was probably commanded by Nabonidus himself, in July 539. Sippar fell on 10 October, and within two days the Persian troops entered Babylon without meeting any resistance, possibly owing to the assistance offered by the priests of Marduk. Cyrus himself made his triumphant entry into Babylon on 29 October, greeted by the population with expressions of jubilation. No Babylonian tablets are dated with Nabonidus as king later than 13 October 539 B.C.[17]

Cyrus took over the administrative organization of the Neo-Babylonian kingdom, and evidently left the governors in their offices. His policy was to act in everything as a real Babylonian ruler. Babylonia itself formed together with Ebir-nāri a huge satrapy (OP Bābiru). In his proclamation (in the so-called Cyrus Chronicle) Cyrus retained the old regnal formulas of the Babylonian kings. He reorganized the cults which Nabonidus had tried to reform. The statues of the deities of various cities which Nabonidus had carried to Babylon were transported back to their sanctuaries.[18] Marduk regained his position as the undisputed city-god of the capital and as the chief deity of the Babylonian assembly of gods (*puḫur ilāni*).

Further, in Babylon there were several foreign deities, taken captive and carried away to the capital, together with the most prominent of the inhabitants of the conquered cities. The cult-images of all these deities, as well as their deported adherents, were gathered and sent back to their own cities. In carrying out this policy Cyrus followed the example set by such former rulers as Esarhaddon, for this was a traditional motif in the royal ideology of Mesopotamia—'the gathering of the dispersed'.[19]

Cyrus in his proclamation does not specially mention the Jews among those whom he sent back to their homeland. We know, however, that he dispatched the Jewish prince Sheshbazzar (Shamash-apal-uṣur) to Jerusalem with precious temple vessels, which had earlier been taken by the Babylonians and carried away to Babylon (cf. Ezra 1: 7 f.). He also ordered that the Jerusalem temple should be rebuilt. These measures are known from the authentic Aramaic documents in the O.T. There has been much discussion whether Cyrus had already sent back to Palestine deported Jews belonging to the kingdom of Judah. The arguments adduced against the actual practicability of sending back Jewish deportees within the span of a single year are hardly conclusive, for Cyrus in his own proclamation expressly mentions that he sent back other people who were in the same situation as the Jews.[20] Therefore, presumably Sheshbazzar had already brought back a considerable number of exiled Jews. If we accept as authentic the list of returning exiles given in Nehemiah 7, the number of such people who returned to Judah cannot have been more than 50,000.[21]

The policy followed by Cyrus regarding the deported ethnic groups and their deities meant a new attitude in the history of the Ancient Near East. His policy of toleration was dictated by political reasoning which implies that with him politics counted for more than religion. Also the fact that Cyrus in Babylon assumed the position of a Babylonian ruler, one chosen by Marduk for this office, can only mean that he held a comparatively detached view as far as his own national religion was concerned. We may see a tendency in the same direction in that in his own country of Persia we find a marked syncretism, in so far as Persian and Elamitic elements were mixed together.[22] Cyrus accordingly would seem to have been accustomed to adopt broad-minded views in religious affairs.

It is not surprising, then, that the unknown Jewish prophet could see in Cyrus the Anointed of Yahweh, for obviously his attitude towards the Jews could inspire such feelings. This expectation, as seen from the general Jewish point of view, is more surprising, for it meant that the hope of a Davidic Messiah was given up and the national Messiah changed for a foreign, not even Semitic, ruler. Deutero-Isaiah, with his universalistic outlook, may have been alone in his views,[23] since the hope of a Davidic Messiah was soon revivified in the person of Zerubbabel (Zēr-Bābili).

When Cyrus had organized his new empire—the greatest empire created in the Near East up to that date—he turned again to the east. But we are badly informed about the expedition undertaken by him. Some assume that it was only after the conquest of the Babylonian kingdom that he included the eastern parts of Iran in his empire. This would seem, however, to be unlikely, for Herodotus (i. 177) mentions that Cyrus, immediately after the victory over Croesus, conquered 'the upper parts of Asia'. Parallel passages show this expression to signify Asia as far as the Indus. When Cyrus, after the conquest of Babylon, again turned to the east, he ultimately suffered a defeat in a battle against some nomadic northern people of Iranian origin, either (and most probably) the Massagetae (Massakata, 'the Great Sakas' in general), or the Dahae (a special sub-tribe of the Sakas), or—less credibly—the Derbicae (whose identity in this case is more difficult to ascertain).[24] These three partly-conflicting possibilities point to the north-eastern frontier of the Achaemenid empire, on the other side of the Oxus. If the eastern provinces of Iran had been recently conquered by Cyrus, it would be natural to find them rebelling immediately after his death, but we hear nothing of such a revolt. Presumably, then, they were conquered earlier and comparatively pacified, and accordingly had already been organized as satrapies before the fall of Babylon some fifteen years earlier.

The news of the death of Cyrus reached Babylon in August 530, for the first document dated in the reign of his son and successor Cambyses (Kanbujiya) is from 31 August 530. Since March 530 he had been the co-regent of Cyrus.[25] Like his father, Cambyses was a very capable general and organizer, but he was a difficult character and lacked his father's undeniable ability to hold people loyal to his person.

Cambyses had his eyes on the expansion of the empire to the west, where Egypt was the only great power capable of resisting the Persian advance. The reigning pharaoh, Amasis, had carried through an anti-priestly political programme, leaning heavily on Greek support, above all upon the Greek mercenaries. These foreign soldiers fought well against Cambyses and his Persian army, but were ultimately conquered.[26] There followed the treachery of the admiral Udjahorresne, who surrendered the important city of Saïs.[27] Amasis had died before the war started in 528, and had been succeeded by his son Psammetichus, who now fled to Memphis. That city was taken in 525, and with the fall of the capital Cambyses had completed the conquest of Egypt. This meant that the Persian king now possessed an undisputed command of the eastern Mediterranean, where he from now on disposed of the combined fleets of the Ionian city-states of Asia Minor, of the Phoenician coastal towns, and of the Egyptian navy. From an economic point of view Egypt, with its great resources and flourishing trade with Greece, was a great gain. On the other hand, it seems obvious that the Persian dominion was resented by Egyptian patriots, and, as will be seen, serious and repeated revolts ensued.

After extending and securing his rule in Egypt Cambyses returned home. Rumours of his madly cruel acts against Egyptian religion were soon spread by the priests, and later told to Herodotus. However, they probably lack all foundation, for it is quite obvious that Cambyses in Egypt followed the same policy of toleration as had his father Cyrus in Babylonia. The Egyptian inscriptions are clear on this.[28]

Before Cambyses embarked upon his Egyptian expedition he had had his brother Bardiya killed. This is the first time, but not the last, we hear of such acts in the Achaemenid family. Probably Cambyses feared an insurrection led by him while he himself was absent in Egypt. The death of Bardiya was, however, kept secret, and was known only to a very few people. To understand such an act of fratricide in the royal house it must be remembered that the princes were mostly born of different mothers and brought up separately, so that no natural ties of attachment existed.

When Cambyses returned from Egypt in 522, he left Aryandes there as his satrap. On his way home news reached him that a usurper, calling himself Bardiya, had seized power in Persia and Media. This was the so-called 'false Smerdis' (Smerdis = Bardiya), who in reality was a Median Magian called Gaumāta.[29] He began his revolt on 11 March 522, and documents dated by his reign continue only to April 14. Cambyses learnt of the insurrection when he was in Syria, but died before he was able to deal with the new development. He did not commit suicide, as Herodotus (iii. 63 ff.) relates. The wording of the Behistun inscription (i. 43) indicates only that he was not killed (OP *uvāmaršyuš amaryatā*).

The insurrection was an endeavour by some Median groups, especially the Magian priests, to regain supremacy and dictate the policy of the empire, not least in religious and social affairs. Gaumāta actually carried through some drastic measures in both the religious and social fields, and obviously aimed at gaining the support of subjugated peoples (Herodotus, iii. 67 and D.Bh. i. 63–71).

The Achaemenid Darius (Dārayavauš), who belonged to a branch of the family other than the reigning house, had been the spear-bearer (*arštibara*) of Cambyses, that is, he had belonged to his bodyguard. He had returned to his home in Persia when the army was dissolved after the death of Cambyses, and there he started a conspiracy with six other noblemen. On 29 September 522 he and his fellow conspirators succeeded in entering the Median fortress of Sikayauvati, where Gaumāta resided, and killing the usurper. Since there had been an interregnum, Darius was elected and proclaimed king by his confederates in accordance with an age-old Indo-Iranian omen practice.[30] The sun-god, by means of his special animal, the horse, chose Darius as king. Herodotus, who tells the story (iii. 85 f.), has only partly understood it, but states the essential facts correctly. The helpers of Darius formed together with him the Seven Houses, the noblest families of Persia. The members of the six non-royal houses were given free access to the King.

The military capacity and vigour shown by Darius on this occasion was to be tested later.[31] The newly created empire was, indeed, near disintegration. Darius had at his disposal some Persian and Median levies, forming his army (*kāra*; the word also means 'people'), but it was small (D.Bh. ii. 18 f). In some provinces he had other reliable troops. Darius crushed several revolts in Babylonia, where national resistance against the Persians was strong, and where two usurpers, calling themselves Nebuchadrezzar III and IV, held Babylon in October–December 522 and August–November 521 respectively.[32] Media also rebelled under a member of the old royal house, Phraortes (Fravartiš). Parthians and Hyrcanians sided with the Medes, and the Sakas, understandably enough, revolted. Even in Persia itself there was a revolution under Vahyazdāta, who claimed to be the dead (real!) Bardiya. Armenia too fell away. In the west the satrap of Sardis remained independent and Egypt used the opportunity to liberate itself.

It is something of a miracle that Darius was capable of mastering this desperate situation. With the assistance of some capable generals and his father Vishtāspa, who was the satrap of Parthia, he overcame all the rebellions. He was helped by the fact that every usurper acted in isolation, there being no collaboration between them. At the end of the year 521 B.C. Darius was undisputed ruler of the whole empire, with the exception of the peripheral satrapies of Asia Minor and Egypt. His next task, therefore, was to win back these countries.

To reach Egypt Darius had to march through Syria and Palestine. There the governor was Zerubbabel (= Zēr-Bābili), the grandson of Jehoiachin.[33] He had his seat in Jerusalem, but was a purely secular leader, in contrast to his Davidic ancestors. His arrival had created great expectations in nationalist circles, as can be seen from the prophecies proclaimed by Haggai. The work on the reconstruction of the Jerusalem temple had ceased. Thanks to the inspiring words of Haggai work was resumed on 21 September 520. But this action aroused the suspicion of Tattenai, the Governor of Ebir-Nāri, to whose satrapy Palestine belonged. He asked the Jews who had given them permission to rebuild the temple. Their answer was that Cyrus had earlier commanded the reconstruction of the temple. Tattenai reported to Darius, who had an investigation made in the archives of Ecbatana. The document in question was found, and Darius therefore issued an order to continue the work, to put the necessary means at the disposal of the Jews, and to promote the cult in Jerusalem. The authenticity of these documents is not to be disputed.[34] Both piety towards the commands of the great founder and above all political reasons demanded that this policy should be followed, for it was imperative to have a quiet Jewish population in Palestine on the flank of the army, when Darius marched against Egypt.

But Zerubbabel disappears from the political scene after the prophet Zechariah had exhorted him not to engage in political actions (Zech. 4: 6). This was in February 519, and Darius shortly afterwards appeared in Palestine on his expedition against Egypt.

When Darius had regulated affairs in Palestine, he continued his march to Egypt, which he visited in the winter of 519–518 B.C.[35] He had earlier sent Udjahorresne there, who had once taken refuge with him. This trusted Egyptian prepared the way for Darius, who acted in accordance with the general policy of his predecessors. He knew how to gain the hearts of the Egyptians by respecting their national and religious customs. Darius therefore was soon accepted in Egypt, where he acted as an indigenous Egyptian ruler, assuming the full titles of such a monarch. Before he returned to his capital, Darius had a canal dug through at

Suez, using an older construction started by Necho. By means of this canal he created a link between the Mediterranean and the Indian Ocean. He also sent out ships to investigate the Eastern coasts from Indus to Suez. The Carian naval captain Scylax who commanded this expedition left stories, from which Herodotus took some of his statements about Arabia and India.

Darius managed to regain the satrapy of Ionia, where Oroites (Huraita?) had acquired an independent position. He achieved this by appealing to the loyalty of the garrison (Herodotus, iii. 127 f.). He also conquered the Indus territory shortly before 519, and added it as the twentieth satrapy to his eastern provinces. This satrapy brought a considerably increased financial income, because of its richness in gold.[36] It is probable that in the east Darius also tried to gain a firmer grip on the Sakas, who had taken part in the great revolts of his accession-year, but had since been brought back to order, evidently by Darius himself (D.Bh. v. 74).

It is understandable that Darius wanted to incorporate other tribes of the Saka people, living in South Russia and known by the Greeks as Scythians. On the western and northern coasts of the Black Sea there were Greek colonies, mostly founded from Miletus, the first city to submit to the Great King's suzerainty. These Greek colonies had established close contacts with the Scythians, both economic and cultural, and were flourishing cities, exporting corn in great quantities. Military and financial reasons both spoke for such an expedition, which could make the Great King overlord of the other side of the Hellespont and the Black Sea, and extend his influence over the Greeks of Europe.[37] The date of this expedition is not known, but must be assigned to some time before 513, which is the latest possible year. The size of the army brought by Darius against the Scythians is not known, but was considerable, though he probably underrated the difficulties of the undertaking. The optimistic goals were not reached, though Darius in the course of the campaign had Thracia conquered by Megabyzus (Bagabuxšā), the satrap of Dascylium, and was recognized as the overlord of Macedonia. In this way Darius not only extended his empire along the coasts of the Black Sea and the Aegean, but henceforth was also a neighbour of Hellas. It was now possible to play a role in Greek politics. In doing so he at first relied on the tyrants of the Greek cities of Asia

Minor (later, however, on 'democratic' governments) as well as on the dispossessed tyrants and adventurers from Greece, who had taken refuge with his satrap in Sardis and at his own court in Susa. From now on Persian and Greek politics were each dominated by concern with the other. The struggle between Greeks and Persians was to continue for nearly 200 years. The idea of a universal empire as inherited from the ancient oriental monarchies had within it the will not to desist from constantly trying to enlarge its territory, until thwarted by a resistance which would prove impossible to overcome.[38]

The course of events is well known. Some dates and facts only need to be emphasized. The defeat at Marathon in 490 followed after the revolts of the Ionian cities had been mercilessly crushed. This was important, since it demonstrated to the Greeks that it was possible for the Greek hoplites to conquer the Persian light cavalry. The lance proved stronger than the bow. It also underlined the tactical advantage of choosing a battle-ground where cavalry had great difficulties in manœuvring.[39]

Xerxes, the son of Darius, who first had to suppress a revolt in Egypt (Herodotus, vii. 7), was infinitely less capable than his father, who was one of history's truly great rulers (Plate VIII). Xerxes was neither a statesman nor a general, and lacked the magnanimity his father was at times capable of showing. The expedition against Greece, however, was well organized and, from the diplomatic point of view, shrewdly prepared, for in many Greek states the Great King had a majority of adherents and friends.[40] Moreover, Xerxes concluded a treaty with Carthage in order to prevent Magna Graecia in Sicily and South Italy from assisting the Greeks. But from the military point of view several mistakes were committed. The most serious was to burn Athens, a misdeed which drove not only the Athenians but also other Greek states to a determined resistance. After the land-and-sea victory at Thermopylae–Artemisium it was a mistake to let the fleet attack in the narrow strait of Salamis on 22 September 480 B.C. Xerxes there lost half his fleet, according to Herodotus' probably exaggerated account. It is calculated that the Persians were hardly superior in number to the Greeks. The Persian fleet was composed of Ionian Greeks, Phoenicians, and Egyptians, the crews being mixed with Persian soldiers as marines. They were all as capable seamen as the Greeks, but they lacked unity and cohesion, and the fleet was prone to break up into its three national groups. Above all, the Persian fleet needed room to manœuvre. The losses of the Persian fleet were probably not so serious as to make it impossible to renew the battle next day, but morale was shaken, since the best sailors in the world, the Phoenicians, had been beaten and the loyalty of the Ionians could no longer be trusted.

The battle of Plataea (479)—where Mardonius had at his disposal slightly more than 20,000 men—provides the same general picture as do the other battles lost by the Persians during the Greek wars. Owing to unfortunate circumstances Mardonius (= Marduniya), who possessed a certain numerical superiority, was induced to fight at close quarters on ground favourable to infantry, but not to cavalry. Arms better suited to hand-to-hand fighting, and superior tactics, determined the issue of the day. The Persian losses were considerable, but Artabazus saved the greater part of the army, with which he retreated to Asia.

The Greek fleet landed in Asia Minor, and at Mycale inflicted serious losses both on a comparatively small Persian fleet and on an army corps composed of local levies. But this was a minor battle and its importance has been grossly exaggerated.[41]

Even before his expedition against Greece Xerxes had to suppress a revolt in Babylonia, when two rebels successively assumed power and had tablets dated by their names. The King's general Megabyzus crushed the revolt and Babylon was severely punished. Its fortifications were demolished, temples destroyed, the golden statue of Marduk melted down, and estates confiscated and given to Persians. Syria was made an independent satrapy and Babylonia incorporated with Assyria as a special satrapy. Xerxes and succeeding kings no longer styled themselves 'King of Babylon, King of lands'.

The war with Greece straggled on, while Xerxes more and more lost energy—the victim of life in his harem, which seems to have been the dominating interest of his life—even if we need not take at its face value all the gossip that Herodotus and Ctesias have recorded of cruelty and harem intrigues. It is this aged Xerxes who is the Ahasuerus of the Esther novel.[42]

It was as a consequence of this decay that Xerxes in 465 was murdered by his chiliarch Artabanus. After some confusion the younger son Artaxerxes (465–424) ascended the throne. He was a rather passive ruler, but indirectly played a great role in the life of the Jewish community, in so far as it was he who sent his cup-bearer Nehemiah—it is interesting to note that a Jew had arrived at this high position at the Persian court—to Jerusalem to rebuild its walls.[43] He got from the king official documents to secure his expedition and to provide him with building material. Escorted by Persian cavalry, Nehemiah arrived at Jerusalem and with skill and vigour completed his task in spite of all difficulties. In this case his position as a royal favourite obviously smoothed the way for the royal commissioner Nehemiah, but the political motives behind the action on the part of the Persian government were the decisive factors.[44] These must be seen in the light of the political situation in the whole empire, which, in the first period of Artaxerxes' reign, was serious. A revolt in Bactria, instigated by his brother Hystaspes immediately after his enthronement, was easily crushed. Much more difficult was a new revolt in Egypt, started by national elements and led by Inarus, who is said to have been the son of Psammetichus. In the year 460 he turned to Athens and its leader Pericles for help, which was given. With the aid of an Athenian fleet Inarus was able to conquer the Persian satrap Achaemenes, who was killed in the battle. Memphis was taken by the rebels in 459. However, the experienced general Megabyzus, who was sent to recover Egypt, met with complete success. The allied Athenians and Egyptians were decisively defeated, and the Athenian expedition ended in catastrophe in 455 B.C. Athens ultimately sent an embassy to Susa, and the so-called peace of Callias was concluded in 449. The outbreak of the Peloponnesian war in 431 gave the Persians a much needed further respite. Actually the empire was already in a state of dissolution. But when a capable general was dispatched, as in 455, to handle the situation he was able by his clever tactics to conquer even the Greek hoplites.

Artaxerxes I was succeeded by Darius II (423–404) after the usual convulsive fighting and murders connected with a change of rule. It is characteristic that some of the chief actors were sons of Babylonian concubines in the Great King's harem. Darius II was under the influence of his consort, the terrible Parysatis, whose name (Pamšyatiš, 'Full of joy') seems sheer irony in the light of all her cruel misdeeds.

The Persian satrap in Egypt employed Jewish mercenaries, who had been there since before the time of Cambyses. It was important for the Persian government to be able to rely on these Jewish soldiers, since Egypt was constantly in a state of unrest and rebellion. To impress them Darius I had an Aramaic translation of his great deeds, as inscribed at Behistun, circulated among his Jewish mercenaries in Egypt, who were garrisoned on the island of Elephantine and in Syene, opposite to it on the eastern side of the Nile.[45] Their task was to protect the southern frontier. Herodotus, who visited Egypt about 450 B.C., reports that one of the three strong Persian garrisons was located in Elephantine itself (ii. 30).[46]

The Jews possessed a small temple where they offered sacrifices to their national god Yahu. Probably these sacrifices, including those of rams offered as burnt offerings, irritated the Egyptian priests of Khnum, whose symbolic animal was the ram. But obviously this was not the chief motive for their destroying the temple in 410. The reason must have been political, for the Jews were loyal to the Persian satrap, and could therefore be used against the Egyptians when they rebelled, as they did that same year (CP 27, 1–2). The opportunity came when Arsham, the satrap, left to report at the royal court in Susa. In concert with Vidrang, the local Persian governor (*frataraka*), who may have been bribed, the Egyptian priests sacked and destroyed the temple. The Jews protested in a letter, probably addressed to Arsham, asking for an investigation and the rebuilding of the altar. In another petition sent to Bagohi, the Governor of Judaea, by the Jewish garrison, they asked Bagohi to give orders for the rebuilding of the temple. It was emphasized that Arsham knew nothing of what was done. This petition, sent in 410, was left without an answer, and was therefore repeated in 407. The petitioners in this second letter mention that they have set forth the whole matter in a letter to Delaiah and Shelemiah, the sons of Sanballat (= Sinuballiṭ), Governor of Samaria. This second letter resulted in an oral reply given by Bagohi and Delaiah to the messenger, who brought the letter, written by himself. This ordered him to tell Arsham that the altar-house of the God of Heaven should be rebuilt on the same site, and that they might offer the meal-offering and incense upon the altar as had been done formerly. Accordingly it was *not* suggested to Arsham that he should allow a renewal of the burnt offerings. In the main, the Jews of Elephantine got the necessary support from Bagohi (CP 30), but to achieve this they had had to bribe the Persian governor (CP 33, 13–14).

The religion of the Jews accordingly caused the Persian authorities some difficulties. They had to intervene, regulating matters relating to the worship of the Jews, not only in Palestine, but also in Egypt. Another proof of this is the so-called Passover Papyrus of the year 419. Here, however, the command given by Darius II to Arsham is lost, and must be restored. It is not likely that the royal command regulated the celebration of the Passover, as has been surmised, but rather that it contained an order to leave the Jewish garrison alone to carry on their cult.[47] In other words, they could celebrate their festivals according to their custom (CP 21). It would have been impracticable for the government to issue regulations concerning foreign cults.

In the Elephantine documents the God of the Jews in a number of passages is called 'God of Heaven' as is the case also in the Persian Aramaic documents of the Old Testament. This is accordingly the name given to Yahweh in the official Persian writings. It has been thought that this phrase was chosen intentionally, to establish a mutual understanding between Jews and Iranians worshipping Ahura Mazdā, who was a god of heaven.[48]

In the following years Egypt rebelled again, and this new revolt started in 405 when Amyrtaeus gained control over some part of Egypt. Aramaic documents, however, clearly show that Artaxerxes II, who succeeded his father Darius II in 404, was still recognized at Elephantine in 402/1 B.C.[49] In this year great internal dissensions troubled the empire. Cyrus the Younger, with the help of the famous 'Ten thousand' Greek mercenaries, tried to seize power from his brother Artaxerxes, whom he hated. But at Cunaxa he lost both battle and life. The Greek soldiers, in the midst of a hostile country, and surrounded by the troops of the Great King, managed, under the leadership of Xenophon, to get back unmolested. This was a great deed, but it shows the terrible confusion and dissolution in the empire, for else such an expedition would have been impossible. Again in the battle itself the Greek hoplites showed themselves vastly superior to the Persian troopers.

It was probably in 398/7 that Ezra came to Jerusalem to carry through cultic and social reforms in accordance with the Law (though it is not known what special law is intended).[50] In this case, too, it has been assumed that Persian initiative played an active part in bringing about his mission, and Ezra's position has been said to be that of a secretary of state for Jewish affairs.[51] This assumption is, however, highly uncertain.[52] We may take for granted that the Persian government wanted peace and order in Judah, as this province was on the border of Egypt, which was now rebelling once more. But there were evidently still some internal dissensions after the time of Nehemiah. Ezra, who was holding some high office in the Persian chancery, and was at the same time a priest (*kāhen*), enjoyed a high reputation among his fellow Jews because of his learning and piety. He was therefore sent out by the Great King as a special commissioner, and provided with royal authorization and financial support. Ezra carried out his commission to the satisfaction of the Jewish community of Jerusalem, and also probably to that of the Persian government. Bagohi was still a governor in Jerusalem, but we hear of no clash between him and Ezra. He is not even mentioned in the book of Ezra. In the following period we lose sight of the connections between the government of the empire and the Jews. We may assume that there were no special troubles and that the Jews remained the same loyal subjects to the crown as before. The province of Judah therefore enjoyed the privilege of issuing coinage.[53]

In other respects affairs were more difficult. Egypt was still in revolt and capable of preserving its independence. In other parts of the empire too—and especially in Asia Minor—there were minor revolts, culminating in the great satraps' rebellion under the leadership of the two satraps Datames (Dātama) and Ariobarzanes (Aryabarzana). This caused immense confusion and lasted for ten years, 368–358. At last the cruel but capable Artaxerxes III (358–338) seized power and began his reign by murdering all princes who could claim a right to the throne. After crushing a revolt in Sidon he succeeded in conquering Egypt and its last pharaoh, Nectanebus, in 345.

Artaxerxes III was murdered by his leading minister, the eunuch Bagohi, in 338. This is an example of the fact that the eunuchs at the Achaemenian court over a long period exercised an often pernicious influence. After the short reign of Arses—who was eliminated by the redoubtable eunuch—Darius III (335–330 B.C.) was promoted to the throne. A capable ruler, and possessed of personal courage, he was confronted with a doubly difficult task. On the one hand, he had to fight against the forces which tended to the dissolution of the empire: the efforts of subjugated peoples to liberate themselves, and the constant revolts of the great feudal lords in their positions as satraps. On the other hand, he had to try to resist the attack prepared by Alexander of Macedonia in the great Greek war of revenge against the Achaemenian Empire. One of these tasks would have been enough; both proved too much for him.

On the whole, however, Darius succeeded in keeping most of the empire, and especially its Iranian parts, together, so as to offer a fair resistance against a general who was a military genius in command of a highly efficient army. The battle of Granicus in 334, when Alexander with an army of 40,000 conquered the local levies of the satraps of Asia Minor,[54] demonstrated to the Persian high command that a mobilization of the resources of the whole empire was necessary if the invader was to be held off.

The battle of Granicus gave Alexander undisputed power over Asia Minor. At Issus he met for the first time the Persian field-army under the command of Darius himself.[55] Greek sources give the Great King 600,000 men. Though a tenth of this is more likely, he was probably superior in numbers. The battle-ground was not well chosen by the Persians, for their cavalry could not be fully deployed. But at least some of the Persian troops fought well, and we learn of violent charges by heavy cavalry, obviously well armed (Curtius, III. xi, 14–15). Alexander's excellent leadership, however, secured the day. Many Persian noblemen fell around the chariot from which Darius supervised the battle, but in the end he had to abandon the battlefield.

In a last effort Darius succeeded in mobilizing a new army, in which the troops from eastern Iran added considerable strength to his cavalry. This was again his most effective arm, his infantry, 2,000 Greek mercenaries excepted, being of negligible worth. In numbers Darius was vastly superior in cavalry, where he outnumbered Alexander by some five to one. Alexander's army was about 50,000 strong. Darius had 34,000 cavalry plus 2,000 Greek foot-soldiers. The rest of his infantry was of little use, and it may be doubted whether the Persians were more numerous than the Macedonians and Greeks. On 30 September Alexander's generalship secured for him the decisive victory at Gaugamela, after a very hard and severe battle.[56] Darius fled from the battlefield and some generals at once deserted his cause.

With this final defeat the fate of the Achaemenian empire was sealed. Darius obviously hoped to organize resistance in eastern Iran, but he was treacherously murdered by his Bactrian satrap Bessus. Indeed, a stubborn resistance did face Alexander in the eastern parts of the empire. It lacked, however, a leader able to integrate the fighting forces. After some years of hard fighting Alexander was undisputed master of all the more important eastern provinces. The political role of the Persians had ended, and it was to be 550 years before they were able to stage a comeback.

(ii) *Administrative and Military Organization*

The Achaemenian empire had a feudal basis for its social structure. Upon that basis was built, however, as a superstructure, an administrative system of a very centralized character.

The feudal basis shows itself even in the principles of education.[57] In Iranian society education was organized by classes, according to age. It started at the age of five to seven years, when the boys were taken from their mothers and handed over to certain foster-parents who acted as instructors (Herodotus, i. 136; Strabo, xv. 3. 18; Ps. Plato, *Alcibiades*, 121 f.). Strabo describes how the boys were trained by the teachers to endure hardships, to camp in the open air, and to practise stealing. For this we may also compare the life led by Cyrus in his youth, as told by Herodotus (i. 114). Xenophon's account (*Cyrop*. I. ii. 3–9) agrees in all essentials, but emphasizes above all the military aspects of this education in a warrior society.

This period of education lasts to about the fifteenth year, which is the ideal age of maturity in Iran. Strabo says that the young men are called *kardakes*, since they live from stealing, which is a characteristic trait in the warrior societies. These *kardakes* we know from Polybius (v. 79. 11) as professional soldiers, and Arrian (ii. 8. 6) relates how Alexander in the battle of Issus broke through their lines. They are accordingly the specially trained young warriors who were used as heavily armed soldiers. The training, however, was carried on to the age of twenty, so that the second period was between ages fifteen and twenty. At this age the youth was counted as one of the fully mature men. He left the training school and probably married, though this is not mentioned in our sources.

The members of a warrior society were attached to their Grand Master by means of a special bond of loyalty, and this bond was symbolically marked by the girdle, which signified the warrior's attachment to his superior.[58] When these societies assumed feudal traits by the members' being given domains, or supported in other ways, the girdle was looked upon as the symbol of vassalage. The unfaithful vassal was seized by his girdle and dragged away to be executed (Xenophon, *Anabasis*, i. 10) or his girdle was cut through. When the vassal broke his bond of vassalage this found an outward expression in the loosening of his girdle. Because of this bond the vassal was a 'bondsman' (*bandaka*), not free, but rather a serf. This was true also of the crown vassals, as shown in the Behistun Inscription, but *bandaka* should never be rendered 'slave'.

Another designation, still in use in Achaemenid times, was *marīka*, expressing the fact that the member of a lord's retinue was a 'young man', which is the proper meaning of the word. *Marīka* became obsolete, but *bandaka* remained in use. The word *anušiya* was also used.[59]

Strabo says that the boys lived in platoons of 50, and this was in fact the number of a unit's strength in the Persian army. The organization was built upon the decimal system,[60] the basic unit being the group of 50. Such units could be combined in various ways (2×50, 3×50, up to 20×50 = 1,000). The smallest unit was the group of 5, commanded by a *pascadasapati*. Then comes the 10-group, the commander of which was the *dasapati*. Two 50-platoons formed a company, called *drafša*, 'flag'. In the Aramaic of the Elephantine papyri it is called either *degel* or *me'āṯā*, 'a hundred'. Ten companies formed a regiment, probably **gunda* > MI. *gund*, whose commander was the *hazahrapati*.[61] Ten regiments constituted a division whose commander was possibly a **baivarpati*. These designations were conventional. A unit seldom reached its nominal strength, and its deficiency was revealed in the rolls used at the yearly mustering (**handaisa*).[62] The Median term presumably was **hama-spāda*, for *spāda* is the Median term for 'army', whereas the Persian name is *kāra*.[63] The muster-scribe (**handaisaka* > (*h*)*andēsak*) recorded the real strength of the troops to be mustered.[64] We know the names of several places where musterings were held, and probably every satrapy had at least one such centre.

A cuneiform document from the reign of Darius II records the armament and equipment of a horseman who had to present himself at Uruk, the mustering-place of Babylonia.[65] He should carry with him provisions and one mina of silver.

The concentration of troops was facilitated by the excellent road system, with its numerous stopping-places.[66] There stores were established for the troops. The so-called 'royal road' from Susa to Sardis (itself considerably older than the Persian empire) played a central role in road communications. Another major road was the 'Silk Road' leading from the Euphrates to China. These roads were equally important from the military and from the economic point of view.

Fiefs were distributed to various people.[67] Cyrus the Great, according to Xenophon, had handed over domains and houses to his followers (*Cyrop.* VIII. iv. 28), but the system was much older. It was probably taken over from the Medes, who had it from the Assyrians, who in their turn had inherited the traditions of the Mitannian kingdom. From the Nuzi and Alalakh documents we know something of this early feudal distribution of royal domains.[68] In Achaemenid times there was a development in the direction of *allodium* (which means that the fiefs were inherited within a certain family).[69] This sometimes had bad consequences, for the fiefs could change their character and be made the object of economic speculation. This had already happened in the Mitannian period. Such a development is obviously connected with the fact that in principle the fiefs were free from tribute, in return for the duty to put one or more soldiers at the king's disposal. Xenophon has preserved a complaint that in his days the holders of fiefs were all kinds of artisans and workmen, but few were keen soldiers: 'Now the rulers make knights out of their porters, bakers, cooks, cup-bearers, bathroom attendants, butlers, waiters, chamberlains who assist them in retiring at night and in rising in the morning, and beauty-doctors who pencil their eyes and rouge their cheeks for them and otherwise beautify them; these are the sort that they make into knights to serve for pay for them' (*Cyrop.* VIII. viii. 20). This description is in general exaggerated, but we may see here one of the causes of the military decay in the later days of the empire.

The troops were divided into two categories: those who were in garrisons and those who comprised the field-army.[70] The garrison was under the command of a phrourarch (**arkapati* > *arkapat*).[71] The troops composing the field army were commanded by either satraps or chiliarchs (= *hazahrapati*), but it is difficult to say how they were distributed. It would seem natural, however, that the satrap should have commanded the local levies. The satrap also had to provide the necessary provisions for the troops of his satrapy. Both the king and the satraps possessed their own body-guards (cf. Herodotus iii. 12 f.).

The king could appoint a satrap as commander-in-chief of a greater number of troops. He was then called *karanos*.[72] We know of several such commanders-in-chief, but when the Great King was present he was, of course, the chief commander.

The various types of fief correspond with the categories of the army, of which the most important was the cavalry. In cuneiform documents we accordingly meet with the following terms:[73] *bīt narkabti*, a fief raising a war-chariot (now a rather outmoded weapon, but still used in Persian armies); *bīt sīsē*, a fief raising a horseman; and *bīt qašti*, a fief raising a bowman (as a foot-soldier). As well as these fiefs (*bītāti*), we have the royal domain (*bīt šarri*), from which the various fiefs were parcelled out. These terms are Babylonian, the Persian names being unknown, except that we find a hybrid term *bīt aspatum* for *bīt sīsē*.

The cavalry was usually a light cavalry, without protection for the body, carrying either bow or javelin, and a comparatively short spear, and also the famous Persian short sword (the *akinakēs* > Sogd. *kyn'k*). There were also, however, some heavy cavalry.[74] The breeding of the formidable Nisaean horses shows too that a heavy cavalry existed, for without it the training of such horses would have been pointless. Their existence is already demonstrated in a reference from the time of Sargon.[75]

Cavalry tactics are mentioned by Herodotus (ix. 49). It must be noticed that nothing certain is yet known from Achaemenid times about the encircling tactics used by the Parthians. The charge by heavy cavalry is mentioned by Curtius in his description of the battle at Issus.[76] The infantry was weak, except for the king's bodyguard, the so-called 'Ten Thousand Immortals', which was a *troupe d'élite*, and the heavily armed *kardakes*. Slingers were also used (see also Plate V*c*).

The Persians possessed no navy of their own, for in antiquity they were never seamen. The deficiency was made good by the mobilization of the Ionian, Phoenician, and Egyptian fleets. But the handling of such a composite navy was difficult, and though they were all excellent seamen, the result was generally disappointing. The crews were supported by Iranians as soldiers, for naval battles consisted not only in ramming but also in boarding enemy ships.[77]

As has been shown above, the military organization was based on the administrative unit. The empire was divided into satrapies (OP *χšaθra*, Greek *nomoi* or *arkhai*), the number of which differed from time to time with the extension of the empire.[78] They were, however, mostly about twenty. They must not be identified with the 'countries', mentioned in the inscriptions of the Achaemenians (OP *dahyu*), though very often a 'country' may be a satrapy.[79] Such a satrapy was governed by a satrap (*χšaθrapāvan*),[80] but sometimes two or more satrapies were put under one single satrap, or one satrapy was reduced and another increased by transferring one or more districts from one satrapy to another.[81] The satrapy was divided into smaller provinces and such provinces into districts. The loose terminology used, however, makes it difficult to survey in detail the administrative division of the empire. The satrapy was modelled after the empire, the satrap being the representative of the king, with his own court, his bodyguard, his judges, and his coinage.[82] Actually the system is interwoven with the feudal institutions, in so far as the satrap occupies the position of a ruler towards his subjects, but the position of a subordinate official towards the Great King. In Achaemenid times the independence of the satrap was checked by various royal measures of control. He accordingly had at his side both a secretary responsible for the chancery and the finance, and chiefs of garrisons and army commanders. Moreover, the famous 'eyes' of the kings inspected the satrap's administration without announcing their arrival, and a well-developed system of organized espionage served as an ultimate measure of control. An excellent road-system with 'stations' promoted rapid communication between the king, with his central government at Susa, and the provinces.[83]

In spite of all checks on the satrap's authority the history of the Achaemenid empire gives sure proof that the forces tending to disruption were very often stronger than the centralistic bureaucratic spirit and the loyalty of the Persians. From time to time the satraps acted as great feudal lords and not as royal officials. There was always a trend towards looking upon the satrapy as a fief, and sometimes the position of satrap was almost hereditary.[84] When the Achaemenid empire dissolved, independent kingdoms were quite naturally created by satraps, as in Asia Minor, Persia, and other places.[85]

(iii) *Art and Architecture*

The art and architecture of the Achaemenid empire is above all an imperial art. Some remains of Median rock-reliefs, showing a Magian in the act of worshipping, at least demonstrate the existence of a religious art.[86] Median art played a great part in transmitting from Assyrian royal art some important iconographic motifs.[87] Among these are the processions of the tribute-bringers at Persepolis, which copy corresponding Assyrian scenes at Khorsabad. Darius sitting on his throne above the peoples of the empire is depicted in the same manner as the enthroned Sennacherib watching the siege of Lachish. The long sceptre is of exactly the same shape. Darius holding his bow, sacrificing before the fire-altar at Naqsh-i Rustam, with the winged symbol of Ahura Mazdā above the scene, is a copy of Ashurbanipal, bow in hand, pouring out a libation. The winged sun-disc of Ahura Mazdā has as its pattern the winged sun-disc of Ashur, the pattern originally being Egyptian.

The practice of cutting rock-reliefs to celebrate the victory of the king over his enemies was of ancient date in Mesopotamia, and the Achaemenid kings inherited the tradition which had been inaugurated by Narām-Sīn.[88]

The palace architecture in other places, especially Persepolis, is of Assyrian type. The dependence of the Persians on the Medes in this field is demonstrated by the Median royal palace at Ecbatana, which shows the same construction as the palace built by Cyrus at Pasargadae.[89]

It is remarkable how little influence was exercised by Neo-Babylonian art. This influence is, however, to be observed in Susa in the friezes of enamelled bricks, where we find the typical Babylonian serpent-dragon monster (*mušḫuššu*) and also the winged bulls.[90] In the palace of Susa the architecture too is of Babylonian inspiration,[91] with inner courtyards to which access is given from living-rooms and halls, surrounded by long corridors. The throne-hall (*apadāna*) is a separate building at the side of the palace proper. The throne-hall was covered by a roof supported by six rows of six columns of a height of about 20 m. To the north, east, and west the hall was surrounded by three peristyles of twelve columns. Three large staircases led up to the hall.

Old Persian art was also influenced from other quarters. Contact in the west with the Greeks could not fail to impress the Persian kings and satraps as well as the artisans in their service. The tomb of Cyrus at Pasargadae may already show Lycian and Greek traits.[92] The tombs of the Persian kings are of two types: one older, similar to a house, represented by the tomb of Cyrus at Pasargadae, and exhibiting clear influences of Greek art—though perhaps also continuing traditions of the original northern home of the Medes and Persians. Another later style is represented by the rock-tombs of Darius and his successors. This also shows influences from Greece and Asia Minor.[93]

The most impressive of the existing royal monuments are found in the palace-town of Persepolis, built by Darius and Xerxes.[94] Here too we have an *apadāna* and a royal palace. But Xerxes added his own palace, larger than his father's, to that of Darius. The throne-hall, situated on a terrace, to which one broad staircase leads, is constructed according to the same principles as those used at Susa. In both places a carefully planned system of canals provided fresh water. In the construction, both at Susa and Persepolis, influences from various regions are conspicuous. Urartu, Assyria, Babylonia, Egypt, and Greece have all made their contributions. We know from the texts that several countries of the empire had to furnish both material and artisans. In his inscription from Susa Darius says of the palace built at Susa:

The stone-cutters who wrought the stone, those were Ionians and Sardians.
The goldsmiths who wrought the gold were Medes and Egyptians.
The men who wrought the wood, those were Sardians and Egyptians.
The men who wrought the baked brick, those were Babylonians.
The men who adorned the wall, those were Medes and Egyptians.[95]
(Susa *f.* 47–55)

The resources of the whole empire were utilized, and this fact was known also by the classical authors (e.g. Diodorus, i. 46).[96]

(iv) *Language, Script, and Literature*

The language of the Persians is called Old Persian (OP), the vernacular of the province of Persis, the language of the Persian tribes who settled there It is attested in the cuneiform inscriptions of the rulers of the Achaemenian dynasty, in proper names and titles found in other languages (Babylonian, Hebrew, Aramaic, and Greek), and in loanwords in those same languages. In the Achaemenid empire in the west the Medes spoke a closely related dialect of OP, known only from loanwords in OP,[97] place-names, proper names, and loanwords in other languages. In the east we have the language of the Avesta, not yet extant in a written form, the older stages of the Sogdian and Saka languages, and also Chorasmian.[98] With the exception of Avestan, these eastern dialects are not known to us from the period with which we are concerned.

OP was spoken by all such officials and soldiers as did not speak Median or other dialects. But it was Aramaic that was used in the chanceries for correspondence within the empire from Egypt to the Indus. OP seemingly served as a written language only in royal monumental inscriptions.

The system of cuneiform script used for OP inscriptions was in all probability invented during the reign of Darius I, who was the first ruler to use OP for literary purposes.[99] His inscriptions, especially that of Behistun, are written in a very simple style, the syntax being undeveloped and chiefly built upon temporal clauses and paratactic constructions.[100] Nevertheless, these inscriptions are impressive; they lack neither majesty nor pride, piety nor humility before the High God Ahura Mazdā. In details we find some agreement with the inscriptions of Babylonian and Assyrian rulers, but on the other hand some details are typically Indo-Iranian, e.g. the proclamation formula: 'Says Darius, the King' (*θāti Dārayavauš χšāyaθiya*). The description of Darius as a warrior, given by himself, is highly characteristic too:

Trained am I both with hands and with feet. As a horseman I am a good horseman. As a bowman I am a good bowman, both afoot and on horseback. As a spearman I am a good spearman, both afoot and on horseback. (Naqsh-i-Rustan *b*. 40–5)

Equally characteristic is his declaration of his attitude to right and wrong:

By the favour of Ahura Mazdā I act so that I am a friend to right, I am not a friend to wrong. It is not my desire that the weak man should have wrong done to him by the strong, nor is it my desire that the mighty man should have wrong done to him by the weak. What is right, that is my desire. I am not a friend to the man who follows a lie. I am not hot-tempered. What things develop in my anger, I hold firmly under control by my mind. I am firmly ruling over myself. (lines 5–15)

The Behistun (Bh) inscription, the *res gestae* of Darius, was written on the rock in Elamite, Babylonian, and OP. A translation of it into Aramaic was distributed to the various parts of the empire to be read by the subjects. One copy has been found among the papyri of Elephantine.[101]

All literature, both religious and secular, was transmitted exclusively in oral tradition, in true Indo-European manner. Therefore we know this literature only through what has been preserved of such tradition by Greek authors (Herodotus, and especially Ctesias). They obviously had access to popular oral traditions about Cyrus the Great and other heroes of popular tales (Aelian, xii. 21 has a tale about Achaemenes). Other tales, too, of an epic type were widespread, such as that about the prince Zariadres and the king's daughter Odatis, preserved by Chares of Mitylene.

The Aramaic used by the scribes in the royal chanceries is called 'Imperial Aramaic'. Both the Aramaic portions of the Old Testament and the Jewish papyri and ostraca from Egypt are written in this kind of Aramaic. A special method was used in order to facilitate its use by the king, the satraps, and other officials who did not master this language. The Persian dictated the document in his own language to his scribe, who wrote it down in Aramaic. The document was sent to its addressee, a Persian, to whom the letter was read by one of the scribes in Persian thus 'interpreted' (*mᵉp̄āraš*, Ezra 4: 18).[102]

The choice of Aramaic as the language of the chanceries was due to the fact that this language was written in a convenient alphabetic script.[103] Because of the intimate relation between language and script, Aramaic was preferred to the three official languages of the royal inscriptions. In practice Aramaic had acquired an undisputed position as the international language of diplomacy and commerce well before 700 B.C. (cf. 2 Kings 18: 26 (= Isa. 36: 11)). It has been assumed that Darius initiated the introduction of Aramaic into the Persian chanceries. This assumption is hardly probable, for the Assyrian kings earlier used scribes writing Aramaic, as is seen from a fresco found at Til Barsip, dated *c.* 750 B.C. That the use of Aramaic spread more and more in the Assyrian chanceries is shown by a letter written on an ostracon, dating from about 650. This Aramaic is not a dialect but a literary language, the precursor of Imperial Aramaic. Juridical and economic documents from the Assyrian territory testify to the rapid spread of Aramaic at the expense of the cuneiform script and Akkadian language. Within the Neo-Babylonian kingdom Aramaic gained ground. When the Median empire succeeded to the Assyrian as the dominating power, it was presumably natural for the Median rulers to have their correspondence conducted in Aramaic. The Persians, in their own province used to Elamite traditions, were accustomed to the use of Babylonian and Elamite. This is demonstrated not only by their royal inscriptions but also by the thousands of account tablets found at Persepolis and written in Elamite language and cuneiform script.[104] When Cyrus the Great conquered Media he must, however, have met there the use of Aramaic in the royal chancery. And when he was the lord of Babylonia he was confronted there too with Aramaic, used for writing diplomatic documents, as shown by the Saqqara papyrus from the year 605 B.C. From this we may assume that already Cyrus and Cambyses made use of Aramaic as the official language of their chanceries, while Babylonian and Elamite were still used for inscriptions and official proclamations, such as the Cyrus Chronicle. Darius I carried on this tradition, but introduced OP as one of the three languages for his own monumental inscriptions. The Aramaic used in the empire spread from the west into the eastern provinces and north-west India (inscriptions of Kandahar, Pul-i Darunteh, and Taxila from post-Achaemenid times).

As time passed and the Persian language gained more ground the scribes introduced Persian words and phonetic complements into the Aramaic they were writing. In this practice they followed an ancient scribal custom in Mesopotamia, for in that way Sumerian in private contracts had been ultimately supplanted by Akkadian, leaving only some Sumerian words and expressions as ideograms.[105] The final result was the emergence of various scribal systems, where some kind of Middle Iranian language was written, but Aramaic ideograms left in the script. This development, which must have begun towards the end of the Achaemenid period, when OP was in a state of grammatical decay (as in inscriptions of Artaxerxes II), is not observable until after the end of our period.

In spite of the official use of Aramaic the Persian language exercised a deep influence on other languages. A great number of Iranian loanwords are found in Elamite, Babylonian, Aramaic, Hebrew, and Greek. It stands to reason that the number of Iranian words is especially high in Aramaic, since that language was the foreign language most used by the Persians. The Aramaic documents of Ezra–Nehemiah as well as the Egyptian papyri and ostraca therefore contain a high percentage of Iranian loanwords. The Aramaic portions of the book of Daniel do not exhibit nearly so many, and by the time of the Aramaic texts of the Dead Sea Scrolls the percentage of Iranian words is low. This is due to the different character of these texts, for the books of Ezra–Nehemiah contain official Persian documents.

In the Aramaic portions of the Old Testament a number of Iranian loanwords are employed. These are terms usually belonging to the sphere of administration and official correspondence, though a few represent specific items of clothing or utensils.[106] In Jewish papyri from Egypt there are several other loanwords belonging in the main to the same range of activity, with the addition of words relating to art and religion.[107] Other loanwords are found in leather documents from Egypt containing Persian administrative correspondence, or in Aramaic texts of a later period.[108] There are, of course, in the Hebrew of the Old Testament a few Iranian loanwords which must have entered Hebrew from Aramaic.[109]

In the Aramaic inscriptions from the east, in part found during recent years, the percentage of Iranian loanwords is still higher. Owing to the religious character of these inscriptions, as edicts of the Emperor Aśoka, known for his Buddhist sympathies, the glossary there has another character.[110]

These words also occur in the inscriptions of Kandahar and Taxila; the inscription of Pul-i Darunteh is, however, too broken to add any useful knowledge.

In all, we may count about eighty Iranian loanwords in Imperial Aramaic, as known to us from Old Testament times. In eastern Aramaic dialects such as Syriac, Talmudic Aramaic, and Mandaic they are still more numerous,[111] and we may safely assume that many of these words were once also part of the glossary of Imperial Aramaic. We should not forget that our source-material for Imperial Aramaic is very restricted, so that the picture we get of it is rather fragmentary as far as the glossary is concerned. In conclusion we may therefore say that Iranian language and culture exercised a strong influence on the Semitic peoples of the west, the Jews included, and that this influence was probably greater than we are now in a position to evaluate.

(v) *Religion*

Three of the Iranian loanwords registered above belong to the sphere of religion: Mazdā-worshipper, Magian, and holder of the barsom-twigs. The occurrence of these three words is no mere accident, but rather significant. Actually these three words probably connote the three most important phenomena in the religion of the Persians in Achaemenid times.

A Mazdā-worshipper is a Persian who worships Ahura Mazdā, so often mentioned by Darius in his inscriptions. It is interesting to note that the form of the word belongs to Median, not to OP, where the worshipper of Mazdā was called *Mazdayasna*.[112] It looks therefore as if the word for Mazdā-worshipper had already entered Aramaic from Median quarters before the time of Cyrus the Great.

At any rate this word well characterizes the religion of the Persians and Medes as above all the worship of Ahura Mazdā, the God of Heaven (Herodotus, i. 131). Now his principal priests were the Median Magians, whom we met in connection with the revolution started by Gaumāta. Already in the days of Darius I they had regained the position they had lost when they supported Gaumāta, and were slaughtered *en masse* after his fall (Herodotus, iii. 79). The Persepolis treasury tablets show that the Magians were still acting as the official priesthood.[113] In their worship of Ahura Mazdā barsom-twigs were used, and a Magian is always depicted as holding the bundle of barsom. Hence the loanword for 'barsom-holder' is really significant and demonstrates the importance of this rite. When sacrificing, the Magian chanted a ritual song, but nothing is known of its characteristics, except that Herodotus (i. 131) says that it was a theogony. This song must have been something similar to our *yašt*-texts in the form in which they were reshaped, in the Zoroastrian spirit.[114]

Sacrifices played an important part in the cult, but probably equally important was the service involving fire. The Magians functioned too as priests of fire. They also acted as libation priests, using the mortar (*havana*) to press the sacrificial draught (*haoma*). Both fire and *haoma* possessed a divine status in Iranian religion, but they were not among the most prominent deities. The latter included Mithra and Anāhitā, who ranked beside Ahura Mazdā. Both divinities seem to have received a special worship in the days of Artaxerxes II. But Mithra as the *baga*, 'god', *par excellence* is the god to whom the month Bagayādiš was already dedicated in the early period. Among theophoric personal names in cuneiform documents Mithradāta is attested. In the Elephantine papyri a Magian with a Mithra-name has been found. Mithra's festival, the ancient New Year's festival, is Mithrakāna, in which the king played a central role. Mithra was above all the deity who protected the royal dynasty. The worship of Mithra is possibly more of Median than of Persian origin, for this form of the name is Median. Later we meet with the true Persian form, e.g., in Vahumissa.[115]

Both Ahura Mazdā and Mithra are deities belonging to the first social function, that of the sovereignty. To the third function, that of fertility and nourishment, belongs Anāhitā, whereas we find no representative of the second, the warrior's function. Mithra's function, however, always had a close affinity to the warrior's, and this may explain the gap. The goddess Anāhitā enjoyed much worship in the empire and statues were erected in her honour in several cities of both eastern and western provinces (Clement, *Protreptikos*, v. 65, 3). Such statues have not been found, but we have representations of an enthroned goddess on gems dated to the Achaemenid period.[116]

The inscriptions further mention the clan-gods of the royal house. A comparison with Xenophon (*Cyrop*. I. vi. 1; III. iii. 22; VII. i. 1) shows that these included also the High God Ahura Mazdā. And obviously Mithra too was such a *theos patrōos* of the royal house.

The elements, according to Herodotus (i. 131), were the object of divine worship. Heaven, Sun, Moon, Fire, Air, Water, and Earth were deified. But it is impossible to say how far they were conceived of as personal beings, or whether there was a pantheistic outlook on the universe—according to which the universe was thought of as divine, being seen as the god's cosmic body—an idea attested elsewhere in Iranian religion.[117]

Much discussion has been going on concerning the problem whether the Achaemenian kings were Zoroastrians or not.[118] A careful examination of the arguments leads to the conclusion that they were not. The cult practised by them, especially the bloody sacrifices so abhorred by Zoroaster, speaks definitely against their being Zoroastrians. And we miss altogether in their inscriptions any reference to the 'Holy Immortals', the Amesha Spentas, so characteristic of the new doctrine preached by Zoroaster. However, the Magians had adopted Zoroastrianism in a syncretistic form, and no doubt the new religion in that form was gradually gaining ground in the empire.[119]

In the religion of the Persians a special position was occupied by the king.[120] An elaborate court-ceremonial served to stress the fact that he was elevated above ordinary mortals. Only the members of the seven great Houses (the descendants of Darius' companions when the assassination of Gaumāta was carried out) had free access to the Great King. When ushered into the presence of the king by the *hazahrapati*,[121] one had to do obeisance to him by throwing oneself prostrate before him, and kissing the ground. This ceremony, called *proskynēsis*, was especially repulsive to the

Greeks, as unworthy of free men. As a ceremony it goes back to the Mesopotamian custom called *labān appi*. Themistocles, the victor of Salamis, when (as a refugee) seeking audience at Susa with the Great King, did not, however, hesitate to carry out the *proskynēsis*. The *hazahrapati*, Artabāna, explained to him the meaning behind the ceremony: 'we Persians', he said, 'worship the King as an image of God' (Plutarch, *Themistocles*, 27). The ruler, accordingly, is divine, and this idea prevailed in Iran until the fall of the Sasanian empire.[122] At his coronation the king took part in certain religious ceremonies, eating sacred food and drinking a sacred drink, probably symbols of the immortal food of the gods.[123] Moreover he was invested with a robe once worn by Cyrus.

The garment usually worn by the Achaemenian king was a symbol of his association with two social functions: the priest's and the warrior's. He belonged to the warrior class and therefore wore the scarlet colours of that class, but he also exercised priest's functions, and for that reason his scarlet garment was striped with white, the colour of the priests.[124] The gods with whom he had special connections, therefore, were Ahura Mazdā and Mithra. These priestly functions the ruler exercised above all at the Mithrakāna, as has already been noted. He carried out a cultic dance, and on this day got himself ritually drunk.[125]

As a divine being the king—in accordance with Indo-Iranian traditions—should not take an active part in combat. He should direct the battle and be present, but not fight. This idea, preserved into late Sasanian times, has often been misunderstood, and has led scholars to accuse Xerxes and Darius III of being cowards—which they were not.[126] A good picture of the Great King as seen by his Jewish subjects is furnished by the book of Esther. Here we meet with many specific details showing his very human—sometimes too human—traits.

There were many points of contact between the Persian and the Jewish religion, and it is highly probable that the Jews in their official correspondence with Persian authorities intentionally and exclusively used, as a designation of their deity, the formula 'the God of Heaven(s)'.[127] Jewish religion indeed did receive strong influences from Iranian religion, but that Iranian influence belongs primarily to a later period, the time of the Parthians.

In conclusion, it may be said that the empire created by the Persians was the most important empire created in antiquity to last for a considerable period. It set the model for both the Parthian and the Sasanian empires, as well as for many subsequent political structures. In principle the Caliphate did not add anything new to its civil and military organization. The causes of its fall have been shown. There were very many factors tending to disintegration, and the King alone was not sufficient to serve as the unifying force. Moreover, the Persians, including the Medes, were never a numerous people, and they were not able to transform all the Iranian tribes into one single Iranian nation. Too few to be able to carry the burden of a huge empire, and not able to reform their military tactics, the Persians had to leave the leading role first to the Macedonians and Greeks, and then to the Romans. But they were to come to power again with the foundation of the Sasanian empire.

NOTES

1. Cf. M. Mayrhofer, *Die Indo-Arier im alten Vorderasien* (Wiesbaden, 1966), esp. pp. 28 ff.

2. E. Ebeling, *Bruchstücke einer mittelassyrischen Vorschriftensammlung für die Akklimatisierung und Trainierung von Wagenpferden* (Berlin, 1951); A. Kammenhuber, *Hippologia Hethitica* (Wiesbaden, 1961).

3. Cf. the literature listed in Widengren, *Der Feudalismus im alten Iran*, p. 9 n. 2.

4. For the following cf. Widengren, op. cit. 10 ff.

5. Cf. Widengren, op. cit. 37. What is said in the text will be worked out in detail in another connection; cf. my remarks in the Swedish edition of C. H. Gordon, *Before the Bible* (Stockholm, 1966), pp. 1 ff.

6. Cf. K. Ghirshman, *Sialk* (Fouilles de Sialk, i–ii, Paris, 1938–9).

7. For the most ancient history of the western Iranian tribes cf. G. Cameron, *History of Early Iran* (Chicago, 1936); A. T. Olmstead, *History of the Persian Empire*, 2nd edn. (Chicago, 1959), pp. 16–33.

8. For the history of Cyrus see P. J. Junge, *Dareios I, der König der Perser* (Leipzig, 1944), pp. 19–38, in addition to Cameron, op. cit., and Olmstead, op. cit.

9. Cf. Widengren, 'La légende royale de l'Iran antique', in *Hommages à Georges Dumézil* (Brussels, 1960), pp. 225–37.

10. Cf. K. Galling, *Studien zur Geschichte Israels im persischen Zeitalter* (Tübingen, 1964), pp. 23 f.

11. Cf. Olmstead, op. cit. 40.

12. Emphasized by Olmstead, op. cit. 43.

13. We do not possess any specific details of these conquests.

14. For Deutero-Isaiah and his oracles cf. S. Smith, *Isaiah, Chapters XL–LV: Literary Criticism and History* (London, 1944).

15. Cf. Galling, op. cit. 7.

16. Cf. Galling, op. cit. 5–20.

17. These dates are those given by Parker–Dubberstein, *Babylonian Chronology*, (Providence, 1956) 13 f.

18. For these measures cf. the Cyrus Chronicle, lines 26–30, 34–5.

19. Cf. such passages as Meissner-Rost, *Die Bauinschriften Asarhaddons*, p. 252: 12–41; *VAB* 14, p. 174: 31–2; *Codex Hammurabi* ii. 9–50 (Hammurapi is *mupaḫḫir nišī sapḫāti*).

20. My conclusions are in conflict with the arguments adduced by Galling, who has not observed the implications of what is said in the Cyrus Chronicle, lines 34–5.

21. Cf. E. Meyer, *Die Entstehung des Judentums* (Halle, 1896), pp. 94 ff.; Galling, op. cit. 89–108 (who thinks that this authentic list concerns those who returned in 521/520).

22. Cf. W. Hinz, 'Die elamischen Buchungstäfelchen der Darius-Zeit', *Or.* xxxix (1970), 427.

23. For Deutero-Isaiah's views cf. *inter alia* Smith, op. cit. 74.

24. Junge, *Saka-Studien* (Aalen, 1962), pp. 70 f., argues for an identification with the Saka Tigraxaudra.

25. Dates given by Parker–Dubberstein, op. cit. 14.

26. Cf. Olmstead, op. cit. 88; Herodotus, iii. 11.

27. Posener, *La Première Domination Perse en Égypte* (Cairo, 1936), pp. 165 ff.

28. Cf. Posener, op. cit. 170 ff.

29. For the following cf. Widengren, 'Über einige Probleme der altpersischen Geschichte', in *Festschrift für Leo Brandt* (Köln–Opladen, 1968), pp. 517–22.

30. Cf. Widengren, 'The Sacral Kingship of Iran', in *La Regalità sacra* (Leiden, 1959), p. 244 with p. 255.

31. For the following cf. Junge, op. cit. 48 ff.

32. Dates as given by Parker–Dubberstein, op. cit. 15 f.

33. For Zerubbabel cf. Meyer, op. cit. 75 f., 79 ff.

34. The merit of having proved this goes to Eduard Meyer, op. cit. 8–70.

35. Junge, op. cit. 90, argues for the year 516 and considers the expedition as entirely peaceful, assuming that the Persian satrap Aryandes had crushed all resistance long before the arrival of Darius. For the date 519/518 cf. R. A. Parker, *A.J.S.L.* lxviii (1941), 373 ff.

36. Cf. A. Foucher, 'Les satrapies orientales', in *C.R.A.I.B.L.* (1938), 336–52.

37. Cf. M. Rostovtzeff, *Iranians and Greeks in South Russia* (Oxford, 1922), pp. 61 ff., where he describes the situation of the Greek colonies and their trade; on p. 84 he argues that the Persian expedition was dictated by purely strategical considerations.

38. Cf. the Mesopotamian idea that the king is *šar kiššati*, 'king of the totality', or *šar kibrat irbittim*, 'king of the four world-quarters'.

39. Cf. How & Wells, *A Commentary on Herodotus* (rep. 1950), ii. 401–10.

40. For the following cf. Olmstead, op. cit., 248 ff.; and Burns, *Persia and the Greeks* (London, 1962); and *inter alia* Hignett, *Xerxes' Invasion of Greece* (Oxford, 1963).

41. I cannot accept Olmstead's view, op. cit. 260 (seemingly accepted by Nyberg, *Das Reich der Achämeniden*, p. 100) that this battle was the decisive one. Actually it was not a great battle, for only minor Persian forces were engaged; cf. Herodotus, ix. 89 ff.

42. Others would prefer to see in him Artaxerxes I.

43. On Nehemiah cf. H. H. Rowley, 'Nehemiah's Mission and its Background', *B.J.R.L.* xxxvii (1955), 528–61.

44. Cf. Galling, op. cit. 156, who rightly points to the necessity of having a reliable governor in the province bordering on Egypt.

45. Cf. A. E. Cowley, *Aramaic Papyri of the Fifth Century* (Oxford, 1923), pp. 248 ff.

46. Cf. E. G. Kraeling, *The Brooklyn Museum Aramaic Papyri* (New Haven, Conn., 1953), pp. 83 ff.

47. Cf. P. Grelot, *V.T.* iv (1954), 349–84; v (1955), 250–65; Galling, op. cit. 152 f. (who accepts Grelot's opinion).

48. Cf. E. Meyer, *Der Papyrusfund von Elephantine* (Leipzig, 1913), p. 67.

49. Cf. Kraeling, op. cit. 111.

50. Cf. H. H. Rowley, 'The Chronological Order of Ezra and Nehemiah', in *The Servant of the Lord*, 2nd edn. (Oxford, 1965).

51. Cf. H. H. Schaeder, *Esra der Schreiber* (Tübingen, 1930), p. 48 f.

52. Galling, op. cit. 166 f.

53. Cf. M. Noth, *Geschichte Israels*, 3rd edn. (Göttingen, 1956), p. 310; W. F. Albright, *The Archaeology of Palestine* (Penguin Books, 1956), p. 143.

54. For the battle of Granicus cf. Olmstead, op. cit. 497.

55. For the battle of Issus cf. Olmstead, op. cit. 503 f.; to be supplemented and corrected by Widengren, 'Über einige Probleme', pp. 529 f.

56. Cf. the analysis of numbers and tactics in E. W. Marsden, *The Campaign of Gaugamela* (Liverpool, 1964), esp. pp. 24–64.

57. Cf. Widengren, *Der Feudalismus im alten Iran* (1969), pp. 64–95.

58. Cf. Widengren, op. cit. 21–9.

59. Cf. Widengren, 'Über einige Probleme', p. 524.

60. Cf. Widengren, 'Recherches sur le féodalisme iranien', *Or. Suec.* v (1956; Uppsala, 1957), 160 ff.

61. For this term cf. Widengren, ibid. 162, and especially P. Junge, *Klio* xxxiii (1940–1), 13–38.

62. For this term cf. H. H. Schaeder, *Iranische Beiträge I* (Königsberg, 1930), pp. 256–8 and the survey below, p. 353.

63. For *kāra* cf. Widengren, 'Die Begriffe "*populorum ordo*" und "*ram*" als Ausdrücke der Standesgliederung im Partherreiche', in *Festschrift*

Walter Baetke (Weimar, 1966), pp. 288–91; and for **hama-spāda* the observation of Eilers referred to in Widengren, 'Über einige Probleme', p. 533.

64. For this term cf. Widengren, 'Recherches sur le féodalisme iranien', pp. 155 f.

65. Cf. Widengren, op. cit. 149–52.

66. Or 'stations' (OP *avahāna* > MI. *'āwān*, Greek *monai* or *stathmoi*); cf. G. Widengren, *Iranisch-semitische Kulturbegegnung in parthischer Zeit* (Köln–Opladen, 1960), p. 90. For the 'Royal Road' (Herodotus, v. 52) see E. Meyer, *Geschichte des Altertums*, iv, 4th edn. (Stuttgart, 1944), pp. 61 f.; How & Wells, op. cit. ii. 21 f.

67. Cf. Widengren, 'Recherches sur le féodalisme iranien', pp. 95–108 (chiefly for Parthian and Sasanian times, but cf. p. 101 for Achaemenid conditions).

68. Cf. the literature referred to in Widengren, *Der Feudalismus*, p. 9 n. 1.

69. Cf. Widengren, 'Recherches sur le féodalisme iranien', p. 105.

70. Cf. Widengren, ibid. 158 f.

71. For this term see (most recently) M. L. Chaumont, *J.A.* (1962), 11–22. As a loanword in Aramaic: *'ar kapṭā*, Widengren, *Kulturbegnung*, p. 33.

72. There is no satisfactory analysis for this term. It must, however, be connected with *kāra* and mean 'army-commander', but the form of this noun is not clear to me (formation in *-ana*?).

73. For these Babylonian terms cf. W. Eilers, *O.L.Z.* xxxvii (1934), col. 94 f.; *Z.D.M.G.* xc (1936), 196; Widengren, 'Recherches', pp. 148 f.

74. Herodotus, vii. 61; viii. 113 (Persians); Xenophon, *Cyrop.* VI. i. 50 f., VII. i. 2; Curtius, III. xi, 15. Cf. Widengren, 'Über einige Probleme', pp. 529 f.

75. F. Thureau-Dangin, *Une Relation de la huitième campagne de Sargon* (Paris, 1912), ll. 50, 55.

76. III. ix, 15. Cf. Widengren, op. cit. 530.

77. Cf. How & Wells, *A Commentary on Herodotus* i–ii (1950), pp. 410 ff.

78. An account of the changes, as far as they can be ascertained, is given by P. Junge, 'Satrapie und Natio', *Klio* xxxiv, no. 19 (1941), 1–55. The oriental satrapies are treated by Foucher, *Les Satrapies orientales* (see n. 30).

79. Emphasized by Junge, op. cit. 5 f., 27 ff., against many earlier expositions, e.g. O. Leuze, *Die Satrapieneinteilung in Syrien und im Zweistromlande von 520–320* (Halle, 1935), esp. pp. 45 ff.

80. This term is Median, cf. n. 97.

81. Cyrus the Younger was in charge of the satrapies of Lydia, Greater Phrygia, and Cappadocia (Xenophon, *Anabasis*, i. 9. 7); cf. G. Cousin, *Kyros le Jeune* (Paris, 1904), pp. 14 ff.

82. Cf. E. Meyer, *Geschichte des Altertums*, iv, 4th edn. (Stuttgart, 1944), pp. 45 ff.

83. See n. 66.

84. Cf. Widengren, 'Recherches sur le féodalisme iranien', pp. 95–108

(chiefly for post-Achaemenid conditions, as correctly observed by Judeich, *Kleinasiatische Studien* (Marburg, 1892), p. 222).

85. In this way the kingdoms of Armenia and Pontus emerged out of the chaos.

86. Cf. E. Herzfeld, *Iran in the Ancient East* (London, 1941), pp. 204 f.

87. Emphasized as *communis opinio* by F. W. von Bissing, *Ursprung und Wesen der persischen Kunst* (München, 1927), p. 3. Cf. Sarre–Herzfeld, *Iranische Felsreliefs* (Berlin, 1910), pp. 14–56. Herzfeld rightly says that Darius is shown in the old Mesopotamian *niš qāti-* gesture.

88. Cf. A. Christensen, 'Die Iranier', in *Kulturgeschichte des Orients* iii. 1, 3, 3: 1 (München, 1933), p. 297.

89. Cf. von Bissing, op. cit. 4.

90. Cf. von Bissing, op. cit. 3.

91. Cf. von Bissing, op. cit. 3.

92. Cf. von Bissing, op. cit. 8 f.

93. Cf. Sarre–Herzfeld, op. cit. 166–80, 57–66.

94. Cf. Sarre–Herzfeld, op. cit. 100–46; E. Schmidt, *Persepolis*, i (Chicago, 1953).

95. Cf. Kent, *Old Persian* (New Haven, Conn., 1950), p. 144.

96. For the Ionian artisans at work, especially in Pasargadae, cf. C. Nylander, *Ionians in Pasargadae* (Uppsala, 1971), where also general reflections on the Greek artistic influence are presented. In addition, a general reference should be given here to the relevant parts of A. Upham Pope & Rh. Ackermann, *A Survey of Persian Art* (1938).

97. Personal names and place-names are not considered. Cf. such words as *χšāyaθya*, 'king' (E. Benveniste, *Gramnaire du Vieux-Perse* (Paris, 1931) *_χšāyaθay-puθra_, 'crown prince' (B. *Titres*); *_baga-puθra_, 'son of God' (=*deva-putra*, B. *Titres*); *_vispuθra_, 'prince' (E. Benveniste, *Titres et noms propres en Iranien ancien* (Paris 1966)); *χšaθra-pāvan*, 'satrap'; *āzāta*, 'nobleman' ('free'); *vispa-zana* and *paru-zana*, 'of all races, of many races'; *vazṛka*, 'great'; *farnah*, 'glory'; *taxma*, 'strong'; *aršti*, 'spear'; *arštā*, 'rectitude'; *ufrašta*, *zūra*, 'evil' (these three B. *Gr.*); *aspa*, 'horse'; *spāka*, 'dog'; *asan*, 'stone'; *kāsaka*, 'a precious stone'; *patisazbayam*, 'I proclaimed'; *vasi*, 'much, the name of the God Mithra' (cf. p. 344 and n. 115).

98. Cf. H. W. Bailey, 'The Persian Language', in *The Legacy of Persia*, ed. A. J. Arberry (Oxford, 1953), pp. 174–98, where a survey of both chronological and local developments of the Iranian languages is presented in a clear and readable form.

99. Cf. W. Hinz, *Neue Wege im Altpersischen* (Göttingen, 1970), where on pp. 1–3 a short survey is given of the research leading up to the conclusion indicated here.

100. Easily accessible in R. G. Kent, *Old Persian* (New Haven, Conn., 1950), text with notes and translation, pp. 116 ff.

101. Cf. Cowley, op. cit. 248 ff.

102. Cf. H. H. Schaeder, *Esra der Schreiber*, pp. 51 ff., and, in more detail, *Iranische Beiträge*, i (Halle, 1930), pp. 1–14.

103. For Aramaic cf. A. Dupont-Sommer, *Les Araméens* (Paris, 1949), pp. 79–104, where the dates referred to in the text are to be found.

104. Published by G. G. Cameron, *Persepolis Treasury Tablets* (Chicago, 1948); R. T. Hallock, *Persepolis Fortification Tablets* (Chicago, 1969).

105. I think of such expressions in the contracts of the Hammurabi period as enim nu.um mal.mal.a for the Akkadian *ul iraggam*, or šam til.lá.bi.šu for *ana šumišu gamrim*, and other such expressions. In these business documents we find Sumerian expressions and whole phrases left as memories of an earlier period.

106. In the Aramaic portions of the O.T. the Iranian loanwords are terms for:[1]

English	Aramaic	Persian
satraps	*aḥašdarpᵉnayyā*	*χšarapāna*
chief ministers	*sārᵉḵīn*	**sāraka*
counsellors	*aḏargāzrayyā²*	*andarzgara²*
companions	*haddāḇᵉrīn*	**hadabara³*
treasures	*ginzayyā*	*ganza*
treasurers	*gᵉḏāḇrayyā*	*ganzabara*
messengers	*aparsaṯkāyē*	**frastāka⁴*
police-chiefs	*tiptāyē*	*tāyupāta⁵*
law	*dāṯ*	*dāta*
law officials	*dᵉṯāḇrayyā*	*dātabara*
corporal punishment	*šᵉrōšī*	*sraušyā*
written order	*ništᵉwānā*	**ništavana⁶*
copy	*paršegen*	**patičagna⁷*
message	*piṯgām*	**patigāma*
exactly	*asparnā*	**asparna⁸*

[1] In F. Rosenthal, *A Grammar of Biblical Aramaic* (Wiesbaden, 1961), W. B. Henning explained the Iranian loanwords. His explanations have been accepted, except when other etymologies are offered. The explanation of *šᵉrōšī* was given by F. Rundgen, *V. T.* vii (1957), 50 f.

[2] It is remarkable that this form of the word shows the MP. development of **handarzakara*. The curious Aramaic form is explained by Bauer–Leander, *Grammatik des Biblisch-Aramäischen* (Halle, 1927), p. 56, § 15 d, as due to metathesis. It could, however, be due to a simple miswriting.

[3] Explanation accepted by Henning.

[4] This is the explanation accepted by Henning. W. Eilers, *Iranische Beamtennamen in der keilschriftlichen Überlieferung* (Leipzig, 1940), pp. 38 f., proposed **fraistaka* > MI. *frēstak*. In that case we must assume that the development *ai* > *ē* had already taken place.

[5] This explanation is owed to Henning, *Ein Manichäisches Bet- und Beichtbuch* (Berlin, 1934), p. 90 n. 1. I accept it provisionally.

[6] Bauer–Leander, op. cit., § 15 d, gave a wrong explanation. Henning rightly compared the Ossetic form *nystwn*.

[7] Cf. the discussion in G. Widengren, *Iranisch-semitische Kulturbegegnung in parthischer Zeit* (Köln–Opladen, 1960), pp. 97 f.

[8] Already explained by H. Hübschmann, *Armenische Grammatik*, i (Leipzig, 1895), p. 239. (This is a good treatment of many loanwords.)

English	*Aramaic*	*Persian*
diligently	*aḏrazdā*	**drazdā*
publicly known	*azdā*	*azdā*

All these words belong to the sphere of administration and official correspondence.

Other terms represent dress, utensils, abstracts, etc.:

English	*Aramaic*	*Persian*
belt	**hamyān^{e}ḵā*	**hamyānaka*[1]
trousers	*sarbālīn*	**šaravāra*[2]
furnishings	*uššarnā*	**usčarna*[3]
sheath	*n^{e}ḏān*	*nidāni*
lamp	*neḇraštā*	**nibrāšti*
kind	*zan*	*zana*
secret	*rāz*	**rāza*
ration	*paṯbāg*	**patibāga*[4]
limbs	*haddāmīn*	**handāma*

107. Persian loanwords in Jewish papyri from Egypt:

English	*Aramaic*	*Persian*
governors	*prmnkry'*	*framānākara*[5]
commander	*prtrk*	*frataraka*
ship's captain	*nwpt'*	**navapati*
partner	*hngyt*	*hangaita*
accountants	*hmrkry'*	*hamārakara*
companion	*hnbg'*	*hanbāga*
informers	*gwšky'*	*gaušaka*
mustering	*hndz*	*handaiza*
ration	*ptp'*	*pitaf-*[6]

1 We must assume that the *k^{e}ṯīḇ* is miswritten for *hmynk*. More usual is the word *hamyān*, for which cf. Widengren, op. cit. 94.

2 Cf. Nyberg, *M.O.* xxv (1931), 180 ff.

3 Henning proposed *āčarna*, which is inadmissible. For *usčarna* cf. Nyberg, op. cit.

4 Cf. P. de Lagarde, *Gesammelte Abhandlungen* (Leipzig, 1866), p. 73; W. Eilers, *Iranische Beamtennamen* (Leipzig, 1940), pp. 79 f. This proposal still seems the best one. This word, found in the Hebrew portions of Daniel, must have entered Hebrew from the original Aramaic and is therefore listed here.

5 Eilers, op. cit. 122, argued for the reading **framānādāra*. But from a palaeographical point of view the reading *dr* instead of *kr* does not recommend itself. Further it must be stated that—contrary to what Eilers has said—in New Persian it is associated with the root *kar-*, for in Firdausi we have *farmān kardan* in many passages; cf. F. Wolff, *Glossar zu Firdosis Schahname* (Berlin, 1935; rep. 1965), s.v. *kardan* 42.

6 Cf. Eilers, op. cit. 77 f., and G. R. Driver, *Aramaic Documents of the Fifth Century B.C.* (Oxford, 1954), p. 22 b.

English	Aramaic	Persian
living	*zywk*	**zīvaka*[1]
weight	*krš*	*karša*
payment	*ptyprs*	*patifrāsa*
protection	*hnpn'*	*hanpāna*[2]
information	*'wdys*	*avadaisa*
informer	*'zdkr'*	*azdakara*
in concert with	*hmwnyt*	*hamvanīt*
fine	*'bygrn*	**abigrāna*[3]
misdeed	*dwškrt'*	*duškarta*

The words listed above are concerned with public life. A few words fall within the sphere of art or architecture:

English	Aramaic	Persian
repairs	*'wpsd*	**upasada*[4]
preparation	*'wpkrt'*	**upakarta*
painting	*hndwn*	**handauna*
arsenic	*zrnyk*	*zarnīka*

And finally there are some terms from religious life:

English	Aramaic	Persian
Mazda-worshipper	*mzdyzn*	*mazdayazna*
Magian	*mgšy'*	*maguš*
holder of the barsom-twigs	*brzmdn'*	*brazmadāna*

108. In leather documents from Egypt, containing Persian administrative correspondence, there are several Iranian loanwords not listed in nn. 106–7 above.

English	Aramaic	Persian
chief treasurers	*knzsrym*	*ganzasara*
mounted officer	*wršbr*[5]	*varšabara*
sculptor	*ptkrkr*	*patikarakara*
sculpture	*ptkr*	*patikara*
gang	*grd*[6]	*garda*
domain	*bg*	*bāga*

1 From **ǰīva-ka* (cf. Avestic *jīva-*), thus 'what belongs to the living'. I am not aware of any previous proposal of this.

2 Cf. B. Geiger, in Kraeling, op. cit. 241. Obviously correct.

3 Cf. Schaeder, *Iranische Beiträge*, p. 66 [264].

4 Cf. Schaeder, op. cit. 65 [263], where the proposal of Scheftelowitz is rejected without any sufficient reason, for the letter *ś* is used in these texts in some words indicating *s*, contrary to what Schaeder says.

5 Cf. Driver, op. cit. 26 a f. The explanation is given by Nyberg (or by Bailey ?).

6 Cf. Driver, op. cit. 24, and for the word *gardapat(u)* in Babylonian documents Eilers, op. cit. 67; *C.A.D.* v. 50.

English	*Aramaic*	*Persian*
stage of journey	*'dwn*[1]	*advana*
from all nations	*wspzn*	*vispazana*
notification	*hndrz*	*handarza*
gift	*dšn*	*dašna*
disturbance	*ywz*	*yōza*
adversity	*gst*	*gasta*

From the Aramaic texts of a later period may be quoted the following terms, since these loanwords have presumably entered Aramaic at a fairly early stage, being of a kind most characteristic of Persian administration and custom:

English	*Aramaic*	*Persian*
muster-scribe	*'ndysk*[2]	*andaisaka*
stopping-place (road station)	*'wn*[3]	*ārāna*
palace	*'pdn*[4]	*apadāna*
hunting park ('paradise')	*prdys*	*paridaisa*

109.

English	*Hebrew*	*Persian*
horses from the herds	*rmkym*[5]	*ramaka*
litter	*'prywn*[6]	*aparyāna*
silo	*prbr*[7]	*paribara*

110. Here I have followed the results arrived at by E. Benveniste, *J.A.* (1958), 36–43. I have also compared the remarks presented by Pagliaro in *Un editto bilingue Greco-aramaico di Aśoka* (Rome, 1958). This was the *editio princeps*, and in several cases the proposals are identical or nearly so. Cf. also the revised English edition, *A bilingual graeco-aramaic edict by Aśoka* (Rome, 1964).

[1] Cf. Driver, op. cit. 22 b.

[2] This word was explained in Widengren, *Recherches*, pp. 155 f.

[3] For this word cf. Widengren, *Kulturbegegnung*, p. 90. Attempts to deny the Iranian origin of this word are based on a highly artificial etymology once proposed by Noeldeke. The word is found also in ancient Syriac Texts, and in E. Iran.

[4] This word is also found in ancient Syriac texts; cf. Widengren, op. cit., p. 30 with n. 109.

[5] Also in ancient Syriac texts; cf. Brockelmann, *Lexicon Syriacum*, 2nd edn. (Halle, 1928), p. 734 b.

[6] In spite of the arguments against this etymology advanced by F. Rundgren, *Z.A.W.* lxxiv (1962), 70–2, I uphold it for two reasons. The Greek *phoreion*, usually proposed as the basis of *'prywn*, is found already as *poryōn*. It is highly improbable that the same Greek word has been borrowed twice in two different forms. Further, the Indian word for vehicle, *yāna*, is actually found in the Khotan Saka language, and may well have wandered westwards at an early date.

[7] For this word cf. W. Hinz, *Or.* xxxix (1970), 436, where the explanation 'silo' is given.

English	*Aramaic*	*Persian*
duration (?)	*ptytw*	**patitava*
peaceful living	*r'm šty*	*rāmō.šiti*
forbidden	*ptyzbt*	**patizbāta*
unbridled	*prbst*	*frabasta*
being unbridled	*prbsty*	*frabasti*
good obedience	*hwptysty*	*hupatyāsti*
oldest	*mzyšt*	*mazišta*
good increase	*hwwrdh*	*huvardah*
good edict	*hwnštwn*	*huništavan*

111. In Widengren, *Kulturbegegnung*, a collection of Parthian loanwords was given. It is my intention to carry further these studies on Iranian loanwords in Aramaic-Syriac.

112. Cf. G. Widengren, *Die Religionen Irans* (Stuttgart, 1965), p. 147. In n. 50 there is a misprint in the Hebrew transliteration; it should be *mzdyzn*.

113. Cf. Widengren, op. cit. 141, referring to G. G. Cameron, *Persepolis Treasury Tablets* (Chicago, 1948), pp. 6 f.

114. Cf. Widengren, op. cit. 125 f.

115. Cf. Widengren, op. cit., p. 119 n. 11.

116. Cf. Widengren, op. cit., p. 122 with n. 23 a (reference to *Survey of Persian Art*, iv. 124, Figs. w and y; cf. i. 392 ff.).

117. Cf. Widengren, op. cit. 8–11.

118. Cf. Widengren, op. cit. 134–49, where a detailed survey of the problem is given.

119. Cf. Widengren, op. cit. 141.

120. Cf. Widengren, op. cit. 151–5.

121. For this official cf. P. J. Junge, *Klio* xxxiii (1940), 13–38.

122. Cf. Widengren, op. cit. 153, 207 ff., 234 f., 237, 314 f.

123. The text found in Plutarch, *Artaxerxes* 3, demands a detailed commentary which cannot be given here.

124. Cf. Widengren, op. cit. 154.

125. Cf. Widengren, *Hochgottglaube im alten Iran* (Uppsala, 1938), pp. 159–61.

126. Cf. Widengren, op. cit. 153.

127. Cf. above, p. 329.

BIBLIOGRAPHY

BAILEY, H. W., 'The Persian Language', in *The Legacy of Persia*, ed. A. J. Arberry (Oxford, 1953).

BENVENISTE, E. *Grammaire du Vieux-Perse* (2nd edit. of A. Meillet), (Paris, 1931).

—— *Titres et noms propres en Iránien ancien* (Paris, 1966).

BURNS, A. R., *Persia and the Greeks* (London, 1962).
CAMERON, G. G., *History of Early Iran* (Chicago, 1936).
GHIRSHMAN, R., *Iran: The Story of Persia from Earliest Times* (Harmondsworth, 1954).
GRAY, G. B., in *The Cambridge Ancient History*, vol. IV (1926), Chs. i, vii.
HERZFELD, E., *Iran in the Ancient East* (London, 1941).
HIGNETT, C., *Xerxes' Invasion of Greece* (Oxford, 1963).
KENT, R. G., *Old Persian* (New Haven, Conn., 1950).
MEYER, E., *Geschichte des Altertums*, 4th edn., iii–iv. 1 (Stuttgart, 1939–44).
—— *Die Enstehung des Judentums* (Halle, 1896).
NYBERG, H. S., *Die Religionen des alten Iran* (Leipzig, 1938), rep. 1966.
OLMSTEAD, A. T. E., *History of the Persian Empire* (Chicago, 1948; paperback, 1959).
SCHMIDT, E. F., *Persepolis*, i–iii (Chicago, 1953–70).
UPHAM POPE, A., *A Survey of Persian Art* (Oxford, 1938), i, iv.
WIDENGREN, G., *Die Religionen Irans* (Stuttgart, 1965).
—— *Der Feudalismus im alten Iran* (Köln–Opladen, 1969).

CHRONOLOGICA

EGYPT

Circa B.C.

2686–2160 OLD KINGDOM

2494–2345 FIFTH DYNASTY

2181–2040 First Intermediate Period

2160–1786 MIDDLE KINGDOM

2133–1991 ELEVENTH DYNASTY

1991–1786 TWELFTH DYNASTY

1786–1567 Second Intermediate Period

1786–1633 THIRTEENTH DYNASTY

1750–1550 HYKSOS PERIOD

1567–1085 NEW KINGDOM
- 1567–1320 EIGHTEENTH DYNASTY
  - 1570–1546 Amosis
  - 1546–1526 Amenophis (Amenhotpe)
  - 1504–1450 Tuthmosis III
  - 1450–1425 Amenophis II
  - 1425–1417 Tuthmosis IV
  - 1417–1379 Amenophis III
  - 1379–1362 Amenophis IV (Akhenaten)
  - 1361–1352 Tutankhamūn
  - 1348–1320 Harmhab
- 1320–1200 NINETEENTH DYNASTY
  - 1320–1318 Ramesses I
  - 1318–1304 Sethos (Sety) I
  - 1304–1237 Ramesses II
  - 1236–1223 Merenptah
  - 1214–1208 Sethos II
- 1200–1085 TWENTIETH DYNASTY
  - 1198–1166 Ramesses III
  - 1166–1160 Ramesses IV
  - 1156–1148 Ramesses VI

945–730 TWENTY-SECOND DYNASTY
- 945–924 Sheshonq I (Shishak)

715–664 TWENTY-FIFTH DYNASTY
- 715–702 Shabaka
- 690–664 Taharka

664–525 TWENTY-SIXTH DYNASTY
- 664–610 Psammetichus I (Psamtik)
- 610–595 Necho II
- 595–589 Psammetichus II
- 589–570 Apries (Hophra)

404–399 TWENTY-EIGHTH DYNASTY
- 404–399 Amyrtaeus

MESOPOTAMIA

3100–2700 URUK IV–EARLY DYNASTIC II PERIODS

2600–2370 THIRD EARLY DYNASTIC PERIOD

2370–2228 OLD AKKADIAN (AGADE) PERIOD
- 2306–2292 Maništusu
- 2254–2230 Šar-kali-šarri

2113–1991 THIRD DYNASTY OF UR
- 2113–2096 Ur-Nammu
- 2037–2029 Šu-Sin
- 2028–2004 Ibbi-Sin

1991–1786 ISIN–LARSA DYNASTIES
- 2017–1985 Išbi-Erra
- 1934–1924 Lipit-Ištar

1894–1595 OLD BABYLONIAN PERIOD (FIRST DYNASTY OF BABYLON)
- 1792–1750 Hammurabi
- 1646–1626 Ammi-ṣaduqa

1605–1150 KASSITE PERIOD

1157–1025 SECOND DYNASTY OF ISIN

1116–1110 Tiglath-pileser I

1073–1056 Ashur-bel-kala

911–612 NEO-ASSYRIAN PERIOD
- 911–891 Tukulti-Ninurta II
- 883–859 Ashurnaṣirapli II
- 859–824 Shalmaneser III
- 810–782 Adad-nirari III
- 745–727 Tiglath-pileser III
- 727–722 Shalmaneser V
- 722–705 Sargon II
  - 721–710 Marduk-apla-iddina II
- 705–681 Sennacherib
- 681–669 Esarhaddon
- 669–627 Ashurbanipal

625–539 NEO-BABYLONIAN PERIOD
- 625–605 Nabopolassar
- 612 Fall of Nineveh
- 605–562 Nebuchadrezzar II
- 562–560 Amēl-Marduk
- 560–556 Neriglissar
- 556–539 Nabonidus
- 539 Fall of Babylon

539–331 PERSIAN EMPIRE
- 539–530 Cyrus
- 530–522 Cambyses
- 522–486 Darius I (Hystaspes)
- 486–465 Xerxes I
- 465–423 Artaxerxes I
- 423–404 Darius II (Nothus)
- 404–359 Artaxerxes II (Mnemon)
- 359–338 Artaxerxes III (Ochus)
- 336–331 Darius III (Codomannus
- 331 Alexander the Great

:HART

SYRIA-PALESTINE

0–2300 EARLY BRONZE AGE III
0–2100 EARLY BRONZE AGE IV

0–1900 MIDDLE BRONZE AGE I
Patriarchal Age

0–1750 MIDDLE BRONZE AGE IIA

0–1650 MIDDLE BRONZE AGE IIB
Mari 1775–1761 Zimri-Lim
Alalah VII 1720–1650

Alalah IV 1550–1473
1500 Idrimi

0–1300 LATE BRONZE AGE IIA
(Amarna Age)

HITTITES

1740–1460 OLD KINGDOM

1680–1650 Labarna(s)
1650–1620 Hattušili(s)
1620–1590 Muršili(s)
1590–1560 Hantili(s)
1525–1500 Telepinu(s)

1460–1200 EMPIRE

1380–1346 Šuppiluliuma I
1345–1310 Muršili(s) II
1286–1265 Hattušili(s) III
1265–1230 Tudhaliya IV
1215–1190 Šuppiluliuma II

1250 Period of Exodus
1230 Israelite Settlement

0–900 IRON AGE I (IA)
1200–1020 Period of Judges
1190 Philistines in Palestine
1020–1000 Saul
1000–960 David
960–930 Solomon
930–913 Rehoboam 930–909 Jeroboam I

-843 Benhadad I (Damascus)
-796 Hazael

-600 IRON AGE II

ISRAEL	JUDAH	
-874 Omri	870–848	Jehoshaphat
-853 Ahab	848–841	Jehoram
-814 Jehu	796–767	Amaziah
-798 Jehoahaz	767–740	Azariah (Uzziah)
-782 Jehoash	740–732	Jotham
-753 Jeroboam II	732–716	Ahaz
-742 Menahem	716–687	Hezekiah
-732 Pekah	687–642	Manasseh
-723 Hoshea	640–609	Josiah
Fall of Samaria	609	Jehoahaz
	609–597	Jehoiakim
	597–587	Zedekiah
	587	Fall of Jerusalem
	587–538	Exile in Babylon

-165 HELLENISTIC PERIOD
175–163 Antiochus IV (Epiphanes)
-63 MACCABAEAN PERIOD

INDEX

(a) BIBLICAL REFERENCES

(*b*) FOREIGN WORDS

AKKADIAN

aḫlamatti/aḫlamu, 150
aḫum, xix
^{KUR}*A-ma-na-a-a*, 144
^{al}*ammia*^{ki}, 49
^{KUR}*A-mur-ri-i*, 104
Amurru(m), 102, 127
Amurrû/Amurrîtu, 127
ana šumišu gamrim, 352
ana warduti, 10
anāku, 35, 36
ʿapiru, 21
apu, 215, 216
apuarra, 13
arame mār ḫabbāti, 154
Aramu/Arumu, 137
ardāni, 312
aribi, 290
$^{m\bar{a}t}$ *Arime*, 137
armû, 153
aspastu, 314
āšib kuštari (*āšibūtu kultare*), 132
awīlu, 7, 13

balū taḫlipi, 313
^{KUR}*Basar*, 104
$^{m\bar{a}t}$ *Bît* (*Ban*)-*Ammanaia*, 144, 239
bīt aspatum, 335
bīt-ḫilāni, 120, 159
bīt kili, 10
bīt narkabti, 335
bīt sisē, 335
bīt qašti, 335
bīt šarri, 335

dimtu, 14

ebēru, 17
egirtu armitu, 147
emantuḫlu, 9
epēru, 16, 17
epru, 16
ewurutu, 10

gardapatu, 354
girû, 240

ḫabātu/abātu, 13, 154
ḫab(b)atu, 6, 12, 15, 17
ḫab/piru/i/a, 4, [5, 6, 7, 8 ff., 9, 10, 11, 12, 14, 15, 16, 17, 18, 19, 20, 21, 22, 23, 25, 26,] 117
ḫabru, 17
ḫalbi SA.GAZ, 5
ḫalqu, 12
ḫumūṣam, 50
ḫa-a-nu-ú-nu, 239
ḫana, 113
ḫapāru(m), 16 f.
ḫāpar, 21
ḫarbi-si-HU, 16
$^{m\bar{a}t}$ *Ḫatti*, 199
ḫatti/û, 197, 199
ḫa-wi-ru, 16
ḫazan(n)u, 12, 152
ḫilānu, 132, 174
ḫubullu, 17
ḫupšu, 21

Ia-ʾa-su, 153
DUMU *Ia-mi-na*, 113
^{mat}*Ia-ú-da-a-a*, 239, f.
Ia-û-di, 239
Ia-u-ḫa-zi, 238
igisû, 239
ili bîti, 11
iššakku, 111
Iu-ʾa-su, 153

kaša/u, 13
MÍ.MEŠ *kat-ra-aš*, 202
$^{m\bar{a}t}$*ke-en-a-ni*, 49
ki-in-a-nim^{ki}, 49
$^{m\bar{a}t}$*ki-na-a-ni* ^{ki}, 49
kinaḫayu, 32
$^{m\bar{a}t}$*kinaḫḫi*, 32, 263
$^{m\bar{a}t}$*kinaḫna*, 32
kinnaḫḫu/iu/ayu, 34
kumirtu, 292

labān appi, 346
labbu, 312
$^{\check{s}ad}$*Labnani*, 150

EDOMITE

EGYPTIAN

GREEK

HEBREW

HITTITE

PHOENICIAN

(c) AUTHORS CITED

(*d*) GENERAL

Šeri, 213
Sethnakhte, 93
Sety (Sethos) I, 26, 59 f., 91
— texts, 49
— and *ʿprw*, 4, 14
Sety II, 74, 231
Shabaka, 95
Shabbetai, 149
Shabwa, 302 f.
Shahar, 270
Shala, 168
Shalmaneser III, 120, 138, 141 f., 144 f., 158 f., 236, 277, 290
Shalmaneser IV, 146
Shalmaneser V, 161
Shamash, 122, 148, 167, 184, 270
Shamash-shum-ukin, 291, 314
Shamgar ben ʿAnath, 63
Shamshi-Adad V, 313
Sharā, mts., 296
Sharkuhe, 9
Sharon, 61
Sharru-lu-dari, 66
Sharuhen, 61
Shasu, 12, 25 f., 231
— of Mt. Seir, 231
Shayʿal-Qawm, 297
Sheba, xviii, 29, 299, 308
Shechem, 13 f., 40 f., 44 f., 86, 225
Sheklesh, 58, 61, 72
Shelemiah, 328
Shem, xvi, xviii, 22, 139
Shephelah, 60
Sherden, 57 f., 61, 69, 72 f.
Sheshbazzar (Shamash-apal-uṣur), 318 f.
Sheshonk I (Shishak), 95, 235, 252
Shigata, 12
Shiloh, 63
Shimei, 65
Shinar, 156, 174
Shishak, *see* Sheshonk
Shukru-Teshub, 18
Shulgi (Šulgi), 7, 110
Sialk, 313
Siamun, 65, 76, 94
Siano, 48
Sibitti-baʿali, 275
Sicilians, 92
Sicily, 60
Sidon, 29, 35, 43, 63, 119 f., 158, 233, 236, 241, 261 ff., 277 f., 330
Sidonians, 126, 262
Sidqi, 66 f.
Sihon, 125, 133
Sikayauvati, 322
Sil-Bel, 67
Šimike, 213
Simyra, 261
Sin, 122, 148, 167, 184, 293, 303, 317
Sinai, 41, 75
— covenant, xxi
— desert, 32
— script of, 41, 266
Sinites, 29
Sin-kašid, 112
Sin-shar-ishkun, 165
Sinuhe, Tale of, 37, 85
Sippar, xix, 111, 158, 318
Siptah, 74
Sirwāh, 300
Siyan, 30, 35, 48
Smendes, 75
Snefru, 85, 264
Solomon, 3, 59, 64, 95, 143, 213, 221, 235, 245, 259, 268, 274 f.
— temple of, 44
Song of Songs, 94
South Arabia, script of, 289
— languages, 299
Sparta, 96
Spartans, 316
Strabo, 298, 332 f.
Subartu, 120
— as North, 103
Ṣubatu (Zobah), 143, 146
'Substitute King', 173
Suez, 75, 85
— canal, 324
Suhu (Shuah), 137 f.
Sumer, 105, 112
— as South, 103
Sumerians, xv, 180, 182 f., 191
— and Habiru, 6
— king-list, 196
Sumhurām, 302
Sumu-abum, 111
Sumu-ditana, 111
Sumu'il, 294
Sumu-la-El, 111
Sumu-Numim, 111
Ṣumur, 12, 30, 33, 48
Sumura, 118 f.